U.S. Foreign
Intelligence

U.S. Foreign Intelligence

The Secret Side of American History

Charles D. Ameringer

Penn State University

Lexington Books

D.C. Heath and Company/Lexington, Massachusetts/Toronto

Library of Congress Cataloging-in-Publication Data

Ameringer, Charles D., 1926–
U.S. foreign intelligence: the secret side of american history /
Charles D. Ameringer.
p.   cm.
Includes bibliographical references.
ISBN 0-669-21491-4 (alk. paper).   ISBN 0-669-21780-8 (pbk. :
alk. paper)
1.   Intelligence service—United States—History.   I.   Title.
JK468.I6A84   1990
327.1'2'0973—dc20   89-13159
CIP

Copyright © 1990 Lexington Books

Published simultaneously in Canada
Printed in the United States of America
Casebound International Standard Book Number: 0-669-21491-4
Paperbound International Standard Book Number: 0-669-21780-8
Library of Congress Catalog Card Number: 89-13159

The paper used in this publication meets
the minimum requirements of American National Standard
for Information Sciences—Permanence of Paper
for Printed Library Materials, ANSI Z39.48-1984.

90 91 92 8 7 6 5 4 3 2 1

To Caroline and Katherine

Contents

Figures

Preface

I began this work in the wake of a scandal that involved illegal and improper activities by U.S. intelligence agencies, and I am finishing it in the midst of a new scandal caused by wrongdoing on the part of many of the same elements. This observation may signal that I am writing another book that is critical of U.S. intelligence, specifically the Central Intelligence Agency, but I mean to convey a different message. Considering that these two events occurred twelve years apart, they demonstrate that the problem of secrecy in American democracy is chronic. Intelligence—its functions including the collection and analysis of information and clandestine operations in support of foreign policy and military objectives—has been vital to the growth and preservation of the United States. At the same time, since intelligence requires secrecy to be effective and therefore limits openness, it has represented a threat to democratic society.

The founders of the American republic recognized this dilemma, even though intelligence contributed significantly to the achievement of American independence. They made no provision for "spying" in the Constitution, and they guaranteed that government was not to violate the privacy and freedoms of individuals. This fundamental rejection of intelligence—especially clandestine operations—contradicts the fact that intelligence has been used at every stage of the development of the United States and has evolved as part of the machinery of U.S. government. Intelligence played a crucial role in continental expansion and in the United States' rise to world power. In wars, it assumed ever-increasing importance, until in World War II it may have made the difference between victory and defeat. As intelligence proved its value, Americans formally adopted it and made it a legitimate function of government. U.S. intelligence agencies developed in response to imperatives of the nation's international position—a position that intelligence itself helped create. This may explain why the United States maintains a multibillion-dollar intelligence apparatus, despite that apparatus's history of errant behavior and despite the fact that it has threatened the constitutional order.

This book examines the historical nature of the problematic relationship between intelligence and American society. It acknowledges the outstanding achievements of intelligence, while it deplores its contradiction within a society of law and principle. A comprehensive history of U.S. foreign intelligence, it follows three tracks simultaneously in order to sort out and merge the rich detail and complex contradictions. It provides, first and foremost, a narrative history of U.S. intelligence, recounting the spy stories and Americans' clandestine activities in building a nation, to show the nature and scope of America's intelligence experience. The book charts, second, the evolution of the intelligence apparatus, describing the functions of intelligence and determining in what order and for what reasons they became permanent responsibilities of the U.S. government. The third track is historiographic: it seeks to establish the significance of intelligence as a factor in American history, employing new documentation and perspectives. Revelations twenty-five years after the fact of the cryptanalytic breakthroughs made during World War II (MAGIC and ULTRA) have fundamentally altered the historical interpretations of that war. More secrets have come to light as a result of congressional investigations of intelligence activities during the last fifteen years. Though most of the data pertain to recent events, the exposure of clandestine techniques has created new perceptions and provided clues for reexamining the past and assessing the quality of U.S. intelligence.

In the contemporary period, the wealth of source material provides the book with the opportunity to break new ground. It analyzes the reforms of the U.S. intelligence community of the mid- to late 1970s, confirming what earlier times taught—that the secrecy factor enables a president to abuse his power and authority.

Reforms of Presidents Gerald Ford and Jimmy Carter reorganized the executive structure for authorization and review of clandestine operations and imposed restrictions on intelligence activities, but these were undone by Ronald Reagan in the pursuit of distinct foreign policy objectives. The events of the 1980s, particularly the illegalities and improprieties of the Iran-contra affair, lead to the conclusion that the search for accountability and control over intelligence activities will require the effort of the American people for a long time to come.

In arriving at this conclusion, as well as others stated herein, I recognize a certain presumption on my part. As Rhodri Jeffreys-Jones observes in a more specific context, ''A historian writing about the CIA is, in some significant ways, at a disadvantage compared with an intelligence expert. The latter may, for example utilize his intimacy with colleagues and his familiarity with complex weapons systems in manner which the historian cannot match.''* I have not had access to secrets, nor do I have the peculiar insights that may come from doing the job. What I do possess are the open mind and skills of an active scholar, with the flexibility and perspective that enable one to remove the topic from the confines of a single lifetime and place it in the sweep of broad experience. Someday, the historian and the intelligence professional together may write the perfect book.

---

*Rhodri Jeffreys-Jones, *The CIA and American Democracy* (New Haven: Yale University Press, 1989), p. 8.

Abbreviations

AEC	Atomic Energy Commission
AEF	American Expeditionary Force
AFIN, A-2	Air Force Intelligence
AFL	American Federation of Labor
AFSA	Armed Forces Security Agency
AFSC	Air Force Systems Command
AFTAC	Air Force Technical Applications Center
AIFLD	American Institute of Free Labor Development
AP/NSA	Special assistant to the president for national security affairs
ASA	Army Security Agency
BNE	Board of National Estimates
CA	Covert action; Covert Action Staff (CIA)
CAT	Civil Air Transport
CFI	Committee on Foreign Intelligence
CI	Counterintelligence; Counterintelligence Staff (CIA)
CIA	Central Intelligence Agency
CIG	Central Intelligence Group
CIU	Combat Intelligence Unit
COI	Coordinator of information; Office of the Coordinator of Information
COINTELPRO	Counterintelligence program (FBI)
COMINT	Communications intelligence
COMIREX	Committee on Imagery Requirements and Exploitation
COMSEC	Communications security

CORDS	Civil Operations and Revolutionary Development Staff
CRS	Central Reference Service (CIA)
CSS	Central Security Service
CT	Counterterror program
DA	Directorate of Administration (CIA)
DCI	Director of central intelligence
DCID	Director of Central Intelligence Directive
DCS	Domestic Contacts Service (CIA)
DDA	Deputy director for administration, Directorate of Administration (CIA)
DDCI	Deputy director of central intelligence
DDI	Deputy director for intelligence, Directorate of Intelligence (CIA)
DDO	Deputy director for operations, Directorate of Operations (CIA)
DDP	Deputy director for plans, Directorate of Plans (CIA)
DDS	Deputy director for support, Directorate of Support (CIA)
DDS&T	Deputy director for science and technology, Directorate of Science and Technology (CIA)
DI	Directorate of Intelligence (CIA)
DIA	Defense Intelligence Agency
DO	Directorate of Operations (CIA)
DOD	Department of Defense; Domestic Operations Division (CIA)
DS&T	Directorate of Science and Technology (CIA)
ELINT	Electronic intelligence
ERDA	Energy Research and Development Administration
FBI	Federal Bureau of Investigation
FBIS	Foreign Broadcast Information Service
FI	Foreign Intelligence (Espionage) Staff (CIA)
5412 Group	Or Special Group; succeeded 10/5 Panel (1955)
FN	Foreign Nationalities Branch (OSS)
40 Committee	Succeeded "303" Committee (1970)

FRUPAC	Fleet Radio Unit—Pacific
FTD	Foreign Technology Division (AFSC)
G-2	Military Intelligence Division (U.S. Army)
GID	General Intelligence Division (FBI)
HUMINT	Human intelligence
IAC	Intelligence Advisory Committee
IAS	Imagery Analysis Service (CIA)
IC	Intelligence community
ICFTU	International Confederation of Free Trade Unions
ICS	Intelligence Community Staff
IEC	Intelligence Evaluation Committee
IG	Inspector general
IGs	Interagency groups
IILR	Institute for International Labor Research
INADESMO	Inter-American Democratic Social Movement
INR	Bureau of Intelligence and Research (State Department)
IOB	Intelligence Oversight Board
IOD	International Organizations Division (CIA)
IRAC	Intelligence Resources Advisory Committee
ITT	International Telephone and Telegraph
J-2	Joint Intelligence Group
JCS	Joint Chiefs of Staff
JN	Japanese Navy codes
KGB	Komitet Gosudarstvennoy Bezopasnosti/ Committee for State Security (USSR)
KH	Keyhole satellite series
KIQ	Key Intelligence Question
MAGIC	Intercepted Japanese messages (World War II)
MI-8	Code and Cipher Section (G-2)
MID	Military Information Division
MIT	Massachusetts Institute of Technology
MO	Morale Operations Branch (OSS)
MU	Maritime Units Branch (OSS)
NFAC	National Foreign Assessment Center
NFIB	National Foreign Intelligence Board

NIA	National Intelligence Authority
NIC	National Intelligence Council
NIE	National Intelligence Estimate
NIO	National intelligence officer
NIS	National Intelligence Survey
NIT	National Intelligence Topic
NITC	National Intelligence Tasking Center
NPIC	National Photographic Interpretation Center
NRC	Nuclear Regulatory Commission
NRO	National Reconnaissance Office
NSA	National Security Agency; National Students Association
NSAM	National Security Action Memorandum
NSC	National Security Council
NSCID	National Security Council Intelligence Directive
NSDD	National Security Decision Directive
NSDM	National Security Decision Memorandum
NSPG	National Security Planning Group
OAG	Operations Advisory Group
OCI	Office of Current Intelligence (CIA)
OCP	Office of Current Production and Analytical Support (CIA)
OG	Operational Group (OSS)
OMB	Office of Management and Budget
ONE	Office of National Estimates
ONI	Office of Naval Intelligence
OPC	Office of Policy Coordination
OP-20-G	Code and Signal Section (U.S. Navy)
ORE	Office of Research and Evaluation
ORIT	Inter-American Regional Labor Organization
ORR	Office of Research and Reports
OSI	Office of Scientific Intelligence (CIA)
OSO	Office of Special Operations
OSS	Office of Strategic Services
OWI	Office of War Information
PBCFIA	President's Board of Consultants on Foreign Intelligence Activities
PD	Presidential Directive

PFIAB	President's Foreign Intelligence Advisory Board
PHOTINT	Photographic intelligence
PICKLE	President's Intelligence Checklist
PRC	Policy Review Committee
R&A	Research and Analysis Branch (OSS)
RAF	Royal Air Force (Great Britain)
RIG	Restricted interagency group
SCC	Special Coordination Committee
SFHQ	Special Force Headquarters
SI	Secret Intelligence Branch (OSS)
SIG-I	Senior Interagency Group—Intelligence
SIGINT	Signals intelligence
SIS	Signal Intelligence Service
S/LPD	Office of Public Diplomacy for Latin America and the Caribbean (State Department)
SLU	Special Liaison Unit
SNIE	Special National Intelligence Estimate
SO	Special Operations Branch (OSS)
SOD	Special Operations Division (CIA)
SOE	Special Operations Executive (British)
SOG	Special Operations Groups
SPADATS	Space Detection and Tracking System
SSTR	Strategic Services Transmitter-Receiver
SSU	Strategic Services Unit
TECHINT	Technical intelligence
TELINT	Telemetry intelligence
10/5 Panel	Succeeded 10/2 Panel (1951)
10/2 Panel	NSC committee (1948) for reviewing high-risk covert action proposals
303 Committee	Succeeded 5412/Special Group (1964)
TSD	Technical Services Division (CIA)
UCLAs	Unilaterally controlled Latino assets
ULTRA	Intercepted German messages (World War II)
USIB	United States Intelligence Board
X-2	Counter-Espionage Branch (OSS)

1

The Craft of Intelligence

The Craft of Intelligence is a borrowed phrase, taken from the title of Allen Dulles's 1963 book, but it defies improvement and is the ideal concept with which to begin. It affirms that there are elements and principles of intelligence that enable one to identify and perceive it in the study of history. It means that the presence of intelligence may be determined over the span of time and that its influence may be evaluated. Accordingly, the first task is to define *intelligence* and review the general terminology, without getting into the semantics of "spookspeak."[1]

In modern terms, *intelligence* is "the product resulting from the collection, collation, evaluation, analysis, integration, and interpretation of all collected information."[2] Historically, it has had further dimensions. Intelligence is information gathered by a _____ about another _____ in order to deal more effectively with that _____. In the study of U.S. foreign intelligence, the blanks may be filled in with the word *country* or *nation,* but in different contexts the words *company* or *football team* could be used. The purpose remains the same—only the actors change. In this sense, intelligence is the collection and processing of information as well as the product itself, and it includes actions done to influence events in a nonattributable or surreptitious manner.

As *information,* intelligence may be categorized as either raw or finished. *Raw* intelligence is the crude information as collected. It may be a photograph taken by a man-made satellite orbiting the earth, or it may be a report of a conversation overheard in a bar. The information may be reliable and valid, but until it is processed, its usefulness is limited. *Finished* intelligence is the product of processing and analysis, stages in the intelligence cycle.

After raw intelligence is collected, it must be processed, analyzed, and disseminated in a clear and understandable form for
those who are going to use it for making decisions or for compiling
more detailed reports. Raw intelligence is rated in the field and at
headquarters for the reliability of its source and the validity of its
content. The greater control one has over collection, the better one
can judge the reliability of the source. An aerial reconnaissance
photograph is likely to be more reliable than a tidbit from a paid
informant. The validity of the content is harder to judge and generally can be better determined at headquarters, where there is an
opportunity for cross-referencing and checking against similar data
from distinct sources. In some cases, a report compiled from con-
versations by untrained observers may be more valid than intercepted radio messages in cipher because the latter could be a
planned deception.

After reliability and validity ratings are assigned, analysts must
then put the raw intelligence into usable form. An aerial photograph, for example, must be analyzed by a photo interpreter who
has the skills to identify objects on the ground even if they are camouflaged and photographed from miles above the earth. A cryptanalyst must render a message in cipher into plaintext, and if the
plaintext is in a foreign language, it must then be translated. The
production of finished intelligence from raw intelligence requires
sophisticated research and analysis, employing specialists in politics,
economics, and virtually every academic discipline, field, and
profession.

Finished intelligence may be a one-page document based upon
a single item or a lengthy report based upon extensive research and
data from many sources. But when disseminated, it generally
appears in one of three forms: basic, current, or estimates. (These
forms may also be described, respectively, as past, present, and
future, or as static, dynamic, and prognostic.) *Basic* intelligence
is encyclopedic or file data that is relatively permanent, which
changes slowly or requires only periodic up-dating. Basic intelligence is information about land and resources, transportation and
communications, and systems of government. Basic intelligence
that involves political parties or leaders, manufacturing or agricultural production, census data, or military order of battle is subject
to change—but not dramatic change. One of the purest forms of

basic intelligence was the National Intelligence Surveys, classified encyclopedias of the nations of the world, which the U.S. intelligence community prepared for some time.

Current intelligence consists of daily reports on developments of interest to intelligence consumers. It is up-to-date and follows events as they unfold. The reports may arrive in a daily bulletin, like a newspaper, or a weekly summary of events, like a newsmagazine, but they are changing and dynamic, and their timeliness is critical. Current intelligence analysts are much like newspaper reporters, except that they are highly trained country specialists or desk officers rather than journalists.

Estimates intelligence usually appears in the future tense. It is the effort by analysts, drawing upon experience, expert knowledge, and intelligence resources, to assess the attitudes and capabilities of other countries in order to predict what they will do in certain policy areas or how they will react to possible diplomatic, political, or military initiatives. Historically within the U.S. intelligence community, estimates intelligence has taken the form of National Intelligence Estimates, but other formal instruments have also been used, in which the community responds to queries from the National Security Council about possible developments in world affairs. One of the best-known estimates of this nature is the Special National Intelligence Estimate that predicted in September 1962 that the Soviet Union would not install offensive missiles in Cuba. Estimates are, in essence, educated guesses and are fallible, but they represent the top of the line of finished intelligence.

The general forms of finished intelligence contain more specific categories, such as political, economic, scientific, or military intelligence. Intelligence consumers have particular needs and responsibilities, and finished intelligence is disseminated accordingly.

As an *activity,* intelligence consists of four broad functions: collection, production, protection, and covert action. Although there have been exceptions, especially in earlier times, in today's intelligence community no one person is involved in all four functions. This makes for a division of labor among intelligence specialists.

Collection is the gathering of information. It is achieved in two ways—either by persons or by machines. Collection from human sources is referred to as human intelligence (HUMINT), and it is done either overtly or covertly. Approximately 80 percent of HUMINT is collected overtly from published or open sources, such as newspapers, magazines, journals, almanacs, manuals, legislative proceedings or hearings, maps, radio or TV broadcasts, or reports. Overt collection is the work of diplomats and attachés, and although discretion may be advisable, it is generally regarded as legal. Covert collection by humans is, of course, espionage and is illegal, risky, and often dangerous. Although only a small number of people are involved, covert or clandestine collection is the stuff of spy novels and is the most sensationalized intelligence function. (Espionage will be treated in detail in chapter 2.) To be successful, covert collection must have no perceivable effect.

Today, a high volume of collection is carried out by machines. Almost all technical intelligence collection is ''covert'' in the sense that even if the act of surveillance is known or suspected, the degree of effectiveness remains hidden. Today's technology provides for every kind of surveillance, monitoring, and eavesdropping. Stations and platforms of all types—satellites, high-altitude reconnaissance aircraft, mobile vans, or spy ships equipped with heat, sound, photo, pressure, motion, or ''sniffer'' sensors—routinely collect information that dazzles the imagination, and they reduce the glamorous spy to life size. The variety of technical collection programs is spectacular.

Communications intelligence (COMINT), for example, is intelligence derived from intercepting messages transmitted by radio or similar means. Electronics intelligence (ELINT) is information gleaned from nonliteral signals emitted by electronic devices such as radar. Infrared cameras mounted in satellites may photograph (PHOTINT) the heat shadows of long-departed objects on the ground. The seismograph may detect underground nuclear explosions and similar earth-shaking events. As will be seen, technical collection's awesome capacity has become a problem.

Production is the conversion of raw into finished intelligence. Production is what turns out basic, current, and estimates intelligence. It employs specialists, such as photo interpreters and cryptanalysts, and analysts trained in the arts and sciences. This intense form of research and reporting enjoys access to the most complete and current data possible. The economists, area specialists, military historians, foreign language experts, and physicists in production are far from the world of espionage and intrigue, and the only moral dilemma they face is the secrecy imposed upon their research. Theirs is a specialized form of scholarship because ideally, intelligence reporting is objective and accurate and serves to guide policy. Indirectly, the production analyst also contributes to general knowledge and science. The scientist, for example, monitors developments globally to make certain that the United States is up to date and that there are no technological surprises out there. Eventually, the outside scientific community benefits from the production function of intelligence.

Protection is the function concerned with defending the intelligence apparatus against illegal penetration and with preventing its secrets from being compromised. It is responsible for both physical security and personnel security. It protects the workplace from intruders by installing fences, alarms, sensing devices, and guards. It keeps sensitive documents in secure areas when they are in use and locked in safes when they are not. Physical security—that is, keeping out unauthorized persons—is relatively easy to achieve. The more difficult task is personnel security, or assuring that everyone who is privy to intelligence is loyal.

All intelligence personnel are subject to a security clearance. In today's U.S. intelligence community, this means a background investigation on the basis of one's Personal History Statement. In certain sensitive areas there is a follow-up polygraph test. In the Personal History Statement, the applicant must provide data involving previous employment, education, residence, affiliations, and financial status, and make personal declarations about the use of intoxicants and drugs and any brushes with the law or potentially embarassing situations. Much of this information (except the personal declarations) is also requested about the applicant's spouse and blood relatives (especially if the applicant has a relative living or residing in a foreign country). The purpose of the investigation is to establish the applicant's character and stability, as well as to determine whether there are circumstances that may render him or her vulnerable to betrayal, blackmail, or subornation.

The protection process does not end after a person has been cleared and provided with appropriate identification and badges to enter secured areas. Clearances do not permit personnel to handle every secret. As part of protection, intelligence documents are classified according to their sensitivity, ranging from confidential (relatively small damage if disclosed) to secret, top secret, and additional compartmentation classifications such as ULTRA (unauthorized disclosure of which could be severely damaging to the national security). Even personnel who receive top secret and additional compartmentation clearances do not have access to every classified document but are provided access on a "need to know" basis: that is, they can receive only information that is directly related to their problem or project. This compartmentalization, although it is considered necessary from a security standpoint, may frustrate the interaction of analysts.

Beyond defending the intelligence apparatus against its own personnel, protection is also concerned with the needs of personnel operating in foreign countries, especially those in clandestine service. These personnel must be provided with "cover" to conceal their true activities or identities. This aspect of protection frequently involves giving personnel diplomatic or private sector cover, whether they are involved in collection or operations.

Another special form of protection is communications security. Governments use cipher systems of various degrees of sophistication to protect the contents of messages transmitted to installations and posts worldwide. Cryptography is the devising of codes and ciphers and the enciphering of messages in order to conceal their meaning (as opposed to cryptanalysis, the breaking of codes and ciphers). Cryptography, then, is the process of concealing the contents of a message. In circumstances where even the effort to conceal the contents of a message would be compromising (as in espionage, for example), steganography is employed. This is a method for concealing the very existence of a message. Steganographic systems include invisible inks, microdots, and specialized forms of signaling to hide the fact that a message is being transmitted.

Within the protection function of intelligence, counterintelligence plays a major role, since it is concerned with preventing foreign intelligence operations from penetrating an intelligence apparatus. Allied to counterintelligence (but not synonymous with it) is counterespionage, a specialized clandestine collection activity whose target is specifically the other side's intelligence apparatus to determine if it has indeed penetrated your own. Hence, although counter-espionage is a specialized collection function, it is a subset of counterintelligence and falls within the purview of protection. This may be a fine point, but the two terms are often confused and used interchangeably.

A final aspect of the protection function (although overlapping with the covert action function) are deception techniques. These may involve creating disinformation, forgeries, and dummy instal-lations and mockups to mislead other governments and conceal intelligence activities. Where the purpose is to protect intelligence, it is principally a protection function. Where the purpose is to influence events covertly, it constitutes covert action.

Covert action as an intelligence function has received the widest attention in recent times and is the most controversial. It is covert intervention in the affairs of another state to try to produce a result that is nonattributable. The so-called department of dirty tricks runs the gamut from simple bribery to assassination. It includes making propaganda and carrying out psychological warfare, subsi-dizing individuals and organizations, trying to influence elections, engaging in subversive and conspiratorial activity, and conducting paramilitary and guerrilla operations. An operation may be intended to enable a regime to survive or to cause its overthrow. It may pro-mote foreign leaders and political groups or thwart their ambitions, depending on the circumstances. Although the covert action func-tion has been stealing the headlines of late, it is not necessarily new. Covert action employs some of the same techniques as espio-nage, a collection function, and an organizational structure similar to a spy net.

2
The Art of Espionage

G ood sources on how to conduct espionage are not easy to come by: there are no "spy manuals" as such. However, Miles Copeland's 1974 book, *Without Cloak or Dagger,* comes very close to filling the need, as one of the few works of nonfiction to concentrate upon the techniques of spying. It would have been very difficult to write this chapter without it. Though Copeland's book received unfavorable reviews for hyperbole and allegedly inaccurate details about specific operations, he himself is a former clandestine operator, knowledgeable in tradecraft, and he conveys the sense of espionage as an art, stressing the human factor. Copeland reinforces the poignancy of the novels of John Le Carré. Although predictability is the bane of the spy trade, successful espionage requires someone routinely being on the inside, who shuns James Bond–style adventures.

An espionage network is built upon an *agent-in-place*—a person who has the right to be where the secrets are, who is cleared to handle them, and who can pass them along without detection. The network avoids conducting break-ins as counterproductive. An intruder is likely either to be spotted or to leave behind clues. If the other side becomes aware that its secrets have been compromised, the mission is a failure. Foreign intelligence officers, therefore, do not engage in actual spying. They employ agents—persons who for one reason or another are moved to betray their country. This is where espionage becomes an art.

How can a trusted citizen of another country be induced to commit treason? As Copeland points out, espionage is cruel and exploitative. Some people spy for money, but more often they are victimized and their lives are ruined because espionage preys upon a weakness or adversity.[1] The person may be vulnerable because of addiction to alcohol, drugs, or gambling, or because of sexual habits, life-style, or debt. The person may have a sick spouse or child, or relatives in the "old country." Any one of these vulnerabilities may provide the opportunity for "recruitment" (a fact that explains the necessity for background investigations of personnel hired for sensitive jobs). There may also be other, less obvious vulnerabilities, including a variety of psychological, moral, and ideological factors that would impel one toward defection. An appropriate pitch may convert wrongdoing into a noble cause. Blackmail and threat of exposure may work in some cases, but indulging or enhancing someone's problem and providing a sympathetic shoulder to cry upon, while making society in general the villain, may work in others. Sometimes a person may be "rescued" from danger or embarrassment in a cleverly staged happening. The espionage net is both a web and an organization.

It is important to point out that there is a distinction between peacetime and wartime espionage. Much of what is described here pertains to peacetime espionage, when normal diplomatic, commercial, and cultural relations exist. Espionage is greatly facilitated under these conditions, as Copeland explains, in three important areas: increased security measures, control and management of agents, and communications.[2] Since wartime espionage lacks these advantages, it is more difficult.

Espionage begins with a *target*. In the broadest sense, a target may be an entire country, but it is generally a particular ministry of government, a military installation, an industrial plant, a research laboratory, or a shipping or communications facility within a specific country. In selecting a target, specific *requirements* are established; that is, specific information is sought that may not be acquired in any other way (since espionage is usually the means of last resort). The target is studied intensively to establish an "operational environment" and to produce (to use U.S. intelligence terminology) a Related Missions Directive, with reference to an entire country, or a Field Project Outline, concerning a specific site.[3]

The target is then assessed as to its degree of sensitivity. Is it a "denied" or "hot" area? What is the nature of its physical security (guards and fences)? What is the nature of its personnel security (badges, IDs, background investigations)? When the target study is completed, the foreign intelligence officers begin their work.

Espionage operations abroad are directed by a *station*. Clearly, a station does not identify itself as such but operates under some form of *cover*. The cover may be diplomatic, in which case the station is housed within a country's diplomatic mission; it may be commercial, housed in an import-export firm or mining company; or it may be cultural, housed in a reading room or instructional center. Diplomatic cover is best from the standpoint of security, since that way the station is immune from police search and is generally protected against intruders. It also provides advantages for communications, since the station can send messages through diplomatic channels, including pouch, and in cipher.

Within the station, the *station chief* is the officer in charge of all operations. He or she also has administrative responsibilities connected with any office or organization. Under the station chief are the *case officers;* their number depends upon the size and extent of the operations. Case officers manage the espionage operation in accordance with the requirements and tasking established by headquarters and the *desk officers/analysts* therein, but they may not have direct contact with the agents engaged in on-site spying. Procedures may vary, but generally a case officer works through a *resident agent,* a citizen or longtime resident of the target country who has numerous contacts in political, social, or commercial circles. The resident agent is normally a businessman whose place of business can routinely be visited by all sorts of persons without arousing undue suspicion. Hence, the cabaret owner of spy novels and films has a place in the real world of espionage. The resident agent serves as a buffer or *"cut-out,"* separating the agent-in-place from the case officer. An espionage net, in fact, may have numerous cut-outs to avoid any sort of contact between agent and case officer, including *principal agents,* or persons whom the resident agent employs in running a spy ring, and *dead letter drops,* whereby instructions and reports are passed without personal contact. In addition, *safe houses,* where case officer and agent may meet without endangering the operation, are maintained. The less any particular agent knows about the espionage net, the better, since he or she has less to reveal under interrogation, should that occur.

The key to the espionage operation is the *agent-in-place*—the person who does the actual spying. According to Copeland, there are four basic kinds of spies: recruited, walk-in, mole, and unwitting.[4] The *recruited agent* is what the name implies: a person working within the target whom the espionage net identifies and induces to spy. The *walk-in* is someone who literally walks into a foreign diplomatic mission or makes contact with foreign officials and volunteers his or her services. In practice, a walk-in may be a person who wants to defect and is persuaded to spy, especially if he or she is in a sensitive position. The *mole* is a native agent who has been recruited years before in anticipation of espionage work. The mole, or "sleeper," avoids all suspicious behavior and purposefully takes a sensitive position in order to burrow deeply into the organization. After possibly years of loyal and even noteworthy service to his native country, the mole may be activated to commit treason. The most dramatic example of a mole—and the damage he can do—is Kim Philby. Finally, the *unwitting agent* is someone who spies for a foreign government but is unaware that he or she is doing so. For example, a person may be persuaded that he is helping a crusading journalist expose wrongdoing and corruption within his government when, in fact, he is turning over documents to another nation. Also, a person may find it palatable to spy for one country, but not for the one that is actually running the operation.

In the operation of an espionage net, relations between the station and its agents may vary according to these distinct types of agents, but operations generally involve the following procedures or areas.[5]

Spotting. Spotting is the first step in recruiting. The espionage net, generally through a principal agent, identifies personnel employed by the target. The contact is casual and low-key, even indirect.

Evaluation. Once a person has been spotted or has volunteered, the case officer conducts a background investigation to determine the person's vulnerabilities, the kind of information he or she might yield, and the potential for risk or embarrassment. Is the person recruitable? If a walk-in, is he or she legitimate?

Recruiting. If the case officer decides to go ahead, the method of recruitment is determined. The actual recruiting may be done by a principal agent or even by an officer of the intelligence service with appropriate talents or techniques. According to Victor Marchetti, depending upon the urgency of the requirements or other circumstances, the station will use various "pitches" ranging from blackmail to the very subtle, where the person is hooked very gently and reeled in slowly.[6] Copeland describes the recruiting of an agent whom he calls Emily, a secretary in a government office who was developed over the course of many months. The recruiter avoided coming on strong, gained her confidence, provided a helping hand from time to time, and got her to give him some very low-level information (an in-house telephone book). The first time she removed it from the office, she was nervous; her "friend," posing as an insurance agent, had said he wanted the directory to develop potential clients for his business. The second time he asked her for a look at the directory, saying he needed to verify a few names, she had fewer qualms about taking it. Her area of conscience had been "expanded."[7] The man thereupon dropped out of her life, but another soon confronted her and threatened to expose her. Technically, she was already a spy, and the espionage net reeled her in. The recruiting phase is described in a multitude of stories, but each story reinforces the conclusion that espionage is an art, if generally a tragic one.

Testing. Once an agent has been recruited (or the *bona fides* of a walk-in established), there is no assurance that he or she will remain "loyal." The person may tell security officials on the other side what has happened, and the security officials may then instruct him or her to play along with the situation and pretend to be a spy. This person is, in effect, *turned,* that is, is a *double agent* or a *controlled enemy agent.* (Allen Dulles preferred the latter term.) In order to detect or avoid this situation, the case officer asks a new agent to provide information that he—the case officer—already has or can corroborate from another source, so that he can tell if he is being given false or misleading information. In some cases, a polygraph test may be administered.

Training. The new agent may need to be trained, especially in filming and concealing documents, but Copeland writes that training should be kept to a minimum, that it is important to keep things normal, to neither frighten nor "inflate" a new agent.[8] Some agents may show signs of stress, and others may go out and buy a trenchcoat. Similarly, Copeland adds, there must be "no overpayment." If a person begins to make unusual purchases, the suspicions of security officers are likely to be aroused.

Handling. Agent handling is the ongoing process of reinforcing the agent's motive for spying. It means maintaining normal appearances when the person is undergoing hardships from living a lie, experiencing mental stress and possibly imagining danger and ruin. Payments or threats may help, but generally the case officer or principal agent must convince the agent that his or her interests are uppermost in their minds. Handling is very tricky because the spy apparatus functions within a hostile environment and must prevent slipups and avoid penetration by the other side's security forces.

Termination. The time may come when an agent is no longer useful or worth the risk or the potential embarrassment. Termination may be as simple as cutting off contact without notice; it may also involve a "debriefing" and a final payment. In some cases, particularly in recent U.S. experience, providing an opportunity to migrate ("to come to America") has been a principal inducement for many agents and may provide a happy ending to the affair. For others, termination requiring "permanent elimination" is the most final solution of all and a sinister reminder that espionage is a dirty business.[9]

Many additional examples of these procedures and practices could be cited. Although the focus and principal reference of this discussion has been espionage, the organization and methods described here may be applied to other kinds of clandestine operations in foreign countries, including covert political influence, subversion, and insurgency.[10] A station can conduct covert action and so-called dirty tricks in the same way that it carries out espionage. For this reason, even though espionage itself may be limited in scope, it is worth the effort to understand its nature.

Having glanced at the fundamental principles of the craft of intelligence and the art of espionage, we can now examine them in the context of U.S. history, to assess the historical influence of intelligence and possibly to gain insights about the United States' past. At the same time, we will trace the development of the U.S. intelligence community and observe its changing role within the American political system.

3

The Secret American Revolution

The history of the American Revolution is rich in cases of intelligence and espionage. It is ironic, given Americans' long-standing aversion toward spying and secrecy, that the nation should have originated in conspiracy and intrigue. Two of the most admired heroes of the revolutionary war—Nathan Hale for the Americans and Major John André for the British—were spies. And James Fenimore Cooper's *The Spy,* one of the classic stories about the American Revolution, is based upon the real-life exploits of American agent Enoch Crosby. The United States' achievement of independence owed much to espionage and covert operations.

The same may be said of the British successes. One author insists that the "clandestine service" rendered by colonists loyal to the crown was "indispensible" and enabled the British to prolong the war for eight years.[1] Parties on both sides of the conflict were "residents" and had no distinguishing characteristics of language or ethnicity to separate them and give them away. They could easily blend in and infiltrate each other's organizations. For this reason, virtually from the beginning the patriots developed a strong "security consciousness" and created organs of internal security.

In each of the colonies they established Committees of Safety and Committees of Correspondence. The Committees of Safety were charged with security and counterintelligence functions. They prevented the infiltration of the patriot organizations by, in effect, running a security check on all members and providing them with bona fides and "clearance." They were responsible for cover in the form of passwords, pseudonyms, and safe houses, and they penetrated Tory bands, a counterespionage function, to uncover the other side's agents-in-place. Governed by similar security concerns, the Committees of Correspondence were the only channels the conspirators had authorized for communication among the colonies. The network of committees ran from Georgia to New England (and to agents abroad as well), employing couriers and mail drops and using cryptography and steganography. James Lovell, who eventually sat in the Continental Congress, was a cryptographer for the rebellion, and Dr. James Jay, the brother of John Jay, formulated an invisible ink. The patriots also engaged in cryptanalysis; Elbridge Gerry (of "gerrymander" fame) successfully cracked British ciphers and produced important intelligence.

These committees were functioning well before the Declaration of Independence was issued. They were particularly active around the port of Boston, where many of the first episodes of the rebellion occurred. After the famous Tea Party (December 1773) and the closing of the port, the patriots formed one of America's first spy rings, the Revere gang or the Mechanics, to observe the movements of British general Thomas Gage. Paul Revere and the Mechanics, a band of about thirty persons, were legals in that they belonged in Boston. They violated a cardinal principle of espionage in that they knew each other's identity, but they were sworn to secrecy. They also performed paramilitary operations, including sabotage and the theft of gunpowder and muskets.

Their espionage was simple. It consisted of taking strolls and walks (reconnoitering) to observe British troop movements. When Gage made preparations for a march inland to capture "subversives" Sam Adams and John Hancock (who were reported to be in the vicinity of Lexington) and to seize a suspected arms dump in Conçord, the Mechanics provided an early warning. Revere was a neighbor of Major John Pitcairn, the second-in-command of the planned march. This enabled him to alert Adams and Hancock on April 16, two days before his famous midnight ride.[2] On the night of the eighteenth, he flashed the signal from the steeple of Christ's (Old North) Church that the British were coming by land (via the Boston Neck) rather than across the Charles River (never by "sea"; Longfellow was a better poet than historian). Revere rode to warn the Minutemen, thereby ending his masquerade, and, though detained part way, his spying activities contributed to the first military victory of the American Revolution.

After Lexington and Concord, during the siege of Boston, the patriots learned that they themselves had been the victims of espionage. Dr. Benjamin Church, the director of hospitals for the Continental Army and a member of the Massachusetts provincial congress, was a spy for General Gage. Among other things, he had furnished the information about the Concord arsenal. George Washington had difficulty believing that a person as prominent and apparently as dedicated as Church could be guilty of treason, but the evidence was overwhelming. Elbridge Gerry and his team of cryptanalysts deciphered an intercepted message from Church to his British case officer that contained military information. Church denied that he was an enemy agent, but he was eventually banished and lost at sea on a vogage to Bermuda.[3]

After the British evacuated Boston on March 17, 1776, action shifted to the New York area, as did the functions of intelligence. Although we may think that political assassination is a "dirty trick" of only recent use, the British plotted to murder Washington by putting poison in a dish of green peas—a favorite food of his. The plot was accidentally overheard by a jailed counterfeiter; it implicated a member of Washington's guard, Sergeant Thomas Hickey, who was publicly hanged on June 28, 1776.[4] Although Washington escaped this and a later plot to abduct him, he could not prevent the British from occupying New York in September.

The British seizure first of Long Island in August led to one of the best-known spy missions in American history. After retreating to Manhattan, Washington needed to learn British plans. But he had withdrawn from Long Island so abruptly that he had had no time to arrange for espionage in his wake. He asked for a volunteer to go behind the enemy line, and Captain Nathan Hale came forward. The Hale mission was poorly planned and badly executed, by all professional standards. Hale was an infiltrator, a resident of Connecticut, and he did not know Long Island well. After he crossed Long Island Sound in a small boat, he had no contacts on the other side, and he carried incriminating papers and the wrong kind of money. As an amateur, he did not know how to either avoid suspicion or to elude capture. His cover as an art teacher was good—except that his silver shoe buckles were a bit above his station and his sketchbook included too many drawings of gun batteries. The mission was extremely short, lasting from September 15 to 22, 1776, and there is little information about Hale's movements, except that when the British occupied Manhattan on the 15th, he followed them there, where he was caught. General Sir William Howe ordered him executed without a trial. Hale earned a coveted place in spydom and a niche in the American pantheon of heroes with his immortal words, "I only regret that I have but one life to lose for my country," before being hanged. However, General Washington had learned a bitter lesson and he swore, if possible, not to use an infiltrator again.

Actually, Washington himself was a skilled intelligence chief in his own right. Modern-day intelligence professionals give him high marks for his intelligence instincts and methods. He had learned to appreciate the value of intelligence as a young officer in the French and Indian War. He had observed that the French made effective use of their Indian allies as scouts, and he attributed "Braddock's defeat" to the failure of the English to do likewise. As commander in chief of the Continental Army, if there were going to be any surprises, Washington intended to "spring" them.[5]

George Washington paid for intelligence from his own pocket, submitting an expense account to Congress for $17,617 at the war's end. He established precise "requirements" for his agents, insisted upon written rather than oral reports, preferred residents over infiltrators, and was extremely cautious about using walk-in Tory defectors.[6] Learning from the Hale misadventure, he left behind a string of agents-in-place as he retreated across New Jersey and into Pennsylvania in late 1776. These helped him end his flight and resume the offensive.

Washington's bold crossing of the Delaware and capture of Trenton on Christmas night 1776 was greatly facilitated by his agent John Honeyman, a Trenton butcher. Honeyman supplied the Hessians with meat and reported to Washington that they were partying and could be caught unawares. When Washington took Princeton on January 3, he was aided by a map pinpointing British artillery and barracks locations that resident agent John Cadwalader had sketched for him. Lewis Costigin was Washington's man in New Brunswick, and John Messereau and Elias Dayton ran a spy ring on Staten Island from across the river in New Jersey.

When Washington established his headquarters in Morristown after these successes, he continued to demonstrate his intelligence sense with a series of deceptions.

The Washington of cherry tree fame ("I cannot tell a lie") was, in the words of one observer, "one of the most experienced and skillful liars that ever lived."[7] At least, he knew that it was vital to mislead the enemy by feeding them false information. While Washington was wintering in Morristown, weary and outnumbered, he sought to persuade the British that he was a formidable foe and thereby avoid an attack. He knew that there were spies in his camp, and he intentionally left phony strength reports and other disinformation lying around for their prying eyes. He had only about four thousand men in his tiny army, but he managed to convince Howe that he had three times that number, and some reports reached the British with the inflated figure of forty thousand. This deception probably prevented a frontal attack from being made upon Washington's weak forces and induced Howe to make an end run and occupy Philadelphia.

Howe captured Philadelphia on September 26, 1777, with the aid of intelligence furnished by British agent Joseph Galloway. (Galloway's information and maps were also instrumental in the British victory at Brandywine.) Despite the British intelligence successes at Philadelphia, Washington had made provisions for the operation of an espionage ring in the Quaker city before the British arrived. This ring operated effectively during the entire British occupation, from September 1777 to June 1778, and enabled Washington to avoid disaster during his most difficult days in Valley Forge. He always knew Howe's capabilities, and he almost always had several days' advance notice of his movements.[8]

Major John Clark ran the Philadelphia net, which he had organized with Washington before the British occupation. Clark was, in effect, the case officer, but his method was slightly unorthodox in that he operated the net from outside Philadelphia. He rendezvoused with his agents at various points on the perimeter of the city. He also used black marketeers as messengers—an inspired move, since the British, who partially depended on them for supplies, rarely interfered with their movements. Clark's net is credited with saving American forces "from surprise and probable annihilation" on at least three occasions.[9]

The Battle of Whitemarsh, on December 4, 1777, was one of those occasions, and a woman agent deserves the credit. The stereotype of the female spy as a vamp, stemming from the Mata Hari legend, does not at all fit the women agents in American history, and especially does not fit Lydia Darragh of Philadelphia. Although American women agents have been aided by men's chauvinistic attitudes toward women, this chauvinism rarely involved seduction itself. Lydia Darragh benefited from men's chauvinism, as well as from the assumption that old ladies do not spy—especially old Quaker ladies. Provided with this ready-made cover, Darragh was handed the opportunity to spy. Her home was opposite British headquarters, and the occupying army requisitioned a portion of it for meeting rooms and visiting officer quarters. All she had to do was look and listen. She passed intelligence to Clark and Washington by way of her fourteen-year-old son, whom she sent with food packages for his older brother, who was in the Continental Army at Valley Forge (although Quakers were supposed to be pacifists). She did not put the messages in the packages (which gave the British something to search) but concealed them in the cloth buttons on the boy's jacket.

While hiding in a closet one day, Darragh overheard the British making plans to attack the rebels. There was not enough time to prepare her son for the mission. So, taking a sack of grain, she passed through the lines herself, seemingly in search of a miller. She brought Washington the vital intelligence. He had suspected that the British were planning an assault, but he did not know from what direction they would advance. Darragh informed him that they were coming up the east bank of the Schuylkill and intended to build a pontoon bridge to cross the river and outflank him. With this information, Washington moved to the east side of the river as well and met the British full strength there at Whitemarsh. He caught them unprepared for battle, with a burden of heavy equipment and canoes for the river crossing. This victory ended the British threat to Valley Forge in the desperate winter of 1777–78.

In the meantime, another spy had helped turn the course of the war. Alexander Bryan was an American agent who managed to go within the lines of the English general, John "Gentleman Johnny" Burgoyne. Bryan gathered the critical information that enabled General Horatio Gates to ambush British forces at Bemis Heights on October 7, 1777, which led to Burgoyne's crushing defeat and surrender at Saratoga ten days later. According to author John Bakeless, "It is possible . . . that Alexander Bryan was the man who really won the American Revolution."[10] This is extravagant praise. But Bryan, carrying a piece of cloth and claiming to be looking for a tailor, wandered about Burgoyne's camp and learned the English plans to occupy Bemis Heights. The Saratoga victory convinced the French that the Americans had a chance, which contributed directly to the Franco-American alliance of February 1778.

In negotiating the French alliance, Benjamin Franklin earned a place in the annals of American intelligence. Franklin was the American confidential agent in France and was deeply involved in intrigue and secret dealings. At the outbreak of the American Revolution, France had been unwilling to risk war with England by openly aiding the Americans but, as a bitter rival of England, was disposed to render discreet assistance. Franklin employed all the stratagems of clandestine operations and managed to secure loans, weapons, and gunpowder for the rebel cause. But British diplomatic representatives and agents kept him under surveillance and succeeded in recruiting his personal secretary and confidant, Dr. Edward Bancroft, as an agent-in-place. Bancroft routinely reported to the British by leaving messages in the hollow trunk of a tree in the Tuileries Gardens, causing one historian to assert that Franklin was "the most duped representative of America ever sent to a foreign power in time of war."[11] Allen Dulles dissented from this opinion; he suspected that Franklin was aware of Bancroft's duplicity and gave him only the information that he wanted the British to have.[12] Whenever Franklin had information that he wanted to keep secret, he wrote the message personally in invisible ink on the blank pages at the beginning and end of a book and sent it directly to his library in Philadelphia.

After Saratoga and the French alliance, the British evacuated Philadelphia, and New York again became the major British stronghold in the North. As the war moved to a close, Washington, who knew the critical role of intelligence, recognized the need to organize it better. He appointed Major Benjamin Tallmadge, Hale's classmate (Yale '73), as chief of the "bureau of secret service" and instructed him to establish a spy ring on Long Island and in the

New York port area. Tallmadge, operating somewhat like John
Clark, established his headquarters in Westchester County and ran
his net by remote control. He created the best espionage organization of the Revolutionary War. He recruited a string of resident
and principal agents and agents-in-place who provided a steady
flow of intelligence about the size, disposition, armaments, morale,
and movements of the British forces in New York under General
Sir Henry Clinton (Howe's successor).

   This espionage organization operated successfully for five years
(1778–83) and was called the Culper Net. The name *Culper* derived
from the pseudonym of its chief resident agents, Abraham Woodhull ("Samuel Culper, Sr.") and Robert Townsend ("Samuel Culper, Jr."). Townsend (another Hale classmate) directed the net in
New York City, and Woodhull operated from his farm in Setauket
on Long Island. Townsend owned a dry goods store, which enabled
him to gather information from customers (including British officers) and to rendezvous with his agents without suspicion. His
agents included merchants, domestics, clerks, barmaids, and especially James Rivington, the King's Printer and proprietor of a
coffee house. Rivington collected intelligence from British revelers
and passed it along even "before the convivialists had slept off the
effects of their wine."[13] As the publisher of the *Royal Gazette,* Rivington managed to remain above suspicion by his highly offensive
denunciations of the American cause.

   Crucial to the success of the Culper Net were its effective communications. Either visiting his father at Oyster Bay, or using a
courier, Townsend reported to Woodhull, who, in turn, informed
their case officer, Tallmadge ("John Bolton"). Woodhull used
Long Island Sound fishermen, especially boatman Caleb Brewster,
to carry messages to the northern shore. Woodhull and Brewster
established a simple but efficient signaling system. When Woodhull went out for his morning ride (carrying dispatches in cipher
or invisible ink), he observed the washline at Brewster's house.
The number of items on the line indicated what boat landing to
use. But when the wash included a black petticoat, he rode on,
forewarned of danger. Aside from a stream of tactical intelligence,
the Culper Net uncovered a British scheme to flood the rebel zones
with counterfeit notes and create economic chaos, as well as a
British plan to attack the French fleet at Newport in July 1779.

The Culper Net also played a role in uncovering the treason of Benedict Arnold. General Arnold was one of history's most notorious walk-ins. Major John André, the chief of Clinton's intelligence service, had not regarded the much-decorated hero as even a possible recruit, and his defection was a windfall for the British. Arnold's action provides clues to people's motivations for betraying their country as they are linked to the factors of personality and character. Arnold's motivation was a combination of conceit and greed. He bitterly resented being passed over for promotion from major to lieutenant general. Actually, Washington had saved Arnold's career after he was court-martialed for embezzlement (which had come about from his and his wife Peggy Shippen's extravagant life-style). Negotiations between Arnold and André dragged on from May 1779 to September 1780, climaxing in a plot to betray Arnold's command at West Point.

In their secret correspondence, Arnold and André used the code names "Gustavus" and "John Anderson," respectively. André's pseudonym "John Anderson" was probably the key factor in his capture and in preventing the fall of West Point. One of the agents in the Culper Net—possibly Townsend's sister, Sarah—overheard another British officer address André as "Anderson." Unaware that his alias had been exposed, André committed the blunder of going behind American lines to complete the arrangements for Arnold's betrayal. He was detained on his return: Townsend had supplied Tallmadge with the name Anderson. Seeing the name on his checklist, Tallmadge had understood almost immediately what was happening. But before he could reach the guardpost where André/Anderson was being held, word had been sent (as it was routinely) to Benedict Arnold at West Point; he immediately fled.

General Washington was incensed by Arnold's treason. He wanted to make a trade of André for Arnold, but Clinton turned him down, not wishing to discourage other would-be defectors. Washington then devised a bizarre scheme to abduct Arnold in New York and return him to American hands. He and Sergeant-Major John Champe agreed upon a plan by which Champe would make a phony defection from the Americans and join Arnold's "American Legion" in New York; once he was in place, he would kidnap Arnold. Washington informed only Champe's commanding officer, General "Light-Horse Harry" Lee, about what was going on. To provide "motivation" for the "defection," Champe was jailed for a series of insubordinate acts. He fled, as planned, and reached the British lines literally in a hail of live bullets from the hotly pursuing Americans. Arnold, too, was apparently convinced by the realistically staged defection and welcomed Champe into his new command. In a game of cat-and-mouse, Champe watched Arnold carefully and determined how he might kidnap him. He observed that before retiring each night, Arnold made a visit to a little house in a garden out back. Champe planned to surprise the general one night in his garden, but on the very evening that he had set for the abduction, he found himself aboard a troop ship en route to the front in Virginia. Eventually, Champe managed to return to American lines, but only with Washington's help was he able to persuade his comrades that he was not a traitor.

Many spies of the revolution shared Champe's dilemma in this regard. Because they had to feign support for the Crown in order to carry out their missions, many American agents were ostracized by their neighbors and subsequently had difficulty clearing their names. One such agent, Sergeant Daniel Bissell, was branded a deserter and considered such for almost a century before his hometown of Windsor, Connecticut, learned the truth and belatedly erected a monument in his honor.[14] Another did not have to wait quite so long to erase the stain: Hercules Mulligan, an agent-tailor who had sacrificed his standing in the community to appear to collaborate with the British, was one of the first persons with whom General Washington dined when he returned to New York. On the other hand, many Tories who had spied for the British by faking support for the rebel cause were never found out, saved their property from confiscation, and even remained in the United States after the war as honored citizens of the new nation. Their true sentiments were never detected. It is an axiom of intelligence that success must often be its own reward, because much depends upon deception.

Deception made possible General Washington's final victory of the American Revolution. Washington was virtually shaping Clinton's plans by permitting Clinton's spies into the American camp and furnishing a constant flow of disinformation to them. When the time came, Washington took advantage of this situation. In midsummer 1781, Washington and French admiral Rochambeau decided to abandon their plans to attack New York City and instead to move their forces to Virginia, there to support the Marquis de Lafayette against the army of General Charles Cornwallis. This meant that Washington had to deceive Clinton and keep him in New York while the allies moved south—Washington from New Jersey and the French from Rhode Island. Washington did this by enabling Clinton's spies to continue to report his "intentions" to attack New York—including planned operations and meetings between American and French commanders. To provide Clinton with evidence that the French were going to join him for a combined attack on New York, Washington installed huge bakery ovens at Chatham, New Jersey. Clinton, knowing that the French live for their croissants at breakfast, was convinced that his intelligence was reliable. Washington's deception kept Clinton pinned down in New York until September, when he could no longer ignore reports of troop movements southward. But by then it was too late, and Cornwallis was overwhelmed the following month at Yorktown.

It is clear that intelligence played a significant role in the American War of Independence. A number of battles were won or lost because of it. Yet the new republic made no provision for the maintenance of an intelligence capability, much less for the creation of a government intelligence agency. Broader concepts prevailed. Secrecy and intrigue were associated with Old World monarchies and, in a sense, represented what the rebels had fought against. If the American government was to be based upon the consent of the governed, it was essential that the public be informed. The American people therefore regarded secrecy as incompatible with democratic government. For over a century, those who argued for a permanent intelligence organization encountered a public notion that intelligence was a function of the military and, like the military, was to be trotted out only in times of emergency. The United States enjoyed this innocence, but in clandestine affairs nothing is ever what it appears to be.

4
Intelligence and
Continental Expansion

A fter the American Revolution, the spies went home, and no agency of the U.S. government was charged specifically with the overt or covert collection of intelligence, nor with the production of national intelligence or clandestine operations. Officers of the State and War Departments performed certain intelligence functions in the course of their duties; those of particular significance became part of the diplomatic or military record. Between the American Revolution and the Civil War, the more dramatic events involving intelligence activity may therefore be found in the general accounts of diplomatic and military history. Some of these events are familiar and essentially episodic but are reviewed here in order to have a complete picture. Other aspects of intelligence—especially on the clandestine side—have been overlooked in more conventional studies or, at least, have not been put in sharp focus. Examination of these aspects may support ascribing a clearer purpose and greater design than has previously been suggested to both national policy and continental expansion in the pre–Civil War period.

Intelligence history has more than its share of ironies. Although the American people abandoned their ''secret service'' after independence, they suffered from intense spy fever in the early days of the republic, imagining that foreign agents were intriguing everywhere.[1] The war between England and France, which was also a test of republicanism versus monarchy, caused much agitation in the United States, particularly because of the controversial status of the 1778 Franco-American alliance. The revolutionary government of France did not invoke the treaty but counted upon receiving U.S. support in its struggle against England. It instructed its diplomatic envoy to the United States, Citizen Edmond Genêt, to proceed under the assumption that it could count on U.S. support. Genêt's mission had all the trappings of a covert action, except that he was highly visible and aggressive. He conspired with American citizens and encouraged them to influence U.S. policy, raised money, purchased arms, recruited men, and issued letters of marque to privateers to raid British shipping from U.S. ports.

The turmoil created by Genêt's activities contributed to the emergence of partisan politics in the United States. The Republicans (Jeffersonians) insisted that the treaty of alliance with France be honored, while the Federalists (Hamiltonians) argued that the treaty was null and advocated a policy of neutrality. The conflict became so acrimonious that the Federalist administration of President John Adams enacted the Alien and Sedition Acts (1798), which were designed to gag the Republicans by threatening to arrest citizens and deport aliens who "conspired" to criticize the government and impede the enforcement of its laws. The measures were aimed at persons like Philip Freneau, who published a woodcut in his *National Gazette* in which the "arch traitor" George Washington was depicted before the guillotine; Freneau was subsidized by Jefferson and also possibly by French agents. The hubbub subsided as U.S.–French relations deteriorated, largely because of Genêt's indiscretions, the insulting behavior of France in the XYZ affair (in which France demanded a bribe as a precondition for receiving U.S. diplomatic representatives in Paris), and the "undeclared" outbreak of hostilities between the two countries on the high seas. American attitudes also changed because U.S. shipping and trade were flourishing under Hamilton's neutrality policy. The Alien and Sedition Acts were permitted to lapse, even though a few editors were imprisoned, and the Franco-American alliance was formally abrogated in the Convention of 1800.

The resulting improvement in Franco-American relations probably contributed to the U.S. acquisition of Louisiana. A great deal of intrigue and secret negotiations were involved in the 1803 Louisiana Purchase, most of which have been treated in detail by diplomatic historians. However, the acquisition of the Louisiana territory led directly to the annexation of West Florida (Baton

Rouge) in 1810, a less familiar event but one that is of particular interest for the study of intelligence.

West Florida was the first of the "lone star republics," in which Americans settled in a foreign territory, achieved political and economic influence, overthrew the existing government, and requested annexation by the United States. Although each "lone star" case must be considered separately, particularly concerning the degree and nature of official U.S. involvement, the West Florida pattern was repeated in Texas, Oregon, California, and Hawaii. President James Madison actively encouraged a separatist movement in West Florida and gathered in the parcel without delay, ignoring the protests of the Spanish government, which claimed sovereignty over the territory. The U.S. President thus served as case officer in one of the first covert actions by the United States.

Madison intended to repeat this action in East Florida. He conspired with George Mathews, a former governor of Georgia, to promote a secessionist movement in the remainder of Spanish Florida. However, Mathews bungled the affair. Instead of organizing a "genuine" insurrection, proclaiming independence, and seeking annexation, he conducted the action like an invasion. He simply claimed the territory for the United States as he advanced from Amelia Island to St. Augustine. Madison was forced to disavow Mathews, providing a lesson in "plausible deniability," in the words of his twentieth-century counterparts. Moreover, within a few days, the United States was embroiled in the War of 1812 against a foe more formidable than Spain.

The War of 1812 would seem to have provided the British with a golden opportunity for covert action. Federalist New England was sharply opposed to "Mr. Madison's War," virtually to the point of treason. The British were aware of this; John Howe, who had been a spy for General Gage before Lexington and Concord and who had settled in Canada after the War of Independence, undertook a spy mission to New England before the outbreak of hostilities. Still familiar with the region, the "old spy" traveled about unsuspected and prepared an excellent intelligence report that accurately described the political temper.[2] But the British failed to capitalize on the favorable situation. In their only known attempt, John Henry, an obscure Irish adventurer who apparently had instructions to encourage the New England secessionists, bumbled, leading to his exposure and flight.[3]

If anyone did significant intelligence work in the War of 1812, it was the pirate allies of the United States. Almost everyone is familiar with the aid that Jean Lafitte rendered General Andrew Jackson at the Battle of New Orleans. Less known is that the Lafitte brothers, along with Renato Beluche and other Caribbean corsairs, reported British and Spanish strengths in Mobile, Pensacola, and the West Indies, as well as ship movements and intentions. The pirates had in place the most complete intelligence network in the Caribbean, with agents in the principal ports from Havana to Cartegena, to report on production, fortifications, cargoes, and sailings. They converted part of their business espionage net into the wartime intelligence network, enabling Jackson to achieve a stunning victory over the British (although after the war was actually over).

In 1836, when Andrew Jackson was president, the Texas secession movement occurred. Although parallels can be drawn between the events in Texas and those in West Florida, there is no parallel between the behavior of Jackson and Madison. Americans had moved into Texas, first under Spanish jurisdiction and then under Mexican, and eventually became dominant in the territory and achieved independence. (The U.S. annexation of Texas is discussed in chapter 5.) But there is no evidence that the Jackson administration conspired with the Texans to seek independence. Despite the close relationship between the Tennesseans Jackson and Sam Houston, Houston had not been sent to Texas by Jackson as his agent. Mexico did have cause for complaint: the United States had failed to enforce its laws that prohibited the recruiting of men for action on foreign soil, and had committed other breaches of neutrality. But there is nothing to sustain a conspiracy theory between Texans and the Jackson administration. (As we shall see, the situation was different when the issue changed from secession to annexation.)

In reviewing U.S. foreign intelligence during this period, the activities of private citizens must be considered. Although unofficial, these actions frequently led to diplomatic crises, particularly when U.S. citizens conspired with foreign revolutionaries or adventurers to overthrow the government or authority of a neighboring state. In a number of cases, moreover, conspirators prepared for invasions of foreign territory from American soil.

The first of these so-called filibustering expeditions occurred in 1806. Francisco de Miranda, a Venezuelan and "precursor" of Spanish–American independence, outfitted the vessel *Leander* and sailed from New York for the Venezuelan coast. He had the support of several Americans, including William Smith (the son-in-law of former president John Adams) and merchant Samuel Ogden. Miranda failed to provoke an uprising on this occasion, but the Latin American wars of independence that soon erupted provided the backdrop for the events in the Floridas.

Such events were not confined to the Caribbean. Since independence, many Americans had expected that Canada would become part of the Union in the natural course of events. Some tried to help nature along by supplying arms to a small band of insurrectionists in the uprising of 1837. British and Canadian authorities crushed the rebellion, rudely destroying the American gunrunner *Caroline* above the falls on the Niagara River. This caused tempers to flare along the southern shore of lakes Ontario and Erie. Groups of Americans then organized Hunters' Lodges—thinly veiled paramilitary bands—for the purpose of "liberating" Canada. The vigilance of the U.S. government stemmed the crisis, but fifteen thousand Americans (some estimates set the figure even higher[4]) had been disposed to invade Canada. Their disappointment contributed to President Martin Van Buren's defeat in his reelection bid.

Subsequent presidents were more sensitive to the popular mood. Ten years later, attention again shifted southward when the notorious filibusters Narciso López and William Walker flaunted American neutrality laws. Between 1849 and 1851, with the connivance of prominent U.S. citizens and some public officials, López, a Venezuelan adventurer, organized three expeditions on U.S. soil to "liberate" Cuba from Spain. U.S. authorities blocked his first expedition, from New York, and brought him to trial. But popular opinion so favored him that it was impossible to find a jury that would convict him. Nonetheless, López switched his base of operations from New York to more congenial New Orleans; from there he embarked on two further expeditions with the aid of sympathetic southerners like Governor John A. Quitman of Mississippi. Although the actions of local and national officials must be clearly distinguished, the willingness of any officials to resort to such extraordinary measures reflects the intensity of Americans' desire to acquire Cuba, beginning as early as 1823. After López was captured and executed, Americans' frustration reached a climax in the abortive Ostend Manifesto (1854), which threatened "to wrest" Cuba from Spain if it were unwilling to sell.

Similar sectional and entrepreneurial interests supported William Walker's forays into northern Mexico and Central America in the 1850s. Although Walker repeatedly violated U.S. laws in mounting his expeditions, he never served time, and he was treated like a hero—even after he had been driven from Nicaragua in 1857 after visiting great pain and suffering upon that land.[5] He raised men and money in the United States, and his departure from San Francisco in 1855 was delayed more by anxious creditors than by government officials. Indeed, federal authorities classified his expedition as a "colonizing" venture, not as a "military" effort, enabling him to sail. This aroused the suspicions of the British (a rival on the isthmus) that Walker was actually advancing U.S. territorial interests in Nicaragua.

The events described so far appear to have little relationship with one another. But seen in the context of American westward expansion, they constitute a consistent pattern. Even without a specific intelligence agency, the United States was supplementing its normal diplomatic and military actions with clandestine operations. The great explorations of the trans-Mississippi West are classic examples of the collection of basic intelligence for advancing the national interest. They even have all the ingredients of a good spy story. Parts of the territory were claimed by the United States; parts were in dispute; and still other parts were clearly under foreign jurisdiction. At one point or another, certain American explorers were thus engaged in espionage. Moreover, native inhabitants of the entire territory were spied upon.

The great expedition of Captain Meriwether Lewis and Lieutenant William Clark (May 1804–September 1806) fits this interpretation. President Thomas Jefferson described the expedition as "commercial," but he requested funds for the undertaking in a "confidential" message to Congress. Whether he was seeking to conceal his real intentions from political opponents or from the British or Spanish, Jefferson clearly conceived of it as an intelligence mission that would serve the broadest interests of the nation. He planned it to its finest detail, and he chose soldiers rather than scientists to carry it out.[6] He instructed Lewis and Clark to consult with the leading scientists of the day and to train themselves in the use of scientific instruments and techniques for measuring the earth's surface, identifying rocks and minerals, and collecting specimens of flora and fauna, among other things. These preparations and the motivation behind them may be compared with twentieth-century missions to explore space and the race to the moon. It made sense to use individuals in good physical condition and with frontier experience; they were instructed "to study the Indian inhabitants very carefully, including . . . their economic and military pursuits."[7] Strengthening the argument that Jefferson was not interested only in commerce and science is the fact that his administration issued no official report for the expedition and that a private edition of the journals of Lewis and Clark (edited by Nicolas Biddle) was first published as late as 1814.

In explorations of the Southwest, Jefferson's aims were more straightforward. After acquiring Louisiana from France, the United States had a new western neighbor: Spain. Jefferson was eager to determine the true extent of the lands that he had purchased. He ordered expeditions to explore the Arkansas and Red rivers so that he might "bargain intelligently" with Spain.[8] The lower Mississippi valley was a caldron of intrigue; Casa Calvo, the Spanish boundary commissioner, conspired with the treacherous General James Wilkinson and the embittered Aaron Burr in a confused situation of national and personal ambition. Wilkinson, the territorial governor of Louisiana and an agent in the pay of Spain, instructed Lieutenant Zebulon Pike in 1805 to locate the source of the Red River, instructions that overtly conformed with the wishes of President Jefferson. But Wilkinson, by his own account, also issued secret instructions to the lieutenant "to continue on to Santa Fe and spy out its approaches and defenses."[9] After discovering

Pike's Peak and enduring a Rocky Mountain winter, Pike reached the Rio Grande River, claiming he thought it was the Red. He was detained there by Spanish authorities in February 1807 and taken to Santa Fe and thence to Chihuahua. The Spanish had handed Pike an opportunity to fulfill his espionage mission. Before he returned to U.S. territory, his "captors" had enabled him to learn virtually everything there was to know about Spanish defenses and military posture in those regions. According to historian William Goetzmann, "No more successful espionage operation has ever been conducted in recorded American history."[10]

Not all intelligence contributed to the unrelenting westward march of the United States. Pike's report, published in 1810, described much of the Southwest as an arid plain and gave rise to the myth of the Great American Desert. This finding was reinforced by the observations of Major Stephen H. Long, a participant in the ill-fated Yellowstone Expedition of 1819. Both tended to lessen the Americans' interest in moving west. Long proclaimed the region "unfit" for settlement, and the War Department placed further major explorations on hold for about a decade.

In the meantime, mountain men and fur trappers were roaming the western reaches. One of them, Jedediah Smith, discovered the South Pass, which opened up the Pacific via the Oregon Trail. He recorded his travels and sent them in a letter to the U.S. secretary of war in 1830. This letter, described as "an excellent intelligence report,"[11] was published as Senate Document Number 39 and received widespread attention. In addition to its enthusiastic description of the territory, it included information about the strength and armaments of the British at Fort Vancouver. The War Department, made aware that the Far West held promise for settlement and concerned about the British presence, now needed better intelligence.

Captain Benjamin Bonneville got the assignment to undertake a major espionage mission into the West beginning in 1832. Taking a "leave of absence" from the army, he assumed the cover of a fur trapper and announced that his interests were purely commercial. But the War Department had instructed him fully about what he was to do on his "leave."

He was to explore the country to the "Rocky Mountains, and beyond with a view of assertaining the nature and character of the various tribes of Indians inhabiting those regions: the trade which might profitably be carried on with them: the quality of soil, the productions, the minerals, the natural history, the climate, the Geography and Topography, as well as the Geology of various parts of the Country within the limits of the Territories belonging to the United States, between our frontier, and the Pacific. . . ."

Moreover, in his spare time he was to devote his attention to what has come to be called the strategy of "small wars." That is, he was to note the number of warriors in each Indian tribe, their alliances, their state of war or peace, etc., and most important, their manner of making war: "of the mode of subsisting themselves during a state of war, and a state of peace, their Arms, and the effect of them, whether they attack on foot or on horseback, detailing their discipline, and maneuvers of the war parties, the power of their horses, size and general description; in short, every information which you may conceive would be useful to the Government."

Perhaps the most significant thing about his official instructions was the fact that he was commanded to collect information about such a wide variety of subjects—far beyond the needs of commerce, the fur trade, or even the requirements of a military campaign against the Indians. Thus, in an "unofficial" capacity, Bonneville was to serve the cause of national expansion.

He was to do all this, General [Alexander] Macomb's letter of instructions made clear, at his own or his backer's expense. The government would have no official part in it.[12]

Bonneville explored American territory, entered the Oregon country (then jointly occupied with Great Britain), and continued into the Mexican provinces of New Mexico and California. Commenting upon his 1833 report to the War Department, Goetzmann states, "as a field intelligence report, it ranks with the best that the government had ever received from the West."[13] Bonneville put to rest all doubts that California was a great place to settle.

After Bonneville's expedition, the pace of U.S. intelligence collection in the West quickened and its organization improved. In 1838, the government reorganized the Army Corps of Topographical Engineers. The corps is a likely candidate for the origin of the U.S. intelligence community: from the very beginning, its functions were intelligence gathering and production. Moreover, since the corps was out on the frontier, facing hostile inhabitants and exploring lands that were either in dispute or definitely under foreign possession, it was engaged in foreign intelligence. The officers of the corps included some of the legendary names in American exploration: Colonel John Abert, Lieutenant James W. Abert, Colonel Stephen Watts Kearny, and Captain John C. Frémont.

The Topographical Engineers blazed the trails and cleared the way for the westward migrations of the next half-century. They mapped these trails, as well as Indian campsites and possible battlegrounds, and they planned campaigns and field operations. Kearny, a cavalry officer, argued that a few principal army forts would be more effective in pacifying the Indians than a string of outposts along the western trails, and he tested the feasibility of cavalry forays. Frémont, a maverick, entered Mexican territory repeatedly between 1842 and 1845, ignoring official orders or carrying out those of his father-in-law, Thomas Hart Benton, the expansion-minded senator from Missouri. Goetzmann characterizes these "secret missions" as "the outstanding examples, in American history, of the calculated use of exploring expeditions [intelligence collection] as diplomatic weapons."[14] Frémont's actions in California in 1846 during the Bear Flag revolt were probably even more spectacular (see chapter 5).

The army collected most of the intelligence that would enable the United States to conquer the continent, but a naval officer also made an important contribution. In 1836, Congress authorized Lieutenant Charles Wilkes to undertake an expedition to Antarctica, the South Seas, and the Pacific Northwest. Wilkes sailed in 1838 and reached the Columbia River and Puget Sound three years later. He collected an enormous amount of data about the region, and his information supported the forty-ninth parallel as the sine qua non of the U.S. position in the Oregon question (despite controversy about the influence of his findings upon the 1846 Oregon Treaty with Great Britain). Similarly, in the 1848 Treaty of Guadalupe-Hidalgo with Mexico, when the U.S. demarcated the Californias, it drew a line west from the junction of the

Gila and Colorado rivers. This line ran not due west along the parallel but westward, to a point on the coast one nautical mile south of San Diego Bay. U.S. intelligence had served U.S. diplomacy well.

Continental expansion was virtually complete by 1848. Almost all the great explorations of what came to be the American West had been led by military officers and were strongly suggestive of clandestine operations.

Captain Meriwether Lewis and Lieutenant William Clark (1804–1806)

Lieutenant Zebulon Pike (1805–1807)

Major Stephen H. Long (1819–1820)

Captain Benjamin Bonneville (1831–1835)

Lieutenant Charles Wilkes (1838–1841)

Captain John C. Frémont (1842–1846)

Colonel Stephen W. Kearny (1842–1846)

When seen as intelligence missions, these expeditions have a sense of national purpose more consistent than is usually portrayed in general history texts. Seen in the context of the covert activities in the adjacent borderlands and the not-so-private filibustering expeditions, this impression is even more manifest. Manifest Destiny, however, received a helping hand. Even as expansionism was causing war with Mexico to loom, the administration of James K. Polk used covert action to ensure that it got its way.

5

Secret Agents
of Manifest Destiny

Texas remained the Lone Star Republic for nine years, from its independence from Mexico until its annexation to the United States. Private American citizens had participated in the independence movement, but the administration of Andrew Jackson rebuffed the overtures of Texas for annexation, almost as if to demonstrate its innocence. Whigs and Democrats steered clear of expansion, fearful that it might threaten the fragile unity of their respective parties. Martin Van Buren avoided the issue, and William Henry Harrison seemed ready to do the same. But Harrison's untimely death in 1841 elevated John Tyler to the presidency, and Tyler viewed the situation from a different perspective.

"Tyler too"—a Virginian and only nominally a Whig—was a president without a party. Tyler needed a political miracle to succeed himself and was therefore willing to risk taking a pro-annexationist stance. After Secretary of State Daniel Webster resigned in disgust, Abel P. Upshur negotiated the Texas annexation treaty. The work was Upshur's, but he died in an accident before completing it, and the treaty was submitted to the Senate by his successor, the controversial John C. Calhoun. This probably ended any chance it had for approval. The matter stood still until the election of 1844.

As had been foreseen, the Whigs dumped Tyler and nominated Henry Clay, the longtime presidential aspirant. The veteran states-man, confident at last of victory, decided to play it safe and hedge on the annexation issue. His Democratic opponent, James K. Polk—

the original "dark horse" candidate—with everything to gain and little to lose, seized upon the expansion issue. Moreover, Polk offered something to both sides on the slavery issue: Oregon for the North and Texas for the South. Expansion proved to be popular and overcame concerns about renewing the sectional crisis. Polk was elected, making Clay a three-time loser. However, before Polk reached the White House, Tyler acted to have Congress settle the Texas annexation question by joint resolution. Requiring only a simple majority vote in each house, the joint resolution narrowly passed in both, and Tyler signed it on March 1, 1845—virtually on the eve of Polk's inauguration.

The resolution, however, left a number of loose ends. Although Tyler had achieved his purpose and as far as Polk was concerned Texas was "in," the U.S. action had been unilateral. The annexation was not really consummated until June, when Texas took a complementary action. In the meantime, the Mexican government declared that it would not recognize the legality of the situation, and even if it did, the territory of Texas extended only to the Nueces River and not the Rio Grande, as the Texans claimed. In other words, the United States could not annex Texas because it belonged to Mexico, and even if Mexico consented, the boundary had to be resolved.

Polk believed that Mexico would come around in time, but he could not risk giving either the Mexicans or the Texans the impression that the Rio Grande boundary was negotiable. In order to overcome any opposition in Texas to annexation, Polk had to show that he would back the Texans' extreme claims. Besides, he had ambitions in California. Under these circumstances, Polk conceived a plan of covert action that was designed to bring Texas into the Union, acquire additional territory, and yet avoid the stigma of aggression.

Polk's plan called for a band of Texas volunteers to cross the Nueces, penetrate the disputed territory, and attack the town of Matamoros at the mouth of the Rio Grande. (There was no Brownsville as yet.) The Texans would become involved in a war with Mexico, and the United States would come to their rescue and, along with annexing Texas, would "annex" the war. Polk sent Archibald Yell, the former governor of Arkansas, and Charles

A. Wickliffe, Tyler's postmaster general, as advance agents to set the scheme in motion. His case officer was Commodore Robert F. Stockton, who arrived off Galveston on May 12 with a fleet of four vessels.[1] (Incredibly, Stockton—an officer of the U.S. Navy in command of a squadron of American warships—was supposed to make it appear that he was financing the operation out of his own pocket.) These operatives easily recruited Major General Sidney Sherman of the Texas militia, who favored annexation and was eager to assert Texas' claim to the Rio Grande.

They were less successful in enlisting the cooperation of the Texas president, Anson B. Jones, who allegedly opposed annexation. Jones was collaborating with the British chargé, Charles Elliot, in a plan to secure Mexico's recognition of Texas in return for Texas's promise to remain independent. Despite these maneuvers, Polk instructed Stockton to obtain the "sanction" of the Texas government to give their project credibility. This meant approaching Jones. On May 28, Dr. John H. Wright, the surgeon on board Stockton's flagship, the *Princeton*, acting as Stockton's spokesman and accompanied by General Sherman, met with Jones and described the plan. They sought authorization for Sherman to raise an army of two or three thousand men for the purpose of marching on Matamoros. They pledged that Stockton would provide arms and provisions and pay for the services of the volunteers. Sherman stated that he approved of the operation, as did the people of Texas in general. Although his testimony may be suspect because of his attitude, Jones subsequently published the following version of the affair, which reveals all the ingredients of a classic covert action plan.

> I asked Dr. Wright if he had written instructions from the Commodore, or any communication from him to me; that the matter was a grave one, and I did not well see how, without them, if disposed even, I could undertake such weighty responsibilities. As I expected, he replied in the negative, but that if I wished, Com. Stockton would visit me in person, and give me the same assurances in person. I asked him if the Minister of the United States [Andrew Jackson Donelson] was cognizant of the matter. He then stated to me that the scheme was rather a confidential and secret one, that it was undertaken under the sanction of the United

States Government, but that the President did not wish to become
known in the matter, but approved Com. Stockton's plan;—that
as an evidence of that to me, Mr. Wickliffe was associated with
the Commodore; that the President of the United States, satisfied
that annexation was in effect consummated, wished Texas to
place herself in an attitude of hostile activity towards Mexico, so
that, when Texas was finally brought into the Union, *she might
bring a war with her;* and this was the object of the expedition to
Matamoras [*sic*], as now proposed. He further stated that Com.
Stockton was . . . very wealthy; that he had means of his own
sufficient to support and carry on the expedition; and that it was
desirable it should appear to the world as his individual enterprise, while at the same time I was given to understand that the
Government of the United States was, in reality, at the bottom
of it, and anxious for its accomplishment and for the reasons
stated. I then said, smiling, "So, gentlemen, the Commodore,
on the part of the United States, wishes me to *manufacture a war*
for them"; to which they replied affirmatively. Subsequently I
had an interview with Gen. Sherman alone. He expressed to me
his own anxiety that I should assent to Com. Stockton's proposals, represented that it was extremely popular among the people,
and that he would have no difficulty in obtaining the requisite
number of men, upon the assurances of Stockton that they should
be provisioned and paid. I obtained all the information in my
power from these parties as to their plans; and although indig-
nant at the proposition . . . I suppressed my feelings, and gave
no expression of opinion, but suggested every objection and difficulty which presented themselves to my mind, and for three days
kept them answering these objections or obviating difficulties,
until they became pretty thoroughly impressed with the belief
that I was thinking very seriously on the matter; and so indeed
I was, but not in the way they hoped.[2]

Jones was, in effect, stalling until his own negotiations with
Mexico were completed. On June 4, after Elliot returned from
Mexico City with a preliminary treaty in which Mexico offered to
recognize the Republic of Texas, Jones issued a proclamation of
peace between the two countries and declared his intention to submit the entire question to the Congress. The Stockton mission was
aborted. But it had achieved part of its purpose nonetheless: on

June 18, the Texas legislature unanimously approved the U.S. offer of annexation and rejected Mexico's belated proposal, as presented by Jones. Stockton had the pleasure of delivering the news to Washington in person. Sailing from Galveston on June 23, he reached Annapolis on the *Princeton,* a steamer, in record-setting time on July 3, 1845. Although Stockton had failed to provoke a war, he led the American forces a year later in California, when the U.S.–Mexican War finally erupted.[3]

The war occurred as a result of Polk's persistence in his expansionism on the Rio Grande frontier and in upper California. Polk was not committed to a particular course to obtain his purpose; he was prepared to purchase the territory if that could be arranged. Learning that Mexico might talk, Polk dispatched John Slidell to Mexico City in December 1845, but the president of Mexico refused to receive him. Polk pointed to this behavior as evidence of Mexico's intransigence, ignoring the fact that the Mexican government had agreed to receive only a "commissioner" but that Slidell had been sent with full credentials as minister plenipotentiary. Mexico considered itself the injured party and expected concessions as a condition for renewing diplomatic relations. To receive Slidell now would be to let the United States back into the game without anteing up. The government of José Herrera had taken a risk by agreeing even to talk; when Polk sent an accredited minister with instructions to, in effect, purchase half of Mexico, General Mariano Paredes staged a coup, proclaiming, "The President is trying to avoid a glorious war." Mexico had its "hawks" and "doves" too.

Satisfied that he had done what he could to settle the matter peaceably, Polk ordered General Zachary Taylor into the disputed zone between the Nueces and the Rio Grande. Polk had finally, on his own responsibility, taken the step that he and Stockton had urged upon the Texans covertly the preceding May and June. It seemed to be Polk's most controversial and provocative action to date, but even so, Mexico did not react. Over the objections of his own cabinet, the frustrated Polk was contemplating drafting a war message that would outline American grievances against Mexico, when in late April he received word that Mexican forces "had crossed" the Rio Grande and clashed with General Taylor, killing a number of his men. Polk went before Congress to proclaim that

Mexico had invaded U.S. territory and "shed American blood upon the American soil." A young congressman from Illinois, Abraham Lincoln, questioned the accuracy of Polk's assertions, but Polk had forced the issue.[4]

In the meantime, Polk had been promoting clandestine operations in California, so as to leave nothing to chance. Along with the Texas border, Polk was concerned about California. The United States consul at Monterey, Thomas Oliver Larkin, had been sending alarming reports to Washington alleging British machinations in the area. Polk, who was already engaged in negotiations with Great Britain over the division of Oregon, was determined that no foreign power would thwart his expansionist ambitions in California. In October 1845, Polk appointed Larkin confidential agent and instructed him "to counteract foreign influence, stimulate separatist tendencies, and encourage annexation to the United States."[5] These highly confidential instructions were entrusted to Lieutenant Archibald Gillespie of the U.S. Marine Corps. Gillespie carried them to Larkin disguised as a merchant representing Bryant, Sturgis, and Company of Boston. Since he had to cross Mexican territory from Vera Cruz to Mazatlán to get there, the presidential spy memorized the message, apparently reciting it faithfully upon reaching Larkin in Monterey in April 1846.[6]

Gillespie then continued northward toward Oregon's Klamath Lake, where he encountered Captain Frémont. He repeated Polk's instructions to Larkin to Frémont "for his information" and delivered a packet of letters from Senator Benton to the captain. Frémont, in command of an armed party of sixty men and assisted by the scout Kit Carson, had been in California since January 1846, ostensibly on an exploring expedition that ranged from the Great Salt Lake to Sutter's Fort. In March, Mexican authorities had objected to his presence in the Salinas Valley near Monterey; he thereafter had withdrawn to the Oregon frontier, where Gillespie overtook him. Apprised of the instructions to Larkin, Frémont turned southward toward Sacramento, where he incited a group of American settlers and eventually took charge of the Bear Flag revolt in June—the first step in detaching California from Mexico.

There is a great deal of controversy about the cause-and-effect relationship between Gillespie's meeting with Frémont and Frémont's role in the Bear Flag revolt. Most historians treat the evidence as circumstantial and ascribe Frémont's actions to his own erratic and impetuous behavior. But his activities nonetheless comported fully with Polk's policy in the region, and the events betray the elements of a standard dirty trick.

Polk was convinced that Mexico's hold over California was tenuous at best and was also concerned about British power and intentions (there being a linkage between the Oregon question and California). He therefore encouraged Americans residing in the region to create a situation that would enable him to intervene without blame. In December 1845, in instructions "heavily marked 'Secret,'" Secretary of the Navy George Bancroft ordered the commander of the Pacific squadron, Commodore John D. Sloat, to move his ships from Mazatlán to waters off Oregon and California. Bancroft instructed Sloat to keep Larkin informed of his location at all times and authorized him to exchange rifles and small arms with American settlers in the Willamette valley for "wheat, flour or other stores."[7] Bancroft sent Sloat separately a copy of Polk's instructions to Larkin and provided the commodore with copies of the Texas Constitution translated into Spanish, instructing him to distribute them at Monterey and San Francisco.[8]

Frémont assumed active leadership of the Bear Flag revolt in June and though the parties concerned were unaware that a state of war existed between Mexico and the United States, he was able to obtain arms and ammunition from a U.S. warship in San Francisco Bay.[9] On July 7, the outbreak of war was confirmed, and Sloat proclaimed that California was "henceforward . . . a portion of the United States," unilaterally terminating the California Republic. Two weeks later, Sloat withdrew, owing to ill health, and was replaced by Commodore Stockton, who completed the conquest of California (with help from General Kearny, who came overland from Kansas and Santa Fe).[10]

Frémont's actions, in combination with the instructions to Larkin and to the U.S. naval commanders operating off California, support the argument that a plan of covert action existed to provide Polk with a pretense for intervention in California. The key factor in this interpretation is the behavior of Gillespie. It is difficult to believe that Gillespie, a U.S. Marine Corps lieutenant entrusted with secret instructions and risking a spy's fate by crossing Mexico in disguise, would have disclosed these instructions to Frémont on his own authority, even if only "for his information." Frémont was a U.S. officer, but the "need to know" principle still applied. Frémont, too, may have exceeded his instructions by his actions; overzealousness on the part of case officers has been a chronic problem in clandestine operations. On the other hand, Frémont's freewheeling nature was known in Washington and may even have been counted upon. By January 1848, when Mexico surrendered to U.S. forces, covert action had already created circumstances for the acquisition of New Mexico and California—far exceeding the original *casus belli* stated in Polk's war message.

Despite the immense role covert action played in the events leading up to the war with Mexico, no move was made to establish a permanent intelligence capability, even a conventional one, either in the fighting or in the peace that followed. Taylor ignored intelligence almost to the point of dereliction in his invasion of northern Mexico. General Winfield Scott, who landed at Vera Cruz and occupied central Mexico, displayed better intelligence sense. He organized a crude but effective secret service known as the Mexican Spy Company under Colonel Ethan Allen Hitchcock. Hitchcock served as case officer for a particularly wily and resourceful resident agent, known only as Domínguez, who recruited several hundred agents and performed guerrilla and espionage operations in and around Mexico City. Domínguez contributed to Scott's capture of the city in September 1847, but Scott's officers seemed prejudiced against the Spy Company; the officers described the Spy Company as "the Forty Thieves" and treated the Mexican agents with scorn and contempt.

Despite its usefulness, then, intelligence emerged from the Mexican War with something of a bad name. As George S. Bryan has observed, "the war with Mexico gave many American officers a certain practical training for Civil War marches and battlefields. But from its extempore secret service little of positive value could have been derived."[11] During the Civil War, this failing certainly showed.

6

The Clandestine War
between the States

The Civil War presented opportunities for intelligence operations, especially espionage and covert action, as the American Revolution had before it. A conflict of divided loyalties fought on common ground once again, it was difficult to tell friend from foe simply by sight; indeed, both sides might be represented in the same family. The war provided opportunities for recruiting resident agents and placed a heavy emphasis upon counterintelligence.

Despite these opportunities—and dangers—intelligence did not play as crucial a role in the Civil War as it had in the American Revolution. Few battles were actually decided by intelligence, and no Civil War general equaled George Washington in good intelligence sense. There was no intelligence bureau in the federal government to coordinate the collection, analysis, and dissemination of intelligence; nor was there any army or navy intelligence, nor even an investigative branch within the departments of Justice or Treasury, strange as that may seem.[1] Before the war, an intelligence operation of sorts had been functioning: the so-called underground railroad, which maintained a network of agents and safe houses to assist the escape of runaway slaves, but there is no evidence that this operation was used by northern officials for clandestine operations after the war started. Generals on both sides who paid attention to intelligence at all simply improvised and operated their own shows.

But necessity is the mother of invention, and this pathetic state of intelligence led to the organization of the first "secret service" within the U.S. government. Beginning in April 1861, under the authority of the War Department, and with Washington under martial law, the detective Allan Pinkerton organized a secret service to protect the capital. In a situation where dissent seemed to threaten the political order and where, as President Lincoln described it, "The enemy behind us is more dangerous to the country than the enemy before us," it is not surprising that an agency concerned with internal security would emerge. Analogies, although not always helpful, may be considered with the Committees of Safety in the American Revolution, the Palmer Raids in the 1920s "Red Scare," and the "plumbers" in the Vietnam War era. The establishment of the Secret Service seemed to arise from "a clear and present danger."

Pinkerton initially attracted attention by uncovering a February 1861 plot to assassinate President-elect Abraham Lincoln. A group of conspirators in Baltimore had planned to intercept and kill Lincoln on his way from Illinois to Washington for his inauguration. Pinkerton, the head of the private National Detective Agency of Chicago, had been hired by Samuel M. Felton, president of the Philadelphia, Wilmington, and Baltimore Railroad, to protect his line against sabotage and vandalism. Felton's railroad connected Philadelphia and the nation's capital; he was aware that it might be disrupted by southern sympathizers residing in Maryland and sought the services of Pinkerton, who already had a reputation as a railroad detective. In fact, Union general George B. McClellan, a director of the Illinois Central Railroad, had recommended him. In the course of his investigation of would-be saboteurs, Pinkerton discovered the Lincoln assassination plot.

Using the pseudonym "E.J. Allen," Pinkerton and several of his detectives infiltrated a rebel band in Baltimore led by "Captain" Fernandina, an erstwhile barber of Barnum's Hotel. The hotel seemed to be the meeting place for about thirty ardent secessionists, including the city's police chief, George P. Kane. The plot called for the assassination of Lincoln as he passed through Baltimore, which was to provide the spark that would set off a general insurrection in Maryland and cut off Washington, D.C., from the North. One of Pinkerton's detectives attended a meeting where the conspirators passed a box of envelopes; one of them contained a red ballot, designating the man who drew it as Lincoln's assassin. As it turned out, there were were eight red ballots; apparently Fernandina was taking no chances with cold feet.[2]

Armed with this information, Pinkerton persuaded Lincoln to let him arrange a clandestine passage to Washington for him. On the night before Lincoln's planned journey, Pinkerton escorted him discreetly from a banquet in Harrisburg, took him undercover to Philadelphia, and placed him in a closed sleeping car on the night train to the federal capital. In the middle of the night, the train carrying Lincoln passed unnoticed through Baltimore, presumably leaving the glorious dreams of a score of would-be assassins unfulfilled. In Washington (a city described as swarming with spies and as a "sieve"), Pinkerton advised Lincoln of the danger to the federal government of subversion and espionage and, as noted, got the job.

Although he was slow and methodical, in accordance with the detective's trade of accumulating evidence, Pinkerton was also good at counterintelligence. Left on his own, he might have performed well and rid the District of Columbia of spies, but McClellan, commanding the Army of the Potomac, wanted him on his staff as intelligence chief. In that role, Pinkerton was out of his element. He had no experience in collecting and evaluating military intelligence, and his investigative techniques were simply too slow for the requirements of a military campaign. He consistently overestimated the strength of enemy forces, tending to compound McClellan's already cautious nature. Pinkerton did run a few spies behind enemy lines and used infiltrators, with tragic results in one case.

Timothy Webster was one of Pinkerton's best operatives. It was he who had infiltrated the secessionist bands in Baltimore and had helped uncover the Lincoln assassination plot. He remained undercover, and as the rebellion developed, he convinced the local Rebels that he was one of them. A man of dash and boldness, he became a courier between the Baltimoreans and their brethren in the Maryland regiments within the Confederacy; he made numerous trips into the South and returned with important information for his chief, Pinkerton. In March 1862, at the very beginning of McClellan's Peninsular Campaign, Pinkerton lost touch with

Webster, who was then in Richmond, and sent two operatives to inquire about him. The two men were English nationals and anticipated that that was all the cover they needed. They found Webster in his hotel, where he was seriously ill with rheumatoid arthritis. That had been the cause of his silence and he was in no other kind of danger, but the appearance of these two men at the hotel blew his cover. He was arrested and hanged as a spy in April 1862.

Lafayette Baker was another daring Union operative, whom fate treated more kindly. Baker operated behind Confederate lines for most of the first year of the war with great success. Although an infiltrator, he established his bona fides by posing as an itinerant photographer. Photography was then in its infancy, and what good soldier would not like to have his picture taken to send to the folks back home? Baker did not have to make excuses to enter military encampments; they invited him in, and he apparently visited "all the regiments of Secession then training in Virginia."[3] After almost a year of such risk, the Southern commanders came to suspect him, and after being detained and released he escaped across the Potomac. Nonetheless, his success enabled him to replace Pinkerton as the capital's secret service chief, when the latter resigned over the firing of McClellan in November 1862.

Lafayette Baker organized the Secret Service Bureau, reporting directly to President Lincoln and Secretary of War Edwin M. Stanton. While operating under military authority, Baker showed himself to be a bully and tyrant. A zealot, he ignored constitutional guarantees in his crusade to preserve the Constitution (although, to some degree, Lincoln, Stanton, and Secretary of State William Seward committed similar excesses). Performing the combined functions of military police and counterintelligence, Baker was at least no amateur, and he introduced many techniques that were employed by European secret police, including "the nation's first police dossier system . . . [and] first criminal photo file."

> He instituted a policy of seizing suspects in the dead of night when their resistance to interrogation and their ability to seek help would be at the lowest ebb.
> He made a science of the interrogation of prisoners, using

teams of detectives to work over a suspect until he was satisfied he either had the full story or he could drag no more information from his victim.

He established a secret fund for building and feeding a vast army of informers and unlisted agents. No one except he knew the full range of his organization.[4]

After he was placed in charge of the Old Capitol Prison, Baker became judge and jailer as well as policeman.[5] His regime tended to confirm the Americans' worst fears about the dangers of secret police. It was apparent that he and his kind of intelligence organization would not survive the end of the war, even before he failed to protect Lincoln's life.

In the meantime, after Pinkerton's departure and with Baker's emphasis upon witch-hunting, military intelligence was unfocused. Some centralizing effort was made in March 1863, when the Bureau of Military Information was created under the direction of Colonel George H. Sharpe. It operated some successful spy rings in the South and eventually achieved respectability, but its service never really extended beyond the Army of the Potomac. For the most part, individual commanders organized their own intelligence services, whose success rested upon the skill of the particular officers assigned.

Civil War commanders seemed to shun the word *spy* and preferred the word *scout*. Indeed, despite the seeming abundance of opportunities for recruiting resident agents, military intelligence employed infiltrators and sent volunteer soldiers behind the lines in disguise on high-risk missions. Their 50 percent survival rate demonstrated just how perilous the job was. The scouts themselves usually belonged to special units that undertook forays or raids behind enemy lines, in the style of the modern-day commandos or operational groups of OSS fame. Since these units wore enemy uniforms while they operated behind enemy lines, they were spies in the technical sense and were treated as such when they were caught. The scouts tended to enjoy a special status within the army, according to George S. Bryan, like the aviators of World War I; they received extra pay and better quarters and were relieved of onerous duties and details. Union scout John Landegon admitted,

There was often enough that I'd think: "Well, by gee! if ever I get back safe from this fool scout I'll never go out again. I'll go back to my regiment. I'll stand guard, I'll do picket, I'll clean camp; but I'm darned if I go in gray out of the lines." But I would get in all right, and loaf around a few days and watch the other boys work, and then I'd get restless or think of the big money, and then the order would come and out I'd go—like as not into worse than before.[6]

Major Harry Young, who served as General Philip H. Sheridan's intelligence chief in the Shenandoah Valley, typified this breed. Young's daring and resourcefulness earned him the respect of both sides. A master of disguise, oblivious of danger, this James Bond prototype seemed to spend as much time in Confederate gray as in Yankee blue. Colonel Harry Gilmor, a Confederate scout captured by Young, remarked, "We never knew when or where to look for him [Young], and yet we knew he or some of his best men were constantly inside our lines."[7] On one occasion in February 1865, Young penetrated as deep behind enemy lines as Staunton, Virginia, in an effort to abduct General Jubal A. Early. Although he failed to accomplish his purpose, his return alone added to the romantic image of the Civil War scout.

Campaigning in the Shenandoah in 1862, General John C. Frémont—no stranger to clandestine operations—named his spy company Jessie Scouts, for his wife, Jessie Benton. The name caught on, and in Virginia, at least, a Jessie Scout was by definition a Union soldier-spy. A mythology sprang up. Just before the second Battle of Bull Run in August 1862, a federal scout posing as a Confederate officer was caught brazenly trying to direct General John Bell Hood's troops down the wrong road. As Hood's men placed the noose around his neck, he proclaimed, "I'll simply ask you to say, if ever you should speak of this, that Jack Sterry, when the rebels got him, died as a Jessie Scout should."[8]

One of the original Jessie Scouts was Grenville M. Dodge, later the builder of the Union Pacific Railroad; he served under Frémont in Missouri in 1861. Dodge attained the rank of general and became the principal intelligence chief in the West, where he rendered important service in the campaigns of U.S. Grant and William Rosecrans in Tennessee and Mississippi. He was probably the Civil War's most professional intelligence officer, organizing a spy network that comprised over a hundred agents. He set specific requirements for these agents in order to obtain precise data on enemy strength, movements, and weapons.[9] Not only did he maintain a command of military scouts, he recruited resident agents and established a chain of messengers made up principally of women and blacks. According to one observer, the female couriers proved especially adept at coaxing a pass "out of some gallant or sentimental Southerner" on the pretense of visiting relatives in Union-occupied territory.[10] Dodge even had an agent acting as a spy for General James Longstreet—one of the few examples of a double agent in the Civil War.

In November 1863, Dodge captured and ordered the execution of Southern spy Sam Davis. Davis could have avoided being hanged by revealing that General Braxton Bragg's intelligence chief, Captain Henry B. Shaw, was present in his group, but he did not. After the war, Dodge, told of this sacrifice, joined with the citizens of Nashville in erecting a monument honoring Davis as "the Nathan Hale of the Confederacy." Captain Shaw, aka "E. Coleman," was the leader of Coleman's Scouts, one of the South's best espionage units.

Confederate commanders organized scout companies for combat intelligence much as their Yankee counterparts did. Among generals of North or South, Thomas J. "Stonewall" Jackson was the closest to George Washington in intelligence sense. He had a virtual obsession with security. To maintain the element of surprise, he did not discuss his plans even with his own staff: "Around his headquarters an air of mystery rested. 'Mystery—mystery is the secret of success' was a remark ascribed to him, as was the more colloquial protest, 'If my coat knew what I intended to do, I'd take if off and throw it away.' Believing that Federal spies were everywhere, he took the utmost precaution to keep intelligence from reaching the enemy."[11]

For intelligence gathering, Jackson relied upon Colonel Turner Ashby, who led his scouts and carried out numerous solo spy missions behind Union lines. Usually disguised as a veterinarian owing to his knowledge of horses, Ashby had little trouble traveling in enemy-held territory because "horse doctors" were always in demand. On one trip, dressed in homespun and astride an old plow horse, "his saddle-bags laden with an alleged cure for ringbone or spavin," he ranged as far north as Chambersburg, Pennsylvania, and visited the camp of Union general Robert Patterson at Harpers Ferry. Jackson, precise in his intelligence requirements, instructed Ashby to learn "the position of the enemy's forces, his numbers and movements, what generals are in command and their head-quarters, especially the headquarters of the commanding general."[12] Presumably, he returned with valuable information. At the same time, according to one observer, "whatever damage Ashby may have done the Union Army, he did its horses a great deal of good."[13]

For sheer derring-do, Colonel John S. Mosby, the leader of Mosby's Rangers, outdid even Turner Ashby. Although not a typical spy chief in that he refused to wear a "false uniform" and operated principally as a guerrilla, Mosby collected intelligence on his forays, and his men, when captured, met the same end that scouts and spies did. Mosby operated as a partisan in support of the conventional military forces. He succeeded to the extent that he dominated a portion of northwestern Virginia and the Shenan-doah, known as Mosby's Confederacy. His operations may be regarded as a nineteenth-century prototype for integrating intelligence operations with resistance movements in occupied territories (which later was exactly William J. Donovan's purpose in the OSS).

Regular army officers, then as later, professed strong misgivings about partisan guerrilla warfare. Confederate general Thomas L. Rosser regarded the guerrilla bands "as a nuisance and an evil to the service." He castigated them as "thieves, stealing, pillaging, plundering and doing every manner of mischief and crime."[14] Robert E. Lee wanted to abolish them, seeing "the whole system as an unmixed evil."[15] Despite these attitudes, Mosby generally was looked upon as an exception, as being "highly effective" and "courageous."

Among his scouts were people like Walter Bowie, who, although somewhat mischievous, did not seem to lose control. Bowie was already a legend in his native Prince George's County,

Maryland, by the time he joined Mosby in the spring of 1864. He constantly sought permission to return to Maryland to "stir things up." Given the green light, Bowie and several Rangers attempted a raid on Annapolis, hoping to abduct Maryland's pro-Union governor or, if that failed, to rob the local bank. But they miscalculated: the governor was away, and the place was swarming with federal troops. Bowie, who had escaped from Lafayette Baker's Old Capitol Prison, could not get away. Pursued into Montgomery County, he was killed in a fire-fight before he could reach safety in Virginia.[16]

In recent wars, machines like aircraft and sensors have largely replaced these adventurous scouts. But Civil War intelligence, too, was not entirely without technological innovation. The telegraph, a new means of communication, was used, and the wiretap was introduced as a method of intelligence collection. Recognizing the military significance of the telegraph, the federal government took control of commercial telegraph for the duration and created the U.S. Military Telegraph under Anson Stager, the former general superintendent of Western Union. Stager successfully tapped Southern lines and read Confederate messages, even those in cipher; and he quickly saw the need for communications security. The telegraph did for cryptography what the radio later did for cryptanalysis.[17] Stager created a new cipher system that made Union communications secure. The fledgling U.S. Army Signal Corps assumed these communications intelligence functions after the war, when the Military Telegraph was phased out.

The scouts did not have even human intelligence all to themselves. In fact, many of the best Civil War spies were women. Espionage, like nursing, seemed to be an acceptable way for a woman "to do her part." As a noncombatant, her presence on the home front was, so to speak, "normal," and she could blend in. Although some writers have described Southern spy Belle Boyd as a "charmer in crinoline," the female spies of the Civil War again did not fit the Mata Hari stereotype. These women were diverse in age, appearance, and method of operation. Their gender may have facilitated their missions, but they did not use sex to achieve their purposes.

Rose Greenhow, for example, a wealthy Washington society

matron, spied for the Confederacy. The widow of Robert Greenhow, an officer of the State Department in the Buchanan administration, she had important contacts in government circles, and
her niece was married to Senator Stephen A. Douglas. As a
Southern sympathizer, she willingly became a member of a spy
ring that had been created by agents of General Pierre G.T.
Beauregard. Pinkerton infiltrated the ring and discovered that this
popular hostess was making use of her dinner parties, but not
before she gave the Confederacy the timely warning about Yankee
troop movements that enabled it to defeat the North at Manassas
Junction (the first Battle of Bull Run) on July 21, 1861—probably
the only Civil War battle to be determined by intelligence. Pinkerton placed Greenhow under house arrest, transferred her to Old
Capitol Prison, then permitted her to depart for Richmond. As a
woman, she did not face the gallows even though her case officer
had written to her, "Our President and our General [Beauregard]
direct me to thank you. The Confederacy owes you a debt." In
Richmond, Jefferson Davis personally acknowledged that "but for
you there would have been no battle of Bull Run."[18]

The same leniency befell Belle Boyd, who also spent some time
in Old Capitol. Boyd was probably the best-known female spy of
the Confederacy—not because she was the most effective but
because she publicized her exploits. She was one of the first spies
to go on the lecture circuit after the war. Although she has been
described as a femme fatale, "Miss Belle wasn't really an especially
pretty girl. Surviving portraits show that she looked rather like one
of those horses she rode so perfectly—a long face, a very long nose,
and prominent teeth."[19] It is likely that on the lecture circuit, her
stories "got better" with the passage of time.

As a resident of Martinsburg, Virginia/West Virginia—a town
variously occupied by the North and South—this young woman,
age seventeen at the war's outbreak, gathered intelligence for
Turner Ashby and Stonewall Jackson. Her information was probably capricious and inconsistent, derived from routine rides
through the countryside and "from young officers, who always
find it hard to keep from talking too freely to smiling young
sirens."[20] She was essentially a lone operative, but she may have
served as a contact for other Confederate agents, sending messages

through the lines via her black servant, Eliza. Her boldest adventure occurred in May 1862 at Front Royal, Virginia, where she literally ran across the battlefield, "shot at by snipers, with an artillery duel screaming and crashing overhead, a hail of iron around her, a shell-burst seven yards distant drenching her with earth,"[21] to inform Jackson of a weakness in the Yankee line, thereby contributing to the Southern victory. Belle Boyd was arrested on three occasions on charges of espionage, but the headstrong woman so intimidated her captors that they eventually permitted her to go free on the condition that she depart for Richmond and not return.

Opposing Boyd in the Shenandoah Valley, Rebecca Wright of Winchester served the Union cause. A Quaker, Friend Rebecca was a known Yankee sympathizer in a Rebel town, which led General Sheridan to recruit her as a spy. Sheridan sent a message to Wright by means of an elderly black man, a peddler and a reliable courier, saying that he was seeking information about the strength and disposition of General Early's forces. With no training as a spy but fortuitously having entertained "a convalescent Southern officer" in her home the night before, the young woman recalled some of the conversation and informed Sheridan,

> I have no communication whatever with the rebels, but will tell you what I know. The division of General [Joseph B.] Kershaw, and Cutshaw's artillery, twelve guns and men, General [Richard] Anderson commanding, have been sent away, and no more are expected, as they cannot be spared from Richmond. I do not know how the troops are situated, but the force is much smaller than represented.[22]

This information was vital, especially the fact that Kershaw was gone, and Sheridan's famous "ride" (October 1864), in which he crushed the Confederate forces in the Shenandoah Valley once and for all, was made possible in part by what has to be one of the most outstanding "one-shot" intelligence reports in history.

Perhaps not as decisive but of longer duration was the clandestine activity of Pauline Cushman, "the Spy of the Cumberland." Cushman provided useful information to federal commanders in Tennessee. As an actress in a theatrical company in Louisville, she established her bona fides by toasting "Jeff Davis and the Confederacy'' onstage. Banished to Nashville, she performed in stock companies throughout the region, reporting to her case officer, William Truesdail, the head of the police office of the Army of the Cumberland. A woman of tremendous valor, she held the rank of major in the Union army. Her principal object was to determine the size and disposition of Bragg's forces at Shelbyville and Tullahoma. However, she committed the error of making notes; Bragg discovered her true identity and ordered her execution. She escaped the gallows only by chance, when federal forces overran Shelbyville in late summer 1863 and the retreating Rebels were forced to leave her behind. Afterward, she returned to the stage, but like Belle Boyd, to tell about her adventures in the war.[23]

But not all spies who survived were able to profit from their experiences. Elizabeth Van Lew of Richmond, the greatest of Civil War spies, male or female, sacrificed everything for her principles. A member of a socially prominent and well-to-do merchant family, Van Lew abhorred slavery and refused to conceal her abolitionist sentiments, even though it caused her to become an outcast in her home city, the Confederate capital. One would think that it would have been impossible for her to be a secret agent under these circumstances, but ''Crazy Bet'' turned the situation into a perfect cover for her intelligence operations. Unmarried in her mid-forties, she lived in a big mansion with her widowed mother and fit the spinster stereotype; she cultivated a reputation as an eccentric. Her neighbors—and Confederate officials—looked upon her pro-Union sentiments as disagreeable but essentially the ravings of a madwoman. In this way, she threw everyone off the scent. She was one of the few persons in Richmond who could visit Union soldiers in the POW camps and hospitals without arousing suspicion. The prison guards and hospital orderlies had no idea that she was debriefing the Yankee soldiers fresh from the front, who had just passed through the lines, and that she was dispatching intelligence reports in invisible ink on the letters she was sending back home for the poor wretches. After the war was over, General U.S. Grant acknowledged, ''You have sent me the most valuable information received from Richmond during the war.''[24] But ''Miss Lizzie'' now had nowhere to hide. Her wartime acts had impoverished her; the family hardware business failed, and she lost the mansion. But she took it in stride, saying that it was her neighbors who had been disloyal, not she: "The government of the Confederacy was never established," she affirmed. "I recognized only the United States."[25]

Beneath the mask of Crazy Bet, the brilliant Miss Lizzie had run a spy net that consisted of the slaves in the households of the Confederate leaders. For the same reasons that whites ostracized her, blacks adored her. She refused to have slaves and even purchased the freedom of some in bondage in order to reunite families, and she employed only free blacks as servants. One of her agents served the table in the home of Jefferson Davis, the president of the Confederacy. Her black couriers were very effective: flowers cut from her garden in the evening adorned the breakfast table of Grant the next morning, along with her intelligence. Her great mansion had secret rooms in which she sheltered escaped Yankee prisoners. At the same time, her home occasionally served as a visiting officer quarters for the Confederacy—a situation that simultaneously placed her in jeopardy and relieved her of tension and suspicion. After the war, President Grant appointed her postmistress in Richmond, but she could not overcome the opprobrium of her neighbors. She might have died in poverty except for aid provided by Colonel Paul Revere, a Boston Yankee who returned a favor.[26] Essentially, the United States abandoned Elizabeth Van Lew, its crack secret agent.

The U.S. also abolished the Bureau of Military Information that she had served. Despite the usefulness of intelligence during the war, the U.S. government retained little of the apparatus afterward. In fact, Lafayette Baker's excesses in directing his secret service strengthened the position of those who argued that secrecy in government endangered the Constitution. Moreover, Baker's own laxity in protecting the life of President Lincoln was so incredible that he was even suspected of being part of a conspiracy. In July 1865, the U.S. Congress established a Secret Service that resembled Baker's barely more than in name and placed it in the Treasury Department with greatly reduced functions.

This new Secret Service was charged with responsibility for the detection and arrest of counterfeiters, a concern that had arisen during the war and which Baker's group had actually investigated.

In 1902, the Secret Service officially assumed the duty of protecting the President. The U.S. Army Signal Corps, in the meantime, maintained a limited communications intelligence capability, as one remnant of wartime intelligence. But beyond this, the spies of the Civil War "folded their tents," as Allen Dulles liked to say, and went home. Approaching the centennial of American independence, the U.S. government still had no formal apparatus for collecting and evaluating intelligence. But that would soon change, as the nature of U.S. government and society changed.

7

Developing the Capability

F or three decades after the Civil War, the United States turned its energies inward. It underwent a period of tremendous internal development, of industrialization, urbanization, population expansion, railroad building, and the closing of the frontier. During this time, the nation's interest in foreign affairs slackened, and in the absence of an external threat, the challenges and opportunities at home absorbed the country's attention. This overwhelming interest in domestic affairs tended to support the disbanding of most U.S. intelligence activities at the close of the Civil War. The new Secret Service performed limited intelligence functions, and U.S. diplomats abroad overtly collected intelligence as part of their normal reporting duties.

But the modernization of American society also developed the resources that would be used for an activist foreign policy in the future, eventually causing America's entry into world affairs. At the same time, modernization also contributed to its development of a foreign intelligence capability. There were signs during these years of where the United States would assert its power in time, and it took preliminary steps toward the systematic collection of information about other nations.

In the meantime, the United States discovered that scrapping military intelligence had been premature. The country was not really at peace. Its "longest war," which had begun in 1848 and lasted for over thirty years, was still going on. This campaign against the Plains Indians kept a force of about twenty-five thousand men in the field. Its commanders required intelligence.

Lieutenant General William T. Sherman commanded the

Division of the Missouri, the territory from the Mississippi River to the continental divide. Headquartered in St. Louis, his task was to enforce the government's policy of placing Indians on reservations, out of the way of white settlement, and keeping them there. To subjugate and control the Plains Indians, the army carried out surprise attacks against their villages. This kind of warfare required the kind of scouting and reconnaissance missions that had been so much a part of the Civil War. "White frontiersmen and friendly Indians, wise in wilderness and Indian lore, were hired or enlisted to provide these services: 'California Joe' Milner, 'Buffalo Bill' Cody, 'Lonesome Charlie' Reynolds, 'Yellowstone' Kelly, Frank Grouard, Al Sieber, and Crow, Arikara, Osage, Shoshoni, and Apache scouts proved indispensible in locating the objective and easing a command into striking position."[1] In recognition of the importance of these services, the Army Act of 1866 authorized the enlistment of a thousand Indian scouts.

Although the scouts used for intelligence purposes received most of the attention, the Indian wars demonstrated the value of the least glamorous form of intelligence—the workhorse basic intelligence. One of the most successful Indian fighters, General George Crook, studied the habits and customs of the Indians in order to defeat them: "He knew the Indian better than the Indian did."[2] He understood the diversity and rivalry among the tribes and used this knowledge to recruit Indian allies and auxiliaries and to induce Indian to fight Indian. Even more effective was Crook's awareness of the factionalism inherent in tribal organization itself. He would seek allies within the very tribes he was fighting: "The efficacy of this method lay not only in matching the enemy's special skills but also in the psychological impact on the enemy of finding his own people arrayed against him. 'To polish a diamond there is nothing like its own dust,' Crook explained."[3] Crook had much knowledge of how to fight and manage Indians, but there was no central archive or mechanism for the dissemination of intelligence, so his insights had little impact beyond his own command. If the situation had been otherwise, a disaster might have been averted.

The defeat of General George Armstrong Custer, "Custer's Last Stand," at Little Bighorn River on June 25, 1876, was a classic intelligence failure. Although Custer's defeat has been

ascribed to a number of causes, it is clear that Custer himself provoked a battle "without knowing the strength and position of the
enemy."[4] His appalling disregard for the most elementary information about the opposing force contributed to the disaster in
which he and 215 men were wiped out. The army subsequently
complained that the Bureau of Indian Affairs had failed to accurately report the number of Indian defectors from the reservations. But that was nothing new: the bureau's agents frequently did
not report when Indians left the reservations, especially for the
spring hunt, when the absence would only be temporary. The
Bureau feared that the army, if informed, would pursue these
Indians and treat them as outlaws. Lacking a specific intelligence
department within the army, the commanders of the Indian wars
were limited to intelligence collected by their own staff and to
possibly false and misleading information provided by others.

Just as the army was completing the continental expansion, the
navy was stirring in contemplation of new expansion into the
Pacific. This had important consequences for the development of
intelligence. As America rose to world power, the navy was mod-
ernized and enlarged. Among the best-known advocates of the
large navy policy was Captain Alfred Thayer Mahan, author of
The Influence of Sea Power upon History in 1890. But even before
Mahan, naval officers had chafed against the small navy and coast
defense concept that had dominated naval affairs since Thomas
Jefferson's time. Although Americans maintained an isolationist
spirit toward Europe, the Pacific and the Far East were something
else. U.S. naval planners promoted a "blue water" navy that
could aid in expanding trade and showing the flag in these regions.
Commodore Matthew Perry "opened" Japan in 1854. Captain
William Reynolds took possession of Midway Island in 1867. By
the 1870s, naval commanders were casting covetous glances
toward Samoa and Hawaii. And in 1876, after conducting extensive surveys in Central America, Admiral Daniel Ammen recommended Nicaragua as the best location for an interoceanic canal.

Commodore Robert W. Shufeldt was a precursor of these
ambitions. While circumnavigating the globe in command of the
Ticonderoga in 1878, Shufeldt paid particular attention to Africa and
the Pacific basin. Instructing his paymaster to keep a thorough

log, he "investigated" commercial opportunities in places like Liberia, the Congo, and Madagascar. He recorded, for example, that the United States provided half of Madagascar's imports in 1879.[6] In 1882, Shufeldt negotiated the first U.S. trade treaty with Korea, in effect duplicating Perry's achievement in Japan. From these experiences, Shufeldt developed the idea that the navy might serve as the "pioneer of commerce"; that is, a built-up navy could be the vanguard of American commercial expansion into new areas.[7]

While some dreamed of American naval greatness, the reality was far less promising. Ten years after the Civil War, the U.S. Navy was a floating museum. It had failed to keep up with foreign navies' conversions from sail to steam and from wood to steel. American ships still relied upon muzzle-loading, smooth-bore cannon, whereas "the German development of the sliding wedge breech block made muzzle-loading obsolete and permitted fixed gun mounts and more accurate aiming."[8] Even the Chilean navy, as American officers observed during the War of the Pacific (1879–83), possessed more advanced ordinance and armor.[9] The navy had begun sending special missions abroad for the purpose of acquiring new technology, but it clearly needed to mount a more systematic collection effort and establish a clearinghouse for information. Faced with this technology gap, the navy created the Office of Naval Intelligence (ONI) within the Bureau of Navigation in 1882.[10] The navy thus took the lead in establishing a permanent U.S. military intelligence agency.

But the army was not far behind. The same circumstance that had compelled the navy to act—the lack of a specific unit responsible for collecting and compiling foreign intelligence—caused the army to organize the Military Information Division (MID) within the adjutant-general's department in 1885. The MID and the ONI were both very modest organizations, staffed by only a handful of officers and clerks. Nonetheless, now that production offices were in place, steps to improve the collection function could be taken.

In September 1888, responding to the need for a consistent flow of technical information, the U.S. Congress authorized the assignment of service attachés to diplomatic missions abroad. In doing so, it imitated the practice of other nations, the first of which was probably Napoleonic France. Diplomatic representatives had traditionally "spied" as part of their reporting function, and ambassadors had been referred to as "honorable" or "public" spies.[11] But diplomats' lack of expert knowledge, especially in military affairs, led their governments to assign military officers to diplomatic missions as "the spy of the spy."[12] Service attachés also performed functions related to ceremonies, protocol, and arms procurement and sales, but these were essentially cover. Their principal function was "to see and report on everything of military relevance."[13] Straddling the worlds of espionage and protocol, service attachés represented the elite of the services, both in intellectual qualities and in social skills.

Alfred Vagts, in *The Military Attaché* (1967), described the frequently contradictory roles of the service attaché. His observations were based upon a remarkable document, "Instruction for an Officer of the General Quartermaster Staff Attached to a Legation Abroad," which had originally been prepared by Austrian general von Radetzky in 1810. Vagts provided rare insight into secret intelligence requirements and how a case officer must operate. Although drafted for the military attaché, the "Instruction" is practically a spy manual and is as timely now as it was when first issued. It tasked the general staff officer and provided thoughtful guidance on how to be a successful spy. The "Instruction" requested "detailed knowledge of the forces of the foreign state," seeking not only their numbers but also the "quality, morale, training and military address" of their troops: "their manner of marching, maneuvering, camping and fighting, their food supply, recruiting and interior administration; and, in particular, information about their leaders and other military chiefs, whose character and intellectual qualities were to be given to the last detail."[14]

Although the Austrian command suggested that it "cannot be too difficult to obtain the necessary data," it assured the officer that the chief of legation "will know how to lighten" his regular work load for the purposes of his mission. The "Instruction" observed that the officer might "obtain such data in an unobjectionable indirect manner through the nearest neighbors of the country in which he is stationed," but it admonished him to "observe the greatest wisdom on the choice of his means in order to avoid altogether the impression of being a spy and thus compromising the Imperial service."[15]

The "Instruction" next required "indications and measures pointing to a war," advising the officer to pay close attention to newspapers and "other prints and public papers" for reports of "the forming of depots, . . . concentration of troops. . . , and generally [of] all similar preparations." It recommended that the officer gather this information discreetly by making the right contacts "under the guise of sociability": "Quite often a good connoisseur of men and an adroit observer, through confidential relationships with carefully selected individuals, will more easily obtain the knowledge of a state secret than in another manner which might expose him in the hateful role of a spy."[16]

As his "main object," the "Instruction" enjoined the officer to provide "definite and prompt knowledge of truly warlike movements," as well as "the closest possible survey" of military operations against a third state. To these ends, the Austrian command instructed the officer to have "confidants" at key locations who might report on troop movements and "war operations" or, if "of supreme usefulness," to seek permission to go to the front himself. "A diary is to be kept about this and about all other important military occurrences in the State under observation; the diary is to be submitted either periodically as a contribution to military history or, in the case of important and momentous incidents, without loss of time."[17]

Under less urgent circumstances, the "Instruction" directed the officer to describe the host country's offensive and defensive posture, including "military positions and posts and the most promising method of making war on it." It told the officer to collect basic intelligence, particularly military and scientific data, so that "useful inventions" and "anything worthy of imitation . . . can be transplanted to our own country." "Hence the need of submitting the relevant literary works, including military almanacs, army lists, decrees about improvements and the arrangement of the military budget, textbooks used in military establishments, valuable new maps and plans, publications on geography and statistics."[18]

In accomplishing these tasks, the "Instruction" stressed the officer's education, modesty, prudence, and wisdom—but informed him that funds were available "when payment of bribes may be required." In essence, the "Instruction" made its needs clear and acknowledged that the business was dirty, but it repeatedly advised that discreet behavior was necessary to prevent disgrace, concluding as follows:

> If, now, this officer of the embassy proceeds with wisdom and modesty, which cannot be recommended too much, and always keeps the All-Highest interest before his eyes, and endeavors in his language and actions as well as by the strictest prudence in his correspondence to avoid all that is compromising, he will find the ways and means to be useful to the military administration by becoming acquainted and connected with persons whose influence, knowledge and service should prove useful in case of the outbreak of war, and on other occasions.
>
> In addition, confidence is placed in every officer who is employed on such service: he will know how to judge with wisdom in all cases not specifically mentioned here, and all his steps will be in keeping with the views and directions of the ambassador.[19]

One may assume that the instructions given to the first American service attachés were not as aggressive, particularly with reference to preparations for war, and that they emphasized obtaining information about scientific and technical developments applicable to military strategy and hardware. In time, the objectives of U.S. attachés expanded. But the advice contained in these instructions to Austrian general staff officers was appropriate for Americans from the start, particularly the admonition against being compromised. The idea of being exposed "in the hateful role of a spy," no matter how vital the mission, terrified military officers, who had been trained to do nothing that would discredit their uniform or lessen the credibility of the military institution. Nonetheless, although an officer might succeed as a "connoisseur of men" in making contacts and recruiting agents, he was informed that bribe money was available if necessary. Organizing groups for possible future subversion and conducting espionage in anticipation of possible future circumstances were not yet American practices, although George Washington and John Clark's preparation of spy rings before the evacuation of Philadelphia in 1777 was a precedent.

Finally, the insistence that the officer be guided by the "views and directions" of the ambassador was not that simple to carry out. Nondiplomatic personnel who were using diplomatic missions as cover for intelligence functions had a relationship with the chief of mission that was distinct from those of foreign service personnel. This tended to diminish the authority of the lead diplomatic officer. The issue became more serious in time, especially when the OSS was created and the U.S. foreign intelligence effort was intensified.

Obviously, time changed much. But the assignment of the first U.S. service attachés reflected the specific interests of the United States, especially its lack of involvement in European affairs. They were sent to the capitals of the major powers of the period: London, Paris, Berlin, Vienna, and St. Petersburg. By the turn of the century, the United States had also posted service attachés to Rome, Brussels, Madrid, Tokyo, and Mexico. The number of positions increased to thirty-one in 1914. That ten of them were in Latin America indicates that the nature of the assignments, as well as U.S. interests, had undergone a transformation.

This transformation resulted from the United States' emergence as a major power at the beginning of the twentieth century. After three decades of internal growth, the United States was ready to flex its muscles and exercise its economic power abroad. Its search for markets and raw materials complemented the theories of the Mahanites, exciting the evangelical fervor of Josiah Strong and the political ambitions of Theodore Roosevelt. As the United States began to dream of empire, its intelligence establishment was still only developing, but the U.S. had already demonstrated an ability to improvise when the president was willing to resort to covert action.

8
Intelligence and Empire

T he United States' arrival on the international scene coincided
with the completion of the partitioning of Africa and Asia by
the major powers of Europe. Although the United States claimed
that it was concerned by this only because it threatened "to close
the door" on its emerging export trade, the country's restlessness
actually ran deeper. The American success story was just beginning. Having settled a continent, it was now preparing to expend
its energies elsewhere.

The United States felt superior to other nations, and it believed
that its motives were loftier. During the debate over the acquisition
of the Philippine Islands in 1900, Senator Albert Beveridge of
Indiana expressed what many Americans had been feeling for over
a decade:

> God has not been preparing the English-speaking and Teutonic
> peoples for a thousand years for nothing but vain and idle self-
> contemplation and self-admiration. No! He has made us the
> master organizers of the world to establish system where chaos
> reigns. He has given us the spirit of progress to overwhelm the
> forces of reaction throughout the earth. He has made us adepts
> in government that we may administer government among savage
> and senile peoples. Were it not for such a force as this the world
> would relapse into barbarism and night. And of all our race He
> has marked the American people as His chosen nation to finally
> lead in the regeneration of the world. This is the divine mission
> of America, and it holds for us all the profit, all the glory, all the
> happiness possible to man. We are the trustees of the world's pro-
> gress, guardians of its righteous peace.[1]

In the last decade of the nineteenth century, this kind of thinking got the United States involved in the Open Door in China and led to the acquisition of overseas territories. Not all Americans felt this way, of course, so that the advocates of the new Manifest Destiny had to proceed with caution. Secrecy had already been employed by presidents Madison and Polk, as much to avoid public criticism and head off embarrassing congressional debate as to conceal U.S. action from foreign powers. In 1893, officials of Benjamin Harrison's administration resorted to secret dirty tricks to promote an annexationist movement in Hawaii (another example of covert action taken long before the CIA).

Competing with Germany and Japan, the other rising powers of the time, the United States focused its attention upon the islands of the Pacific, especially Hawaii. It had already carried on a lengthy courtship with Hawaii. New England whalers and missionaries had started visiting the islands in the 1820s, and their sons and daughters had since put down roots and become the mainstay of the planter class. By midcentury, the United States had virtually extended the Monroe Doctrine to Hawaii, and after the acquisition of California, it became Hawaii's principal market for sugar. A reciprocal trade treaty was negotiated between the United States and the Kingdom of Hawaii in 1875, bringing the islands further into the American orbit. On renewing the treaty a dozen years later, the United States also acquired the lease of Pearl Harbor for a naval base. The steady march toward union hit a snag in 1890, when the United States negotiated a reciprocity treaty with Cuba that provided Cuban sugar with the same duty-free status that Hawaiian cane enjoyed. At the same time, Congress granted a bounty of two cents per pound to domestic producers.

Reeling from this economic blow, the American planters in Hawaii suffered still another setback. The new Hawaiian monarch, Queen Liliuokalani, proclaimed a policy of "Hawaii for the Hawaiians." Resentful of the economic and political power of the white planters, "Queen Lil" sought to restore the authority of the native monarchy by revoking the constitution that had been imposed upon her brother and predecessor in 1887. Under these circumstances, the planters concluded that their interests would be better served by annexation by the United States.

Some U.S. officials welcomed this prospect. James Garfield's secretary of state, James G. Blaine, had expressed his views on the matter ten years before. Concerned about Chinese immigration and its possible effects upon political control, Blaine had stated in 1881, "if [the Hawaiian Islands] drift from their independent station it must be toward assimilation and identification with the American system, to which they belong by the operation of natural laws, and must belong by the operation of political necessity."[2] He described the islands "as the key to the dominion of the American Pacific" and affirmed that the United States would meet any change in their situation "by seeking an avowedly American solution" to the problem.[3]

After a ten-year interruption of his "premiership," Blaine, the practitioner of "spirited diplomacy," returned as secretary of state under Benjamin Harrison and recommended John L. Stevens, another "man from Maine," to be the U.S. minister in Hawaii. Blaine could hardly have picked a better agent than Stevens, an outspoken annexationist, to precipitate an "avowedly American solution." Even after Blaine resigned in June 1892, Stevens wrote to the new secretary of state, John W. Foster, in language that signified no change in policy. Commenting upon the dire economic straits of the American planters and the lack of responsible government in the islands, Stevens asked, "What should be done?" and responded to his own question:

> One of two courses seem to me absolutely necessary to be followed, either bold and vigorous measures for annexation or a "customs union," an ocean cable from the Californian coast to Honolulu, Pearl Harbor permanently ceded to the United States, with an implied but not necessarily stipulated American protectorate over the islands. I believe the former to be the better, that which will prove much the more advantageous to the islands, and the cheapest and least embarrassing in the end for the United States.[4]

Stevens himself made this communication public; as the former editor of the *Kennebec Journal* of Augusta, Maine, he revealed its contents in an unsigned editorial in November 1892. The editorial was widely reprinted in the United States; the source was obvious, and it was easy to conclude that Stevens was sending signals to the planters in anticipation of their action and encouraging them. In fact, Lorrin A. Thurston and Sanford P. Dole, leading planters and members of the secret Annexationist Club, said as much, insisting that they had Stevens's "assurance of sympathy, if not aid."[5]

With such assurances, and reacting to the queen's professed intention to revise the Constitution of 1887, a small group of planters, constituted as the "committee of public safety," met on January 14, 1893, "to consider the situation and devise ways and means for the maintenance of the public peace and the protection of life and property."[6] The committee acted on the sixteenth to create a provisional government "to exist until terms of union with the United States of America have been negotiated and agreed upon" and quickly dispatched a note to Stevens explaining that "the lives of the people were in peril" and beseeching his aid. "We are unable to protect ourselves without aid, and therefore hope for the protection of the United States forces."[7] Without delay, Stevens requested the commander of the USS *Boston*—which happened to be in Honolulu harbor—to land forces to protect the U.S. legation and American lives and property. But they took up positions opposite the Royal Palace, so that the so-called provisional government, meeting with Queen Lil on the seventeenth, could threaten that resistance on her part would involve conflict with the United States. The queen abdicated under protest, and Stevens extended de facto recognition to the newest lone star republic on January 18. It immediately sent a delegation consisting of "four Americans and one Englishman" to Washington to request annexation.[8]

The sequence of events indicates that U.S. forces played a critical role in the success of the Hawaiian Revolution of January 1893. The real story might have remained secret, and Stevens, Dole, and the other conspirators might have pulled an annexation treaty off, except for the fact that their timing was bad. In March 1893, Grover Cleveland would become president. Harrison was not able to get the treaty of annexation through the Senate before Cleveland's inauguration, nor before Queen Lil arrived in the United States to protest what had happened. Cleveland, a Democrat, sensed an opportunity to embarrass the Republican Harrison but was also concerned that an injustice may have been done. He withdrew the treaty from consideration and appointed James H. Blount as special commissioner to Hawaii to ascertain the facts. Blount's report—undoubtedly partisan—excoriated Stevens and the white planters for their actions, and Secretary of State Walter Q. Gresham submitted it to Cleveland with the observation, "Should not the great wrong done to a feeble but independent State by an abuse of authority of the United States be undone by restoring the legitimate government? Anything short of that will not, I respectfully submit, satisfy the demands of justice."[9]

In the events in Hawaii in 1893 can be seen both the effectiveness and the perils of covert action—as well as the wonderful complexity of the American democratic system. It is rare that a nation admits to playing dirty tricks, but rarer still that a nation's chief executive publicly and personally confesses doing so. Cleveland made such a confession to Congress in December 1893 in explaining why he did not intend to resubmit the treaty for the annexation of Hawaii. Even with allowances made for Cleveland's partisanship, he had a reputation as a person of unusual integrity. His statement testifies to an early dirty trick, the "other functions" of intelligence. As Cleveland put it, "we are brought face to face with the following conditions:

> The lawful government of Hawaii was overthrown without the drawing of a sword or the firing of a shot by a process every step of which, it may safely be asserted, is directly traceable to and dependent for its success upon the agency of the United States acting through its diplomatic and naval representatives.
>
> But for the notorious predilections of the United States Minister for annexation, the Committee of Safety, which should be called the Committee of Annexation, would never have existed.
>
> But for the landing of United States forces upon false pretexts respecting the danger to life and property, the committee would never have exposed themselves to the pains and penalties of treason by undertaking the subversion of the Queen's Government.
>
> But for the presence of the United States forces in the immediate vicinity and in position to afford all needed protection and support, the committee would not have proclaimed the provisional government from the steps of the Government building.

And finally, but for the lawless occupation of Honolulu under false pretexts by the United States forces, and but for Minister Stevens's recognition of the provisional government when the United States forces were its sole support and constituted its only military strength, the Queen and her Government would never have yielded to the provisional government, even for a time and for the sole purpose of submitting her case to the enlightened justice of the United States.[10]

Although he withdrew the treaty, Cleveland did not act to restore Queen Liliuokalani to her throne. Even though the leaders of the revolt had been "led to their present predicament . . . by the indefensible encouragement and assistance of our diplomatic representative," Cleveland was unwilling to abandon them to their fate in the absence of a pledge of amnesty from the Queen.

The Republic of Hawaii, like the Republic of Texas before, required a change in circumstances for actual annexation to take place. This change occurred in July 1898, during the Spanish–American War. Arguing that the islands were a strategic necessity, the expansionists finally had their way, and the House and Senate resolved jointly to "take them in." The new president, William McKinley, observed, "Annexation is not change; it is consummation."[11]

American expansionism, which the events in Hawaii only foreshadowed, reached its apogee toward the end of the nineteenth century. The United States needed a catalyst that would combine the numerous elements favoring an expansionist foreign policy, and the Cuban insurrection became that catalyst. The United States seized this opportunity to expel the last vestige of Spanish colonial rule from the Western Hemisphere and assume a protective and hegemonic position itself. Despite all its bravado, however, the nation was unprepared for war, and the state of American intelligence was woeful. Only the Secret Service, under John E. Wilkie, was functioning well, enjoying success in internal security matters.[12] The United States was fortunate to be fighting a power that was no longer of the first rank.

Intelligence thus contributed little to the United States' victory over Spain, but it produced a legend and accounted for two heroes. In print and on the screen, "A Message to García," relates the legendary mission of Lieutenant Andrew Summers Rowan of the Military Intelligence Division in April–May 1898 to make contact with Cuban insurgent General Calixto García. Although Americans designated their conflict with Spain the Spanish–American War, the Cubans had already been fighting for over three years with a force of approximately ten thousand armed men. Rowan's "message to García" was actually not a message but an oral request for "the numbers, location, and morale of the Spanish troops, the character of their officers; the topography, the condition of the roads in all seasons; how well each side was armed, and what the *insurrectos* were most in need of until an American force could be mobilized."[13]

According to Elbert Hubbard's highly imaginative story, President McKinley himself served as Rowan's case officer, but it was actually Colonel Arthur Wagner, the chief of the MID, who briefed the young officer about his assignment. Rowan encountered enough real adventure and danger to establish him as a hero and enable him to earn the Distinguished Service Cross. He was an infiltrator in the style of Nathan Hale, except that Cuban guides met him on the beach and escorted him to García's headquarters at Bayamo. Sailing in a small fishing boat from Jamaica, Rowan came ashore on Cuba's south coast and traveled for five days over rough terrain and through dense jungles, eluding Spanish patrols, to reach the Cuban general. García, badly in need of modern rifles and ammunition, sent the young spy on his way within six hours, in the company of three Cuban officers who were to personally assist the Americans in their invasion plans.[14] After another five-day journey through jungles and enemy lines, traveling north this time, they reached the coast and set out in a tiny boat for Nassau, 150 miles away. General Nelson A. Miles described Rowan's accomplishment as "an act of heroism and cool daring . . . rarely excelled in the annals of warfare."[15]

Another young officer, Lieutenant Victor Blue of the U.S. Navy, duplicated Rowan's feat during the same war—twice, in fact. For some time after the outbreak of hostilities, Americans had been gravely concerned about the whereabouts of the Atlantic squadron of Spanish admiral Pascual Cervera. They feared possible attacks upon east coast cities and were reluctant to commit troop transports to the open sea for Cuba. On May 19, however, an agent-in-place in the employ of the U.S. Army Signal Corps in the Havana telegraph office reported that Cervera had arrived in Santiago Bay.[16] At the same time, ships under Admiral Winfield S. Schley observed two Spanish warships entering the bay. Ten days later, the North Atlantic Squadron under Admiral William T. Sampson established a blockade of the harbor.

In the absence of aerial reconnaissance, Admiral Sampson was still uncertain whether all of Cervera's ships were in the harbor— hills screened the inside of the bay from the blockading fleet. He requested Victor Blue to go ashore in enemy-held territory and, in the company of Cuban guides, penetrate the Spanish lines to gather the needed intelligence. To evade Spanish patrols and reach a point overlooking the bay, Blue had to traverse difficult terrain, including wading through waist-deep snake- and insect-infested swamps. He carried out his mission and reported to Sampson that all of Cervera's ships were there. This enabled American troop transports to embark from Tampa for the invasion of Cuba.[17]

Blue was not permitted to rest on his laurels. Sampson, deciding to launch a night attack upon the besieged Spanish fleet, ordered Blue to repeat his mission and draw a chart showing the exact locations of the ships at anchor. Blue was rowed ashore for another run through the Spanish lines. This time he had to toast a number of "Cuba Libres" to persuade the Cubans to assist him—the Spaniards had heard about "an American officer being within their lines."[18] Blue succeeded in preparing an excellent map, but his second mission served no purpose because Cervera decided to make a run for it. As Cervera's ships came out of the narrow opening of the bay in single file, they were destroyed by the waiting Americans.

The Spanish–American War had a few other espionage episodes, but the most significant development in intelligence took place after the war. The war had more than its share of confusion and mismanagement: troops had been sent to fight in the tropics in woolen winter uniforms and the lack of transportation had forced Teddy Roosevelt's Rough Riders cavalry regiment to sail for Cuba without its horses. As a result, in 1903, the U.S. Army adopted the European "general staff" concept, and intelligence was one of the beneficiaries of this change. The Military Information Division became the second division, or G-2, of the U.S. Army General Staff. With the creation of G-2, the army's principal intelligence organization was in place. But G-2 did not acquire immediate respectability, nor did intelligence become an accepted career field for a long time. G-2 generally withered in peacetime and was revived during the two world wars. Up until the outbreak of World War I, G-2 was housed in the Army War College as a kind of research and archival unit.

In the meantime, the United States had acquired a number of possessions either directly or indirectly as a result of the war with Spain—including Hawaii, Samoa, Guam, the Philippines, and Puerto Rico—plus a protectorate over Cuba. To police and protect its new empire, U.S. naval strategists stressed the urgency of building a canal across the Central American isthmus. This need had been further dramatized during the Spanish–American War by the voyage of the USS *Oregon* around Cape Horn from Puget Sound to Key West. This thirteen-thousand-mile odyssey began on March 19 and ended sixty-eight days later—barely in time for the new battleship to participate in the battle of Santiago Bay. How much time and anxiety a canal would have saved!

The United States' acquisition of the Panama Canal is still another early example of the use of covert action by the executive branch before the CIA. Unable to achieve his purposes through normal diplomatic means and yet unwilling to go to war, President Theodore Roosevelt obtained the right to construct, operate, maintain, and protect the Panama Canal by supporting the Panama Revolution of 1903. He enabled a group of residents of the Isthmus of Panama to carry out a separatist movement against the Republic of Colombia and create an independent state.

The acquisition of the Panama Canal is a complex and controversial story. After a lengthy and acrimonious debate over the relative merits of Panama and Nicaragua as the site for an isthmian canal, the U.S. Congress recommended the Panama route in 1902. Two men were largely responsible for bringing this decision about. William Nelson Cromwell, of the prestigious Wall Street law firm Sullivan and Cromwell, represented the New Panama Canal Company of Paris, which held the rights over the Panama route; Philippe Bunau-Varilla, a French engineer, represented the "penalized" stockholders of the Paris company (the alleged profiteers of the failed enterprise of Ferdinand de Lesseps) who had chosen to invest in the New Company rather than go to jail. Cromwell and Bunau-Varilla lobbied brilliantly to persuade Congress to choose Panama. Although they had a huge financial stake in the outcome, Bunau-Varilla insisted that he was striving "to vindicate French genius."

After Congress selected the Panama route, the United States negotiated a canal treaty with Colombia—at the time, the sovereign power in the isthmus. But in the summer of 1903, the Colombian Senate rejected the treaty, leaving Roosevelt with the options of either renegotiating the treaty or turning to Nicaragua. Roosevelt, however, regarded the Colombians as "contemptible little creatures" and "inefficient bandits"; he weighed the possibility of seizing the territory under a sort of "international right of eminent domain." But he then learned that the Panamanians, also disgusted by Bogotá's action, might act in their own behalf and secede. The people of Panama, separated from the Colombian heartland by mountains and jungle, were in a position to gain control of their destiny if they could subvert the small local Colombian garrison and prevent the arrival of fresh troops by sea. The amount of collaboration between Panamanians and U.S. officials to achieve this purpose has never been established, but that there was contact between private persons actively involved in the secessionist movement and U.S. officials in a position to render support and encouragement is well documented.

Cromwell was the lawyer not only for the French canal company but for the Panama Railroad, a subsidiary and a principal enterprise in Panama. He took the lead in promoting the separatist movement through his subordinates on the isthmus. In fact, the isthmian leaders of the movement were all connected with the railroad in one way or another. In October, however, the Colombian legation in Washington got wind of Cromwell's activities and threatened to act against his clients in the event that a subversive movement emerged. Cromwell lowered his profile and departed for Paris for consultations, passing Bunau-Varilla coming the other way.

There is no evidence that Cromwell had sent for Bunau-Varilla to step in where he left off. But the latter immediately contacted Manuel Amador Guerrero, an isthmian leader and also the railroad company's physician. (He would later be the first president of the Republic of Panama.) After consulting with Amador in New York, Bunau-Varilla went to Washington, where he met with Roosevelt, Secretary of State John Hay, and Assistant Secretary of State Francis B. Loomis (a key figure in the affair). Bunau-Varilla later insisted that he had received no assurances of aid from these or any other American leaders; rather, he said, he had described the preparations on the isthmus for a revolutionary movement, and the reactions he had received made him "thoroughly convinced . . . that [his] friends would be protected against the crushing load of the Colombian forces."[19] President Roosevelt later observed that Bunau-Varilla would have to have been "a very dull man" not to guess his intentions. At about the time of these meetings (October 10–16), American warships received orders to sail for the isthmus.[20]

Bunau-Varilla returned to New York and told Amador to make his revolution. He gave him a cable code for secret communications and exacted a promise that Amador would appoint him Panama's first minister to the United States. On October 18, two days before he sailed from New York to Panama, Amador wrote to his son, a U.S. Army doctor stationed in Fort Revere, Massachusetts, saying,

> The plan seems to me good. A portion of the Isthmus declares itself independent and that portion the United States will not allow any Colombian forces to attack. An assembly is called and this gives authority to a minister to be appointed by the new Government in order to make a treaty without need of ratification by that assembly. The treaty being approved by both parties, the new Republic remains under the protection of the United States and to it are added the other districts of the Isthmus which do not already form part of the new Republic and these also remain under the protection of the United States.[21]

Amador informed his son that Bunau-Varilla was a man of "great influence," and that he had promised to get him—the son—a place on the medical commission that was slated to begin early work at

Panama. Amador had related "that my name is in Hay's office and that certainly nothing will be refused you."[22]

But when Amador arrived in Panama, his fellow conspirators seemed unwilling to risk everything based on the assurances of a Frenchman who claimed to be an insider in Washington. Accordingly, Amador cabled Bunau-Varilla in code, insisting that an American warship be sent to the isthmus in anticipation of the revolutionary movement. Bunau-Varilla hurried to Washington, where he discussed the entire matter with Acting Secretary of State Loomis. Again, Bunau-Varilla later asserted that he had received no pledges of any kind but that Loomis's behavior had convinced him that the United States would intervene. Returning to New York by train, Bunau-Varilla read in the *Baltimore Sun* a short notice saying that the USS *Nashville* had departed Kingston, Jamaica, for an undisclosed destination. Bunau-Varilla guessed that the vessel was bound for Colón, Panama's Caribbean port, and calculated its speed and the distance it would have to cover. He then cabled Amador that a U.S. warship would arrive in Panama in two and a half days. That was October 30. On November 2 at 6:30 P.M., the USS *Nashville* steamed into Colón harbor, where it received instructions from the Navy Department to prevent the landing there "of any armed force, either Government or insurgent, with hostile intent."[23] Since the possible arrival of Colombian government reinforcements by sea was the principal concern of the isthmian insurgents, the mission of the *Nashville* was clear. The *Marblehead* and the *Boston* were converging on the isthmus from the Pacific side and had received identical instructions, with the additional order: "if doubtful of the intention of any armed force, occupy Ancon Hill strongly with artillery."[24]

The Panama Revolution took place at 6:00 P.M. on November 3. A slight delay had occurred because of the unexpected arrival of five hundred Colombian troops on the morning of the third, before the captain of the *Nashville* had had time to act on his instructions. But the general superintendent of the Panama Railroad had moved all the rolling stock over to the Pacific side, keeping the Colombians in Colón and under the *Nashville's* guns until the Panamanians achieved independence. Nonetheless, Acting Secretary Loomis jumped the gun and sent the following cable to Panama a little after 3:00 P.M.: "Uprising on Isthmus reported. Keep department promptly and fully informed."[25] Felix Ehrman, the U.S. vice consul-general in Panama, was fully in touch with the separatists and dispatched the reply, "No uprising yet. Reported will be in the night. Situation is critical."[26]

The Panamanians finally acted, coming under the protection of an increasing number of American warships. The United States extended de facto recognition to the Republic of Panama on November 6. A week later, President Roosevelt received the credentials of Bunau-Varilla as Panama's minister to the United States, and on the eighteenth, Bunau-Varilla and John Hay signed the treaty that established the Canal Zone and gave the United States the right to construct, operate, and defend the Panama Canal.

Successful covert operations are rarely documented; only the failures receive publicity. In the case of Panama, however, it is perfectly clear that the leaders of the conspiracy had access to the highest officials of the U.S. government and kept them fully informed in every detail. It stretches the imagination to think that Bunau-Varilla relied on intuition alone to fulfill his pledge that U.S. warships would be on hand to protect the rebels. The Panama affair eventually stirred a controversy in which certain hitherto secret matters leaked out. Roosevelt started the revelations himself with a public "confession" in 1911. He told an audience at the University of California,

> I am interested in the Panama Canal because I started it. If I had followed traditional, conservative methods I would have submitted a dignified State paper of probably 200 pages to Congress and the debates on it would have been going on yet; but I took the Canal Zone and let Congress debate; and while the debate goes on the Canal does also.[27]

Roosevelt's "I took Panama" statement caused the inevitable congressional investigation. Representative Henry T. Rainey of Illinois argued that Roosevelt's action at Panama had violated U.S.–Colombian treaty provisions and international law, and he introduced a resolution expressing his dismay. This resulted in hearings before the Committee on Foreign Affairs of the House of Representatives in 1912. The committee's principal witness was

Henry N. Hall, a staff correspondent for *The New York World*. In 1908, the *World* had published a story describing the Panama episode as a stock speculators' scheme to make millions. This had incurred the anger of President Roosevelt, who had sought to stretch the law so that the U.S. government could sue the paper for libel. The courts quashed the indictment on First Amendment grounds so that the case was never heard, but during the hearings on the Rainey Resolution Hall presented the evidence that the *World* had gathered for its defense.

Hall's testimony shed new light on Roosevelt's involvement in the Panama Revolution and U.S. covert operations there. Hall began by quoting from an address delivered by Roosevelt on January 4, 1904, in which the President had defended U.S. actions in the Panama affair:

> I think it proper to say . . . that no one connected with this Government had any part in preparing, inciting, or encouraging the late revolution on the Isthmus of Panama, and that save from the reports of our military and naval officers, . . . no one connected with this Government had any previous knowledge of the revolution except as was accessible to any person of ordinary intelligence who read the newspapers and kept up a current acquaintance with public affairs.[28]

The contacts with Bunau-Varilla alone jeopardized the President's credibility in this statement. But Hall continued to use TR's own words to indict him. In the same speech, Roosevelt had declared, "Suffice it to say that it was notorious . . . that revolutionary trouble of a serious nature was impending upon the Isthmus. But it was not necessary to rely exclusively upon such general means of information."[29] Elaborating, Roosevelt revealed that on October 16, 1903, he had met with Captain Chauncey B. Humphrey, Twenty-second Infantry, U.S. Army, a drawing instructor at West Point, and with Second Lieutenant Grayson Mallet-Prevost Murphy, Seventeenth Infantry, U.S. Army, a June graduate of the U.S. Military Academy. They

> had just returned from a four months' tour through the northern portions of Venezuela and Colombia. They stopped in Panama

on their return the latter part of September. At the time they were sent down there had been no thought of their going to Panama, and their visit to the Isthmus was but an unpremeditated incident of their return journey.[30]

According to Roosevelt, the two officers had learned for the first time that the people on the isthmus were stockpiling arms for a revolution and that they would probably act at the end of October if the Colombian Congress adjourned without approving the canal treaty. Hall, having used Roosevelt himself to verify the presence of these officers on the isthmus, described them as "Mr. Roosevelt's military spies" and noted that they had traveled out of uniform and had been registered at the Hotel Central in Panama from September 16 to 20 as "C.B. Humphrey, New York" and "G. Mallet-Prevost Murphy, New York." He added that Captain Humphrey was the son of General Charles F. Humphrey, who was then the quartermaster-general of the army and who on September 15–17, 1903, "came up from Washington and occupied rooms adjoining that of Dr. Amador, the revolutionary conspirator, in the Hotel Endicott, New York."[31] Hall permitted the congressmen to draw their own conclusions and proceeded to challenge President Roosevelt's version of the Humphrey–Murphy mission. He testified,

If the visit of these young officers to the Isthmus "was but an unpremeditated incident of their return journey," why did they return in the roundabout way by Curaçao? If they had not been spoken to by anyone at Washington regarding the possibility of a revolt, why their amazing initiative in acquiring the wealth of detailed military information, part of which is contained in Document No. 217, War Department, Office Chief of Staff, a book of 286 pages bearing the stamp of the Government Printing Office of November, 1903, under the heading "No. 1, Notes on Panama"? . . .

The extracts from Capt. Humphrey's report published in the "Confidential Notes on Panama" contain an astonishing wealth of information concerning interior points in Panama which never could have been obtained in the four days these military spies remained at the Hotel Central, in Panama City. . . .

One feature alone of Capt. Humphrey's "unpremeditated"

investigations in Panama must have consumed a week's time.
. . . It is a report on each of the 25 stations between Panama and
Colón on the railroad. Distance from Panama, population,
topographical features, and capacity of sidetrack at each station
are given.[32]

The confidential report "Notes on Panama," to which Hall
referred throughout his testimony, had been prepared by G-2 and
issued in November 1903. This extremely detailed document is
itself an excellent example of basic intelligence. The portions that
quote directly from the report of the Humphrey–Murphy mission
sustain Hall's contention that there was nothing casual or hap-
hazard about their visit to the isthmus. Rather, there is convincing
evidence that it was a well-executed espionage mission:

An advance across the Isthmus from Colón toward Panama
would be, of course, easiest by the railroad line, as the trails are
all generally very difficult and overgrown with brush. . . . The
railroad is ballasted with rock nearly the whole distance from
Colón to Panama. . . . Three equipped men could march abreast
on foot along the railroad line. . . . The railroad is quite well
equipped with rolling stock. . . . About 150 small cart mules and
horses could be obtained at Panama, about 70 pack mules at
Chorrera, while not more than 60 or 70 animals could be obtained
at Colón. . . . About one-half mile from the city of Panama is a
large hill, about 600 feet (Ancon). . . . Modern artillery could be
placed upon this hill and command the city of Panama and harbors; also the anchorage at Culebra Island.[33]

Hall further pointed out that "Notes on Panama" contained
reproductions of maps Humphrey had drawn of La Boca, on the
south side of the isthmus, and Ancon Hill, which, as he emphasized, was the exact position that the commanders of the *Marblehead*
and the *Boston* had been instructed to "occupy strongly with artillery."

Every student of American diplomatic history is familiar with
the events of the Panama Revolution—particularly the Amador-
Bunau-Varilla–Loomis connection, the timely arrival of the *Nashville* at Colón, and Teddy Roosevelt's boast, "I took Panama."

They have generally concluded on the basis of circumstantial evidence that the United States appreciably helped out in the birth of the Republic of Panama. The Humphrey–Murphy spy mission renders speculation unnecessary. Their mission shows premeditation by the Roosevelt administration and reveals a high level of determination. The White House was on top of developments, and Roosevelt left nothing to chance. He did not rely upon the coincidence of events, as Bunau-Varilla asserted, but intervened and influenced events without appearing to do so, in a clear example of covert action.

The United States did not play a dirty trick of that sort for almost fifty years after the Panama affair. One reason for this is that the United States now exercised power overtly, intervening directly in the internal affairs of neighboring states, especially in the Caribbean and Central America. In the so-called big stick policy, or Roosevelt Corollary to the Monroe Doctrine, the United States "sent in the Marines" to handle troublesome situations, making covert operations unnecessary. Only after this policy was discredited and the United States accepted the principle of non-intervention did the U.S. again resort to covert action. But that was another time and a different set of circumstances. In the meantime, U.S. foreign intelligence continued to evolve, shaped by new technologies and two world wars.

9
A Short Lesson in
Secret Writing

A merican intelligence changed radically in the twentieth century, not only quantitatively but qualitatively, in relation to
advances in science and technology. The qualitative change was
particularly striking in the development of Communications Intelligence, which affected both the making and the breaking of codes
and ciphers. To understand the significant role played by CO-
MINT in twentieth-century American intelligence, it is important
to understand the fundamentals of *cryptology,* the science of secret
writing. Very few books have been written about this science for
the merely curious or moderately interested. The notable exception
is David Kahn's *The Codebreakers,* a major contribution to popular
understanding of this topic. Those who wish to know more should
consult his works.

Cryptology is a divided science that consists of three conflicting
fields: *cryptography,* the devising of codes and ciphers; *cryptanalysis,*
the breaking of codes and ciphers; and *steganography,* the conceal-
ment of the existence of a message itself. In cryptography, a
message is rendered unintelligible by altering the *plaintext* in one of
two ways, either by *transposition*—that is, the scrambling of the normal order of plaintext letters—or by *substitution*—that is, the
replacement of plaintext letters, words, or phrases with other letters, words, phrases, characters, or code groups in accordance with
a *cipher alphabet* or *code.* In cryptanalysis, the cryptanalyst attempts
to undo the work of the cryptographer by recovering plaintext from
cipher text. Thus, although the two fields are antagonistic, both
must master the principles of language and mathematics.

Steganography, which seeks to maintain the secrecy of a message by concealing the fact of its physical existence, is used especially in espionage. It is accepted practice for businesses and governments to transmit messages in cipher, but private individuals sending enciphered messages are likely to arouse suspicion. Persons involved in clandestine operations, therefore, conceal messages by using steganographic devices such as invisible inks and microdots (photographically reducing a message to microscopic size, so that it can be concealed in the dot of an *i* imprinted by a standard typewriter), or by using ordinary items as signaling devices (Caleb Brewster's black petticoat, for example). Governments, especially the armed forces, may achieve transmission security by various technical means, such as burst transmissions and frequency-hopping,[1] so that the line between steganography and cryptography is not always exact. The present discussion focuses mainly upon codes and ciphers.

A transposition cipher, as we have seen, rearranges or scrambles plaintext letters in a systematic way. For example, rearranging the letters of the word *cipher* in alphabetical order produces the *cryptogram* CEHIPR. The transposition cipher that employs a grid composed of five rows and five columns (see figure 9–1) is more complex. A message (*This is a confidential cipher*) is entered by rows and then extracted by columns in accordance with a numerical *key*. (A key of 1 through 5 produces the cryptogram TSFTI HAIIP ICDAH SOELE INNCR, and a key of 5 through 1 produces INNCR SOELE ICDAH HAIIP TSFTI). The message may also be extracted according to the alphabetical order of the letters of a given *keyword* (such as WORLD, in figure 9–2), which produces the cryptogram INNCR SOELE HAIIP ICDAH TSFTI.

Knowing the key, the recipient of the message inserts the cipher text into the appropriate columns of a blank grid and reads across. For longer messages, more grids are employed. For messages of less than twenty-five characters, *nulls* in the form of X's or nonsense complete the text. (Plaintext is written in normal upper and lower case, whereas cipher text is written in UPPER CASE.)

A transposition cipher is relatively easy to break because the cryptogram displays the same characteristics of language as plaintext, particularly in letter frequencies. But it has the advantage of being simple and therefore less vulnerable to error in encipher-

1	2	3	4	5
t	h	i	s	i
s	a	c	o	n
f	i	d	e	n
t	i	a	l	c
i	p	h	e	r

Figure 9-1. *Transposition Cipher*

W	O	R	L	D
t	h	i	s	i
s	a	c	o	n
f	i	d	e	n
t	i	a	l	c
i	p	h	e	r

Figure 9-2. *Transposition Cipher (with Keyword)*

ment. Under some circumstances, the contents of a message may not have to be kept secret forever; in a battlefield situation, for example, the message may have to be secret only until an action is taken, perhaps no more than an hour. In such circumstances, simplicity may take priority. The transposition cipher in figures 9-1 and 9-2 requires no more equipment than sheets of paper with keys and blank grids and a pencil to decipher, so that a young, relatively unschooled code clerk under the stress of combat can encipher and decipher messages quickly, with less possibility of error. If keys are changed hourly or daily or even with each message so that the volume of traffic in any single key is greatly reduced, a transposition cipher may do the job.

Transposition, however, can be devilishly tricky when used to achieve a double or super encipherment—that is, when it is used to scramble a message already enciphered by *substitution.*

In substitution, a message is enciphered either by substituting each letter of the plaintext with another letter or character—in which case a cipher alphabet or alphabets is/are employed—or by substituting whole words or phrases with other words or groups of letters or characters, in which case a *code book* is required. There are three types of substitution ciphers: monoalphabetic, polyalphabetic, and code.

A *monoalphabetic substitution cipher* uses only one cipher alphabet in substituting the letters of plaintext. Since this cipher does not change the characteristics of language, particularly with reference to the appearance of high-frequency vowels and consonants, it is easy to solve. In a message written in English, for example, if x is substituted for *e* and s for *k* in a monoalphabetic cipher text, the letter frequency count of x and s will be the same as the letter frequency count of *e* and *k* in plaintext, depending upon length and subject matter. Monoalphabetic substitution ciphers are of historical interest and generate fascination in puzzle enthusiasts, but they are also useful learning tools to introduce the basics. They

	1	2	3	4	5
1	a	b	c	d	e
				i	
2	f	g	h	j	k
3	l	m	n	o	p
4	q	r	s	t	u
5	v	w	x	y	z

Figure 9-3. *Polybius Square*

	E	A	R	T	H
W	p	l	a	n	e
O	t	b	c	d	f
			i		
R	g	h	j	k	m
L	o	q	r	s	u
D	v	w	x	y	z

Figure 9-4. *Polybius Square (with Keyword)*

have been around a long time, since ancient Greece and the *Polybius square,* around 200 B.C.[2] (figures 9–3 and 9–4).

In this monoalphabetic substitution cipher, the plaintext alphabet is placed within a 5-by-5 grid (*i* and *j* occupy the same cell). The cipher alphabet serves as coordinates for the rows and columns (figure 9–3), so that each plaintext letter is substituted by two characters (a *digraph*), such as $a = 11$; $b = 12$; $m = 32$; and $z = 55$. Therefore: *Boston* = 12344 34434 33555, and *Chicago* = 13232 41311 22344. (Cipher text is generally transmitted in five-character groups. This is in accordance with international telecommunications practice. It provides additional security by eliminating normal word length as a clue for solution.) Because the cipher alphabet is reduced to only five numbers, the cipher appears difficult. But once its digraphic character has been determined, the cipher reveals itself as merely monoalphabetic and the solution is simple. It can be made more complex by using keywords as coordinates within the plaintext alphabet (figure 9–4). If changed frequently, hourly or daily, these ciphers may resist quick solution. In figure 9–4, a = WR; b = OA; m = RH; and z = DH. *Detroit* would be enciphered as OTWHO ELRLE RROEX.

A less complex system, although it appeared later in history than the Polybius square, is *Caesar's alphabet.*[3] This is probably the most venerated and best-known monoalphabetic substitution cipher. The cipher alphabet is achieved by starting someplace in the alphabet other than the beginning, somewhere beyond A. Caesar would begin with D and use that displacement throughout the message as a substitute for plaintext (figure 9–5). One could also use a keyword (figure 9–6) or random alphabet to achieve the same effect.

---

p: *a b c d e f g h i j k l m n o p q r s t u v w x y z*

C: D E F G H I J K L M N O P Q R S T U V W X Y Z A B C

I came.   I saw.   I conquered.

LFDPH LVDZL FRQTX HUHGA

Figure 9–5. *Caesar's Alphabet*

keyword: JULIUS CAESAR

p: *a   b   c   d   e   f   g   h   i   j   k   l   m   n   o   p   q   r   s   t   u   v   w   x   y   z*

C: J   U   L   I   S   C   A   E   R   B   D   F   G   H   K   M   N   O   P   Q   Z   Y   X   W   V   T

I have crossed the Rubicon.

REJYS LOKPP SIQES OZURL KHWW

Figure 9-6. *Caesar's Alphabet (with Keyword)*

Despite the many ways that Caesar's alphabet and its clones may be made more secure, such as changing keywords and scrambling alphabets, cryptographers eventually learned that working with two or more alphabets gives more security than working with one. Hence they created the *polyalphabetic substitution cipher.*

The technologies used in polyalphabetic substitution ciphers range from relatively limited cipher cards and disks to complex cipher machines and computer-generated systems. The systems they produce may be unbreakable. But other factors need to be weighed as well, such as mobility or portability and user friendliness. Two polyalphabetic systems that are portable and easy to use, the cipher disk and the cipher card, may be traced to the fifteenth and sixteenth centuries. The cipher disk of L.B. Alberti (c. 1466),[4] and the Vigenère square, derived from a treatise written by Blaise de Vigenère in 1585,[5] contain the essential concepts of polyalphabetic substitution ciphers and have been handed down to the present time.

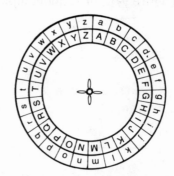

Figure 9-7. *Cipher Disk (Alberti's Disk)*

Alberti's *cipher disk* system consists of two disks with different circumferences. (A modified version appears in figure 9–7.) The smaller disk lies on top of the larger and is joined to it in the center by a pin, enabling it to rotate. Each disk is divided into equal segments (twenty-six for English). A plaintext alphabet is inscribed on the larger disk, or outer edge, and a cipher alphabet is inscribed on the rim of the smaller disk. Messages are enciphered by lining up plaintext letters with cipher letters in accordance with a setting that is normally determined by a keyword. Keywords are of varying lengths and thus bring into play varying numbers of cipher alphabets. Each letter of the keyword is lined up with plaintext *a* in sequence as each letter of plaintext is enciphered by its corresponding letter in the cipher alphabet. For example, the keyword BED, with three letters, would use three alphabets to encipher the word *cede* and produce the cryptogram DIGF, whereas the keyword DOCUMENT would employ eight cipher alphabets. Although this method is tedious, a user basing the settings upon a *keyphrase* or random alphabet could utilize up to twenty-five alphabets to encipher a message, appreciably reducing letter frequencies and other linguistic clues to plaintext.

The *Vigenère square* (figure 9–8) has the same cryptographic capabilities as the cipher disk and differs principally in design. Cipher alphabets (up to twenty-five) are placed beneath the plaintext alphabet in rows and arranged progressively. Encipherment is achieved in accordance with a keyword or keyphrase, the letters of which are matched sequentially with the initial letter of one of the cipher alphabets. This determines which alphabets to use and how many. The keyword DOG tells the user to select three alphabets, those in row D, row O, and row G, in that order. If the word to be enciphered is *Fido,* the user reads down the column headed by plaintext *f* to where it intersects with row D and inscribes the cipher letter occupying that space, which is I. Continuing this procedure, column *i* to row O produces W, column *d* to row G yields J, and column *o* to row D encounters R. *Fido* is enciphered as IWJR. Using the keyword DICKENS, the title *A Tale of Two Cities* would be enciphered as follows: DBCV IBXW EQMM GAHA. In this example, note that the high-frequency vowels, *a e i o,* and even the high-frequency consonant *t* are not enciphered by the same letter. A cryptanalyst would require a high volume of traffic to overcome

	a	b	c	d	e	f	g	h	i	j	k	l	m	n	o	p	q	r	s	t	u	v	w	x	y	z
a	B	C	D	E	F	G	H	I	J	K	L	M	N	O	P	Q	R	S	T	U	V	W	X	Y	Z	A
b	C	D	E	F	G	H	I	J	K	L	M	N	O	P	Q	R	S	T	U	V	W	X	Y	Z	A	B
c	D	E	F	G	H	I	J	K	L	M	N	O	P	Q	R	S	T	U	V	W	X	Y	Z	A	B	C
d	E	F	G	H	I	J	K	L	M	N	O	P	Q	R	S	T	U	V	W	X	Y	Z	A	B	C	D
e	F	G	H	I	J	K	L	M	N	O	P	Q	R	S	T	U	V	W	X	Y	Z	A	B	C	D	E
f	G	H	I	J	K	L	M	N	O	P	Q	R	S	T	U	V	W	X	Y	Z	A	B	C	D	E	F
g	H	I	J	K	L	M	N	O	P	Q	R	S	T	U	V	W	X	Y	Z	A	B	C	D	E	F	G
h	I	J	K	L	M	N	O	P	Q	R	S	T	U	V	W	X	Y	Z	A	B	C	D	E	F	G	H
i	J	K	L	M	N	O	P	Q	R	S	T	U	V	W	X	Y	Z	A	B	C	D	E	F	G	H	I
j	K	L	M	N	O	P	Q	R	S	T	U	V	W	X	Y	Z	A	B	C	D	E	F	G	H	I	J
k	L	M	N	O	P	Q	R	S	T	U	V	W	X	Y	Z	A	B	C	D	E	F	G	H	I	J	K
l	M	N	O	P	Q	R	S	T	U	V	W	X	Y	Z	A	B	C	D	E	F	G	H	I	J	K	L
m	N	O	P	Q	R	S	T	U	V	W	X	Y	Z	A	B	C	D	E	F	G	H	I	J	K	L	M
n	O	P	Q	R	S	T	U	V	W	X	Y	Z	A	B	C	D	E	F	G	H	I	J	K	L	M	N
o	P	Q	R	S	T	U	V	W	X	Y	Z	A	B	C	D	E	F	G	H	I	J	K	L	M	N	O
p	Q	R	S	T	U	V	W	X	Y	Z	A	B	C	D	E	F	G	H	I	J	K	L	M	N	O	P
q	R	S	T	U	V	W	X	Y	Z	A	B	C	D	E	F	G	H	I	J	K	L	M	N	O	P	Q
r	S	T	U	V	W	X	Y	Z	A	B	C	D	E	F	G	H	I	J	K	L	M	N	O	P	Q	R
s	T	U	V	W	X	Y	Z	A	B	C	D	E	F	G	H	I	J	K	L	M	N	O	P	Q	R	S
t	U	V	W	X	Y	Z	A	B	C	D	E	F	G	H	I	J	K	L	M	N	O	P	Q	R	S	T
u	V	W	X	Y	Z	A	B	C	D	E	F	G	H	I	J	K	L	M	N	O	P	Q	R	S	T	U
v	W	X	Y	Z	A	B	C	D	E	F	G	H	I	J	K	L	M	N	O	P	Q	R	S	T	U	V
w	X	Y	Z	A	B	C	D	E	F	G	H	I	J	K	L	M	N	O	P	Q	R	S	T	U	V	W
x	Y	Z	A	B	C	D	E	F	G	H	I	J	K	L	M	N	O	P	Q	R	S	T	U	V	W	X
y	Z	A	B	C	D	E	F	G	H	I	J	K	L	M	N	O	P	Q	R	S	T	U	V	W	X	Y
z	A	B	C	D	E	F	G	H	I	J	K	L	M	N	O	P	Q	R	S	T	U	V	W	X	Y	Z

Figure 9–8. *Vigenère Square*

this flatness and, in the absence of data processing equipment, many painful hours of work.

Although polyalphabetic substitution originated in the fifteenth century with Alberti, almost three centuries elapsed before Thomas Jefferson conceived of a device that took away the drudgery and reduced the error inherent in most hand systems. Jefferson invented a cipher "machine" (figure 9-9), probably while he was secretary of state, between 1790 and 1793, that consisted of twenty-six wooden wheels. A random alphabet was inscribed on the circumference of each wheel, and the wheels were mounted on a common axle, giving the appearance of a cylinder. Jefferson enciphered messages by rotating each wheel to produce a line of plaintext. He then locked the cylinder into place with a wing nut that was attached to the end of the axle. He rotated the entire device and selected at random any one of the other twenty-five lines as the cipher text. The recipient of the message, who was in possession of a similar device, merely reproduced the line of cipher text on his own cylinder, tightened the wing nut, and rotated the cylinder until—eureka!—he encountered the plaintext line. For some reason, Jefferson's cipher machine gathered dust for over a century until its principle was rediscovered and put to use in modern cipher machines. The only difference between today's machines and Jefferson's is that today the cipher wheels, or rotors, are activated by an operator using a keyboard, causing the rotors to turn and produce a printout in accordance with electronic settings and circuitry.

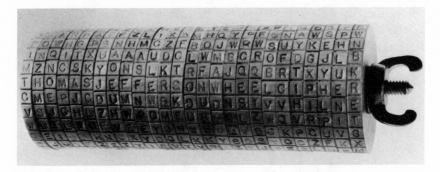

Exact reproduction. Courtesy of Silvio A. Bedini, Washington, D.C. Reprinted with permission.

Figure 9-9. *Thomas Jefferson's Wheel Cipher Device*

According to David Kahn, Jefferson merits the title "the father of American cryptography."[6]

In the meantime, the search for a hand or field cipher that combined convenience and security continued. Among the systems devised, the Playfair cipher (1854), used by the British in the Crimean War, deserves particular mention because it was still in use during World War II and may have saved the life of Navy Lieutenant John F. Kennedy. Australian coast-watchers observed the sinking of Kennedy's *PT 109* in the Solomons in 1943 and used the Playfair cipher to report the incident and guide the rescue of Kennedy and his crew from behind Japanese lines.[7]

As a polyalphabetic substitution cipher, *the Playfair system* (figure 9–10) has a number of attractive features. It is simple to use and difficult to solve. It requires no more equipment than paper and pencil and a list of keywords or keyphrases. The same alphabet is used for both plaintext and cipher text. Playfair adds another degree of difficulty by enciphering letters in pairs (digraphs), which increases the number of substitutions for a single letter to the extent of its possible combinations with all other letters. A cipher alphabet (which is usually modified in accordance with a keyword or keyphrase so that it can be changed periodically) is inscribed within a 5-by-5 grid, or checkerboard. The user enciphers two letters at a time, guided by their relative positions within the grid. If the letters are in the same row, the letters immediately to the right of each are substituted; if the letters are in the same column, they are enciphered by the letters immediately below; when they are neither in the same row nor in the same column, they are enciphered by moving along the row of the first letter to its intersection with the column of the second, and the row of the second to its intersection with the column of the first. For example, using the alphabet in figure 9–10, *as* = SH; *te* = EP; *rn* = LB. To decipher, one reverses the procedure.

After the coming of the telegraph and the underseas cable, no manual polyalphabetic substitution cipher could provide the necessary convenience and security for the increasing volume of governmental traffic. Governments thereafter adopted the third form of substitution, the code. Codebooks are bulky and must be stored in a secure area, but this posed no difficulty for governmental offices

	w	a	s	h	i j
	n	g	t	o	b
	k	f	e	d	c
	l	m	p	q	r
	z	y	x	v	u

Keyword: WASHINGTON

Plaintext:	The nation's capital								
Encipherment:	*th*	*en*	*at*	*io*	*ns*	*ca*	*pi*	*tx*	*al*
	OS	KT	SG	HB	TW	FI	RS	ES	WM
Cipher text:	OSK	TSG	HBT	WFI	RSE	SWM			

Figure 9-10. *Playfair Cipher*

and permanent overseas missions. Codes are more secure than hand or field ciphers because in codes (although they are based on the principle of substitution), whole words or phrases are enciphered by code groups, which eliminates entirely the giveaway of letter frequency. (Certain common words or punctuation marks are repeated frequently and thereby provide clues to solution, but this is corrected by having several distinct code groups for *comma* or *stop*.) In practice, to break a code the cryptanalyst must reconstruct an entire code book that consists of thousands of words instead of a cipher system based upon variations of twenty-odd letters of an alphabet. Breaking such messages requires a very high volume of traffic and a great deal of time.

There are two types of codes. In the codebook of a *one-part code* (figure 9-11), plaintext letters, syllables, words, and phrases are listed in alphabetical order alongside code groups arranged in alphabetical or numerical order. Only one book is needed for encoding and decoding. A *two-part code* (figure 9-12) is more secure but requires two books: one for encoding—in which plaintext is listed alphabetically—and another for decoding—in which the code groups are listed in order.

Plaintext	CODE GROUP
cab	YABC
cabal	YBCD
cabin	YCDE
cable	YDEF
cache	YEFG

Figure 9–11. *One-Part Code*

encode:

Plaintext	CODE GROUP
cab	FZMH
cabal	CBTJ
cabin	VRLL
cable	APKX
cache	QCCG

decode:

CODE GROUP	Plaintext
APIV	minister
APJW	Washington
APKX	cable
APLY	toward
APMZ	however

Figure 9–12. *Two-Part Code*

Codes and ciphers and the breaking of them have had a long history. But once American intelligence got involved with them, it soon became very effective. The cipher systems and codes described in this chapter are relatively simple, but studying them provides insights into the science of secret writing applied by U.S. foreign intelligence in the modern age. Beginning with World War I, cryptanalysis in particular came into its own.

10
Intelligence Goes to War, 1914–18

I n World War I, cryptanalysis rose from playing a bit part to having a starring role in the production of intelligence. The wireless, or radio, brought this transformation about. Radio enabled military commanders and general staffs to conduct operations on a scale grander than ever before—to move whole armies and supplies around like pieces on a gigantic chessboard. It also provided the enemy with access to every message transmitted. With the telegraph, the enemy had had to infiltrate behind the lines to set up a wiretap. But with radio, anyone could listen in from almost anywhere. Even so, signal officers who had used the telegraph had recognized the risk of interception and taken steps to ensure cryptographic security. If the telegraph had promoted the development of cryptography, radio promoted the development of cryptanalysis, which for a long time maintained the upper hand.[1]

The radio made available a steady stream of enemy communications in World War I, enabling cryptanalysts to break most of the existing codes and ciphers and providing decision makers with reliable and timely intelligence. English cryptanalysts cracked messages that revealed German intrigues with Irish revolutionaries, leading to the arrest and execution of Sir Roger Casement on charges of treason. An intercepted cipher message exposed history's most notorious female spy, Mata Hari.[2] French codebreaker Georges Painvin lost thirty-three pounds in three months while solving the ADFGVX system, a transposition of cipher text (superencipherment) that was described as "the toughest field cipher the world had yet seen,'' just in time to provide the key information that enabled the Allies to turn back the last major German offensive of the war in June 1918.[3] As significant as these contributions were, none equaled the significance of the Zimmermann telegram, both as an accomplishment of cryptanalysis and as an example of the influence of intelligence upon history.

On January 16, 1917, the German foreign minister, Arthur Zimmermann, sent a coded message to the German minister in Mexico, Heinrich J.F. von Eckhardt. Zimmermann informed Eckhardt that Germany had decided that it would resume unrestricted submarine warfare on February 1—an action that would likely provoke war with the United States. He instructed Eckhardt to seek an alliance with Mexico, offering Mexico the understanding that it would reconquer its ''lost territory'' in Texas, New Mexico, and Arizona.[4] In making this brazen proposal, Germany was taking a calculated risk.

Germany had originally proclaimed submarine warfare back in February 1915. It had established a ''war zone'' around the British Isles and threatened to sink all enemy vessels, merchant or war, on sight, but it had retreated because of the protest of President Woodrow Wilson. Wilson declared that he would hold Germany to ''strict accountability'' if American lives or ships were lost. He insisted that submarines must observe the same rules of naval warfare as surface ships, which meant, among other things, that the lives of noncombatants aboard any merchant ship or passenger liner, regardless of registry, must be guaranteed. Over the course of the next two years, a number of incidents had occurred, the most spectacular being the sinking of the ocean liner *Lusitania*. But for the most part Germany had kept its ''ultimate weapon'' on a leash.

In 1917, however, Germany decided that the price of American neutrality was too high. Its leaders concluded that Wilson's concept of neutral rights and ''freedom of the seas'' favored the Allies and possibly even kept them in the war. Anticipating the collapse of the czar's government in Russia and observing the growing weariness and even defeatism in France and England, Germany prepared to launch a major offensive in the spring of 1917. Even if the United States entered the war, Germany's generals reasoned, the fighting would be over before the Americans could train and send a force to Europe. In the meantime, German submarines would deprive the Allies of food and supplies in their most desperate hour. In the context of delivering this "knockout blow," Germany regarded the United States as more menacing as a neutral than as a belligerent.

But just to be sure, to slow down the Americans and distract them, Germany proposed the alliance with Mexico. U.S.–Mexican relations had been strained since 1913, stemming from events in the Mexican Revolution. Wilson had intervened at Vera Cruz in 1914, and at the very time when Zimmermann sent his message, troops under General John J. Pershing were in northern Mexico pursuing the Mexican revolutionary Francisco "Pancho" Villa. Germany had been conducting covert political action in the United States and Mexico for some time, supporting American leaders who criticized Wilson's "watchful waiting" and trying to stir up trouble in the border regions.[5] When Venustiano Carranza rose to power in Mexico, Germany exploited his nationalistic fervor and general anti-American attitude. Hence, the Zimmermann telegram.

But the Germans had not counted upon the fact that the British were reading their diplomatic traffic. In fact, the British received a copy of Zimmermann's encoded dispatch before Eckhardt did. Although they had not completely reconstructed the code (it was a tough two-parter), they recovered enough of the plaintext to realize that it could be the means to bring the United States into the war. The British had worked hard for this success. At the outset of the war, they had severed most of the underseas cables that connected Germany with the rest of the world, forcing the German government to communicate either by cables that passed through the British Isles or by the wireless. In this way British cryptanalysts became privy to almost every German international message, as well as to the radio traffic that was being used to conduct German military operations. British Naval Intelligence had assumed the task of breaking German codes and ciphers, initially with a small staff of cryptanalysts in Room 40 in the Admiralty's Old Building. By 1917, the unit had expanded to include eight hundred radio-intercept operators and over seventy "cryppies." Although it moved to larger quarters, the name "Room 40" was still used by insiders to identify the operation.[6] During World War I, Room 40, under the direction first of Sir Alfred Ewing and then of Admiral William Reginald Hall, solved an estimated fifteen thousand German intercepts.[7]

Although the Zimmermann telegram was critical, Admiral Hall did not act upon it immediately. He faced a dilemma that is not unusual in the craft of intelligence: How could he use the information without disclosing its source? If the Germans discovered that the British had breached their code, they would change it and a vital source of intelligence would be lost. Not only would his cryptanalytic edge be compromised, Hall also faced a potentially embarrassing situation with the Americans. The original Zimmermann telegram, encoded in Germany's top Code 0075, had been sent from Berlin to the German ambassador in Washington, Count Johann von Bernstorff, for forwarding to Eckhardt in Mexico. It had been sent through a channel that President Wilson's adviser and confidant Edward M. House had set up for Wilson's peace efforts. Wilson's anger at the contents of the telegram would certainly be compounded by this abuse of the special communications link and by the evidence that Germany had been deceiving Wilson by only feigning interest in his peace initiatives while all along planning a military solution. But it would also expose the fact that Room 40 had been reading U.S. diplomatic traffic.

Under these circumstances, Hall did not reveal even the existence of the message to Foreign Secretary Arthur Balfour until February 5. When he did, he may have been hoping that Germany's renewal of submarine warfare alone would cause an American declaration of war, in which case Room 40 would not be compromised. Or perhaps he thought that the Americans had cracked the German code, but this does not seem likely, given the sorry state of American cryptanalytic efforts at the time. Hall ultimately concluded that to solve his dilemma, he had to acquire a copy of the Zimmermann telegram at the receiving end, that is, in the form that Eckhardt received it from Bernstorff. Luckily for Hall, a British agent obtained a copy of the note from the telegraph office in Mexico City. Moreover, Bernstorff had encoded it in a lower-level code since Eckhardt did not possess 0075.[8] Hall could now produce a text that would neither jeopardize Anglo–American relations nor compromise the code-breaking activities of Room 40. On February 22, Secretary Balfour and Admiral Hall delivered a copy of the Zimmermann telegram to Walter Hines Page, the American ambassador in London.

Within a few weeks, the United States entered World War I against Germany. The Zimmermann telegram alone did not cause the United States to go to war; it might have gone to war without it. But according to Barbara Tuchman, its effect was to loosen Wilson's last hold on neutrality: "It left Wilson bereft of the prop of public opinion which had so far sustained his struggle to keep the United States neutral. After the middle of March [1917] there was nothing to hold him back."[9] "And so it came about," adds David Kahn, "that Room 40's solution of an enemy message helped propel the United States into the First World War. . . . No other single cryptanalysis has had such enormous consequences. Never before or since has so much turned upon the solution of a secret message. For those few moments in time, the codebreakers held history in the palm of their hand."[10] Ironically, despite these claims that the Zimmermann telegram was "history-making," if left up to Hall it would have remained locked in his safe.

Hall's behavior shows the intelligence mind at work and raises the question of accountability. He withheld critical information from policymakers so that he could continue to serve them. Admittedly, it took until February 19 to reconstruct the entire telegram, including the most sensational part dealing with the intention to dismember the United States; but Hall did not inform either the foreign secretary or the prime minister of the existence of the message for almost three weeks. (One has to wonder if there have been other "Zimmermann telegrams" in the netherworld of intelligence that never had a chance to "alter" history.) Nor did he even alert Fleet Operations about Germany's intention to launch submarine warfare. On the other hand, there is no evidence that Balfour chastised Hall for not informing him sooner, and for his part, Balfour took no action himself until Hall had sanitized the document and it was clear that the United States was not going to act without a push.

The United States apparently did not solve the message on its own, even though it had both the original Zimmermann telegram and access to Bernstorff's version in a lesser code; U.S. crypt-analytic capability apparently had not been sufficient. Yet although the United States entered the war with an inadequate intelligence establishment, it had been sensitized to foreign espionage and subversion. Between 1914 and 1917, the belligerent nations had attempted through propaganda and covert action to influence the policy and behavior of the United States, owing to the fact that it was the most productive agricultural and industrial nation that was also not in the war. The Allies, the principal beneficiaries of American production, stuck to propaganda and saw no purpose in disruptive action, but the Central Powers engaged in covert action— and incredibly clumsy covert action, at that.

In August 1915, the American people learned that Germany and Austria were planning propaganda, strikes, and sabotage in the United States, when the German commercial attaché, Dr. Heinrich Albert, left his briefcase on a New York streetcar and an alert Secret Service agent picked it up. Then the British seized a German courier, John J. Archibald, onboard the transatlantic liner SS *Rotterdam*.[11] These purloined plans implicated the German ambassador, Bernstorff; the Austrian ambassador, Constantin Dumba; and German attachés Franz von Papen (military) and Karl Boy-ed (naval). They "woke the State Department with a shock of surprise to the fact that the Germans were dangerous."[12] Afterward, through its office of the counselor, the State Department "increasingly concerned itself with intelligence matters" and undertook to coordinate the counterintelligence activities of the "various American intelligence services."[13] At year's end, the United States demanded the recall of von Papen and Boy-ed, presenting evidence that they and another German agent, Captain Franz von Rintelin, were engaged in a plot to restore to power the former Mexican dictator Victoriano Huerta, whom they had brought to the United States from exile in Spain. Even before the Zimmermann telegram became public, the Huerta affair alerted the United States to German efforts to cause trouble with Mexico. It provoked speculation that Germany had been involved in the Plan of San Diego, which had called for a rebellion and secessionist movement by Mexican-Americans in the Southwest in 1915 and in Pancho Villa's raid on Columbus, New Mexico, in March 1916.[14]

In 1917, Lothar Witzke, the notorious saboteur responsible for the destruction of the Black Tom munitions plant in New Jersey the year before, turned up in Mexico, causing Senator Albert B. Fall of New Mexico to think he saw a connection among all these events.[15]

The United States' entry into the war intensified the emotions aroused by these foreign intrigues. Government agencies concerned with internal security and intelligence expanded rapidly, even over-zealously. Even as President Wilson despaired that democracy could survive the war, the abuse of authority at home seriously affected the functions of intelligence in the long run. Wrapped in the mantle of patriotism, extremist groups such as the American Protective League and the Sedition Slammers threatened to wipe out political dissent and nonconforming behavior. Acting as self-appointed vigilantes and espousing "100% Americanism," these groups persecuted so-called hyphenated Americans—German-Americans especially but not exclusively—causing Beethoven's music to be banned and menus changed to read "liberty cabbage" instead of sauerkraut: "In self-defense," writes Robert K. Murray, "towns and individuals with German names . . . appealed to the courts for relief and Schmidts became Smiths while Berlins became Bellevilles. For a time there [was] congressional talk of passing a 'no strike' law in order to compel greater labor cooperation than already existed, and in the nation at large men [were] beaten and tarred and feathered for failure to buy war bonds or support Red Cross drives."[16]

Far from protecting persons against such attacks upon their freedoms, the U.S. government seemed to encourage them. The Committee on Public Information, a wartime agency created by executive order, set standards for loyalty and encouraged Americans to spy on one another. Its director, George Creel, boasted, "Not a pin dropped in the home of any one with a foreign name, but that it rang like thunder on the inner ear of some listening sleuth."[17] The Justice Department's Bureau of Investigation and G-2's Counterintelligence Police expanded and grew bolder, forti-fied by laws that impinged heavily upon civil liberties. The Espio-nage Act of 1917 declared it unlawful to make "false statements" with intent to obstruct U.S. military operations, including enlist-

ment and recruiting activities. Although peace activists' opposition
to the war was not popular, the Espionage Act threatened them
with twenty years' imprisonment if they seemed to persist. The
Sedition Act, passed the following year, further stifled dissent by
making it a crime to "utter, print, write, or publish any disloyal,
profane, scurrilous, or abusive language" about the American
form of government, the Constitution, or the U.S. military uniform.

More than a thousand people were arrested and convicted in
accordance with these laws. Among them, Socialist leader Eugene
V. Debs, an outspoken critic of the war, received a ten-year jail
sentence for making a speech in which he denounced the Espionage
Act as "a despotic enactment in flagrant conflict with democratic
principles and with the spirit of free institutions."[18] Not even the
Supreme Court offered relief. In *Schenck v. U.S.* in 1919, Justice
Oliver Wendell Holmes delivered the opinion that First Amendment rights were not absolute: "Free speech," he stated, "would
not protect a man falsely shouting fire in a theater and causing
panic."

Even after peace was restored, tolerance was not. In fact, violations of civil liberties and even human rights increased in the
United States in the immediate postwar period. Two circumstances combined to make this happen: an economic recession,
caused by the conversion from war to peace, and the Bolshevik
Revolution in Russia in 1917. As production was cut back and four
million men under arms were quickly demobilized, unemployment
rose, contributing to a series of strikes and acts of violence across
the country from Seattle to Boston, especially in the steel industry.
These economic setbacks and terroristic attacks alarmed Americans, and the strong antiforeign feelings engendered during the
war shifted from an old threat to a new one. The "dreaded Hun"
was replaced by the Communist International: "As labor unrest
increased and the nation was treated to such abnormal events as
general strikes, riots, and the planting of bombs, the assumption
that the country was under serious attack by the Reds found a wide
acceptance. In the long run, each social and industrial disturbance
was received as prima-facie evidence of the successful spread of
radicalism."[19]

Toward the end of the war, in October 1918, Congress passed the Alien Law, which prohibited anarchists and those who advocated the violent overthrow of the U.S. government from entering the country and provided for the deportation of aliens already in the country who held such beliefs. After the war, armed with this and the earlier enactments, U.S. attorney general A. Mitchell Palmer undertook a campaign against radicalism—and radicalism, according to one observer, included even "the most innocent departure from conventional thought."[20] Declaring that the United States was being consumed by a "blaze of revolution," Palmer helped incite the Red Scare of 1919–20, which led to arbitrary arrests and deportations. Within the Justice Department's Bureau of Investigation, Palmer created the General Intelligence Division (GID) and instructed the young J. Edgar Hoover to compile a card index of radical leaders and organizations.[21] Acting on information gathered by Hoover, Palmer ordered the famous "raid" of January 2, 1920, that was carried out simultaneously in thirty-three cities against the Communist and Communist Labor parties: "Virtually every local Communist organization in the nation was affected; practically every leader of the movement, national or local, was put under arrest. Often such arrests were made without the formality of warrants as bureau agents entered bowling alleys, pool halls, cafés, club rooms, and even homes, and seized everyone in sight. Families were separated; prisoners were held incommunicado and deprived of their right to legal counsel."[22]

The excesses committed in these acts, the revelations of overcrowding and inhuman conditions in the detention centers ("Palmer Houses"), and the numerous cases of false arrest caused a public reaction against Palmer, and the Red Scare eventually subsided. Palmer slipped from being a presidential possibility in 1920 to being a pathetic joke who exemplified the public's loss of confidence in the Wilson administration. When prosperity returned and concern about the bolsheviks and world revolution abated, a new president, Warren G. Harding, pardoned Gene Debs in December 1921 and even had him to the White House for a chat. As the pendulum swung from hysteria to apathy, the craft of intelligence fared poorly at both ends.

In the meantime, U.S. military intelligence had undergone significant if fleeting changes. In 1917, when the United States entered World War I, the Military Intelligence Division (G-2) was a "minor appendage" of the War College Division, consisting of two officers and two clerks. By November 1918, it had expanded to 282 officers, 29 noncommissioned officers, and 948 civilian employees.[23] Major (later Major General) Ralph Van Deman and Lieutenant Colonel (later Brigadier General) Marlborough Churchill were largely responsible for the transformation. Van Deman rescued G-2 from the file card section of the War College in May 1917 and brought it to life, developing in particular a counter-intelligence capability that concentrated upon the home front and matters of subversion and espionage. In a way, he did not have much choice; U.S. commanders overseas tended to rely upon British and French resources for combat intelligence, and General Pershing organized his own intelligence staff within the American Expeditionary Force (AEF). Nonetheless, when Van Deman went to France after a year and Churchill succeeded him as head of G-2, he inherited a vital organization that enabled him to fight to restore intelligence to its central status on the general staff. He succeeded, in part, owing to the fact that G-2 had earned a reputation for excellence in cryptology.

According to General Peyton C. March, U.S. Army chief of staff during World War I, "we were babes-in-the-woods" in cryptology in April 1917. By war's end, MI-8 "was the equal of any on the globe."[24] MI-8 was section eight of the Military Intelligence Division, or the Code and Cipher Section, which had been created by Van Deman in June 1917. Van Deman had recruited Herbert O. Yardley, a $900-a-year code clerk in the State Department who had been solving U.S. diplomatic codes for fun. In May 1916, Yardley had shocked his superiors by cracking an enciphered message from Colonel House to President Wilson in just two hours.[25] An obsessed puzzle-solver, Yardley became one of America's most famous—and infamous—cryptologists.

Yardley was transferred to G-2 with a second lieutenant's commission. Within MI-8, he created subsections and bureaus to deal with every aspect of secret writing. Having demonstrated the inadequacy of American ciphers, he organized the Code and Cipher Compilation Bureau to produce new and secure cryptosystems. Within the strong counterintelligence thrust of Van Deman's G-2, he set up a bureau to handle secret inks, steganography being a critical part of the spy's trade. MI-8 also assumed responsibility for instructing and training army cipher clerks before assignment overseas with the AEF. But Yardley's greatest passion was cryptanalysis, and his Code and Cipher Solution Bureau solved over ten thousand messages, reading the diplomatic traffic of Argentina, Brazil, Chile, Costa Rica, Cuba, Germany, Mexico, Spain, and Panama.[26]

When the fighting neared its end in August 1918, Yardley traveled to Europe, where he had the pleasure of meeting Hall and Painvin. These three together symbolized the flowering of cryptanalysis in World War I. No longer wishing or needing to rely upon the British or French, Yardley subsequently served the U.S. peace delegation at Versailles by producing cryptanalytic intelligence. Besides Yardley himself, twenty of G-2's specialists accompanied President Wilson to France, including General Churchill. Their presence indicated that army intelligence had come very far in less than two years.

The reorganization of the army general staff in August 1918 provided further measure of the success of the Military Intelligence Division. The reorganization specifically recognized G-2's status as one of the four principal divisions of the general staff and made it responsible for planning, coordinating, and supervising military intelligence, both *positive* (the collection and production of foreign intelligence) and *negative* (internal security and counterintelligence). G-2's organizational structure in 1918 reveals both its activities and its sophistication. The Military Intelligence Division comprised an Administrative Section with three branches, subdivided thus:

Military Intelligence Division Administrative Section (M.I. 1)

   (a) Records, Accounts, and General Section.
   (b) Interpreters and intelligence police sections.
   (c) Publication (Daily Intelligence Summary, Weekly Summary, Activities Report).

The Positive Branch.

   (a) Information Section (M.I. 2. Prepared the strategic estimate which attempted to answer the questions, "What is the situation today?'' [current intelligence] and ''What will it be tomorrow?'' [estimates] by analyzing the situation in each country under the military, political, economic, and psychological headings.)

(b) Collection Section (M.I. 5. Administered the military attaché system.)
(c) Translation Section (M.I. 6).
(d) Code and Cipher Section (M.I. 8).
(e) Shorthand Bureau.
(f) Secret Ink Bureau.
(g) Code Instruction Bureau.
(h) Code Compilation Bureau.
(i) Communication Bureau.
(j) Combat Intelligence Instruction Bureau.

The Geographic Branch (maps and military monographs of all countries). [basic intelligence]

(a) Map Section (M.I. 7).
(b) Monograph and Handbook Section (M.I. 9).

The Negative Branch (collects and disseminates information upon which may be based measures of prevention against activities or influences tending to harm military efficiency by methods other than armed force).

(a) Foreign Influence Section (M.I. 4).
(b) Army Section (M.I. 3).
(c) News Section (M.I. 10).
(d) Travel Section (M.I. 11).
(e) Fraud Section (M.I. 13).[27]

By the conclusion of World War I, U.S. military intelligence was performing most of the functions of a modern intelligence organization, except for clandestine operations. It appeared that G-2 had come of age. Just before the 1918 reorganization, General Churchill foresaw this development and had raised the broader concept of national intelligence, declaring,

There is hardly an officer who does not recognize that at a GHQ and at the headquarters of every army, corps, division and similar unit, G-3 [Plans] cannot make good plans unless G-2 furnish good information. We take that truth for granted, but what is less often emphasized is the fact that there must be a G-2 in the War Department performing a similar function, not only with the War Plans Division in the initiation and perfection of plans, but also concurrently with the State Department in the work of prediction [estimates] upon which national policy is based.[28]

Nonetheless, neither G-2 nor intelligence in general prospered during the interwar years. In the postwar demobilization, G-2 diminished in size and prestige. Regular army officers discovered that intelligence was not a viable career field, and according to one author, G-2 became a kind of "dumping ground" for incompetents.[29] In the late 1930s, Italian dictator Benito Mussolini remarked that the United States "must have" the best intelligence system in the world "for no one has been able to ever discover it."[30]

The reasons for the decline of intelligence in peacetime are not hard to find. First of all, intelligence in general tended to be associated in the popular mind with the excesses committed during the Red Scare—particularly since G-2, especially under Van Deman, emphasized counterintelligence and internal security matters. Constitutionally, intelligence seemed to have played a sinister role. Secondly, the general American disillusionment toward the entire war experience contributed to antimilitarism and diminished interest in international relations. If the American people did not favor taking a world role, they obviously saw little need for large military, diplomatic, or intelligence establishments. This disillusionment took distinct forms during the "normalcy" of the 1920s and the Depression of the 1930s. Yet U.S. foreign intelligence did not completely disappear between 1918 and 1941; nor did the United States fully withdraw from international involvement.

11
"Gentlemen Do Not . . ."

Despite its isolationism during the years between the two world wars, the United States did not abandon the international arena entirely. It refused to join the League of Nations and it shunned military and political alliances, but it vigorously pursued its interests in Latin America and the Pacific and treated with other nations in matters of disarmament, the pacific settlement of disputes, and trade. Observers tended to confuse America's preoccupation with independent action with an unwillingness to deal at all.

Under these circumstances, the dismantling of the U.S. intelligence apparatus was not as thorough as is normally supposed. The United States especially maintained its cryptologic capability. Communications intelligence had been a success in the Great War, marked by low risk and exceptional reliability, which made it a logical choice for retention. Moreover, Herbert O. Yardley's reputation and persuasiveness helped keep the momentum going. After returning from Paris in April 1919, with the encouragement of General Marlborough Churchill, Yardley prepared a memorandum in which he argued for continuing U.S. codebreaking activities. He focused on cryptanalysis since he was aware that the Signal Corps had a responsibility for cryptographic security and since he was prepared to give up the other functions of MI-8, such as secret inks. Moreover, cryptanalysis served both diplomatic and military interests: taking his cue from General Churchill's views about strategic or national intelligence, Yardley proposed that the Departments of State and War jointly sponsor a peacetime Cipher Bureau.

Yardley won the approval of Acting Secretary of State Frank

L. Polk (who, as counselor of the State Department from 1915 on, had "coordinated" U.S. counterintelligence efforts) and U.S. Army Chief of Staff General Peyton C. March. Yardley became chief of the *American Black Chamber* in May 1919,[1] beginning an episode of triumph and tragedy.

Although the Black Chamber was part of the Military Intelligence Division, Yardley and his staff of about twenty-five cryptanalysts were civilians. The War Department provided only sixty percent of the estimated annual budget of $100,000, and the Department of State funded the remainder. Yardley established his operation in midtown Manhattan in "a four-story brownstone front in the East Thirties, just a few steps from Fifth Avenue."

Yardley made this move, he wrote, because "there was a joker in the Department of State special funds: they could not legally be expended within the District of Columbia."[2] Moreover, the New York location placed him near the principal international cable companies. Unable to break one law, he broke another: in violation of the Radio Communication Act of 1912, which guaranteed the privacy of communications, Yardley negotiated secret agreements with the Western Union and Postal Telegraph companies to obtain copies of the diplomatic messages of foreign governments. It was an early example of conflict between U.S. foreign intelligence and American law. According to James Bamford, author of *The Puzzle Palace,* "American cryptology had lost its virginity."[3] As cover, Yardley organized the Code Compilation Company, located on the first floor of his brownstone, a "private" business engaged in the preparation and sale of commercial codes.[4]

The complete cryptanalyst, Yardley worked under the concept that no cipher was unsolvable, with an intensity that codebreakers in time called the "Yardley syndrome": "It was the first thing I thought of when I awakened, the last when I fell asleep."[5] In over ten years of operations, the Black Chamber solved forty-five thousand cryptograms, breaking the codes (as Yardley listed them) of Argentina, Brazil, Chile, China, Costa Rica, Cuba, England, France, Germany, Japan, Liberia, Mexico, Nicaragua, Panama, Peru, Russia and the Soviet Union [sic], San Salvador [El Salvador], Santa Domingo [the Dominican Republic], and Spain.[6]

Yardley's greatest success, a classic example of the effectiveness of communications intelligence, was the decryption of Japanese diplomatic messages during the Washington Conference for the Limitation of Naval Armaments (November 1921–February 1922).

The Warren Harding administration, having spurned membership in the League of Nations, sponsored arms limitation as an alternative way to promote international peace. Regarding the arms race as a major cause of the outbreak of the Great War, American leaders argued that disarmament would ease tensions and free up resources for peaceful goals. They said that it could be achieved objectively, in stages and by categories, without political entanglements. In this spirit, Secretary of State Charles Evans Hughes opened the conference with a proposal to reduce the tonnage in capital ships proportionately, so that the relative size of the navies of the major powers—the number of battleships, specifically—would be the same after disarmament as it was before. Five nations participated—the United States, Great Britain, Japan, France, and Italy—and the United States proposed a 10–10–6–3.3–3.3 ratio, respectively, or one million tons each for the United States and Great Britain and 600,000 for Japan.

The plan satisfied the Americans and the British, since for them it reduced a major military expense while maintaining the status quo. But the up-and-coming Japanese believed that the formula belittled them, even though they would be hard pressed to bear the cost of an arms competition. They felt the need to assert their new status. Unfortunately for the Japanese, Yardley had broken their secret code and was reading their diplomatic traffic.

The Japanese delegate, Admiral Tomosaburo Kato, stated publicly that Japan would accept nothing less than a ratio of 10 to 7. But Yardley knew that Tokyo had instructed him "to avoid any clash with Great Britain and America, particularly America, in regard to the armament limitation question." The Black Chamber had intercepted a cipher message, dated November 28, in which the Japanese government had urged its delegation to do its "utmost," but advised it, if necessary "and in the interests of general policy," to accept the 10–6 ratio, provided the United States and Great Britain agreed to maintain the status quo of Pacific defenses.[7] Although this proviso proved harmful to American interests in the long run, at the time Yardley smelled only victory, observing, "stud poker is not a very difficult game after you see your opponent's hole card."[8]

Secretary Hughes agreed—cryptanalysis had greatly facilitated his task. All he had to do was sit tight and apply a bit of pressure, and the Japanese would accept his formula. Intelligence and policy functions worked together in perfect harmony in this episode: intelligence provided objective and timely information without intruding on policy formulation. Hughes recognized all of this in a letter of commendation to Yardley.

After the Washington arms conference, however, the Black Chamber received few additional kudos. In fact, from that point on it declined. The lack of American foreign policy initiatives deprived Yardley of opportunities to perform dramatically, and cuts in federal spending forced him to reduce his staff to fewer than a dozen in 1924 and to six by 1929. Moreover, the Radio Act of 1927 tightened the law governing the unauthorized disclosure of private communications, making it difficult for Yardley to maintain his arrangements with Western Union and Postal Telegraph; the number of messages available for solution dropped precipitously.[9] Finally, in 1929, the new secretary of state, Henry L. Stimson, withdrew support for the American Black Chamber.

Whereas Hughes had been delighted to receive Yardley's product and Secretary of State Frank B. Kellogg (under Calvin Coolidge) had apparently paid little attention, Stimson was outraged by the Chamber's activities. After Herbert Hoover was inaugurated in March 1929, Yardley became apprehensive about what he perceived as the "high moralism" of the new administration. He waited until May in order to give Stimson time "to lose his innocence," then briefed him about the Black Chamber and provided him with examples of its work.[10] Stimson took the position that was described years later as "Gentlemen do not read each other's mail," and he had to be restrained from dismissing Yardley on the spot. According to David Kahn, Stimson "was shocked to learn of the existence of the Black Chamber, and totally disapproved of it. He regarded it as a low, snooping activity, a sneaking, spying, keyhole-peering kind of dirty business."[11] In time, Stimson would change his mind; ten years later, as Franklin Roosevelt's secretary of war, he eagerly read Japan's secret communications. But the closing of the Black Chamber in 1929 clearly illustrates the ambivalence of Americans toward clandestine operations.

Yardley could have waited for the mood to change, but instead, he decided to write a book about his secret work. In doing so, he encountered a problem that is peculiar to American intelligence: how to reconcile a former intelligence officer's right of free speech with the government's need to protect secrets. Freedom of expression is a foundation of American society, and there is no U.S. law comparable to the British Official Secrets Act, which provides penalties for the unauthorized disclosure of secret information. Yardley set a precedent that was later followed, with variations, by Philip Agee, Daniel Ellsberg, Victor Marchetti, and Frank Snepp; each invoked high purpose in exercising First Amendment rights to inform the public about intelligence matters.

After sixteen years of honored service, Yardley's skill now had very limited demand; his scornful dismissal came at the worst possible time because of the Great Depression, and Yardley was soon almost penniless. In desperation, he wrote *The American Black Chamber,* "the most famous book on cryptology ever published."[12] Critics accused him of doing it for the money, but Yardley insisted that he had written the book to undo the awful mistake of terminating America's cryptanalytic effort; moreover, "now that the Black Chamber has been destroyed there is no valid reason for withholding its secrets." The book did very well, selling twenty thousand copies in the United States and almost twice that number in Japan, where, as one might expect, it became a sensational best seller. It was sufficiently controversial, however, that when Yardley tried to publish another book, *Japanese Diplomatic Secrets,* U.S. authorities seized the manuscript and threatened to prosecute him if he persisted. Moreover, although he had broken no law, his career was ruined and he was treated as a pariah. The United States even denied him the opportunity to work as a cryptanalyst during World War II; Yardley did wartime service as an enforcement officer for the Office of Price Administration.

Yardley claimed, as a justification for writing his book, that the United States had stopped all codebreaking activities, but he was mistaken. Stimson may have adhered to the principle that gentlemen do not read each other's mail, but that principle apparently did not apply to nations. It will be recalled that, in creating the Black Chamber, Yardley had transferred MI-8's Code Compilation Section to the Signal Corps, which under army regulations had responsibility for communications security. There existed, therefore, a tiny cryptologic unit outside the Black Chamber. Its chief was William F. Friedman, a cryptologic genius who had developed his skill at the Riverback Laboratories, a private research organization in Illinois, between 1915 and 1920 and who had served as a cryptanalyst in France in General Pershing's headquarters. In 1921, he had gone to Washington under a six-month contract to consult on U.S. cipher systems but stayed for thirty-four years, reaching the very pinnacle of his field.

During the 1920s, Friedman devoted most of his energies to cryptography. He invented numerous cipher devices and machines and provided the United States with the most secure communications in the world; had he sold these machines commercially, he might have become a wealthy man. At the same time, Friedman observed that no cryptosystem was secure if its users were careless. Determined to eliminate errors, he prepared U.S. Army training manuals on secret communications, instructing, over time, a generation of soldiers in the proper procedures of enciphering and deciphering. As a master teacher, he created a new lexicon, redefining and inventing terms such as *cryptanalysis* and *mono-* and *polyalphabetic substitution cipher.* The Signal Corps had been planning for some time to bring code compilation and codebreaking under one roof, so that when Stimson closed the Black Chamber, it acted without delay to create the Signal Intelligence Service (SIS) and placed Friedman in charge.

Friedman had been operating with only one assistant, a clerk typist, but his new responsibilities required additional personnel. Although the SIS staff remained at about seven until 1937, Friedman's first recruits—three young mathematicians, Solomon Kullback, Frank Rowlett, and Abraham Sinkov—laid the foundation for American cryptanalytic supremacy in the next three decades. J. Robert Oppenheimer and his group of atomic scientists are better known, but no team of scholars ever dominated their field more completely than Friedman, Kullback, Rowlett, and Sinkov; nor did anyone play a role more decisive than they in the organization of the U.S. communications intelligence effort.

Ironically, they established their reputation, as Yardley had, by solving Japanese cipher messages. The Japanese had learned from Yardley of their cryptographic shortcomings and had done what many governments were doing in the 1930s: they used a machine to encipher secret messages. Cipher specialists now rediscovered Thomas Jefferson's cipher wheel, wired it for electricity, and attached a keyboard to it.

> Characteristic of all these [machines] was the wheel or "rotor," around whose circumference would be a series of points or studs representing the letters of the alphabet and cross-linked, within the wheel, by an infinitely complicated arrangement of wires. Imagine, then, an instrument in the front of which there is an ordinary typewriter keyboard but, at the rear, a set of these wheels positioned side by side. Pressure on letter A of the keyboard initiates an electric current or impulse which passes to a letter point or stud on the first rotor, then through its inner wiring to *another* point, representing a different letter. The current then passes into and through the next rotor, and the next. . . . The means of converting that current back into a letter might vary, but one thing was certain. The letter finally produced would not be A but—say—X: and for a cryptanalyst the problem of discovering the original letter which X had replaced would be incredibly difficult.[13]

Although these machines did produce ciphers that were "incredibly difficult," when broken they betrayed every message that was transmitted because governments tended to rely upon them exclusively. Friedman and his team exploited precisely this concept. Attacking the workings of the machines themselves, they used them as a kind of Rosetta Stone for codebreaking. By 1935, they had solved what Friedman called the Japanese Red Machine, enabling them to read all Japanese diplomatic traffic. Two years later, the Japanese introduced a more complex machine, designated Purple by Friedman, which he broke—along with his health—in September 1940. As David Kahn related it,

The solution had taken a terrific toll. The restless turning of the mind tormented by a puzzle, the preoccupation at meals, the insomnia, the sudden wakening at midnight, the pressure to succeed because failure could have national consequences, the despair of the long weeks when the problem seemed insoluble, the repeated dashings of uplifted hopes, the mental shocks, the tension and the frustration and the urgency and the secrecy all converged and hammered furiously upon his skull. He collapsed in December.[14]

Friedman's nervous collapse only enhanced the legendary reputation that he eventually attained: mortal driven to exhaustion, beating a machine of hideous complexity, whose concept was broken before he. But Friedman himself insisted that the cracking of Purple was a collaborative effort: "No one person is responsible for the solution. . . . It was only by very closely coordinated teamwork that we were able to solve it."

In actuality, the navy had had a hand in the unraveling of Purple. A few pioneer cryptanalysts in the Navy, such as Laurence Safford, Joseph Rochefort, and Ellis Zacharias, had been working on codes and ciphers since the mid-1920s. Reflecting the general American attitude of eschewing European affairs, they concentrated on Japanese communications, overseeing the installation of eavesdropping equipment on U.S. vessels operating in Asian waters and promoting the establishment of intercept stations in Guam, the Philippines, and Hawaii. Not until 1939, however, did the navy cryptanalysts and the SIS formally begin to collaborate. At that time Safford, then a commander, became chief of OP-20-G, the navy's Code and Signal Section in Washington. The two groups pooled radio intercepts; this alone facilitated their cryptanalytic work because U.S. communications laws still made it difficult to obtain messages sent via commercial cables. Their cooperation was essentially a matter of deciding who would do what—the navy concentrated on military/naval ciphers and SIS continued the attack on Purple. But even this level of cooperation was rare in the period before World War II.[15]

After Friedman and the SIS team unraveled Purple, they assigned the code word MAGIC to the decrypts and translations of

Japanese diplomatic traffic. When MAGIC appeared on the heading of a document, personnel cleared to receive it knew exactly what they were reading, without need for further explanation. By November 1941, the dissemination list included President Franklin Roosevelt. In time, because of MAGIC, serious questions arose as to how the Japanese could have taken the United States by surprise at Pearl Harbor. These questions are addressed specifically in chapter 12, but it may be noted here that even though the army and the navy were cooperating in collection and cryptanalysis, they collaborated little in other functions of intelligence. In fact, after Purple was cracked, the partners became rivals again for a few months, as each tried to scoop the other by getting to the president first. Such "unseemliness" led to an agreement to split the assignment: OP-20-G processed the Japanese messages dispatched on odd days, and the SIS processed those sent on even days.[16] Although this eliminated bickering and duplication, no one was getting the full picture. Thus, the dominant intelligence was largely departmental, with no centralized or national intelligence structure to set requirements or coordinate production and analysis.

This is understandable, given the mood of America during much of the 1930s. "Head-in-the-sand" isolationism equated talk of strengthening American defenses with warmongering and had little interest in improving U.S. foreign intelligence capabilities. Starting in 1935, the U.S. Congress passed a series of "neutrality" laws, strongly influenced by hearings conducted by Senator Gerald P. Nye in 1934–36. The Nye Committee placed the blame for America's entry into World War I upon arms manufacturers ("the merchants of death"), upon bankers, and upon Woodrow Wilson's defense of the right of "a few Americans" to travel on the high seas. Accordingly, the Congress now forbade Americans to travel on belligerent ships, prohibited the sale of arms to countries at war, and set a policy of "cash and carry" for all other trade with belligerent states. Misinterpreting history and making no distinction between aggressor and victim, the legislation was designed to keep America out of the last war but virtually ensured its involvement in the next.

Although Franklin Roosevelt complied with the letter of the Neutrality Acts, he disagreed with their spirit. He deplored the aggressive actions of Germany, Italy, and Japan and believed that the United States could not escape the breakdown of world peace. He was immediately worried about covert intervention in American affairs, such as that during the neutrality period of 1914–17, and he feared another outbreak of hysteria and vigilantism. Connecting foreign intelligence and internal security, Roosevelt summoned the FBI director, J. Edgar Hoover, to the White House on August 24, 1936.

With the cooperation of Secretary of State Cordell Hull (who under the law had to make the request), Roosevelt explained to Hoover that he wanted the FBI to conduct a "highly confidential" investigation of subversive activities in the United States, "including communism and fascism." He suggested that Hoover coordinate "information upon these matters in the possession of the Military Intelligence Division, the Naval Intelligence Division, and the State Department."[17] Expressing concern about the international linkages of communist and fascist groups and their potential for disloyalty, he cited the unusual amount of travel that Soviet diplomat Constantine Oumansky was doing around the country and observed, "The State Department had a right and a duty to know what was going on in such cases."[18]

With the approval of Attorney General Homer Cummings, the FBI undertook to collect the information requested, coordinating its efforts with G-2, ONI, and the State Department. This particular effort continued until late 1938, when the House of Representatives appropriated $50,000 for the FBI to investigate espionage cases in the United States. Hoover interpreted this action as giving the FBI "primary responsibility" among civilian agencies for the investigation of espionage. He sought to formalize this arrangement, under which he had already been operating, and through Attorney General Frank Murphy requested that nonmilitary departments having investigative responsibilities channel relevant information to the FBI. Although certain officials of the post office and the departments of State and Treasury objected to having to report to the FBI, Hoover argued that "centralization" was "absolutely essential" for the effective investigation of espionage cases.[19] Hoover's argument prevailed to the extent that in June 1939, President Roosevelt placed the investigation of all matters of espionage, counterespionage, and sabotage under the jurisdiction of the FBI, G-2, and ONI and established the Interdepartmental Intelligence Committee (IIC), which consisted of the heads of each, for that purpose.

The creation of the IIC in 1939 was a benchmark in the development of the U.S. intelligence community. The concept of keeping departmental intelligence intact while a mechanism for coordination and tasking produced national or strategic intelligence was the essence of the IIC. The nature of this bureaucracy, reinforced by the particular character of American government, seemed to indicate that the United States would never have a central intelligence agency.

The centralization of intelligence was resisted in foreign functions as well. The creation of the IIC fixed areas of responsibility for domestic intelligence but did not assign areas of responsibilities for overseas operations. This became a critical matter with the outbreak of the war in Europe. In June 1940, the IIC urged Assistant Secretary of State Adolf A. Berle, Jr., Roosevelt's adviser on intelligence matters, to bring the matter before the president. Predictably, Roosevelt divided the field. Leaving the details to the intelligence chiefs, Roosevelt instructed Berle that "the FBI should be responsible for foreign intelligence work in the Western Hemisphere, on the request of the State Department. The existing Military Intelligence and Naval Intelligence branches should cover the rest of the world, as when necessity arises."[20]

Accordingly, the three agencies reached an agreement. The ONI took responsibility for the Pacific; G-2 took responsibility for Europe, Africa, and the Canal Zone; and the FBI took responsibility for the Western Hemisphere except the Canal Zone. These three agencies, along with the SIS and OP-20-G, generally constituted the organization of U.S. foreign intelligence on the eve of U.S. entry into World War II. In staffing, the SIS comprised over three hundred officers and men, and OP-20-G had a strength of seven hundred, but other intelligence units were apparently seriously short of personnel. "Even worse," according to one observer, "the limited numbers involved in intelligence and counterintelligence included many who had neither the qualifications nor the feel for intrigue. Frequently career naval and air officers who demonstrated no special aptitude in other branches of service life were relegated to intelligence work simply to be got rid of.''[21] Mussolini's quip was not wholly accurate but was close enough to the truth to be no laughing matter.

Intelligence had few backers, as the activities of FBI director Hoover tended to demonstrate. From the beginning of his involvement, Hoover saw the need for discretion. He had to be sensitive to isolationists, who reacted against anything that hinted at preparedness, and to civil libertarians, who denounced perceived threats to political freedoms. Hoover had originally apprised Roosevelt of the problems involved in domestic intelligence; he had pointed out, for example, that it was not unlawful to be a member of the Communist party. He instructed his agents in the field to exercise particular care so as not to stir up memories of the Palmer Raids. But despite his precautions, Hoover seemed to attract controversy.

In January 1940, Hoover appeared before a House appropriations subcommittee and described the FBI's intelligence responsibilities, the formation of the General Intelligence Division within the bureau, and the investigation of persons engaged in subversive activity. He added that the GID had compiled a ''general index'' of individuals who ''may need to be the subject of further investigation'' in the event of a national emergency.[22] This information provoked a strong response from one of the leading left-wing politicians of the day, Brooklyn congressman Vito Marcantonio, who declared, in reference to Hoover's testimony, that ''two facts become obvious:''

> First, we are preparing a general raid against civil rights, a blackout against the civil liberties of the American people, a system of terror by index cards such as you have in the Gestapo countries of the world; second, we are engendering a war hysteria which is a menace to the peace of the United States.[23]

Marcantonio changed his tune after Adolf Hitler invaded the Soviet Union, but his statement was another instance of the permanent debate over the proper role of intelligence in American society. It was neither the first nor the last time that Hoover was the object of severe criticism. On this occasion (as they would during the Vietnam War—see chapter 21), critics recalled his part in the excesses of Attorney General Palmer in 1919–20, charging that he had little regard for the rights of individuals or for the Constitution. These attacks subsided a bit after an exchange between Roosevelt and Hoover at a formal dinner in Washington on March 16, 1940. From his seat on the dais, Roosevelt called to Hoover, "Edgar, what are they trying to do to you on the Hill?"

> Hoover shook his head and replied, "I don't know, Mr. President."
>   Roosevelt grinned and turned his thumbs down on the table. "That's for them," he said.[24]

Roosevelt turned thumbs down on the critics of Hoover, and in the political environment of the times, he could do little more to improve the poor state of U.S. foreign intelligence. In the election of 1940, he was moved to pledge that American boys were "not going to be sent into any foreign wars," and in mid-1941, soldiers of the peacetime conscript army were marking walls with the slogan OHIO ("Over the Hill In October"). The attack on Pearl Harbor changed much about the United States. Among other things, it marked a watershed in the history of U.S. foreign intelligence.

12

Pearl Harbor

T he word was not used then in the same way it is now, but *escalation* accurately describes Franklin Roosevelt's policy toward the war in Europe during 1940 and 1941. Despite his 1940 "no foreign wars" pledge, the Fourth Neutrality Act was already in place: it lifted the arms embargo for victims of aggression and enabled him to render military assistance to the Allied powers. At first, Roosevelt devised various schemes to overcome the expense and economic implications of supplying the Allies with weapons, such as trade-in arrangements and the "destroyers-for-bases deal." But he removed the "dollar sign" completely with Lend-Lease in March 1941. Proclaiming the United States the "arsenal of democracy" and prepared to exert all measures "short of war," Roosevelt ordered the occupation of Greenland and Iceland and extended the Western Hemisphere "safety belt" to include them. This made it possible to convoy Lend-Lease supplies all the way to Reykjavik.

Undeclared warfare between U.S. naval vessels and German U-boats followed and became critical in late October, when the destroyer *Reuben James* was sunk and ninety-six men were lost. Roosevelt authorized the arming of U.S. merchant ships and instructed American warships to shoot on sight the "rattlesnakes" of the North Atlantic. One can only speculate on how long this situation could have continued without the United States entering the war, but the question became moot when the Japanese bombed Pearl Harbor on the other side of the world.

Pearl Harbor has many meanings and may be examined from many viewpoints. Nothing is as significant as the fact that 3,681

Americans were killed or wounded while, as Gordon W. Prange phrased it, "at dawn we slept."[1] For the purposes of this book, we shall focus upon the role of intelligence. Indeed, the history of U.S. foreign intelligence in general may be divided into everything that happened before Pearl Harbor and everything that happened afterward. Despite the search for scapegoats and the "back-door-to-war" revisionists, the overriding lesson of Pearl Harbor was that it must not happen again and that the United States must create a national intelligence apparatus to see that it would not. The "back door" conspiracy controversy (that is, that Roosevelt let Pearl Harbor happen because it was the only way he could get the United States into the war) is irrelevant to the postwar decision to reorganize American intelligence. Pearl Harbor was perceived as an intelligence failure, and it was an intelligence failure. The conspiracy theory is what Ronald Lewin politely calls "moonshine."[2]

This is not to exonerate high-level American officials, including Roosevelt, from a share of responsibility for what happened. Nor is it to accept the idea that the commanders on the scene, Admiral Husband E. Kimmel and Lieutenant General Walter C. Short, deserved the ruin that befell them. It affirms only that there was no hidden or specific piece of information that revealed what the Japanese were going to do. The United States collected a great deal of information, but it lacked a clearinghouse for analysis to overcome the nonintelligence factors that were guiding U.S. policy in relation to Japan, especially what David Kahn refers to as "rationalism and racism."[3] The former held that the Japanese would not dare to attack the United States, and the latter that they could not pull it off if they wanted to. Unwilling to believe that the Japanese would start anything and unmindful of the changed situation because of the war in Europe, the United States continued to oppose Japan's aggressive behavior in the Far East.

U.S.-Japanese relations had long been strained, since America's acquisition of the Philippines at the turn of the century and its sponsorship of the Open Door policy in China. The United States had condemned Japan's occupation of Manchuria in 1931 virtually alone, and Roosevelt refused to apply the Neutrality Act when Japan invaded China in 1937. He allowed arms sales to China on the technicality that, since Japan had not declared war, no war existed. After 1940, when Japan was allied with Germany and Italy, and when England, France, the Netherlands, and the Soviet Union were all but powerless in Asia, only the United States stood in the way of Japanese ambitions.

The United States first attempted to restrain Japan by waging economic warfare. Demanding that Japan withdraw from Indo-China and China, the United States cut off sales of petroleum and scrap steel and froze Japanese assets in American banks. Faced with the choice of probably having to fight the United States to establish a "New Order in East Asia" or of giving up its dreams of Asian domination in return for U.S. trade concessions, the Japanese chose the former. In October 1941, when the civilian government of Prince Fumimaro Konoye fell and was replaced by the hard-line cabinet of General Hideki Tojo, the course was set, although Tojo kept negotiations going with the United States, even dispatching special envoy Saburo Kurusu to Washington to assist Ambassador Kichisaburo Nomura. On November 26, while the diplomats were meeting, the thirty-three ships of the Pearl Harbor attack force rendezvoused in the Kurile Islands and set out across the bleak North Pacific to swing south and surprise the American Pacific Fleet at Pearl Harbor on Sunday morning, December 7, 1941. How was it that the Americans did not know they were coming?

The United States did not know, although it had collected a great deal of information from a variety of intelligence sources. In fact, according to Roberta Wohlstetter, the United States had an "embarrassing" quantity of information riches. What it lacked was the organization and personnel to sort out the "signals" (the signs that point to an action) from the "noise" (irrelevant or contradictory information).[4] One source, the U.S. embassy in Tokyo, routinely reported observations by the service attachés. But because the United States did not engage in espionage, these notices constituted the sole form of HUMINT. Ambassador Joseph C. Grew, who was an old hand in Tokyo, having been posted there since 1932, advised with great skill about political and economic developments, but (according to Brigadier General Sherman Miles, the head of G-2) his dispatches "included only 'very indefinite and general' information about Japanese military and

naval movements."[5] Grew nonetheless made an extremely important observation on November 3, 1941, when he warned against
"any possible misconception of the capacity of Japan to rush head-
long into a suicidal conflict with the United States. National sanity
would dictate against such an event, but Japanese sanity cannot be
measured by our own standards of logic."[6]

U.S. news correspondents provided similar insights into Japanese policy and attitudes, but owing to the restraints of censorship,
they could not comment upon military movements or dispositions.
British intelligence furnished information, especially about events
in Southeast Asia, but American leaders tended to be distrustful
of this. First, they suspected that the British might distort the
situation, hoping to influence American policy; second, they were
"uneasy" about British methods—spying, which they regarded
as "underhanded." In a magnificent display of the "gentlemen
do not" syndrome, General Miles affirmed, "We kept above
board."[7]

Although the United States eschewed espionage, its counterespionage efforts gave it a significant brush with the clandestine
world before Pearl Harbor. An important signal involving a British
double agent, Dusko Popov (code-named "Tricycle"), got lost in
noise because J. Edgar Hoover paid more attention to an operational aspect of the mission than to its purpose. Popov, who was
working out of Lisbon for the Abwehr (German Military Intelligence), had been turned by British intelligence (MI-6) and arrived
in the United States in August 1941 with instructions to organize
an espionage net. MI-6 alerted Hoover to "Tricycle's" true identity and arrival, but Hoover distrusted double agents and was
offended by what he judged as Popov's "immoral" character.
(Popov was something of a playboy.) Hoover refused to have anything to do with him or to take advantage of an opportunity to
deceive German intelligence.

But Hoover *was* interested in Popov's instructions, which were
concealed in two microdots that appeared as "tiny smudges or
paper defects" on a telegram blank.[8] That is, he showed interest
in microdot technology. He tended to ignore the message itself,
which contained requirements in the form of a questionnaire. Fully
one-third of these requirements sought detailed information about

military installations and defenses of the island of Oahu and of Pearl Harbor. In this best/worst example of departmental intelligence, Hoover's only external report relating to the Popov affair concentrated upon the Abwehr's use of microdots and omitted any reference to the Pearl Harbor questionnaire. Hoover wrote to presidential secretary Brigadier General Edwin M. Watson on September 3, 1941, "the President and you might be interested in the attached photographs which show one of the methods used by the German espionage system in transmitting messages to its agents." Hoover's letter

> goes on to describe the microdot system, but, instead of discussing the substance of the microdot message, . . . ends by simply stating that the information was "secured in connection with a current investigation being made by the FBI." Hoover used the information to demonstrate how efficient the FBI was rather than to warn of a possible attack.[9]

It is unclear why Hoover did not share the Popov/"Tricycle" questionnaire with the Interdepartmental Intelligence Committee, except that the IIC served to divide the foreign intelligence field rather than as a clearinghouse. Lacking a clearinghouse, Hoover filed away information that might have been important to other units, particularly to persons working in communications intelligence. Lewin suggests that "had [they] been aware of the Hawaii section of the questionnaire some of the MAGIC intercepts ought to have appeared to them in a different and far more menacing light."[10] In fairness to Hoover, he was not a recipient of MAGIC.

The United States relied very heavily upon communications intelligence for information about Japan before Pearl Harbor. Its COMINT consisted of traffic analysis and cryptanalysis. *Traffic analysis* is the process of locating radio transmitters (particularly military ones) by direction-finding, identifying call signs, and reconstructing the network; that is, identifying the lines of communication and chain of command.[11] Even if the messages transmitted are unreadable, the location of armies and ships can be determined and, depending on the nature of the net, a wealth of information may be gathered simply on the basis of the volume of traffic. For the purpose of traffic analysis, the U.S. Navy established

the Mid-Pacific Strategic Direction-Finder Net in 1937. It enabled
Lieutenant Commander John Rochefort, who was placed in command of the Combat Intelligence Unit, or station "Hypo," at
Pearl Harbor in May 1941, to trace the movements of the Japanese
fleet although he could not read its cipher traffic. Unfortunately,
the Pearl Harbor attack force maintained absolute radio silence,
and the Japanese Navy changed its twenty thousand radio call
signs on December 1. Although this told Rochefort something, it
did not tell him "Pearl Harbor." [12]

Twice already in 1941, in February and July, the Japanese carrier fleet had observed radio silence. On both occasions the carriers
had remained in home waters in reserve, while the main fleet units
had moved south in support of the Japanese occupation of French
Indo-China. Believing that if the Japanese were going to make a
move, it would be a thrust into Malaya, Rochefort viewed the carriers' silence as a virtual confirmation, and the fleet intelligence
officer at Pearl Harbor, Lieutenant Commander (later Admiral)
Edwin T. Layton, concurred. [13] They did not know for certain
where the carriers were, but they deduced from previous experience that they were in home waters. If they had had much doubt,
it is unlikely that Kimmel would have had a "twinkle" in his eye
when he joked with Layton on December 1, "Do you mean to say
that they could be rounding Diamond Head and you wouldn't
know it?" [14]

Cryptanalysis did not produce a single message that identified
Pearl Harbor as the target for attack on a specific date, but had its
yield been disseminated appropriately, it might have shaken such
complacency. Cryptanalysis furnished the bulk of U.S. intelligence
about Japan, MAGIC being the principal but not the exclusive
source. MAGIC produced fifty to seventy-five messages daily, too
many for the limited number of "cryppies" and translators. Lower-
priority cryptosystems had to be set aside until the workload eased,
such as systems designated J19 and PA-K2. (The Japanese had a
panoply of lesser codes and hand systems for consular and similar
less sensitive use.) Because MAGIC dealt with diplomatic traffic,
American officials tended to use it "as a guide in diplomatic nego-
tiation" and overlooked its operational value. [15]

This attitude dictated a short dissemination list and placed a
premium on security. Only nine persons in Washington routinely

received MAGIC: the president, the secretaries of state, navy, and war (Stimson!), the army chief of staff, the director of military intelligence (G-2), the chief of naval operations, the chief of the Navy War Plans Division, and the director of the ONI. With security so tight, there was confusion about just who was getting MAGIC. For example, Admiral Harold Stark, chief of naval operations, was "under the impression" that Kimmel was receiving it, and G-2 in Washington believed that Rochefort had a Purple decoder, enabling him to produce MAGIC and disseminate it to Short and other commanders at Pearl Harbor.[16]

Since U.S. government leaders did not have time to read every MAGIC decrypt, Lieutenant Commander Alwin D. Kramer, the top Japanese language officer at OP-20-G, and Colonel Rufus Bratton, head of the Far East section at the SIS, picked out the most important messages and distributed them by courier (sometimes personally). "The messenger officers waited while [the] leaders read them, and then took them back and burned them."[17]

> The system was a hodgepodge. No one was responsible for the continuous study of all material. Recipients would read their portion of intercepts, and then it would be whisked away, never to be seen again. There was very little that could be done to put together all pieces in a cohesive form, or to correlate them with information available from other sources. Though the technical side of COMINT, particularly the breaking of Purple, had been performed with genius, the analytical side had become lost in disorganization.[18]

Lacking a coordinated team of research analysts in production, the United States did not get the full value of the remarkable achievements of collection and cryptanalysis. The highest U.S. officials, themselves performing the functions of intelligence officers, learned a great deal about Japan's intentions from MAGIC. But they were looking for the needle in a haystack, for the telltale signal. (Roosevelt insisted that he see the original decrypts, not just summaries.) They were unable to piece together the relationships between and significance of signals that they saw only in isolation. Considering the thousands of intercepted Japanese messages, the system was bound to break down.

The two most discussed incidents involved not MAGIC but the lower priority J19 code, which other elements were also reading. On September 24, the United States intercepted a message that had been sent to Takeo Yoshikawa, the Japanese spy assigned to the consulate in Honolulu. The message instructed him henceforth to report ship locations in Pearl Harbor in accordance with a suggested grid. At the time, American officials interpreted the message "primarily as an effort to cut down on the length of espionage communications and to get the proper sort of detail of interest to the Japanese Navy,"[19] but it was subsequently labeled the "bomb-plot" message. No one concluded at the time that it marked Pearl Harbor as *the* target for attack because the Japanese sought similar information about Manila, Portland, San Diego, and the Panama Canal, among other places. There was no one in the U.S. foreign intelligence effort who knew both about the "bomb-plot" message and about the Abwehr questionnaire.

The second incident was the "winds code" controversy. On November 19, the U.S. Navy intercept station at Bainbridge Island, near Seattle, intercepted a message from Tokyo to Washington. Because it was a J19 encryption, the cryptanalytic units gave it a low priority and did not have it ready until the twenty-sixth. But when it was read, the message created great excitement because it set up an open code by which the rupture of diplomatic relations would be signaled. If a break with a particular country was imminent, the warning would be repeated twice in the form of a weather forecast. That is, if a break with the United States threatened, the forecast would be "east wind rain"; if with the Soviet Union, "north wind cloudy"; if with the British, "west wind clear." This was not a signal for an attack against any specific place, and only in hindsight could anyone realize its importance to the Hawaii strike force observing radio silence at sea.

But the U.S. radio intercept effort immediately began the search for the "execute." The specialists reacted to the lead with total seriousness and professionalism. Army and navy intercept stations and Federal Communications Commission monitoring facilities tuned into Japanese news and weather broadcasts, and Rochefort assigned his four best language officers to listen to Japanese voice transmissions. U.S. authorities also alerted the British in Singapore and the Dutch in Java.

Soon plain-language intercepts were swamping GZ [the translation section of OP-20-G]. Bainbridge ran up bills of $60 a day
to send them in. Kramer and the other translators, already bur-
dened, now had also to scan 100 feet of teletype paper a day for
the execute; previously only three to five feet per week of plain
language material had come in.[20]

How much difference it would have made if a "winds-code execute" message had been received remains an object for speculation; the information that U.S. foreign intelligence had already
provided about Japanese intentions was sufficient to warrant greater
alertness on the part of U.S. military and political leaders. Nonetheless, even as time was running out, cryptanalysis produced still
another message that might have made a difference if American
intelligence had been up to it.

On November 26, 1941, the United States made its final proposal to the Japanese. It offered to renew trade relations with Japan
if it would withdraw from China, even though it was clear that the
Japanese were no more willing to sacrifice China than the United
States itself was. Japan dispatched its reply, a lengthy fourteen-part
message, to its representatives in Washington in the top-level Purple code. It sent the first thirteen parts on Saturday, December 6,
and the final, operative part on Sunday, the seventh. The United
States intercepted the first thirteen parts, and after a day of frantic
work, Lieutenant Commander Kramer personally delivered the
product to the list of MAGIC recipients on Saturday evening.
Although the Japanese had clearly rejected the U.S. proposal, and
although Roosevelt observed privately to Harry Hopkins that "this
means war," it was only the diplomatic negotiations that appeared
in jeopardy at the moment, which was not unexpected.

At a little after three on the morning of December 7, OP-20-G
received from Bainbridge Island the fourteenth part of Japan's
reply and, shortly thereafter, a briefer, trailer message, also in
Purple. But there were now technical problems with the Purple
decoder and a limited number of personnel on duty; delays and
slip-ups characterized the rest of the day down to the final disaster.
Everyone had worked long and hard on the sixth. Even Kramer
needed sleep, although he reported back on Sunday morning at
7:30. The fourteenth part (which was in English, like the rest of the

Japanese reply) announced Japan's intention to suspend negotiations. But the trailer message, encoded in Japanese, proved to be
more critical: it instructed Ambassador Nomura to deliver Japan's
reply at precisely 1:00 P.M., Washington time. Because OP-20-G
did not have a translator on duty, the watch officer sent the "one
o'clock" message to the SIS but neglected to leave a note advising
Kramer of this. So when Kramer reported back at 7:30, he prepared only the fourteenth part for dissemination and hastened to
deliver it personally.

Consequently, Colonel Bratton over at the SIS was the first
to have the translation of the "one o'clock" message, at around
9:00. He immediately saw its "implications" and contacted Army
Chief of Staff General George C. Marshall. Marshall interrupted
his Sunday-morning horseback ride and met Bratton at the War
Department at about 11:00. Both sensing and not sensing the
urgency, Marshall decided to alert the commanding officers in the
Philippines, Hawaii, the West Coast, and the Caribbean. He considered using the "scrambler" telephone on his desk to call Lieutenant General Short at Pearl Harbor but changed his mind to
avoid possibly compromising the all-important MAGIC.[21] Besides,
the War Department Message Center informed him that it would
deliver his message to all parties in less than a half-hour. Unfortunately, the center experienced interference on its Honolulu frequency and had to send the message via the RCA commercial
channel in San Francisco. It reached Honolulu at 7:33 A.M., when
the Japanese attack planes were only thirty-seven miles away.
Because of the ensuing pandemonium, Short did not receive Marshall's warning until 3:00 P.M. and then "threw it into the waste-
basket."[22]

Short's disgust was understandable. But he himself should have
been more alert in any case, and he had no cause for complaint
about American cryptanalysts. They "had done their duty."
According to David Kahn, "Safford later estimated that OP-20-G
handled three times as much material that weekend as on a normal
one; the GY [cryptanalytic section] log shows at least 28 messages
in Purple alone handled that Sunday."[23] Still, the handling of the
"one o'clock" message demonstrates America's general state of
mind and lack of preparedness. The circumstances only compounded an inadequate intelligence effort.

Nevertheless, in assessing the role of intelligence in the events leading to Pearl Harbor, there is a tendency to emphasize American *failure* and overlook Japanese *success*. The Japanese observed tight security in carrying out the raid. Only a very few of the very highest officials of the Japanese government knew about the decision and the actual preparations to carry out Admiral Isoroku Yamamoto's strike plan. The Japanese made absolutely no reference to the plan or to any stage of its implementation in any communication to their diplomatic or military representatives abroad. Moreover, Vice Admiral Chuichi Nagumo's Pearl Harbor flotilla maintained complete radio silence throughout its voyage of almost three thousand miles. Not even the finest COMINT system in the world could have picked up a message that did not exist.

The Japanese enhanced their tight security with a number of deceptions. They made an overall change in navy call signs on December 1. The ships of the task force left their regular radio operators behind in Japan to send routine messages, so that their " 'fists,' or sending touch, . . . as distinctive as handwriting," might convince the Americans that these ships were in home waters.[24] As the holidays approached, the Yokosuka Naval District approved "large numbers" of shore leaves in Tokyo and Yokohama. The army "reinforced" its garrisons in Manchuria, implying a possible invasion of Russia, and sent "false war plans for Chinese targets" to individual commanders.[25] On November 25, the foreign office announced that the *Tatsuta Maru* would depart on December 2 for Los Angeles and Balboa in order to evacuate Japanese residents from the United States and Panama, which caused the U.S. embassy staff in Tokyo to conclude "that a final break was unlikely while Japan's crack liner was at sea."[26] Additionally, the Japanese kept diplomatic negotiations alive right up to the very end.

These deceptions may have worked partly because the United States was predisposed to accept them. As noted previously, Americans generally did not believe that the Japanese would or could attack the United States, and as Wohlstetter observes, American leaders underestimated the willingness of Japan to take risks.[27] Marshall and Stark, concentrating upon the war in Europe, were anxious to avoid a conflict with Japan. Marshall refrained from using the "scrambler" telephone on December 7 not only because he was concerned about the security of MAGIC but also because he did not want to give the Japanese any justification for going to war with the United States.[28] At Pearl Harbor itself in the weeks before the attack, the navy investigated seven reported sightings of Japanese submarines, and a "fatigue" or "cry wolf" syndrome had set in; Short had even stopped sending Kimmel the "nuisance" reports.[29]

The Pearl Harbor failure demonstrates the three ingredients of intelligence success. First, the system must collect information. Second, it must disseminate the product to those who have the authority to act. And third, those with the authority to act must be willing to act.

At the time of Pearl Harbor, U.S. foreign intelligence was still in its dark ages. Even aside from the fact that Americans did not want to go to war and equated taking steps to strengthen intelligence with preparing for war, they did not like spies or spying. Pearl Harbor changed this attitude because it exhibited in brutal terms the need for intelligence. Intelligence could not have prevented the Pearl Harbor attack, but it might have reduced the extent of the damage. If Roosevelt erred, it was in that he had stretched American political commitments beyond American military capabilities. Even with all possible warnings, the United States was not able to defend the Philippines at the beginning of the war.

Just as America's military power grew, its intelligence effort grew. Intelligence—especially communications intelligence—enjoyed tremendous success during the war, saving lives and making victory possible. Never again would intelligence have a low priority, in either the civilian or the military sector of U.S. government, nor would it again lack coordination and organization. Both the intelligence failure of Pearl Harbor and the remarkable intelligence achievements during World War II seemed to assure that intelligence would have a place in the postwar United States.

13
Secrets of Success:
MAGIC and ULTRA

I ntelligence had been unable to avert the Pearl Harbor disaster, but it contributed enormously to the United States' victory in World War II. Communications Intelligence, especially, played a crucial role. COMINT proved incredibly reliable in the European theater, giving the Allies the critical edge from beginning to end. In the Pacific, COMINT helped turn the tables on Japan within six months and alter the strategy of the war.

American leaders had decided on a "Hitler first" policy, believing that Germany constituted the more serious threat and that Japan could be dealt with in due course. But in mid-1942, aided by the genius of navy cryptanalysts, the United States achieved a stunning victory in the Pacific that enabled it to modify this unpopular policy and pursue the war against Japan more vigorously and sooner.

The Combat Intelligence Unit at Pearl Harbor, station Hypo, went into action within hours of the attack. Before the attack on Pearl Harbor, MAGIC had consisted primarily of Japanese diplomatic messages enciphered with the Purple machine; afterward, it included decrypts of Japanese Navy (JN) codes. Hypo—particularly, but not exclusively—concentrated upon the JN codes. It received an influx of new personnel, many of them seamen who lost their ships in the Pearl Harbor raid. The bandsmen of the USS *Maryland,* for example, served ably as cryppies for Lieutenant Commander John Rochefort. Even as the Japanese reveled in their early victories, Rochefort's codebreakers began creating the circumstances for their reversal.

Admiral Yamamoto, the architect of Pearl Harbor, hoped to

establish a perimeter behind which to consolidate Japanese gains in the Western Pacific and Southeast Asia. He conceived a plan to seize Port Moresby, in New Guinea, in the south and to occupy Midway Island in the Central Pacific. COMINT played a large role in spoiling this plan.

The CIU at Hypo was having trouble with the Japanese naval codes, especially the tough JN25 cryptosystem (a superenciphered code), but it had recovered enough of it by April 1942 that, with traffic analysis, it could inform the new commander of the Pacific Fleet, Admiral Chester W. Nimitz, about the movements of Japanese naval units. Though Yamamoto claimed victory in the Battle of the Coral Sea in May, MAGIC enabled Nimitz to concentrate sufficient force to cause the Japanese admiral to abandon the attempt to occupy Port Moresby. Yamamoto, believing that he had sunk two U.S. carriers (actually, only the *Lexington* was lost), decided that he had achieved superiority and that the opportunity was golden for the invasion of Midway and the destruction of the U.S. Pacific Fleet.

The Japanese were careless in their preparation for the assault upon Midway and not conscious of security, in contrast to their conduct before Pearl Harbor. While assembling a flotilla of a hundred ships, the Japanese communicated extensively by radio and failed to make routine changes in their operational codes. They may have rationalized that distributing new codes to widely scattered units was an immense logistical problem not worth the bother, interpreting their unbroken series of victories as evidence that their codes were secure. Cryptanalysts at Hypo, at OP-20-G, and other stations took advantage of this lapse, as well as of the flood of traffic, to produce a cornucopia of intelligence. On the eve of the Battle of Midway, Nimitz "had a more intimate knowledge of his enemy's strength and intentions than any other admiral in the whole previous history of sea warfare."[1] The only information missing was the place of the attack.

In their messages, the Japanese used the code group AF for Midway, and similar designators for other geographic place names. Rochefort was certain that AF was Midway, but Nimitz, who had to operate in a huge ocean with only limited resources—especially carriers—had to be sure. Rochefort decided upon a ruse:

he secretly instructed the command at Midway to send a message in the clear reporting a breakdown in its freshwater distilling plant and requesting a tanker. The Japanese fell for it. On May 21, the United States intercepted a Japanese message that, stripped of its encipherment, read, *"AF is short of fresh water."*

MAGIC enabled Nimitz to confidently position his three carriers, *Enterprise, Hornet,* and *Yorktown,* at Midway and wait for the unsuspecting Yamamoto to enter his trap. As George Washington once said, if there were going to be any surprises, he preferred to be the one to spring them. Nimitz sprang the surprise and crushed Yamamoto, entirely ending the Japanese threat and sinking the four carriers of the Pearl Harbor attack force, *Akagi, Kaga, Soryu,* and *Hiryu.* More than MAGIC had been needed to win the Battle of Midway; it took a frightful toll of American lives. But according to David Kahn, the cracking of JN25 "forged effects more crucial to the course of history than any other solution except that of the Zimmermann telegram. The codebreakers of the Combat Intelligence Unit had engrossed the fate of a nation. They had determined the destinies of ships and men. They had turned the tide of a war. They had caused a Rising Sun to start to set."[2] Kahn wrote this passage before ULTRA became known, but his claims remain largely valid. As Nimitz himself affirmed, "Midway was essentially a victory of intelligence."

MAGIC continued to be Yamamoto's nemesis. In fact, it sealed his death warrant in April 1943 in "probably the most spectacular single incident ever to result from cryptanalysis."[3] Nimitz had learned from intercepted JN25 messages that Yamamoto planned to fly to and inspect Japanese bases in the Solomon Islands. Nimitz decided to attack his flight and shoot him down. Thanks to Yamamoto's absolute punctuality (and MAGIC had given his precise itinerary), U.S. P-38 Lightning fighters ambushed his squadron and, in what amounted to a political assassination, sent his plane crashing in flames into the Bougainville jungle. Yamamoto's death was regarded by American leaders as the equivalent of a military victory, although ironically, it may have foreclosed the possible emergence of a peace movement in Japan.

Midway and the Yamamoto shootdown are among the more

sensational achievements of MAGIC in the Pacific war. But the accumulated effect of successful communications intelligence day in and day out wore Japan down and contributed to the almost inevitable outcome. According to Lieutenant Commander Thomas H. Dyer, Rochefort's immediate subordinate at Hypo, "American cryptanalysts demolished 75 Japanese naval codes during the war."

> Among them was the four-digit code used by the marus, or Japanese merchant vessels—the *s* code. Presumably this was attacked after the more important combat codes had been resolved. From about 1943, it yielded information of the greatest value: the routes, timetables, and destinations of Japanese convoys.[4]

Because the Japanese Empire relied upon the sea-lanes for survival, Dyer believed that this solution contributed enormously to victory. Guided by MAGIC, American submarines sank nearly two-thirds of the Japanese merchant fleet, causing severe shortages of basic needs, including food and petroleum, and crippling Japan's war effort. Tojo himself stated "that the destruction of the merchant marine was one of the three factors that defeated Japan, the others being leapfrog strategy and fast carrier operations."[5]

One might add to this list of factors the failure of the Japanese to break American cryptosystems, including field ciphers. Admittedly, the United States exercised thoughtful communications security at every level. They used Navajo Indians as radio operators, who developed a code in their native language. The Navajo "code talkers" played an important part in the success of the "leapfrog" or island-hopping strategy. According to one military commander, "were it not for the Navajos, the Marines would never have taken Iwo Jima."* The inability of the Japanese to handle even Playfair, as noted, enabled U.S. forces to rescue the young Lieutenant John F. Kennedy.

In accomplishing these successes, the U.S. cryptologic effort underwent tremendous expansion. In 1943, the navy reorganized the CIU as the Fleet Radio Unit–Pacific, or FRUPAC, and raised its complement to more than a thousand persons. OP-20-G under-

---

*This story is told in a short film, *Navajo Code Talkers,* distributed by One West, Santa Fe, New Mexico 87501.

went even more spectacular growth, eventually comprising a force of six thousand and moving from the overcrowded Navy Department building on Constitution Avenue to the Mount Vernon Academy, a former girls' school, on Nebraska Avenue. Incredibly, Rochefort did not advance with this expansion. Although there was a war on, his achievements had aroused the envy of his powerful rivals in the Navy Department in Washington and they blocked Nimitz's recommendation that Rochefort receive the Distinguished Service Medal. They also arranged to have him reassigned from Hypo to the Floating Drydock Training Center at Tiburon, California.[6] Forty-four years after Midway, in June 1986, the United States finally bestowed the Distinguished Service Medal upon Rochefort, though posthumously.

The U.S. Army's cryptologic effort dwarfed even the navy's in magnitude and equaled and surpassed it in achievement. Circumstances caused the same Henry L. Stimson who had once shuttered the American Black Chamber to begin building this effort as secretary of war. While the wreckage of Pearl Harbor was still smoldering, Stimson appointed Alfred McCormack, a prominent New York attorney, to be special assistant to study the army's COMINT services and to make appropriate recommendations. McCormack's report consisted of a virtual reprise of what had gone wrong on December 7. There he stated,

- intercept facilities were extremely limited;

- arrangements for transmitting material from the point of intercept to the cryptanalytic center were hit-or-miss;

- there was a critical shortage of translators;

- there were neither sufficient personnel nor adequate procedures for studying and checking the translated product to derive the maximum degree of intelligence;

- the method of presenting the intelligence to the responsible authorities in Washington was ineffective; and

- there was no arrangement for getting such intelligence to commanders in the field promptly and in a manner that would ensure security.[7]

During World War II, as the Signal Intelligence Service strove to overcome these deficiencies, it expanded and underwent reorganizations and name changes. It labored under a burden of divided responsibility between G-2 and the Signal Corps. The Signal Corps operated the technical facilities for radio intercept (collection) and maintained communications security (cryptography), while G-2 performed the function of production—specifically analysis, reporting, and estimates. Caught somewhere in between was cryptanalysis, which is a production function, although narrowly specialized and technical in nature. The SIS became the Signal Security Service in 1942, the Signal Security Agency in 1943, and the Army Security Agency in 1945; at the war's end, G-2 finally unified all cryptologic activities into one agency (the ASA) under its control.

In the meantime, by whatever name, the army's Communications Intelligence service got the job done. In Washington alone, the number of personnel increased from 331 on December 7, 1941, to a high of 10,609 on June 1, 1945.[8] It, too, moved its headquarters station from downtown Washington to a former girls' school— Arlington Hall—across the Potomac in northern Virginia. With worldwide responsibilities and with personnel serving in every theater of war, SIS and its successors now dealt with an explosion of radio traffic. On one peak day, August 8, 1945, the War Department's message center handled nearly 9.5 million words, "the equivalent of almost one-tenth the total of French intercepts in all of World War I."[9] In all this expansion, the army did not forsake its pioneers (except for Herbert Yardley). Solomon Kullback was director of the cryptanalytic branch at Arlington Hall, and Abraham Sinkov traveled to Australia to head the so-called Central Bureau, attached to General Douglas MacArthur's command.

> A country whose ingenuity was capable of launching a new Liberty ship every few days tackled the problem of codes and ciphers with the same constructive energy. The British at Bletchley Park, the Germans with their B-Dienst [*Beobachter Dienst,* the German Navy cryptanalytic service], evolved tools for signal intelligence of the highest quality, but in sheer quantitative application the Americans were preeminent.[10]

The British solved Germany's Enigma cipher machine and set up shop at Bletchley Park, and the United States created a mas-

sive cryptologic organization that enabled the two allies to cooperate in the production and exploitation of ULTRA, the COMINT
star of the war against Germany.

With reckless arrogance, Germany had committed virtually its
entire secret communications system to the Enigma cipher
machine. Its concept of a lightweight, portable, user-friendly
cipher machine as a universal cryptosystem was brilliant, but its
very uniformity made it vulnerable to solution and, once solved,
turned it into an agent for those whom it was supposed to deceive.
Not long after the outbreak of the war in Europe in 1939, British
codebreakers (with the aid of Polish and French cryptanalysts)
managed to construct a model of the Enigma machine and, as a
result, to uncover its secrets. They designed so-called *bombes*—
electronic data-processing machines, or early computers—to
recover Enigma's settings and keys. After achieving this success,
the British gave the code name ULTRA to decrypts and translations of intercepted Enigma messages. This enormous advantage
remained a secret not only for the duration of the war but for
almost thirty years afterward.

A French publication revealed the existence of ULTRA in
1973, but it was the publication of Group Captain F.W. Winterbotham's *The ULTRA Secret* the next year that truly brought it to
public attention. By divulging the importance of ULTRA in the
defeat of Germany, Winterbotham's book caused a reexamination
of the military history of World War II. Indeed, the book took
some of the shine off the achievements of U.S. and British commanders since, after all, they had been reading Hitler's mail.

Winterbotham himself had served in the RAF's Secret Intelligence Service at Bletchley Park. It was he who briefed Winston
Churchill and organized the Special Liaison Units (SLUs), the
unique network for disseminating ULTRA to American and
British commanders and to military units in the field. Although
ULTRA provided a steady flow of rich intelligence that gave Allied
units the opportunity to outmaneuver the enemy on a daily basis,
Winterbotham cited a number of specific episodes in which, he
believed, ULTRA provided the decisive element of victory.

ULTRA helped England survive in its "finest hour"—the Battle of Britain (July–October 1940). An ULTRA of June 12 contained hard evidence about the installation of *Knickebein,* a German
radio navigational system that used intersecting beams to guide

Luftwaffe bombers to English targets at any time of day and in all kinds of weather. Additional decrypts enabled British specialists to locate the German transmitters and determine the wavelengths in order to take countermeasures to jam or distort the signals.

> They never "bent" the beams, as was suggested by a rumour not yet dead. Rather, they blanketed or jammed them: initially, and in desperation, by commandeering diathermy sets from hospitals with which they imposed an obliterating crackle of sound on the Knickebein transmissions. By September these improvisations were being replaced by properly constructed jammers called Aspirins (maintaining the hospital connection: and the *Knickebein* beams were suitably called Headaches).[11]

ULTRA told Churchill that Hitler was planning to invade England, and it spoke, too, when he abandoned the idea. ULTRA revealed Hitler's directive of July 16 that informed all military commands to prepare for Operation Sealion, the invasion of England. Two months later, ULTRA revealed Hitler's order to dismantle airlift facilities at Dutch airfields. Knowing what this meant in the overall invasion plan, Churchill's face "beamed" when he read the signal.[12]

In the meantime, ULTRA helped deny Germany control of the air, without which there could have been no invasion. The Luftwaffe's strategy was to draw the Royal Air Force into combat and outlast it in a contest of sheer numbers. On August 8, ULTRA revealed the centerpiece of this strategy: "From Reich-Marshal [Hermann] Goering to all units of Luftflotte 2, 3 and 5. Operation Adler [Eagle]. Within a short period you will wipe the British Air Force from the sky. Heil Hitler."[13] Goering's *Adler Tag*, or Eagle Day, failed because Air Chief Marshal Sir Hugh Dowding, who was in charge of the Fighter Command, refused to be lured into a do-or-die battle. Although criticized and eventually dismissed for his response to Goering's challenge, Dowding "won by parsimony."

> Knowing from ULTRA the staggered pattern of the raids to come, he was able to resist the temptation to commit too many of

his resources too early, to weaken the defences of the north and aid the hard-pressed south, to fail to make his fighters concentrate on the German bombers instead of "mixing it" with their escorts and risking heavy losses. He always kept something in hand to send up against the next raid.[14]

Having failed to smoke out Dowding's fighters, Goering tried another massive raid on September 15, in which he encountered resistance and fresh evidence that the RAF existed. Goering still had not achieved air superiority, but it would soon be too late in the season for a cross-channel invasion. Hitler called it quits on the seventeenth and canceled Sealion, and he demanded secrecy about the cancellation. But Churchill already knew: ULTRA had told him that it was safe to shift his resources to the theater of war in Libya and Egypt.

ULTRA helped Field Marshal Bernard Montgomery cage "the desert fox," Field Marshal Erwin Rommel. The British learned that they had to be careful in using ULTRA against Rommel because he did not always obey orders and sometimes changed his mind after relating his intentions. But ULTRA was consistently rich in detail about his order of battle, and it recorded his complaints about shortages of equipment and fuel. Isolated and feeling neglected—especially after Hitler's invasion of the Soviet Union—Rommel literally poured his heart out in lengthy dispatches describing his needs and circumstances. When his superior, Field Marshal Albert Kesselring, responded from Italy with a convoy of supplies, ULTRA told when and where, and the British navy, after first sending up a reconnaissance aircraft to allay suspicions, did the rest.

No other commander over so prolonged a period was affected so outrageously by the ability of his opponents to look into his cards. . . . The list of occasions on which his triumphs were diminished and his disasters made worse is a staggering one. The climax battle at Medinine in Tunisia offers a graphic example. The message detailing what he intended to do there on the day of encounter reached Montgomery the evening before at approximately the same time that it was received by . . . Kesselring in Italy.[15]

From Alamein to Medinine, ULTRA undid Germany's most charismatic general.

At sea, too, ULTRA proved to be, in the words of Sir John Slessor, marshal of the RAF, "a real war-winner." "Those in the know would agree," affirmed Winterbotham, "that ULTRA was the hub of the whole Atlantic battle."[16] Intercepted messages between units at sea and the U-boat Command of Grand Admiral Karl Doenitz gave precise positions and routes of German submarines and supply ships, the vital "milchcows." Although the German navy's Enigma cipher was the most difficult system to solve and caused occasional shutdowns of ULTRA production, in one good ULTRA month alone—"Black May" 1943—the Allies sank fifty-six enemy submarines. Over two-thirds of the men who served in the German U-boat fleet were killed in action, and during the last eleven months of the war the Allies destroyed close to three hundred submarines, virtually one a day.

ULTRA's role in the Battle of the Atlantic may be understood by comparing the periods of time when it was operative with those when it was not. In the four-day period beginning on March 16, 1943, during which U.S. and British cryptanalysts were grappling with new Enigma settings, a wolf pack of forty U-boats sank twenty-one vessels of convoys SC122 and HX229 while losing only one of its own: "The Germans never came as near to disrupting communications between the New World and the Old as in the first twenty days of March 1943."[17] Less than two months later, after ULTRA had been restored, Germany experienced the "extraordinary reversal" of Black May.

Although the production of ULTRA normally required grueling work, in sea warfare there was always the chance of capturing cryptographic material. This happened in May 1941, when the abandoned U-110 yielded an intact Enigma machine. Lewin hints that this may have occurred again in March 1943, enabling Bletchley to recover new Enigma settings "with astonishing speed" and force Doenitz to retreat from the open Atlantic.[18]

In that joint U.S.-British action, the Battle of the Atlantic, ULTRA was used routinely by U.S. naval and air forces. Winterbotham revealed that Churchill "probably" first told Franklin Roosevelt about ULTRA during the Arcadia Conference (in

Washington, December 22, 1941, to January 14, 1942). He described his own briefings of top American commanders, beginning with General Dwight Eisenhower in July 1942. Winterbotham organized SLUs for American units, following the procedures already in place for British commands, and generally achieved full cooperation for the proper dissemination and safeguarding of ULTRA. For various reasons, the British and the Americans did not make similar arrangements with the Soviets, although they did furnish ULTRA intelligence in sanitized form to the Russians.

Yet Winterbotham's descriptions indicate only that U.S. commands were consumers of ULTRA, not producers of it; there is in fact a paucity of information about American production of ULTRA. Ronald Lewin provides a small clue: "In due course the Americans were actually producing for Bletchley Park the 'bombe,' or machines for automatically processing cryptanalytical data."[19] And James Bamford reports the arrival in England in April 1943 of a special mission that consisted of Alfred McCormack, now a colonel and deputy chief of the Special Branch of G-2 (concerned specifically with COMINT); Colonel Telford Taylor, soon to be G-2's man in charge of the American ULTRA effort in Europe; and William Friedman. During the next two months, these men had complete access to Bletchley Park and negotiated the BRUSA Agreement, by which the two countries pledged to share cryptologic secrets and pool their resources. "The significance of the pact was monumental," Bamford writes. "It established for the first time intimate cooperation on COMINT of the highest level. It provided for exchange of personnel, joint regulations for the handling of supersensitive material, and methods for its distribution."[20] Although the details of cryptanalytic production are lacking, that Americans used ULTRA is manifest in further episodes where Winterbotham asserted its role was crucial: the Allied invasions and campaigns of North Africa (Operation Torch), Sicily (Operation Husky), Italy (Operation Avalanche), and France (Operation Overlord).

In the landings in North Africa in November 1942, Eisenhower got his first lesson in the use and value of ULTRA. As it turned out, the best intelligence that ULTRA provided was "negative"; that is, Kesselring's signals indicated that he did not suspect where the landings would actually take place. Lewin relates, "At the start of his Mediterranean experience, therefore—and thereafter in North Africa, in Sicily and in Italy—Eisenhower and numerous other American officers received clinching evidence that in ULTRA they had an incomparable source of military intelligence."[21] Consider the following:

> Hitler, according to ULTRA, had taken remote control of the Afrika Korps and ordered Rommel to make a stand at El Agheila. . . . Rommel eventually had to abandon his stand. . . . [He] then decided, probably against his own better judgment, to dig in at Buerat. He signaled Hitler to this effect.[22]

Occasionally there were hitches. At Kasserine Pass, ULTRA was uncharacteristically quiet and failed to provide advance warning of Rommel's attack. Problems also arose because of personal quirks, when Allied commanders resisted ULTRA. General George S. Patton usually used ULTRA to great advantage; in fact, it frequently was behind what at the time appeared to be extraordinary boldness. But nonetheless he interrupted Winterbotham abruptly at their first meeting: "[Patton] was delighted at the idea of reading the enemy's signals, but when I got to the security angle he stopped me after a few minutes. 'You know, young man, I think you had better tell all this to my Intelligence staff. I don't go much on this sort of thing myself. You see I just like fighting.' "[23] Patton was here reacting against the restriction placed upon ULTRA consumers that they were not to engage in combat and run the risk of capture. A number of "front-line" commanders and especially "flying" generals objected to this restriction on their movements.

Having assisted the Allies in their advance across North Africa, ULTRA revealed the Germans' evacuation plans. It enabled Allied planes to intercept and destroy the transports and gliders and made possible the total capture of the Afrika Korps. And when the time came to invade Sicily, July 10, 1943, ULTRA laid out in precise detail the strength and disposition of enemy forces—furnished by Kesselring himself—and ensured that surprise would be achieved. Not only did ULTRA relate that Kesselring was uncertain where the blow would fall (even after the invasion armada was sighted), it provided a reliable check on the effectiveness of Allied deceptions. "The Man Who Never Was" (Operation Mincemeat), for example, a deception in which the body of a drowned "British officer" was washed ashore in Spain in May carrying "plans" for the invasion of Sardinia and Greece, clearly took. Hitler himself fell for it, instructing his generals to forget Sicily and concentrate upon Sardinia and the Peloponnese.[24]

In Sicily and Italy, ULTRA continued to perform its miracles, giving constant gifts about order of battle and eliminating guesswork. Detailed information flowed daily from the Enigma intercepts about the movements and state of mind of the Nazi commanders, so that as the September 1945 invasion of Italy drew near, Winterbotham could write, "The Allies knew exactly where the opposition was on the Italian mainland, . . . [and] Kesselring had absolutely no idea where the main landing would take place."[25] In the Italian campaign, according to Lewin, "ULTRA's direct impact . . . was nowhere more evident than at its heart, the command post from which [Field Marshal Harold] Alexander concerted and controlled the operations of Montgomery's (later Oliver Leese's) 8th and Mark Clark's 5th Armies. . . . Into its files and on to its maps there was filtered, of course, all the selected information from other sources that would be of value at the level of an army group, but the essential flow came from ULTRA."[26]

The Western Allies prepared next for their greatest single operation of the war, the D-Day landings in Normandy on June 6, 1944, and ULTRA's star shone really bright. The key to the success of Operation Overlord, the invasion of France, was the achievement of tactical surprise. ULTRA helped attain that goal in two ways. First, it told where the Germans were, and second, it maintained a check on the effectiveness of the Allied deceptions. ULTRA informed Eisenhower and the Allied planners that though Rommel suspected it might come in Normandy, the view of Field Marshal Karl von Rundstedt had essentially prevailed—that the Pas de Calais area would be the place of the anticipated invasion— and that a group of four Panzer (armored) divisions remained in reserve near Paris. If Rommel had gotten his way and had moved the Panzer reserve divisions to positions behind the Normandy beaches, Operation Neptune (the Normandy invasion) would have been jeopardized. ULTRA revealed the debate that went on among Hitler's generals over the Panzer reserves and in May confirmed that they would stay near Paris. In the tradition of George Washington, the Allies carried out numerous deceptions to induce Hitler to make this decision and keep building his Atlantic Wall in the wrong place; ULTRA reported that the deceptions were working.

As historian Harold Deutsch has stated, ULTRA was the "mother of deceptions." ULTRA unfailingly enabled the Allies to twist and distort reality and mislead the enemy. Not only did ULTRA monitor the smooth running of Allied deceptions, it thwarted the Nazis' own attempts at deception. The Double Cross system may be listed among its most sensational achievements; in this system, British intelligence gained control over the entire German espionage network in Britain and "turned" it. Throughout the war, the British fed German intelligence what they wanted it to have, and when it came to D-Day, they put up so much smoke that it took the Germans two months to realize that the real invasion had actually taken place. Without ULTRA, Deutsch concluded, "Double Cross would have been inconceivable."[27]

This conclusion is most clearly seen in Fortitude South, a deception in which a completely bogus army, the First U.S. Army Group (FUSAG), was "created" at Kent, in southeastern England, under Patton's command. FUSAG never existed except as a mockup, complete with camouflage netting, dummy tanks and planes, and amplified recordings of sounds of activity that rivaled the detail and fantasy of a Hollywood backlot. The only real thing was Patton, who ostentatiously walked his white bull-terrier among the phony buildings of his phantom army; the "agents" of Double Cross duly reported everything as it seemed. (The desperate effort to expose this ruse forms the plot of the Ken Follett spy novel and movie, "The Eye of the Needle.") ULTRA established the fact that no spy of any sort ever got through and verified that an entire German army remained in place in the Pas de Calais waiting for Patton—even after the Normandy landings.

After the invasion, ULTRA continued to spew out operational data and command decisions of inestimable value. The Germans never caught on, right to the very end. At only one point did

ULTRA fail, in the Ardennes offensive in December 1944—the Battle of the Bulge, when Hitler unwittingly cut off its flow by imposing a radio ban. If any doubts exist about ULTRA's value, its absence in this tragic event dispels them. As the war neared its conclusion, ULTRA gave the Allies a better picture of German order of battle than Hitler had himself: "All too often for his own clear thinking, he found facts distasteful and would, especially in the final months of the conflict, have pins moved on his war maps representing divisions that had all but ceased to exist."[28]

In reviewing the specific accomplishments of ULTRA, there is a risk of overlooking other factors and of missing the way it affected the war as a whole. Victory would have been impossible without troops and guns and leadership and resolve, but in so many ways ULTRA determined the *quality* of the conduct of the war: "In innumerable not easily measurable ways it impacted on the war efforts of the rival coalitions in such fashion that Allied performances steadily improved whereas those of the Axis underwent an inexorable process of erosion."[29] In assessing ULTRA's contribution to victory, even the most conservative estimate that it shortened the war by a year is a matter for sober reflection. Deutsch, a scholar not given to exaggeration, wrote simply, "Without ULTRA, victory in the spring of 1945 would have been unthinkable."[30] And in the Pacific, MAGIC played a similar role, though surpassed by the atomic bomb. "A Japanese victory at Midway," Kahn reminds us, "would probably have cost the United States more than a year to come back."[31]

U.S. foreign intelligence expanded and improved significantly during World War II, and MAGIC and ULTRA were the star performers. Despite the controversy that had previously surrounded COMINT, it now appeared certain that the U.S. cryptologic capability would be preserved after the war. Other wartime intelligence efforts seemed less likely to survive the transition to peace. The United States had engaged in new intelligence functions, particularly clandestine operations. The history of U.S. foreign intelligence is incomplete without an account of the wartime cloak-and-dagger activities of the Office of Strategic Services. This account is also necessary for an understanding of the debate over the organization of intelligence after World War II.

14

The OSS

Although foreign leaders before the war were joking about the inadequacies of U.S. intelligence, President Franklin Roosevelt was not amused. When war came to Europe in 1939 and as the United States' involvement deepened, Roosevelt recognized that he needed more secret information, that he was not getting the big picture. Roosevelt and his advisers sensed the need for an expanded clandestine service and for a centralized agency to provide strategic and national intelligence. In July 1941, Roosevelt took steps to correct these deficiencies, creating the position of *coordinator of information (COI)* and appointing William J. Donovan to fill it.

Donovan had earned his sobriquet, "Wild Bill." He had been one of America's most daring soldiers in World War I, having served as a colonel in the famous Fighting 69th regiment, been wounded three times, and received the Congressional Medal of Honor. After the war, he practiced law in upstate New York and held various positions in the Justice Department in the Republican administrations of the 1920s. During the thirties, like a real-life counterpart of Upton Sinclair's Lanny Budd or Herman Wouk's Pug Henry, he became a troubleshooter for the U.S. government abroad. He turned up in places like Ethiopia and Spain in the middle of the decade, and in 1940 he observed the Battle of Britain at the behest of Secretary of the Navy Frank Knox. Impressed with British intelligence and security services during the blitz, he traveled next as the president's personal fact finder to the eastern Mediterranean, to Spain, to Portugal, and back again to England. A strong advocate of strategic intelligence, he had urged that just the job that Roosevelt gave him be created.

Roosevelt authorized Donovan as COI "to collect and analyze all information and data which may bear upon national security" and, without saying so explicitly, to engage in espionage. Since a presidential order had established Donovan's authority and funding, much depended upon his relationship with the president, and he had to navigate the Washington bureaucracy with care. A strong personality, Donovan was not always careful: he bruised egos and made enemies. Nonetheless, he had a clear concept of U.S. intelligence needs, and after Pearl Harbor, though he did not get his way entirely, he was hard to stop.

It would have been challenging enough for Donovan simply to coordinate the intelligence activities of the various departments and serve as a clearinghouse for strategic intelligence. But he also sought to expand and direct clandestine operations. From the start, Donovan conceived of a central intelligence agency that performed exclusively the functions of producing strategic intelligence (research and analysis) and performing clandestine operations (espionage and covert action). From Donovan's time to the present, this duality of the central intelligence mission persists as a matter of controversy.

As a man of action, Donovan tended to favor the clandestine side, like so many of the directors of central intelligence after him. He understood that as a type of organization, a clandestine service created for espionage also served the needs of covert action. The world had witnessed the effectiveness of German fifth column activities, and the term *quisling* (from the name of the Norwegian who had betrayed his country to the Nazis) replaced *Benedict Arnold* as the synonym for "traitor." Donovan further advocated a special wartime role for intelligence in the conduct of unconventional warfare, including carrying out commando raids, guerrilla action, sabotage, and linking with resistance movements in occupied countries. In this regard, Donovan was strongly influenced by the secret warriors of Britain's Special Operations Executive (SOE), which had been established in July 1940 to—in the words of Winston Churchill—"set Europe ablaze."

Aided by the wartime emergency, Donovan's conception largely became reality on the creation of the Office of Strategic Services (OSS) in June 1942. By military order, Roosevelt established the

OSS to "collect and analyze . . . strategic information" and "plan and operate . . . special services." He placed it under the "direction and supervision" of the Joint Chiefs of Staff, thereby fixing its military character and enabling it to support and be supported by military operations.

Donovan did not win all the battles in his struggle to achieve an integrated intelligence agency to perform the functions of collection, production, and operations. General Sherman Miles, head of G-2, opposed him, suspecting that he wanted "to establish a super agency controlling *all* intelligence."[1] Although Donovan centralized certain intelligence functions, he came nowhere near to establishing that super agency. G-2, the ONI, and the FBI retained their specific departmental collection and production functions and, as had been agreed in 1940, continued to monopolize certain geographic regions. J. Edgar Hoover, with the support of Nelson Rockefeller in the State Department, preserved the FBI's exclusive jurisdiction in Latin America, and General Douglas MacArthur ran his own show in the Far East. Donovan considered propaganda and psychological warfare as cognates of covert action, but he failed to obtain complete control over propaganda. He was opposed by Rockefeller, again, and by Robert Sherwood (the head of the COI's own Foreign Information Service), who feared the abuse of such power and believed that the truth was America's most effective weapon abroad. Although the OSS had responsibility for "black" (covert) propaganda, Roosevelt created the Office of War Information, under the direction of Elmer Davis, as the public wartime voice of America.

Despite these setbacks, Donovan fashioned an entirely new American intelligence agency—at least for the duration—and he had Europe, Africa, the Middle East, and the China-Burma-India theater in which to operate. He was a doer and an empire-builder. He hired—"Oh, how he hired," wrote Stewart Alsop—eventually recruiting a force of thirteen thousand persons and spending $135 million. The OSS underwent a number of changes and reorganizations, but its structure in May 1944 provides a basis for examining its historic role (see figure 14-1.)

The structure of the OSS can best be traced by highlighting certain technical and support branches and by concentrating upon

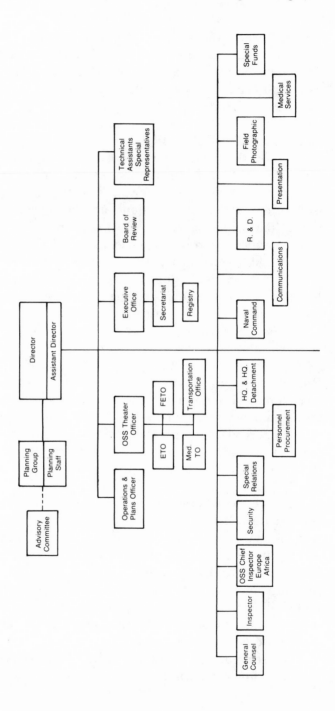

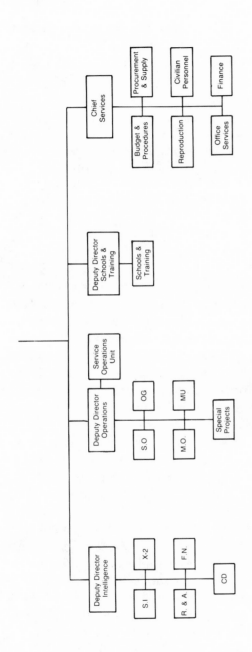

Source: *War Report of the OSS*, with a new introduction by Kermit Roosevelt. Prepared by History Project, Strategic Services Unit, Office of the Assistant Secretary of War, War Department, Washington, D.C., 1947; New York: Walker and Company, 1976.

Figure 14–1. *OSS Organization, 1944*

the directorates (each under a deputy director) of Intelligence and Operations. As Anthony Cave Brown has written, "The structure of OSS was less complicated than it seemed on the Charts.

> There was Donovan's office, the offices of the Assistant Directors, Special Assistants and Representatives, the Office of the Executive Officer, and the Secretariat. The Registry maintained the files, the Theater Officers kept a watchful but benevolent eye on the four areas into which OSS divided the world. But there was one office that had much influence: OSS was formed by lawyers and therefore lawyers dominated much of the superstructure. In a world of illegalities the General Counsel sat supremely powerful, trying, so far as was possible, to keep the game honest, to keep OSS out of trouble.[2]

Though the technical branches had commonplace-seeming names, none of them were ordinary in fact; each supported highly secret and dangerous missions. The *Communications Branch* ran the message center and provided secure communications between OSS/Washington and overseas stations and operatives in the field. For the vital matter of maintaining secret contact with agents operating in occupied countries, Communications developed the famous "suitcase radio," or Strategic Services Transmitter-Receiver, so called because of its small size (which was remarkable in the days before the transistor) and because it was usually camouflaged as an ordinary valise of seemingly local manufacture. This amazing radio, which underwent various model changes, enhanced tremendously the OSS's ability to aid the resistance movements and conduct sabotage and espionage.

Although Communications developed the suitcase radio, the *Research and Development Branch* was responsible for the design and manufacture of a complete line of spy paraphernalia and devices and special weapons for sabotage and subversive warfare. The OSS laboratory was headed by Dr. Stanley Lovell, a sort of mad scientist, and produced a variety of James Bond–style gadgets including pocket-size incendiaries, time-delay detonators, and fuel-line and engine contaminants. It developed silenced weapons and silencers for standard weapons that eliminated muzzle flash as well as noise; it designed the "spy camera," which did not have to be focused, only pointed at an object.[3] Among its more exotic creations was "Aunt Jemima," an explosive that had the appearance and the properties of flour; when mixed with water, it formed a dough and could be baked into "biscuits or loaves of bread."[4] Another explosive charge, the "firefly," a three-ounce device, could be placed in the gas tank of a vehicle and, depending upon the corrosive action of the gasoline itself, produce an explosion one and a half to ten hours later.

Within R&D, the *Documentation* and *Camouflage divisions* were responsible for agent authentication. For persons operating in enemy-held territory, R&D prepared "official" documents—birth certificates, driver's licenses, and ID and ration cards—duplicating authentic documents in minute detail, and it provided "pocket litter" that was designed to deceive the most thorough search. The OSS employed "Jim the Penman," an expert forger "on leave from a federal penitentiary," to reproduce signatures "so exact not one was ever questioned."[5] Everything about an agent's cover had to be right—razors, eyeglasses, dental work; "the manner in which buttons are sewn on—the Americans do it in crisscross, Europeans in parallel; the lining—European linings are full; the adjustment buckles—in Europe they bear the mark of the country of origin; suspender buttons—no matter what European country they come from, they bear the imprint, 'Elegant,' 'For Gentlemen,' or 'Mode de Paris.' "[6] An agent's very life depended upon such attention to detail. (The Alan Ladd film, "OSS," once shown as part of CIA training, contains a scene in a café in occupied France wherein an agent betrays himself by taking up a fork with the wrong hand.)

In order to "collect and analyze strategic information" and "plan and operate special services," the OSS had two principal components: *Intelligence* and *Operations,* each under a deputy director. Though this organization appeared to reflect the missions assigned to the OSS, it had the effect of splitting up the clandestine services. Clandestine collection was placed in Intelligence alongside the production branches (analysis) and not with the covert action branches of Operations. Later, in the organization of the CIA, the division between overt and covert activities would be more "tidy," with all clandestine services "under one roof."

The *Secret Intelligence (SI) Branch,* therefore, conducted espionage under the jurisdiction of the deputy director for intelligence but had no contact with the analysts in the Research and Analysis (R&A) Branch. In the Axis nations and occupied countries that constituted a vast "denied area," the United States carried out espionage from the periphery by remote control, setting up stations in neutral Sweden, Switzerland, Turkey, Spain, Portugal, and for a while, Vichy France. The controversial decision to maintain relations with the Vichy government stemmed from numerous considerations, the opportunity to spy under diplomatic cover definitely among them.

One of SI's most effective station chiefs was Allen W. Dulles, who served in Bern as "special assistant to the American minister" from November 1942 to the war's end. There, Dulles made contact with various German dissident groups, which enabled him to secure valuable intelligence and to have knowledge of anti-Hitler movements within Germany. His top agent was Fritz Kolbe (code name "Wood"), an official in the German foreign office who traveled to Bern periodically as a courier. He delivered top-secret diplomatic cables to Dulles "by the pound."

> Over a period of a year and a half, OSS received from "Wood" more than 1,600 true readings of cables to and from the Foreign Office and some forty German diplomatic and consular missions. They included reports from the military and air attachés in Japan and the Far East, data on the structure of the German secret service in Spain, Sweden and Switzerland, and espionage activities in England and in the British Embassy in Istanbul.[7]

The latter bit of information led to the exposure of the German agent "Cicero," Elyesa Bazna, who was serving as the valet of the British ambassador to Turkey (an episode portrayed by James Mason in the film "Five Fingers").

Because much of what SI did was new to the American experience, misunderstandings occurred between OSS and State Department personnel. The Spanish station, particularly, encountered difficulties. Not only did SI spy on neutral Spain, but OSS/Spain ran more than a thousand subagents in occupied France. The American ambassador, Carlton J.H. Hayes, looked upon such activities against a "friendly" country as "un-American." Moreover, the regular embassy staff generally resented what they perceived to be the free-spending and the irregular hours of the OSS officers. "OSS supplies (which were used for bartering), OSS cars and OSS entertainment (of potentially useful persons) all contributed to the general irritation of embassy personnel. The latter made little effort to conceal from Spanish officials the real activities of OSS representatives. As early as December 1942 an agent leaving Washington was told, 'Good luck, you'll probably have more trouble keeping under cover from Americans than from the Gestapo.'"[8]

Like SI, the *Counter-Espionage (X-2) Branch* was a "fish out of water," a clandestine service housed in Intelligence. X-2, the double-cross, spied on the Axis secret services (in counterespionage, a positive or dynamic function) in order to prevent penetration of U.S. and Allied intelligence (counterintelligence, a negative or security function). Apart from the earlier FBI effort against internal subversion and sabotage, the United States had had little experience before World War II in counterespionage and counterintelligence. If an intelligence service is to undertake serious X-2 work, it must have a registry of persons and organizations of proven or suspected hostile intent; such a vast body of records can only be accumulated over a long period of time. Fortunately, the British were willing to give the Americans a hand.

> Starting at a late date, X-2 developed a CE [counterespionage] organization for wartime service which could take its place among the major security services of the world. No small part of the credit for making this achievement possible was due to the records and experience made available by the British.[9]

Overseas as well, X-2 proved its effectiveness. In Sweden, OSS/Stockholm used controlled or double agents to penetrate Axis intelligence operations, thereby "neutralizing" over 150 German agents (meaning they were either imprisoned or executed) and helping to identify over three thousand agents and officials "of intelligence interest."[10]

Though SI and X-2 engaged in new and adventurous pursuits, the less glamorous *Research and Analysis Branch* constituted the heart of Intelligence. R&A was the first branch to be created by the former COI, a central clearinghouse for information gathered by all sources to produce intelligence of a comprehensive and strategic nature. During the war, R&A produced basic, current, and estimates intelligence dealing principally with political, military, economic, geographic, and scientific matters.

Following the advice and counsel of Archibald MacLeish, the librarian of Congress, Donovan assembled "a galaxy of academic stars" and put them to work initially in an annex of the Library of Congress, an existing storehouse of basic intelligence. William L. Langer, a noted professor of history at Harvard, served as chief of R&A during most of its wartime existence. (James Phinney Baxter, president of Williams College, had occupied the post briefly at the beginning.) Langer recruited the most distinguished scholars of the time and some soon to be, including Sherman Kent (Yale), Preston James (Michigan), Conyers Read (Penn), S. Everett Gleason (Amherst), Edward S. Mason (Harvard), Geroid Robinson (Columbia), Burton Fahs (Pomona), Maurice Halperin (Oklahoma), John K. Fairbank (Harvard), Hajo Holborn (Yale), and a group of young Harvard dons: Arthur Schlesinger, Jr., Carl Schorske, and Ray Cline. It was a list that "would have put the faculty of any one university to shame."[11]

Donovan was extremely proud of his "professors" and a great deal of essential research was accomplished, but the ideal of strategic intelligence was not attained. Ray Cline complained that R&A was not the recipient of "all-source" intelligence. Cline had only "minimal" access to COMINT, for example, which caused him to reflect years later, "It is now clear to me that the OSS work in research, analysis, trend forecasting, and current reporting fell far below the mark in quantity and quality compared to the kind that would have been most useful."[12] The fact that there was a war on and that operational intelligence seemed critical and timely may explain the frustrations of R&A, but Cline complained of an intolerance toward the academic mind and scholarly process. R&A's problems did not bode well for the future of the OSS because experience showed that effective analysis is inexorably linked to centralization but that departments resist external influences (estimates) that affect their pet policies and operations.

The *Foreign Nationalities (FN) Branch* did not encounter these problems. Its work was widely accepted and highly praised. FN established offices in the principal American cities with significant ethnic concentrations (Boston, New York, Pittsburgh, Cleveland, Detroit, Chicago, Milwaukee, San Francisco, and Seattle). These offices overtly collected information from exile and émigré groups to provide intelligence for propaganda and psychological warfare, for secret operations, and to guide foreign and domestic policy on political developments in enemy and occupied countries. As a "domestic contacts" service, FN managed to avoid the issues of "government spying" and "official status."

The FBI appreciated the "leads" it might not otherwise have received as an investigative branch, and the State Department used FN as a go-between, needing the thinking and possible future good-will of refugee leaders, organizations, and governments-in-exile but having to avoid the appearance of extending recognition. FN alerted American leaders to possible developments in postwar Europe.

> For example, it deduced that the new Czechoslovakia would have to be recognized on a basis of much wider local autonomy, it foresaw the problems of the restored Greek Government, and it discerned the great issues affecting Poland and her neighbors.[13]

As a domestic activity linked to central intelligence, FN was potentially controversial, but during World War II no one apparently complained.

If FN collected documents and other material useful for agent authentication, the *Censorship and Documents (CD) Branch* had specific responsibility for "the collection, evaluation, and distribution of documents and related intelligence" for providing cover. CD collected the intelligence that enabled R&D to manufacture accurate copies of the documents, clothing, and accessories needed for successful infiltration. CD acquired a great deal of this intelligence from the Office of Censorship in the form of postal and cable intercepts, telephone summaries, and traveler's interrogation reports. CD also maintained liaison with G-2's documents section and prisoner-of-war branch, gathering information about Axis security procedures and controls. Dependent upon the British and French at first, CD in time independently authenticated nine hundred agents for operations in Europe and North Africa.[14] According to Cline, CD should have been named "Cover and Documentation." He equated it with the Technical Services Division of today's CIA, a veritable warehouse of spy gadgets, indicating that CD (like SI, X-2, and possibly FN) might have been better housed in the Operations Directorate.

Within the Operations Directorate, the *Special Operations (SO) Branch* occupied the very center. Indeed, the daring agents who parachuted into occupied territory to carry out sabotage missions and link up with resistance and partisan groups constituted the very image of the OSS in the popular mind. Though SO agents were infiltrators à la Nathan Hale, their principal purpose was not espionage; nor were they lone operatives. They sought rather to "effect the physical subversion of the enemy" by means of sabotage operations and by supporting and supplying resistance groups in enemy and enemy-occupied countries.[15]

Generally operating in small teams usually of three or four persons, SO agents provided technical and logistical support to resistance movements and tried to coordinate paramilitary and guerrilla activities with conventional military operations. Over their suitcase radios, SOs received instructions from military commanders and reported on the results of sabotage missions and on the effectiveness of Allied bombing. Because SO was primarily military in character, SO/Washington had only a small staff, approximately forty-five persons, with responsibility for recruiting and training. For all practical purposes, SO field activities were under the control of the theater commanders.

Although this hampered Donovan's freewheeling spirit, he had the support and collaboration of the British SOE, who were old hands in prying loose aircraft for "jumps" and in securing other forms of cooperation. In fact, during 1943, SO and SOE became full partners in preparing the French underground for playing a role in the invasion and liberation of France, forming the Special Force Headquarters directly under General Eisenhower's command. On the eve of D-Day, after almost a year of planning and training, SO/SOE began dispatching Jedburghs, or three-person international teams that each included a French operative, to organize and direct the resistance in support of the advancing Allied armies. The fame of the "Jeds" spread widely, and many of the team members later attained prominence, including Stewart Alsop and Tom Braden (both as journalists and writers), William Colby (as director of the CIA), and Michael Burke (as president of the New York Yankees).

A mythology evolved about SO, but its achievements were real enough. During the first half of 1944 alone, SO and SOE, working in cooperation, directed the work of the French resistance in sabotaging factories, causing electric power outages, and disrupting rail and canal traffic.

> Agents pretending to be travelling salesmen, completely equipped with forged documents showing that they were legitimate representatives of existing French firms, called on the managers of a factory, requested that they permit the sabotage of certain machines, and threatened Allied bombing of the plant if they did not agree. Compliance was usual, since it saved the lives of countless French civilians, and prevented the destruction of the entire plant.[16]

SO supplied European resistance movements with twenty thousand tons of ammunition, weapons, and food during World War II and achieved the rescue of nearly five thousand U.S. airmen downed behind enemy lines.[17] Among its "failures," SO had serious problems with and received much criticism for putting the fight against the enemy first, without taking into consideration the political orientations of certain resistance groups (a harbinger of the postwar European situation). There were deep rifts within the French Maquis; Tito and Mihailovich were bitter enemies; and aid to the Greek resistance threatened SO/SOE harmony.

The OSS earned a record of both "brilliance and balderdash," according to military historian Hanson Baldwin, although movies and popular novels tended to emphasize the glamorous and the bizarre. One case in particular achieved notoriety—the "Lake Orta caper," in which Major William Holohan, leader of a three-member SO that parachuted north of Milan in September 1944, disappeared. An Italian court convicted in absentia Lieutenant Aldo Icardi, Holohan's deputy, on charges of murdering the major and dumping his body in the lake in order to steal the team's operational funds. (Holohan had been carrying $16,000 in gold and other sizable sums in lire, Swiss francs, and U.S. dollars.) The case against Icardi was not proven in a series of sensational trials in the United States. Icardi in turn charged that the OSS was pro-Communist and that Holohan had favored the Communist underground over other partisan groups.[18]

Though SOs and *Operational Groups (OGs)* both fought the enemy in the rear, they were quite distinct in concept and character. Whereas SOs were small teams that worked and blended in with the resistance and counted on partisans for numbers, OGs were self-contained guerrilla units. Ideally composed of four officers and thirty enlisted men (though frequently smaller), they were trained to carry on irregular warfare and harassment behind enemy lines. The OSS approached ethnic Americans in the armed forces who had foreign-language capabilities to volunteer for the OGs. Although OGs wore uniforms, they could be expected to be treated as spies or terrorists. They might cooperate with local partisans, but they were capable of fighting alone, much like the Jessie Scouts and Mosby's Rangers of old.

The OGs' reputation for violence and lack of control tended to discredit the OSS. This delighted Donovan's enemies and eventually led to the formation of commando or ranger battalions under direct military command and discipline. OG operations in the Mediterranean were especially controversial when the involvement of the Mafia was alleged; when investigated, the stories produced a few surprises. Actually, it was the ONI that enlisted the support of imprisoned mobster Lucky Luciano, seeking the cooperation of "Mafia-controlled" dock workers' unions in the United States for a counterespionage operation. (See Rodney Campbell's 1977 *The Luciano Project*.) "The OSS in Sicily did benefit," and Luciano was eventually released from prison for his "service to the war effort" and deported from the United States.[19] There was substance, then, to the concern "that OSS was recruiting Mafiosi and, on a smaller scale, hit men from the ranks of Murder, Inc., and the Philadelphia 'Purple Gang.'

> . . . as one OSS training officer for OGs would recall, the OGs
> consisted of "tough little boys from New York and Chicago, with
> a few live hoods mixed in. . . . Their one desire was to get over

to the old country and start throwing knives." By 1945, these groups were considered to be so dangerous that OGs returning from operations were, on the orders of the Allied High Command, confined to a castle near Spezia until they were either returned home or were sent back into the field.[20]

These stories detracted from the substantial achievements of the OSS—and Donovan's own "rash behavior" did not help either. He was "always showing up on landing beaches,"[21] going ashore specifically in the Sicily and Normandy invasions. Because the risk of capture in such situations was high and because of Donovan's knowledge of Allied intelligence services, the atomic bomb, and ULTRA, Anthony Cave Brown has related, the British secret services came to regard their "American comrades-in-arms" with "intense suspicion."[22]

The *Maritime Unit (MU)* managed to avoid these controversies. It did not attract the same attention as SO or OG, probably because its success depended upon stealth and because it did not operate within enemy territory for prolonged periods. It performed four principal functions: "(1) Infiltration of agents for other branches by sea; (2) supply of resistance groups and others by sea; (3) execution of maritime sabotage; and (4) development of special equipment and devices to effectuate the foregoing."[23] As a clandestine service, MU tended to concentrate upon the secret infiltration of agents and supplies and did not compete on a grand scale in underwater demolition and maritime sabotage with military units such as the navy's Frogmen. However, MU did develop new equipment, namely an electrically propelled inflatable surfboard, a folding kayak, a luminous waterproof watch, and the self-contained underwater breathing apparatus (SCUBA).

Rounding out the covert action services of the OSS, the *Morale Operations (MO) Branch* conducted "black" propaganda and psychological warfare. "Persuasion, penetration and intimidation," Donovan believed, were "the modern counterpart of sapping and mining in the siege warfare of former days."[24] Denied control over the attributable or "white" propaganda, the OSS used the covert "black" to confuse, demoralize, and divide the enemy. MO missed no opportunity or trick to create dissension within the Axis nations.

From Stockholm, for example, MO carried out the *"Harvard Project"*—a newsletter supposedly published by German business interests in Sweden. "The publication, named *Handel und Wandel,* sought to impress upon German businessmen the damage to their interests resulting from Nazi policy and leadership. It stressed the effectiveness of Allied industrial efforts and the willingness of Allied businessmen to work with German businessmen once the Nazis were out of the way." [25] During 1944, taking advantage of the fact that Hitler had not appeared in public for some time, MO circulated rumors to the effect that Hitler was variously dead, insane, or a prisoner of Gestapo chief Heinrich Himmler. Even after Hitler made a speech on January 1, 1945, "black" raised doubts, suggesting that it had been delivered by a "double." [26] MO also fabricated and distributed false reports and forged documents implicating high Nazi officials in antigovernment conspiracies, in one instance forcing Field Marshal Kesselring to deny publicly that he was the leader of a plot against Hitler.

One of MO's major achievements was the MUZAC Project, in cooperation with the British. It arranged for American popular music to be sung in German by performers such as Marlene Dietrich and recorded, providing the programming "mainstay" of Soldatensender West, a British radio station that was posing "as a German station relaying entertainment and news to the Wehrmacht." [27] American jazz kept the German army listening to the Allied propaganda. But "black" techniques occasionally had unexpected results. In its campaign to induce defections, Soldatensender West broadcast fake reports of the wholesale flight of Nazi officials to Argentina. When the British learned that the FBI in Buenos Aires was busily engaged in a hunt for the Nazis, the embarrassed broadcasters supposedly exclaimed, "Oh no! Somebody forgot to tell the Yanks."

The Directorate of Operations also maintained the *Special Projects Office,* which had an R&D function but on a larger scale. Special Projects undertook to develop major weapons systems and technologies for conducting unconventional warfare and clandestine missions. One such project, Javaman, involved the development of a drone vessel that could be packed with explosives and disguised as a local harbor craft (a tugboat or junk) and guided to its target by radio. A unique feature of this craft was that a television camera was used for aiming. (TV was still very much an oddity back then, there being no commercial TV). The war ended before Javaman could be used in an operation, but it was one OSS activity that interested even General Douglas MacArthur.[28]

Despite the many separate functions within the OSS, the compartmentalization (for security purposes) and the "need to know," Donovan created a fully integrated intelligence system. The OSS could coordinate all its activities in a single theater or operation. A clear case in which diverse intelligence functions interacted occurred early in the war during Operation Torch, the Allied invasion of North Africa.

As part of its "Vichy gamble," the United States had made an economic pact with General Maxime Weygand, the chief of the Vichy French forces in North Africa. It posted twelve vice-consuls as control officers to see that American goods did not reach the Nazis. COI/OSS sent agents to North Africa to engage in espionage (SI) and covert action (SO and MO), using these positions as cover. Operating from stations in Casablanca, Oran, Algiers, and Tunis, the vice-consuls enlisted the support of French officials and residents and native Arab groups. They secured the cooperation of " 'Strings,' the leader of the most powerful religious brotherhood in northern Morocco, and 'Tassels,' one of the most influential undercover tribal leaders in Er Rif."[29] In preparation for future contingencies, they established clandestine radio stations in those four cities and organized an underground for sabotage and resistance.

As they moved about the area, the vice-consuls collected important military, physical, and political data. At the same time, they disseminated propaganda: "A series of photographs of U.S. war materials being produced in factories, loaded on ships, etc., was shown to Frenchmen and natives in cities and outlying areas throughout French Morocco."[30] The vice-consuls even distributed copies of President Roosevelt's "four freedoms" speech in Arabic. Although many French, including military officers, collaborated in this "subversive" activity, they objected to stirring up Arab nationalism and arming anticolonial rebel groups. Donovan's R&A professors in Washington could have pointed out the prob-

lems that were being created for the future, but they were busy producing basic and current intelligence about North Africa to save
American lives for the present.

By the time the invasion took place, on November 8, 1942, the
OSS had established "a new kind of efficiency in warfare." It had
provided the invading forces with the most current information
and had softened up the territory for attack: "U.S. troops were met
on many beaches by friendly guides. On the previous night, an
OSS/Oran agent had removed the caps from demolition charges in
the tunnel connecting Mers el Kebir with Oran. The tunnel was
vital to Allied movement and it was estimated that it would have
required three months to rebuild.

> . . . Allied Army, Navy, and Air officers with the invasion fleet
> received until the last minute of H-Hour, and beyond, detailed
> information on what to expect . . . at every landing point. They
> had maps and diagrams of airport locations and measurements,
> and of port dimensions and facilities. They knew the disposition
> of the French fleet, the batteries actually being manned, and the
> number of planes on every airfield, with the amount of aviation
> gas available at each. They were aware of conditions of wind,
> weather, and tide and they had the expert advice of guides who
> knew the harbors intimately. Before and after the landings, they
> were advised, by OSS representatives who accompanied them,
> on terrain, locations of French headquarters and of German
> Armistice Commission offices, and the officials on whom they
> could rely for assistance in the administration of civil affairs.[31]

After the American forces had landed, however, the OSS had less
success in political intrigue and was implicated in the assassination
of the Vichy leader in Algiers, Admiral Jean Darlan, in December
1942. Although author Stephen Ambrose clears the OSS, this
incident provided an early warning of the possible excesses of clandestine operations.[32]

From Torch to Overlord, Donovan wrote a unique chapter in
American history, and it would be difficult to exaggerate his accomplishment. By creating an organization that gathered the functions
of intelligence in one place and centralizing some, he gave essence
to the concept of intelligence. The main task that he failed to

achieve was the preservation of the OSS—not that he did not try. In November 1944, when Roosevelt requested his thinking, Donovan prepared a memorandum in which he recommended that intelligence control be returned to the president and that a central authority be established under a director of central intelligence reporting directly to the president. This director would have responsibility for setting requirements and for collecting and coordinating national and strategic intelligence. Foreseeing a structure not unlike today's intelligence community, Donovan wrote, "You will note that coordination and centralization are placed at the policy level but operational intelligence (that pertaining primarily to Department action) remains within the existing agencies concerned. The creation of a central authority thus would not conflict with or limit necessary intelligence functions within the Army, Navy, Department of State and other agencies."[33]

Donovan's achievements notwithstanding, his mistakes ultimately caught up with him. He had rubbed a lot of people the wrong way. The heads of G-2 and the FBI, in particular, opposed his plan, and someone (Donovan suspected J. Edgar Hoover) leaked it to the press. Walter Trohan of the *Chicago Tribune* published Donovan's "secret" memo in full, labeling it an attempt to create a "Super Gestapo Agency" and denouncing it under banner headlines: "New Deal Plans Super Spy System: Sleuths Would Snoop on U.S. and the World; Order Creating it Already Drafted."[34] Franklin Roosevelt died with the issue unsettled, and Donovan lost what chance he had.

Harry Truman, the new president, lacked experience and was not attuned to intelligence's expanded role as an instrument of policy and power. He disapproved of espionage and resented Donovan's lobbying activities. The OSS ended even more swiftly than it had begun. On September 20, 1945, Truman executed an order that terminated the OSS effective October 1. It transferred R&A to the State Department and SI and X-2 to the War Department to form the Strategic Services Unit, which had the task of apprehending Nazi war criminals and recovering looted art treasures. As the armed services were cut from twelve million persons in 1945 to three million in 1946 and a million and a half by 1948, few noticed the disappearance of the OSS—"just another wartime agency."

But the United States' demobilization was not commensurate to its new place in international affairs; U.S. foreign intelligence had only gone into remission. In the next three decades, its growth would have dazzled even "Wild Bill."

15

The Great Intelligence Debate

There was something old fashioned and typically American about President Harry Truman's disbanding of the OSS. Like most Americans, he did not like spying, and he distrusted secrecy in government. But eventually, although he never really abandoned these ideals, he changed his mind about the role of intelligence. He learned about its achievements in the war and was called upon to lead in a time when the United States' world position radically changed. A number of factors, working almost simultaneously, caused him to rethink his position. The 1946 congressional investigation of the Pearl Harbor attack concluded that Pearl Harbor might have been avoided if a unified intelligence system had been in place at the time. The wartime alliance, which had worked as an antifascist coalition, disintegrated once the common enemy was removed and the old rivalries and suspicions resurfaced. The executive branch of government had undergone a great deal of improvised growth in response to the emergencies of economic depression and war and now had to be reorganized.

Yet the disbanding of foreign intelligence had been more apparent than real. The OSS was gone, but some of its functions had been transferred to other departments. Military intelligence stayed intact; G-2 and the ONI were larger than ever and enjoyed respect; and the cryptological services were untouchable. Consider the creation of the Army Security Agency in September 1945. The question was not "Would foreign intelligence be done?" but "How would it be organized?" Considerations of the national security apparatus and the structure of the armed forces formed part of the larger issue of government reorganization.

During World War II, American leaders had worried that the Pentagon—old "Fort Five Sides," the world's largest office building—would become the world's largest white elephant after the war ended. It did not; in fact, to this day the Pentagon has not been able to house Washington's entire military establishment. Nonetheless, in 1945 there was much discussion and debate about streamlining and merging the armed forces. James V. Forrestal, the secretary of the navy, was a dominant figure in these debates and advocated many of the changes that ultimately led to the creation of the Department of Defense. An early hard-liner toward the Soviet Union, Forrestal favored a strong defense establishment that would be directed by a supercabinet constantly vigilant on world developments and capable of taking swift and decisive action. These ideas influenced a 1945 report prepared by Ferdinand Eberstadt, Forrestal's close friend, on government reorganization on behalf of the Navy Department. Eberstadt recommended that a National Security Council be created as a permanent means of consultation between the president and the chiefs of the diplomatic and military departments.

The organization of intelligence figured prominently in all of these discussions. Tremendous in-fighting went on; Forrestal favored centralization, while the intelligence services battled to remain separate. The Eberstadt Report recommended that a central intelligence agency be created as an "essential element" of the proposed National Security Council: "Without such an agency, Eberstadt maintained, the NSC 'could not fulfill its role' nor could the military services 'perform their duty to the nation.' "[1] But the report waffled when it also stated that "each Department had its independent needs [for intelligence] which required the maintenance of independent capabilities."[2] Centralization really meant creating a coordinating body that would act to orchestrate—but not assume—the functions being performed by individual departments. Donovan had proposed a similar solution but had urged that the coordinator of intelligence be under the "direction and supervision" of the president. For the moment, the intelligence services overruled this key recommendation.

Following the advice of the Eberstadt Report and pending permanent legislation, President Truman created the *Central Intelligence*

Group (CIG) in January 1946, headed by a *director of central intelligence (DCI)* but operating under the supervision of a National Intelligence Authority composed of the secretaries of state, navy, and war. Although the CIG was given responsibility for the "coordination, planning, evaluation, and dissemination of intelligence," it was largely at the mercy of the departments—even to the extent that it had no budget of its own and relied upon the secretaries for funding. Nonetheless, the concept of central intelligence had been restored, and (although this was not inevitable) it grew to play a key role in the exercise of American power in world affairs. The creation of the office of director of central intelligence gave intelligence a place in the policy-planning process, and the personality and influence of the DCI became a critical factor in the development of particular functions of intelligence.

The first DCI, Rear Admiral Sidney Souers, held the position for only six months, from January to June 1946. This was his choice; he was not a career naval officer and wanted to return to civilian life. But Souers had been deputy chief of the ONI and had written the section of the Eberstadt Report that argued for the preservation of departmental intelligence. He had agreed to stay on to get the CIG started, but despite his general sympathy toward the intelligence services, he found them uncooperative. He organized the central reports staff in an attempt to facilitate the production of national intelligence estimates, but the departments were unwilling to provide it with adequate funds or to permit access to their secrets. Souers had more success in gaining certain overt collection functions. He took in a few holdovers from the OSS that lacked a permanent home: the Domestic Contacts Service, which debriefed persons returning from trips abroad, and the Foreign Broadcast Information Service, which monitored foreign radio transmissions, especially by government news and propaganda stations.

The next DCI was less inclined to be pushed around. Lieutenant General Hoyt S. Vandenberg served as DCI from June 1946 to May 1947. Even though he too looked upon the position as temporary (since he was the likely choice for vice chief of staff of the soon-to-be-independent air force), Vandenberg was not the kind of man just to warm a chair. A former head of army intelligence, a West Point careerist, and nephew of Senator Arthur Vandenberg of Michigan, the "boy general" was a match for the chiefs of the intelligence services. He secured a more independent funding arrangement for CIG, committing the departments to regular lump-sum allotments, and he reorganized the central reports staff into the Office of Research and Evaluation. Frustrated in his efforts to carry out his "primary mission" of coordinating intelligence, Vandenberg found a substitute in production. He expanded his corps of research analysts and started producing intelligence—especially current intelligence. The "bugs" in a weak central intelligence system showed up early, but they were not eliminated, only finessed. President Truman actually encouraged the wayward behavior of the CIG (acting on a false assumption).

> President Truman expected and liked to receive CIG's daily summary of international events. His known preference meant that work on the *Daily,* as it was called, assumed priority attention—every day. The justification for the *Daily* as an addition to other departmental summaries was that CIG had access to all information, unlike the Departments that had only their own. This was not true. Between 1946 and 1949, CIG and later CIA received almost all its current information from State. Although CIG had been created to minimize the duplicative efforts of the Departments, its acquisition of an independent intelligence production capability was now contributing to the problem.[3]

Vandenberg also acquired the former OSS clandestine collection branches, which had been transferred temporarily to the army in 1945. SI (espionage) and X-2 (counterespionage) constituted the army's Strategic Services Unit, but not even G-2 wanted to engage in espionage since career officers perceived it as too controversial and even demeaning. Seizing the opportunity, Vandenberg took in these orphaned branches to form the Office of Special Operations and increased the size of the CIG to over ten times what it had been under Souers. Although this was not a duplication of effort, there had been no specific intention that the CIG would assume these functions (an early indication of the kind of influence a DCI might have). By the time Truman decided to make central intelligence a permanent feature of the U.S. government—anticipating all-source, national intelligence, that could avoid another Pearl Harbor—Vandenberg had already positioned it to resume an independent course, and the Office of Research and Evaluation (renamed Research and Estimates) and the Office of Special Operations followed the OSS model of Intelligence and Operations.

When the National Security Act was passed in 1947, U.S. foreign intelligence entered a new era. Allen Dulles's concern that "we would fold our tents" after World War II was laid to rest. The great intelligence debate had produced a compromise affirming the principle of central intelligence while preserving the status quo in the form of an intelligence community composed of the existing intelligence services. For the moment, central intelligence fit in with the reorganization of the U.S. military establishment and the perfecting of the mechanism for the formulation of strategic policy. The National Security Act created the National Security Council; the office of the secretary of defense, who presided over the National Military Establishment (the forerunner of the Department of Defense), which consisted of the newly formed departments of the air force, army, and navy; the United States Air Force; the Joint Chiefs of Staff (JCS); and the Central Intelligence Agency.

Although the composition of the National Security Council (NSC) would change over the years, its core membership consisted of the president, the vice president, and the secretaries of state and defense. The NSC was a response to Truman's desire to consult specifically with cabinet officers most directly involved in the issues of peace and war. The chairman of the JCS and the director of central intelligence served the NSC as the principal advisers for military and intelligence matters, respectively. The inclusion of the vice president was the particular idea of Truman, who had felt left out during his own vice presidency; he had not been privy to Roosevelt's strategic decisions and top secrets. The NSC was Truman's way of involving more heads and doing things more formally.

The establishment of the office of the secretary of defense was another compromise that resulted from the long debate over military reorganization. In that debate, a merger of the military services had been a possibility. Although after a number of reorganizations the secretary of defense did gain control over the secretaries of the air force, army, and navy, the principal aim was to avoid a merger as impractical and to substitute coordination. The defense secretary was to coordinate the efforts of the service secretaries and the JCS through a rotating chairmanship and permanent staff was to achieve unified military planning and combined operations. After the merger of the army and navy was rejected, an independent air force was created. As one anonymous cynic put it, "Instead of one, you got three." In 1949, the Department of Defense (DOD) was created to unify the armed forces, and the same cynic probably quipped, "Now you have four."

All these changes had great bearing on the history of U.S. foreign intelligence. For the purposes of this study, the key items in the 1947 National Security Act were the establishment of the CIA and the organization of the intelligence community. The act gave the CIA the responsibility

> to advise the National Security Council in matters concerning such intelligence activities of the Government departments and agencies as relate to the national security;
>
> to make recommendations to the National Security Council for the coordination of such intelligence activities of the departments and agencies of the Government as relate to the national security;
>
> to correlate and evaluate intelligence relating to the national security, and provide for the appropriate dissemination of such intelligence within the Government . . . ;
>
> to perform for the benefit of the existing intelligence agencies, such additional services of common concern as the National Security Council determines can be more efficiently accomplished centrally;
>
> to perform such other functions and duties related to intelligence affecting the national security as the National Security Council may from time to time direct.

The act's original intent was that the DCI would use the facilities of the CIA to coordinate the work of the intelligence community for the production of national intelligence estimates (although the so-called elastic clauses—the "services of common concern" and "such other functions"—would virtually dominate the CIA's activities in time). The act assured that the departments would continue to perform intelligence functions to meet specific needs, and the CIA was to serve as a clearinghouse and tasking center to furnish the NSC with national and strategic intelligence. The problem was that the CIA was to serve as a command post for a DCI who lacked the power to command. By shunning centralization, the United States had in fact established a full-blown intelligence system that ran by committee. Because the National Security Act (following Donovan's suggestion) had put the DCI under the direction and supervision of the president, the CIA eventually could go off and "do its own thing," just like any other member of the intelligence community.

16

The U.S.
Intelligence Community

I n the forty years after World War II, the U.S. intelligence community (IC) kept pace with the rest of the federal bureaucracy. It responded to political developments, vastly improved its ability to collect information through advanced technology, and grew in size and sophistication. But it failed to evolve an effective coordinating mechanism, since it was based on the concept that the best way to produce national intelligence was to permit individual departments to maintain independent capabilities and fulfill tactical requirements. The IC was a "loose confederation" in which each member acted in a spirit of competition rather than of cooperation and resisted efforts to achieve central control.

In order to sort out the IC's complex history, it is helpful to understand the participants and their various roles. For this purpose, the chart in figure 16-1 is a useful instrument, depicting the national intelligence community structure as it stood in mid-February 1976 when most of the important intelligence agencies were in place after almost thirty years of development. (For the reorganizations by the Ford and Carter administrations, see figures 24-1 and 24-2, chapter 24; for changes under the Reagan administration, see figure 25-1, chapter 25.)

The IC exists to serve the president and the NSC, who establish national intelligence requirements and receive the national intelligence product. A complex management system has evolved to fulfill these requirements; the system is governed by a whole taxonomy of direction documents, foremost of which are *executive orders*

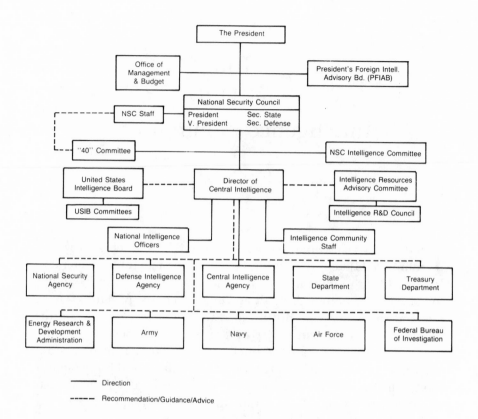

Source: U.S. Senate, Select Committee to Study Governmental Operations. *Foreign and Military Intelligence.* Report no. 94-755, book 1, 94th cong., 2d sess., 1976.

Figure 16-1. *National Intelligence Community Structure (Prior to February 18, 1976)*

and *NSC decision directives.* The executive orders are unclassified and are usually issued by each new presidential administration; they outline the general function and responsibility of the IC elements. The decision directives are classified and generally concern high-risk or highly secret intelligence operations, such as covert action and advanced technical collection. Like executive orders, decision directives have been revised or replaced by incoming presidents. (Their designations have also been changed. They were called *National Security Action Memorandums,* or *NSAMs,* during the Kennedy and Johnson administrations; *National Security Decision Memorandums,* or *NSDMs,* under Nixon; *Presidential Directives,* or *PDs,* under Carter; and *National Security Decision Directives,* or *NSDDs,* during the Reagan administration.[1]

Following these general guidelines, the NSC—with the president presiding—communicates its will to the IC in more specific terms through *National Security Council Intelligence Directives (NSCIDs).* "Enskids," as they are called in intelligence jargon, are the authority under which the DCI assigns tasks to the IC; the DCI also prepares more detailed instructions by means of *Director of Central Intelligence Directives (DCIDs).* Other, less formal types of guidance documents have also been issued from time to time. These include, in the 1960s, the President's Intelligence Checklist (the so-called PICKLE), which were succeeded in the 1970s by the Key Intelligence Questions (KIQs) and, still later, by the National Intelligence Topics (NITs). The purpose of all was the same: "to get all of the intelligence agencies to respond to policymakers' needs rather than just to their own operational requirements."[2] Because of the enormity of the tasking problem, an array of coordinating boards, committees, groups, offices, and panels (not all shown in figure 16–1) have been created. In all of these arrangements, the essential need has been to find a way to coordinate a decentralized system and to overcome the short-circuiting of the process by the secretaries of defense and state, who sit on the NSC.

Two elements not specifically part of the intelligence community are listed under "the president" in figure 16–1: the *Office of Management and Budget (OMB)* and the *President's Foreign Intelligence Advisory Board (PFIAB).* The OMB (the Bureau of the Budget, or BOB, until 1969) has the responsibility for regulating spending by government agencies and could in theory monitor intelligence operations through budgetary accountability. At least through the mid-1970s, it did not achieve this potential. In 1974, Victor Marchetti, a former high-level CIA official, and John Marks, his co-author, asserted that, with reference to the CIA, the OMB "has never been more than a minor irritant." They cited "secrecy and deception" as the ways the intelligence agencies commonly stonewall the OMB's budget examiners.[3] The PFIAB had similar problems.

President Kennedy created the PFIAB in 1961 in an effort to

control the damage of the Bay of Pigs failure. (The PFIAB replaced and was stronger than the President's Board of Consultants on Foreign Intelligence Activities, or PBCFIA, which President Eisenhower had set up in 1956 following a recommendation by the Hoover Commission on government reorganization and acting to head off a congressional move toward intelligence oversight.) Composed of distinguished private citizens, the PFIAB visited Washington routinely to evaluate the work of the IC and reported to the president at least twice a year. The PFIAB has been criticized for its part-time status and for its connection with the "establishment" (corporate executives, university presidents, former high-level officeholders, and retired admirals and generals); in 1972, Patrick McGarvey, a fourteen-year veteran of U.S. intelligence, referred to the PFIAB as "a joke," and Marchetti and Marks characterized it only as "a nuisance." McGarvey described the board's visits of "a day or two" each month as consisting of little more than a morning of boring "world situation briefings" and an evening "of drinks and dinner in town."[4] Marchetti and Marks were more charitable, observing that "Presidents have tended to use the PFIAB as a prestigious but relatively safe 'in-house' investigative unit, usually at times when the chief executive was displeased with the quality of intelligence he was receiving. Whenever an intelligence failure [was] suspected in connection with a foreign policy setback, the Board [was] usually convened to look into the matter."[5]

Lyman B. Kirkpatrick, Jr., who served as inspector general of the CIA and acted as liaison between the CIA and the president's boards between 1956 and 1962, treated the PFIAB with more respect. He defended especially the participation of former public servants: "The argument that the board is simply a mirror of the system ignores the broad experience of the members. It is a grave error to assume that because an individual served in the government he is an advocate of all that the intelligence agencies may do."[6] Kirkpatrick affirmed that it was his experience "that the President's board was one of the severest critics of the intelligence system." Nonetheless, in 1976, when President Ford was presented with evidence of illegal and improper behavior on the part of intelligence agencies, which raised the question of the PFIAB's effectiveness, he reinforced the board with a permanent, three-member Intelligence Oversight Board (IOB)—the head of which was also a member of PFIAB. Two years later, President Carter scrapped the PFIAB altogether, retaining only the full-time IOB as the president's watchdog.

Turning to the NSC and specifically to the tasking process, there have been numerous committees and panels set up to advise on requirements. Many have been temporary, organized to monitor special problems and issues. For example, the Verification Panel, organized in 1971, concerned itself with intelligence relating to compliance and noncompliance with the strategic arms limitation agreements (the SALT treaties). The Net Assessments Group had the task of assessing the relative military strengths of the People's Republic of China, the Soviet Union, and the United States, receiving all-source intelligence to do this job.[7] When in existence, these committees occupied the same line as the "NSC Intelligence Committee" and the "40 Committee" in figure 16-1.

President Nixon created the *NSC Intelligence Committee* in 1971 to "give direction and guidance on national intelligence needs and provide for continuing evaluation of intelligence products from the viewpoint of the intelligence user."[8] Chaired by the special assistant to the president for national security affairs (AP/NSA), the members of the committee include the DCI, the attorney general, the undersecretary of state, the deputy secretary of defense, and the chairman of the JCS. Although it was created to improve the management of the IC, the committee actually strengthened the position of the president's national security adviser—Henry Kissinger, at the time—in relation to the DCI. In the early years, the DCIs tended to dominate, but under Nixon and Kissinger the NSC Staff grew in power, especially in the conduct of covert foreign policy.

The *"40" Committee,* which existed from February 1970 until 1976, was an incarnation of NSC organs concerned with high-risk covert operations. Called successively the 10/2 Panel (1948), the 10/5 Panel (1951), the Planning Coordination Group (March 1955), the "5412" or Special Group (December 1955), and the "303" Committee (1964)—the designations generally originated from the numbers of the decision directives, such as NSC-10/2, NSAM-303, or NSDM-40[9]—the committee's membership included the DCI, the national security adviser, the undersecretary of state for political affairs, the deputy secretary of defense, and the chairman of the JCS. Their purpose was always the same: to plan and carry out covert action in support of foreign policy objectives. These so-called dirty tricks have run the gamut from hidden intervention in the political affairs of other states to the conducting of "secret" wars. This intelligence function has had a dynamic all its own. Because the CIA is the principal IC member that can conduct clandestine operations, it has been criticized for covert action failures, but who was giving orders and who was taking them have changed over time. Allen Dulles, for example, exerted powerful influence over the "5412" Group as DCI, but Henry Kissinger dominated the "40" Committee as AP/NSA. In 1973, Kissinger chaired the "40" Committee as national security adviser and served as secretary of state at the same time; he conducted both covert and overt foreign policy, concentrating in one person the powers once exercised jointly by the Dulles brothers, Allen and John Foster.

For covert action, the DCI put on his other hat and went directly to the CIA, which had the authority to perform "such other functions"; for tasking, the DCI conveyed the NSC's instructions to the IC through the *United States Intelligence Board (USIB),* of which he was the chair. (The USIB was called the Intelligence Advisory Committee, or IAC, until 1960 and was reorganized as the National Foreign Intelligence Board, or NFIB, in 1978—see figure 24–2.) The USIB comprised the heads of the various intelligence agencies; combined, they spent a total of over $6 billion in fiscal year 1972 and employed more than 150,000 persons.[10] The USIB was the DCI's principal means of coordinating the IC's work and served as the tasking center for the production of *National Intelligence Estimates (NIEs).* The NIEs were formal papers prepared collaboratively by U.S. intelligence agencies in response to general questions raised by the NSC, usually in the form of NSCIDs. One of the best-known NIEs was the "Special," or SNIE, of September 19, 1962, one month before the Cuban missile crisis, in which the IC answered an unqualified "no" to the question, "Will the Russians put offensive weapons in Cuba?"

To keep such miscalculations to a minimum, the USIB assigned tasks and pooled resources through a number of interagency subcommittees (as many as fifteen at one time), including the *Watch Committee* and the *National Indications Center (NIC)*. The Watch Committee listed items for priority handling and remained on standby to receive reports from all sources, thereby "institutionalizing," according to Patrick McGarvey, the "Pearl Harbor syndrome"—that is, "getting all tidbits of intelligence to Washington in the shortest possible time."[11] The National Indications Center, whose staff consisted of professional worriers, looked for warning signs and any indicators that might signal preparations for war. Based on the belief that armed attack is only the last move on an aggressor's timetable, the NIC circulated "an elaborate check list of items to look for" in a countdown to the outbreak of hostilities.[12] Among its other subcommittees, the USIB maintained one on overhead reconnaissance to establish priorities and eliminate duplication in the use of this highly specialized and expensive means of intelligence collection.

To prevent the costs of intelligence from getting out of hand, the DCI also chaired the *Intelligence Resources Advisory Committee (IRAC)*, which paralleled the USIB. Organized in 1971, IRAC succeeded the National Intelligence Resources Board (established in 1968), adding the director of the OMB to make it more effective. It was charged with preparing a composite intelligence budget so that the DCI could use the power of the purse to control intelligence activities. But IRAC's role was primarily advisory, and most intelligence agencies had departmental or independent sources of funding. So the DCI's ability to control the IC through spending was seriously limited, especially in technical collection systems linked to military operations.

More directly under his control, the *national intelligence officers (NIOs)* and the *intelligence community staff (ICS)* were further means for the DCI to guide the collection and production of national intelligence. Since these elements also appear on the organization chart (17-4) of the CIA, which is under the command authority of the DCI, they will be discussed in chapter 17, dealing with the CIA. The NIOs, especially, are a function still unfulfilled.

Below the policy-making and managerial levels of the IC are its operating members, the intelligence agencies (most of which opposed centralization, it must be remembered, because they had primary departmental missions to perform). The CIA merits a separate chapter because it alone is a multipurpose, multi-functional, integrated intelligence agency that performs functions of a communitywide character.

Of the IC members treated here, a cluster of them belong to the Department of Defense: the National Security Agency, the Defense Intelligence Agency, Army Intelligence, Naval Intelligence, and Air Force Intelligence. These major agencies account for most aspects of military intelligence. But certain other elements, because of their special character or size, ought also to be mentioned. The *assistant secretary of defense for intelligence,* since 1972, has actually headed the Pentagon intelligence establishment in its table of organization; he represents the DOD on appropriate NSC committees. The *Defense Mapping Agency,* the U.S. military's mapping, charting, and geodetic service, produces basic intelligence derived from the most sophisticated collection systems. The *Defense Investigative Service* is responsible for conducting security clearances of defense personnel. And the *National Reconnaissance Office (NRO),* a supersecret agency tucked away in the air force's table of organization, has responsibility for overhead reconnaissance, meaning essentially for placing in orbit and managing spy satellites. It is not necessary to describe these elements in detail (except the NRO), but they reflect the vast size and complexity of military intelligence in contrast to pre–World War II days.

The *National Security Agency (NSA)* is the United States' premier cryptologic agency. Organized in 1952, it is the latest in a long line of such agencies going back to Herbert O. Yardley and MI-8. During World War II, with MAGIC and ULTRA, U.S. cryptanalytic and cryptographic activities expanded tremendously in size and sophistication. After the war, in 1949, when various efforts were being made to unify or merge the armed forces, Secretary of Defense Louis Johnson established the *Armed Forces Security Agency (AFSA)* to coordinate the work of the various military cryptologic units. Three years later, President Truman reorganized the AFSA and changed its name to NSA to emphasize the production of national intelligence and to overcome the agency's military image.

Centralization and the change in emphasis from departmental to national intelligence enabled the NSA to concentrate genius and acquire a high volume of traffic. But it encountered jurisdictional problems with the three service cryptologic agencies, which had retained control over intercept facilities (collection): the Army Security Agency, the Naval Security Group, and the Air Force Security Service. In 1971, to solve this problem, President Nixon "confederated" the three under a *Central Security Service (CSS)* and placed the director of the NSA in charge: "The mission of NSA/CSS is to provide centralized coordination, direction, and control for the United States Government's Signals Intelligence (SIGINT) and Communications Security (COMSEC) activities."[13]

Because communications intelligence is very sensitive and enjoys huge respect, the NSA has managed virtually to write its own ticket. It is one of the largest and most expensive IC members and one of the most secretive. But the days when Yardley's book, *The American Black Chamber,* could be kept off library shelves are gone. In 1954, when plans were being made to move all the NSA's operations to a site near Fort George G. Meade, Maryland, and construct a multimillion-dollar headquarters, the *New York Times* and the *Washington Post* published background stories that provided a surprising amount of detail about the agency. In 1960, the defection of two NSA employees, William H. Martin and Bernon F. Mitchell, to the Soviet Union brought more unwanted publicity and worse to NSA.

Finally, the publication of such books as David Kahn's *The Codebreakers* (1967) and James Bamford's *The Puzzle Palace* (1982) removed the last aura of mystery from NSA and even emboldened critics to question the agency's effectiveness. Though volume is the key to cryptanalytic success, writers like Patrick McGarvey asked if the NSA was not collecting too much. He estimated that it required "a hundred tons of paper a day" to record the "take" and charged that one program alone, involving the taping of Soviet "scrambler" communications, cost $100 million per year to run. After this information was collected, he affirmed, "it was merely stored away in vaults at NSA headquarters, as NSA's mathematicians had not yet devised a formula for breaking it out."[14] Though memories of MAGIC and ULTRA tend to intimidate most of the NSA's critics, concerns about duplication and possible waste in other defense agencies have not been ignored.

Secretary of Defense Robert McNamara established the *Defense Intelligence Agency (DIA)* in 1961 in an effort to overcome duplication among the military intelligence agencies and to coordinate DOD participation in the activities of the USIB. Charges had been made that the military intelligence agencies were skewing intelligence reports to support budget requests for more weapons, "marching to Capitol Hill each spring to sell fear."[15] McNamara, in response, gave the DIA responsibility for coordinating the DOD's contributions to national intelligence estimates and intended that the DIA alone would represent military intelligence on the USIB. He mandated that the director of the DIA report to the secretary of defense through the Joint Chiefs of Staff. With the same stroke, he replaced the Joint Intelligence Group, or J-2, the JCS intelligence staff. The DIA's principal functions were tasking (particularly the assignment of national intelligence requirements) and coordinating production. Its collection role was modest, limited to administering the defense attaché system.

In many respects, the DIA concept mirrored that of the CIA— the clearinghouse idea. The DIA did not replace the service intelligence agencies; it merely sought to coordinate their activities to achieve a more efficient allocation of resources and to overcome the worst aspects of tribalism (or self-serving intelligence reporting). But the grip of departmental/tactical intelligence persisted, reinforced by the technological explosion. The service intelligence agencies never really relinquished their places on the USIB, nor did they stop expanding.

> The national leaders who established the DIA were alert to the danger that it might evolve into simply another layer in the intelligence bureaucracy, and cautioned against thinking of it as no more than a confederation of service intelligence activities. Nonetheless, a decade later executive branch reviews criticized DIA for perpetuating the very faults it had been designed to avoid— duplication and layering. By 1970, each service actually had a larger general intelligence arm than it had before DIA was created.[16]

Although the service intelligence agencies lost their estimative function,[17] they could continue to report current intelligence to national intelligence consumers because of the increasingly techno-logical nature of warfare. Moreover, the service agencies contrib-uted appropriate basic intelligence to the National Intelligence Surveys, the classified encyclopedias of the nations of the world, on such matters as order of battle, targets, and weapons systems. (The NIS program was terminated in 1974.) But what really stimulated the growth of the service intelligence agencies, enabling them to dwarf the DIA and most other members of the IC in size, was tech-nical collection, with the related capabilities of early-warning and arms control verification.

For example, by the early 1970s, *Air Force Intelligence (AFIN/A-2)* was the IC's largest intelligence agency. It employed fifty-six thou-sand persons and had an annual budget of $2.7 billion.[18] Although it retained responsibility for monitoring order of battle of the world's air forces and kept up to date on potential bombing targets, preventing technological surprise became a major concern and fueled its massive expansion. The Foreign Technology Division of the Air Force Systems Command, for example, undertook to acquire foreign weapons systems for analysis and exploitation.[19] More particularly, the AFIN's management of the USIB's "spy-in-the-sky" programs, through the National Reconnaissance Office, accounted for its huge size and cost. Although the NRO appeared to be an air force component and was usually directed by the under-secretary of the air force, NRO operations are set by the National Reconnaissance Executive Committee, which is chaired by the DCI. Created in 1960, the NRO is the United States' principal "black" space agency, even though "officially" it does not exist.[20] It is a "national-level" intelligence organization and runs the IC's satellite programs only under the "cover" of the air force. Its bud-get was $1.5 billion in the early 1970s and exceeded $3 billion a decade later.[21]

Naval Intelligence (ONI) is the oldest of the service intelligence agencies. Although much smaller than AFIN, it too expanded rapidly during these years. Technical collection spurred the ONI's growth to fifteen thousand hands and an annual budget of $600 million in the early 1970s. While air force eyes looked down from above, navy ears listened in from below as the navy equipped its submarine fleet with electronic listening devices and other types of sensors for intelligence purposes.[22] This was not as risky as using surface ships for intelligence missions.

Army Intelligence (G-2) also got into the act. Marchetti and Marks affirmed that G-2 was the "least mechanized" of the service agencies and that it regarded its principal mission as the acquiring of "tactical intelligence in support of its field forces."[23] But the army did not miss the opportunity to acquire advanced technology through linkage with technical collection. Army Intelligence employed thirty-five thousand persons and expended $700 million in 1974; its heaviest costs were incurred by the electronic and signals intelligence operations of the Army Security Agency.[24]

Thus, the military intelligence agencies expanded through technical collection, while the civilian agencies, for the most part plodding along with old-fashioned overt collection and production, stayed relatively poor and uninfluential.

The *State Department* has a major voice in determining how intelligence influences policy at the NSC level, but its specific intelligence arm, the *Bureau of Intelligence and Research (INR)*, is one of the poorest and weakest members of the IC. The INR has been much maligned, and the sad truth is that much of the maligning has been from within its own department. It is the remnant of the former OSS Research and Analysis branch, brought over to State by William Langer in 1945. State apparently did not want this intelligence function and has never felt comfortable with it since. The cables and reports from U.S. embassies abroad are a principal source of intelligence, but the State Department shies away from any connotations of espionage as incompatible with its diplomatic mission. The INR has no collection function of its own, relying upon State Department cables and the intelligence reports of other agencies to produce current and basic intelligence (usually political and biographical reports) and to represent the State Department on the USIB/NFIB and appropriate subcommittees.

Despite having major responsibilities in the IC, the INR's reputation has suffered because it has never had either the staff (down to about 350 in 1972) or the budget ($8 million in the same year) to be effective. Ray Cline, who served as the director of the INR between 1969 and 1973 after over twenty years of experience in the OSS and the CIA, described the INR's funding as "parsimonious" and expressed resentment at the "haughty" foreign service officers and "State officialdom" who "did not really value an independent analytical approach that sometimes threatened already established policy positions."[25] To be fair, the INR had had a few very good veteran analysts, but a hitch in the INR does not advance one's career in the foreign service, and therefore many on its staff were merely warming chairs between overseas assignments. The INR's desk officers have been competent people, but because of a lack of commitment and experience, they were no match for the current intelligence analysts at the CIA, who made careers of being experts about one country or region.

In the IC trenches, Hamilton's department has been more active than Jefferson's. The *Treasury Department* has been an active IC member, represented on the USIB/NFIB by a special assistant to the secretary [of the treasury] for National Security Affairs. Its intelligence units include the Bureau of Alcohol, Tobacco, and Firearms, the U.S. Secret Service, the U.S. Customs Service, and the Internal Revenue Service. The Customs Service, for example, "has an intelligence potential in such matters as narcotics and munitions control, prevention and detection of terrorism in international transportation facilities, and enforcement of Federal regulations affecting articles in international trade."[26] The Secret Service, which has responsibility for protecting the life of the president, plays a particularly critical role within the IC. It exchanges information relevant to the president's safety and works closely with the CIA and, if possible, with the intelligence services of other nations whenever the president travels abroad. Reciprocally, the Secret Service is responsible for the safety of foreign dignitaries visiting the United States and for the security of foreign diplomatic missions in the United States.

In the area of intelligence production, the Treasury Department provides economic intelligence from attachés posted in U.S. embassies abroad, and its economic and monetary analysts play an important role in estimates intelligence: "Inasmuch as nearly everything costs money, both the Treasury Department and the Office of Management and Budget are frequent contributors to policy papers. Such questions must be answered as: What will our proposed action do to the federal budget for this or the next fiscal year? Or, what impact will it have on the balance of payments?"[27]

In the 1970s, answers to these economic questions also depended upon developments in international energy affairs. Before that time, the IC's principal concern in the energy field had been with nuclear matters. The Atomic Energy Commission (AEC) sat on the USIB, represented by its assistant general manager for national security. But the "oil crunch" of 1973 added new dimensions to energy and national security and resulted in the reorganization and replacement of the AEC by the Energy Research and Development Administration (ERDA) and the Nuclear Regulatory Commission (NRC). ERDA, the more comprehensive of the two new agencies, assumed the AEC's intelligence functions and placed its assistant administrator for national security on the USIB.

Although ERDA was concerned with research and development in every aspect of energy, it continued as both "a consumer and producer of intelligence in the critical national security field of nuclear energy." It established requirements for the technical collection of data to detect nuclear explosions and used all-source information to prepare current intelligence reports and contribute estimates about "the atomic weapons capabilities of foreign powers." [28]

If ERDA was the newest member of the IC in 1975, the *Federal Bureau of Investigation (FBI)* was one of the oldest. The FBI's primary responsibility was to protect the nation from clandestine operations in the United States by foreign powers, specifically espionage, sabotage, and subversion. Although the FBI's overseas operations terminated in 1946, it continued to maintain abroad "liaison agents with other security and intelligence agencies to insure a link between cases or leads which develop overseas but which come to rest in the continental United States." [29]

The FBI was not the only component of the Justice Department with intelligence potential; the Drug Enforcement Administration (DEA), created in 1973, may also be cited. In fact, throughout the executive branch as a whole intelligence potential exists. A U.S. Senate study in 1976 concluded that an "outstanding characteristic" of the IC was "its pervasiveness." It noted that the agencies depicted on the IC organizational chart (figure 16-1) did not exhaust entities of the federal government that "conceivably contribute information relevant to intelligence matters." It cited "Department of Agriculture overseas attachés, National Aeronautics and Space Administration satellite launching systems, and products of the National Weather Service,'' as well as the U.S. Information Agency, ''which maintains numerous overseas offices,'' and the Agency for International Development, ''with missions in Asia, Africa, the Middle East, and Latin America.''[30]

Nor is the extent of the IC exhausted by considering the executive branch alone. In Marchetti and Marks's book, a chart depicting the U.S. intelligence community has a box labeled ''The Congress'' floating off by itself, not attached to anything. While executive agencies have performed the functions of intelligence, constitutional and legal issues are involved, particularly in clandestine operations, the conduct of secret foreign policy, and intervention in the affairs of other states. After Watergate, the Congress fully asserted the concepts of checks and balances and separation of powers in intelligence matters with the creation of the Senate Select Committee on Intelligence in 1976 and the House Permanent Select Committee on Intelligence in 1977. Up until that time, the Congress had acted in a kind of good faith relationship with the executive branch, because of fears of ''leaks'' and because it took time for the system to discover what was happening in clandestine operations. It had entrusted intelligence matters to a select group of senior legislators within the existing Armed Services and Appropriations committees of the respective chambers.

A few ''flaps,'' such as the U-2 shootdown and the Martin and Mitchell defections, had resulted in hearings after the fact, but Congress generally showed little disposition to exercise effective oversight for the first twenty-five years of the IC's operations. During this period, congressional leaders serving on the oversight committees were among the most established and conservative, such as Richard Russell, John Stennis, Carl Hayden, and Allen Ellender; but even Senator Leverett Saltonstall, who had a slightly more liberal outlook, shared the attitude of his colleagues in 1966: ''It is not a question of reluctance on the part of CIA officials to speak to us. Instead it is a question of our reluctance, if you will, to seek information and knowledge on subjects which I personally, as a member of Congress and as a citizen, would rather not have.''[31]

Allen Dulles supposedly once said, in preparing for an annual budget hearing on Capitol Hill, ''I'll just tell them a few war stories.''[32] But Ray Cline, drawing upon his experience in the CIA, insisted that such hearings were ''serious efforts'' to inform Congress about intelligence programs, ''especially when they cost a lot of money or when they might come to public notice in ways that would embarrass the Congressmen if they had not been forewarned.''[33]

Whatever the truth of these statements, it is true that before Watergate, Congress was not particularly attuned to developments in the U.S. intelligence community. Few in the U.S. government foresaw the role that intelligence—especially clandestine operations—would play in U.S. foreign policy after World War II. They especially did not foresee the role that would be played by the CIA, whose charter contained the ''elastic clauses'' authorizing it to perform ''additional services of common concern'' and ''such other functions'' at the behest of the NSC. Stymied in effectively doing the job that it was created to do, the CIA expanded on the basis of its clandestine capability. The chapters in American history that it wrote, the American people, like the members of Congress, read with surprise.

17
The CIA

The CIA was intended to be the nerve center of the intelligence community. But instead, it became just another member—if a very special one. Unable to secure the cooperation of the departments in producing national intelligence, the CIA undertook to produce national intelligence on its own and assumed responsibility for performing clandestine operations. It took about six years (1947 to 1953) for the CIA to carve out its place, but William J. Donovan himself could not have done a better job of combining Intelligence and Operations into a single agency. Harry Truman had killed the OSS in 1945 but had failed to drive a wooden stake through its heart; it rose again as the CIA.

In 1947, when Rear Admiral Roscoe Hillenkoetter was appointed the first director of the CIA, it was already heavily involved in producing current intelligence. The Office of Research and Estimates continued to disseminate the *Daily,* the daily intelligence summary it had been preparing as part of the Central Intelligence Group. Though criticized for producing current intelligence and neglecting estimates, the truth was that the ORE did a good job and filled a role that the State Department's INR, as successor to the Research and Analysis branch of the OSS, was supposed to play but did not. President Truman's "known preference" for the *Daily* created incentives that the ORE's analysts could not resist.[1]

Nonetheless, the CIA's failure to predict the outbreak of hostilities in Korea in June 1950 caused Hillenkoetter's successor, General Walter Bedell ("Beedle") Smith, to abolish the ORE and replace it with the Office of National Estimates (ONE) and the

Office of Research and Reports (ORR). The ONE was created to deal exclusively with estimates intelligence, and ORR was to specialize in economic research on the "Soviet Bloc." Smith brought William Langer back from Harvard to head the ONE and recruited economist Max Millikan of MIT for the ORR, but he could not stem the tide.

Langer managed to keep the ONE small. He assembled a select group of scholars and turned out a high-quality product, but the ONE remained essentially a CIA component. Langer tried to "coordinate" with other departments but without much success; he tended increasingly to rely upon CIA resources, stimulating in turn CIA's research and analysis capability. The ORR responded. Having a broader mission to serve all levels of the IC, its ranks swelled. The ORR quickly established a reputation in economic analysis, and its concentration on the Soviet area facilitated expansion. Its holdovers from the ORE in basic and current intelligence climbed onto the bandwagon. Its continuing responsibility for the *Daily* led to the creation of the Office of Current Intelligence and the birth of the *Current Intelligence Bulletin,* which was essentially a classified daily newspaper. The ORR also organized the Office of Scientific Intelligence (OSI) to monitor nonmilitary developments in science and technology. In less than two years, July 1951 to February 1953, the ORR expanded from 461 persons to 766.

The Korean War stimulated and facilitated this growth. At the same time, the United States' new role in world affairs, the cold war, and the GI bill with its bumper crop of college graduates provided a pool of bright young people interested in careers in international relations. The quip ran that you went to work for the CIA if you flunked the foreign service exam, but the truth was that opportunities in the foreign service were limited and the CIA was hiring. Moreover, the State Department was undergoing a very difficult time as a result of the Alger Hiss trials and the irresponsible attacks of Senator Joseph McCarthy. The quipsters could have their fun, but the time had arrived to formalize intelligence as one of the CIA's principal activities, with a deputy director (DDI) in charge.

In January 1952, CIA's intelligence functions were grouped under the Directorate for Intelligence (DDI). In addition to

ONE, the DDI's intelligence production components included: the Office of Research and Reports (ORR), the Office of Scientific Intelligence (OSI), and the Office of Current Intelligence (OCI). Collection of overt information was the responsibility of the Office of Operations (OO). The Office of Collection and Dissemination (OCD) engaged in the distribution of intelligence as well as storage and retrieval of unevaluated intelligence.[2] [See figure 17–1.]

Within two years, the number of people employed by the DDI had risen to 3,338. This growth, however, was not even half the story, for the CIA's clandestine services experienced an even more spectacular expansion.

The CIA had initially performed only the clandestine functions of espionage and counterespionage, having acquired the CIG's Office of Special Operations. As noted, the CIG had organized the OSO when it took over the army's Strategic Services Unit in 1946, thereby absorbing the former clandestine collection branches of the OSS (SI and X-2). The covert action branches of the OSS were not reassigned, having been abolished with the OSS: that is, Morale Operations (propaganda and psychological warfare), Special Operations (sabotage and subversion in cooperation with local dissident or resistance groups), and Operational Groups (paramilitary and guerrilla operations). Within a year after the covert action branches were eliminated, American leaders began to have second thoughts.

The advent of the cold war created a new urgency for the use of techniques of persuasion and subversion. Neither the United States nor the Soviet Union wanted to risk war, but each believed in a distinct social and world order and each felt seriously threatened by the extension of the other's influence. The United States charged that the Soviet Union had violated the Yalta and Potsdam agreements by covert intervention in support of Communist takeovers in Poland, Czechoslovakia, Hungary, and Rumania, and that it secretly aided Communist-led uprisings in Greece and the Philippines. American leaders had been convinced by "Wild Bill" Donovan of the value of covert action in support of military objectives in wartime, but the Soviet Union demonstrated to them its value in support of political objectives in peacetime. Although the United States successfully stemmed Soviet expansion in

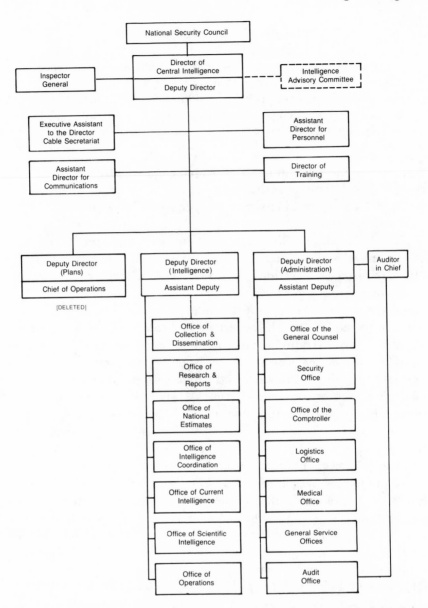

Source: U.S. Senate, Select Committee to Study Governmental Operations. *Supplementary Detailed Staff Reports on Foreign and Military Intelligence.* Report No. 94–755, book 4, 94th Cong., 2d sess., 1976.

Figure 17–1. *CIA Organization, 1953*

Western Europe through its policies of economic and military assistance, the ideological nature of the East-West struggle tended to favor the use of covert action, defined as "something more than diplomacy but still short of war."[3]

Throughout 1947, American leaders discussed ways and means of conducting psychological warfare. Secretaries Robert Patterson (war) and James Forrestal (navy) proposed that the State Department undertake the task, but Secretary of State George Marshall objected, arguing that such activity was incompatible with the diplomatic function. He recommended instead that the CIA, which already had the authority and experience for clandestine operations, be assigned "operational responsibility" for covert psychological warfare, while State would exercise control over planning and execution. Marshall prevailed, and in December 1947 he succeeded in imposing a covert action responsibility upon the CIA. While the influence of the DCIs was a major factor in the CIA's development, in this case DCI Hillenkoetter's lack of influence (he was no match for Marshall or Forrestal) had a profound effect on the mission of the agency. The departments exploited this weakness further during the next year.

In June 1948, in the wake of the Communist coup in Czechoslovakia and growing fears of a Russian invasion of Western Europe that amounted to a "war scare," the NSC issued directive 10/2, providing for covert political intervention and paramilitary operations. Further, it created the Office of Policy Coordination (OPC) to carry out covert political warfare, placing it within the CIA but outside the authority of the DCI: "Responsibility for the direction of OPC rested with the Office's director [Frank G. Wisner], designated by the Secretary of State. Policy guidance—decisions on the need for specific activities—came to the OPC director from State and Defense, bypassing the DCI."[4] George F. Kennan, director of the State Department's policy planning staff, who had helped draft NSC 10/2, explained that he intended only to create a "small contingency force" capable of covert action: "We had thought that this would be a facility which could be used when and if an occasion arose when it might be needed. There might be years when we wouldn't have to do anything like this."[5] If this was the intention, it clearly got out of hand, initially stimulated by the Korean War.

OPC's participation in the war effort [paramilitary activities in Korea] contributed to its transformation from an organization that was to provide the capability for a limited number of *ad hoc* operations to an organization that conducted continuing, ongoing activities on a massive scale. In concept, manpower, budget, and scope of activities, OPC simply sky-rocketed. The comparative figures for 1949 and 1952 are staggering. In 1949 OPC's total personnel strength was 302; in 1952 it was 2,812 plus 3,142 overseas contract personnel. In 1949 OPC's budget figure was $4,700,000; in 1952 it was $82,000,000. In 1949 OPC had personnel assigned to seven overseas stations; in 1952 OPC had personnel at forty-seven stations.[6]

While this expansion was taking place, "Beedle" Smith replaced Hillenkoetter as DCI. Smith brought OPC under his control, not content merely to have it show on his organizational chart. Moreover, tensions existed between OSO and OPC, because, although espionage required more nerve and greater finesse, the faster-action "dirty tricks" resulted in quicker rewards. According to a former clandestine operative, "Collection is the hardest thing of all; it's much easier to plant an article in a local newspaper."[7] After several preliminary moves, Smith duplicated what he had done on the Intelligence side and merged the Operations components (OSO and OPC) to create the Directorate of Plans (DDP) in August 1952. At the same time, by appointing Frank Wisner as deputy director for plans, Smith assured "the maximum development of covert action over clandestine collection."[8]

By 1953 the Agency had achieved the basic structure and scale it retained for the next twenty years [figure 17–1]. The Korean War, United States foreign policy objectives, and the Agency's internal organizational arrangements had combined to produce an enormous impetus for growth. The CIA was six times the size it had been in 1947.

Three Directorates had been established. In addition to the DDP and the DDI, Smith created the Deputy Directorate for Administration (DDA). Its purpose was to consolidate the management functions required for the burgeoning organization. The Directorate was responsible for budget, personnel, security, and medical services Agency-wide. However, one quarter of

DDA's total personnel strength was assigned to logistical support for overseas operations. The DDP commanded the major share of the Agency's budget, personnel, and resources; in 1952 clandestine collection and covert action accounted for 74 percent of the Agency's total budget [this did not include DDA budgetary allocations in support of DDP operations]; its personnel constituted 60 percent of the CIA's personnel strength. While production rather than coordination dominated the DDI, operational activities rather than collection dominated the DDP. The DDI and the DDP emerged at different times out of disparate policy needs. [They] were, in effect, separate organizations.[9]

If the CIA suffered from a split personality, the simple fact was that the dark side was in charge. Though Kennan had spoken of covert action only in terms of "contingencies" and President Truman had insisted, "I never had any thought when I set up the CIA that it would be injected into peacetime cloak-and-dagger operations,"[10] both men were responsible for NSC 10/2, which formalized covert action as an instrument of U.S. foreign policy and assigned to the CIA the principal role in carrying it out.

Despite the swift movement of unprecedented events, the constitutional and moral issues were clear enough, and the U.S. Congress must share a certain responsibility for the later developments. It approved the Central Intelligence Agency Act of 1949 (frequently referred to as the CIA's "secret charter"), which authorized the DCI "to spend money 'without regard to the provisions of law and regulations relating to the expenditure of government funds.' [And it] granted him the unique right to spend the hundreds of millions of dollars in his secret annual budget simply by signing his name."[11] At the same time, Congress exempted CIA from any requirement to disclose the "functions, names, official titles, salaries, or numbers of personnel employed by the Agency." Whether Congress realized it or not, this measure was designated more for Operations than for Intelligence.

It is interesting to note that the 1953 and 1972 organizational charts (figures 17-1 and 17-2, respectively) provide no breakdown of the DDP, even though the source of both is the 1976 report of the U.S. Senate Select Committee on Intelligence and even though organizational charts depicting the DDP in detail had already appeared in Philip Agee's *Inside the Company: CIA Diary* (1973) and in Victor Marchetti and John D. Marks's *The CIA and the Cult of Intelligence* (first published in 1974).

The CIA's basic structure was set by 1953, and it remained essentially the same for approximately twenty-five years (except that the DDP was renamed the Directorate of Operations, or DDO, in 1973). The chart in figure 17–2, "CIA Organization, 1972," is a useful guide, depicting the historic CIA, which is integral to the narrative of the Agency's development. The breakdown of the DDP, as noted, is marked [DELETED]; the clandestine CIA, including the DDP's "slave," the Directorate of Support, will be scrutinized in chapter 18. It is sufficient at this point to review the more public part of the CIA.

At the top is the *director of the CIA*. The positions of CIA director and director of central intelligence are held by the same person, although most Americans think of the DCI principally as the head of the CIA. Of the various persons who have served as directors of central intelligence and of the CIA (figure 17–3), most came from outside the Agency. Those who did come from within all came from the clandestine side, having served first as chief of clandestine services (DDP/DDO). Six directors were high-ranking military officers, and William Casey, a civilian outsider, served in SI at OSS/London during World War II. The only DDI who ever got close to the top spot was Robert M. Gates, who was appointed acting DCI in December 1986, when Casey was stricken with a brain tumor and the CIA needed a "white hat" because of the Iran-contra arms scandal. Gates could not make it all the way to the top, however, because he had also been deputy DCI, which meant that he was not as clear of clandestine operations as the situation required. In the superheated atmosphere of the Iran-contra affair, Gates withdrew his name from consideration for DCI, and President Reagan, looking for a safe bet, went outside the Agency again and nominated FBI director William H. Webster.

Allen Dulles, the DCI who probably had the most influence upon the CIA's development, contended that the director ought to be an intelligence professional. Dulles believed that the DCI ought to be above politics and not linked to a specific presidential administration, even though the president appoints the DCI, subject to congressional approval, and one—Casey—had cabinet status.

Dulles's model was J. Edgar Hoover, who, when Dulles was DCI, had been FBI director since 1924 and had lasted through six presidential administrations, including changes from Republican to Democratic and back again. Dulles almost succeeded in carrying his point, being retained by President Kennedy, but in due course the Bay of Pigs fiasco resulted in his replacement. Richard Helms also managed to survive a change in political parties in the White House, but the Watergate affair proved his undoing. Jimmy Carter and Ronald Reagan both changed DCIs upon taking office, but George Bush kept Webster on, a gesture in the direction of the Dulles concept. But in view of the Gates affair, the chances of a CIA careerist being appointed again are slim.

On the same row as the director in figure 17-2 are lines connecting him to the Office of National Estimates and to the deputy to the DCI, intelligence community. But in figure 16-1, these lines run instead to the national intelligence officers and the intelligence community staff. Moreover, in figure 17-4, the National Intelligence Council (comprising the NIOs in 1987) and the director, IC staff, appear. To explain the NIOs replaced the Office of National Estimates in 1973. The ONE, which had been created in 1950 to coordinate the production of National Intelligence Estimates (NIEs) within the IC, was not able to achieve its purpose. The departments and even the president and high-ranking officials scorned NIEs that did not sustain pet projects or policies. As a result, NIEs, which were supposed to be the highest form of finished intelligence, became pariahs in the IC. This was especially true during the Vietnam War. In 1973, national security chief Henry Kissinger, tired of the hassles that bogged down the estimates function and preferring succinct, short-term evaluations, replaced the ONE with NIOs, a small group of senior analysts, who could make brief assessments of foreign policy problems as they arose.[12] The NIOs were intended to be an IC function of the DCI rather than a responsibility of the CIA, which had previously maintained the ONE as a "service of common concern." The production of national intelligence remains a difficult problem to this day, as will be seen. More successful, the IC staff under a deputy to the DCI had the responsibility for managing interdepartmental intelligence activities and was not specifically a component of the CIA.

Below the director, the *deputy DCI* acts in the DCI's absence

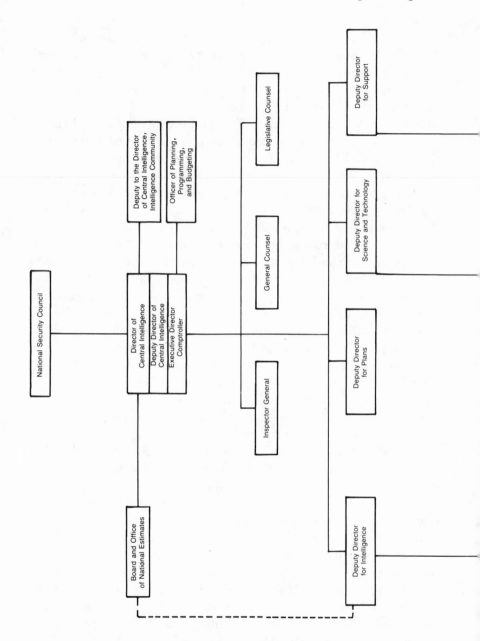

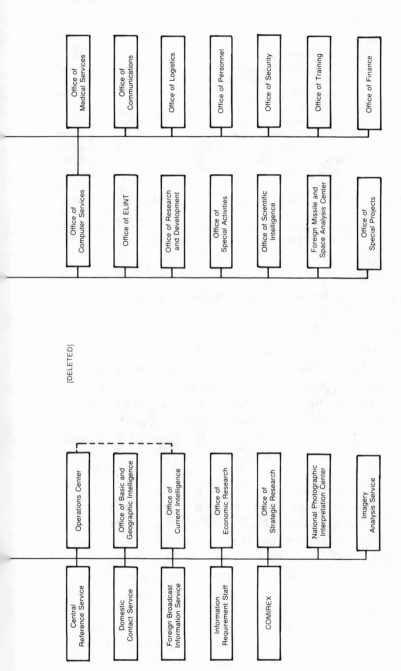

Source: U.S. Senate, Select Committee to Study Governmental Operations. *Supplementary Detailed Staff Reports on Foreign and Military Intelligence.* Report No. 94–755, book 4, 94th Cong., 2d sess., 1976.

Figure 17–2. *CIA Organization, 1972*

DCI/CIG:	RADM	Sidney W. Souers, USNR	(1–6/1946)
	LTGEN	Hoyt S. Vandenberg, USA	(1946–47)
DCI/CIA:	RADM	Roscoe H. Hillenkoetter, USN	(1947–50)
	GEN	Walter Bedell Smith, USA	(1950–53)
		Allen W. Dulles*	(1953–61)
		John A. McCone	(1961–65)
	VADM	William F. Raborn, Jr. (USN, Ret.)	(1965–66)
		Richard Helms*	(1966–73)
		James R. Schlesinger	(2–7/1973)
		William E. Colby*	(1973–76)
		George Bush	(1976–77)
	ADM	Stansfield Turner (USN, Ret.)	(1977–81)
		William J. Casey	(1981–87)
		Robert M. Gates, Acting DCI	(12/1986–4/1987)
		William H. Webster	(1987–)

*Served as DDP

Figure 17–3. *Directors of Central Intelligence and the CIA*

and serves as the CIA representative on IC committees, particularly the USIB/NFIB. The *executive director* is the chief administrative officer of the CIA, charged with the details of running the Agency as an organization. The director's staff includes the inspector general, the general counsel, and legislative counsel.

The *inspector general (IG)* "reports to the Director and assists him in his attempts to assure that CIA activities are consistent with the Agency's charter regulations and the Constitution and laws of the United States. In addition, the Office of the Inspector General has a wide range of responsibilities designed to improve the performance of CIA offices and personnel."[13] The IG requires reports, carries out inspections, has access to any information, and receives complaints and grievances from CIA personnel. Even though it is in-house, the IG's office could be extremely important for oversight if it functioned as intended. But this was not the case, at least for the first twenty-five years. The Rockefeller Commission report stated in 1975, "The Inspector General frequently was aware of many of the CIA's [abuses] . . . and brought them to the attention of the Director or other top management. The only program which was terminated as a result was one in 1963—involving experiments with behavior-modifying drugs on unknowing persons.''[14] But the problem was not just at the top. Former IG Peter Heimann stated in 1976, ''More unfortunate has been the growing tendency of IG reports to adjust their recommendations to the IG's estimate of what might be acceptable under the circumstances.''[15] Nonetheless, the IG has the responsibility to refer to the general counsel ''all matters involving legal questions.''

The *general counsel* serves as the director's chief legal adviser. He and his staff (originally ten attorneys but enlarged to approximately thirty by the mid-1970s) perform the legal tasks that any major organization requires—except that the CIA's mission and the peculiar situations of certain personnel complicate even the most routine case. Moreover, while the general counsel has a primary responsibility to determine ''the legality and propriety of CIA activities,'' he also has an ''obligation'' to assist the Agency in carrying out its programs: ''This dual responsibility with its potential for conflict is not in itself unique—almost any 'inside' counsel is in a similar position—but the secret and often sensitive nature of CIA activities does make protection of the independence of [the general counsel's] judgment particularly important.''[16] This potential for conflict (and opportunity for oversight) was reduced in practice because the general counsel's role has been ''essentially passive.'' Matters may be referred to him for an opinion, but he does not have the authority to initiate an investigation: ''During the 20-year course of the CIA's mail opening program [1952–72], the General Counsel was never asked for an opinion on its legality or propriety.''[17]

The legislative counsel also does the director's bidding. The *legislative counsel* is essentially the DCI's link with Congress. Though prohibited from lobbying, this staff organization monitors legislation on Capitol Hill that may affect the activities and interests of the CIA directly or indirectly. Before the congressional oversight committees were created in the mid-1970s and a more adversarial relationship developed, the CIA did more watching of the Congress than the reverse and probably exercised the greater influence. As Marchetti and Marks observed, ''Congressional control of the

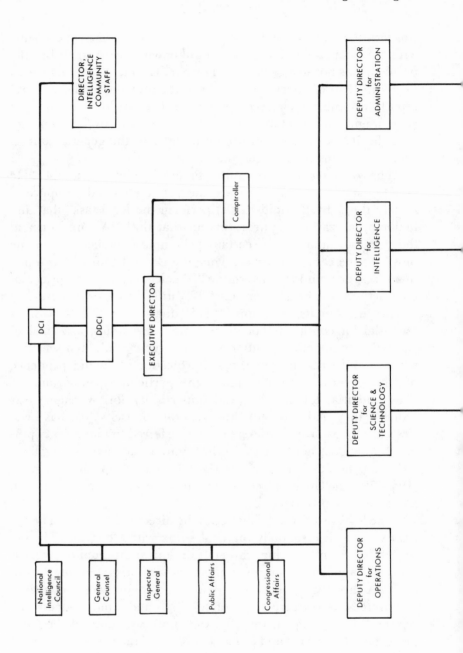

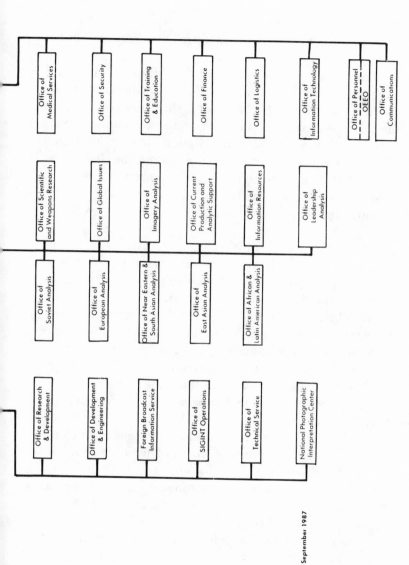

September 1987

Figure 17-4. *CIA Organization, 1987*

Office of Medical Services

Office of Security

Office of Training & Education

Office of Finance

Office of Logistics

Office of Information Technology

Office of Personnel
OEEO

Office of Communications

Office of Scientific and Weapons Research

Office of Global Issues

Office of Imagery Analysis

Office of Current Production and Analytic Support

Office of Information Resources

Office of Leadership Analysis

Office of Soviet Analysis

Office of European Analysis

Office of Near Eastern & South Asian Analysis

Office of East Asian Analysis

Office of African & Latin American Analysis

Office of Research & Development

Office of Development & Engineering

Foreign Broadcast Information Service

Office of SIGINT Operations

Office of Technical Service

National Photographic Interpretation Center

CIA can be broken down into two distinct periods: before and after Watergate.''[18]

Marchetti and Marks also referred to two additional staff units that do not appear on the chart in figure 17-2: the cable secretariat and the historical staff. The *cable secretariat* is the message or nerve center of the CIA, with responsibility for secure communications between Washington headquarters and stations in any location. ''Beedle'' Smith set it up as a staff function within the director's office in 1950, when he learned that the clandestine services were controlling Agency communications. He supposedly said, ''The operators are not going to decide what secret information I will see or not see.''[19]

The *historical staff* writes the official history of CIA. As part of this project, it retains CIA officers as consultants for a year or two after they retire, enabling them to ''tell their story'' and write their memoirs. This exercise preserves a vital record, even if it is secret for now, but Marchetti and Marks suggested that it serves another purpose as well: it provides a catharsis for former officers and helps prevent ''the battle-scared old hands'' from going public: ''[they] have gotten their frustrations out of their systems—with no harm done.''[20] The historical staff also aids in the publication of a professional quarter journal, *Studies in Intelligence,* which provides an outlet for writing and commentary by the Agency's research analysts and scholars. The historical staff has also helped to compile a CIA ''spy'' library, containing works of fiction as well as nonfiction. One of the early curators, ''a senior career official by trade but by avocation a bibliophile of some note,'' received a generous allotment ''to travel around the world in search of rare books and documents on espionage.''[21]

On the line beneath the DCI and his staff are the four deputy directors who divide the labor of the CIA even today (compare figures 17-2 and 17-4): for intelligence (DDI), for science and technology (DDS&T), for support (DDS; renamed ''management and services'' in 1973 and ''administration'' [DDA] in 1975), and for plans (DDP; renamed ''operations'' [DDO] in 1973).

The *Directorate of Intelligence* used the acronym DDI for the first twenty-five years of its existence (1952-77); it became the National Foreign Assessment Center (NFAC) for a while (1978-81), in a

Foreign Assessment Center (NFAC) for a while (1978–81), in a short-lived effort to become the analytical arm of the IC; since 1981, it has been known simply as the DI. The DDI had its roots in the offices that were intended to assist the DCI in coordinating the production of national intelligence. For reasons already discussed, it ended up as an intelligence producer itself, particularly of current intelligence, although it continued to provide certain "services of common concern" for the IC at large. The DDI presumed to fix its own role, but the 1976 report of the Senate Intelligence Committee described it as "by far the best analytical organization for the production of finished intelligence within the Government."[22] In many respects, the DDI was the true heir of the old Research and Analysis Branch of the OSS, comprising scholars from the humanities and the natural and social sciences. Allen Dulles enjoyed projecting this image, with his pipe and tweeds. Before the move to Langley, Dulles's DDI, Robert Amory, a former Harvard Law School professor, referred to the CIA's cluster of "temporary" buildings along the Potomac as his "campus" and compared the DDI to a research institute, though one enjoying special and unique sources.

The distinction between the DDI, described as "the clean tip of the iceberg,"[23] and the DDP, the clandestine side, underscored the CIA's split personality. The DDI differed from the DDP not only in function but in attitude and outlook. While the DDI comprised "academic and contemplative types" and was labeled as "liberal," the DDP was made up of "activists and risk-takers" who had a generally "conservative" political orientation.[24] These differences sometimes had serious consequences, as in the Bay of Pigs affair, wherein Dulles kept Amory in the dark because he was convinced that DDI analysts were sympathetic to Fidel Castro and that they would obstruct the contemplated action. Yet, according to Marchetti and Marks, if the DDI had not existed, the DDP would have had to invent it. The DDI was the DDP's "cover."[25] It was more than that, of course, but within the CIA power structure itself, like comedian Rodney Dangerfield, "it got no respect."

The organization of the Directorate of Intelligence (see figure 17-2 and figure 17-4) reveals that the acronym is not the only difference between the DDI and the DI. Whereas the DDI was a mix of intelligence production and services of common concern, the DI is engaged almost exclusively in production and analysis. Moreover, whereas the DDI principally focused upon the Soviet Union and Soviet bloc, the DI is organized for effective analysis of all world areas. The DDI emerged from the ONE and the ORR, the cold war shops for estimates intelligence and economic research of the Soviet bloc, respectively. The DI focuses on events in Iran, Nicaragua, Libya, and Afghanistan, with a heavy emphasis on current intelligence; it is policy-conscious. The DDI, the scholarly keeper of the estimates flame, was still linked to the Board and the Office of National Estimates in 1972 (figure 17-2), though they would cease to exist in a year.

Throughout the 1950s and 1960s, the ONE was a component of the DDI. Despite its select nature and small size, it seemed to represent the image of the DDI within the IC. The visible presence of such scholars as William Langer and Sherman Kent, as well as the Amorys, Bundys, and Clines, gave a particular Ivy League and "old-school-tie" cast to the ONE. Besides reviving some of the "professors *v.* generals" tensions of the OSS and World War II days, the perceived elitism of the ONE and the DDI had an ugly side as well. A 1964 study by the inspector general revealed that the ONE "had only men with the most proper bloodlines working there."[26] When conflicts subsequently developed over the divergence between NIEs (estimates) and policy, the vulnerability of the ONE contributed to its elimination. Nonetheless, the ONE's "old-boy" network model did not disappear overnight; it seemed to persist at least into the 1970s, when Marchetti and Marks wrote, "While changing times and ideas have diffused the influence of the Eastern élite throughout the government as a whole, the CIA remains perhaps the last bastion in official Washington of WASP power, or at least the slowest to adopt the principle of equal opportunity."[27]

However, the BNE and the ONE did not succumb only because of the CIA's need to become an equal opportunity employer. The ONE fell because of a basic philosophical conflict over the nature and role of research and analysis in the policy-making structure. At Henry Kissinger's insistence, William Colby abolished the ONE in 1973, replacing it with individual national intelligence officers—experts in particular world areas who were capable of providing instant analyses of fast-breaking developments. Kissinger wanted situation reporting, not seminar papers— a view that Colby apparently shared, stating, "I had sensed an ivory-tower mentality in the Board."[28]

Given the persistent difficulties of the ONE, the *Office of Current Intelligence (OCI)* became the centerpiece of the DDI's intelligence production effort and, in time, the model for the reorganization of the DI. Organized into country desks or geographic branches, the OCI's analysts, who were highly trained area and international relations specialists, produced finished intelligence of international political developments on a daily, ongoing basis. Though OCI reports appeared in a variety of forms, the best-known products were the *Current Intelligence Bulletin* (its daily report, covering the world political arena) and the *Current Intelligence Digest* (described as a classified *Time* or *Newsweek*). With the move to even more "relevant" action-oriented intelligence reporting in 1981, the OCI's geographic branches became separate regional analytical offices (figure 17–4), though multidisciplinary in scope.

The regional offices (such as the Offices of Soviet Analysis, European Analysis, and Near Eastern and South Asian Analysis) not only assumed the analytical functions of the parent OCI but merged with certain of the DDI's other functional offices as well (the Office of Basic and Geographic Intelligence and the Office of Economic Research). Each was given a competency in political, geographic, economic, sociological, and biographic analysis. The OCI's editorial and service functions became the DI's Office of Current Production and Analytical Support (OCP), essentially an editorial board and publications service for the DI's intelligence reports and CIA maps, charts, graphics, and documents. The top of the line was the *President's Daily Brief* and the *National Intelligence Daily.* The OCP also took over the OCI's management of the CIA's twenty-four-hour Operations Center, the mechanism and facility for mobilizing "the full information resources of CIA to work in concert with the [IC] in foreign crisis situations."[29]

For most of twenty-five years after 1952, the DDI performed certain services of common concern such as:

Domestic Contacts Service (DCS), for the debriefing of private persons in the United States returning from trips abroad, especially from high-interest or "denied" target areas;

Foreign Broadcast Information Service (FBIS), for the monitoring and transcription of foreign shortwave broadcasts, including foreign government news and propaganda broadcasts and dissident and clandestine radio broadcasts;

National Photographic Interpretation Center (NPIC), a community-wide service in cooperation with the DIA for the analysis of overhead reconnaissance photographs;

COMIREX, or *Committee on Imagery Requirements and Exploitation*, a USIB subcommittee established in 1967 for tasking in the operation of overhead reconnaissance systems;

Imagery Analysis Service (IAS), an in-house photo intelligence service for the CIA, organized in 1967 to supplement the NPIC, with heavy national intelligence responsibilities;

Central Reference Service (CRS), a highly sophisticated storage and retrieval system that served as a national intelligence archive.

Within the DI, only Central Reference and Imagery Analysis remain, upgraded to offices and geared to the analytical mission. The DI also reorganized the former Office of Strategic Research (the CIA's "excuse" for military intelligence)[30] and Office of Scientific Intelligence (recovered from the Directorate of Science and Technology) into the *Office of Scientific and Weapons Research*, which combined the assessment of foreign weapons and space systems with overall analysis of scientific and technological developments throughout the world. The DI also created two more functional analytical offices: *global issues* (for topics such as insurgency, narcotics trafficking, and terrorism that do not fit within national or regional borders) and *leadership analysis* (for biographical studies and methodologies for determining regime/political stability). At various times even before 1981, the DDI's communitywide services involving collection, technical analysis, and tasking were transferred out. "Contacts" went over to the Directorate of Operations, COMIREX and tasking went to the IC staff, and FBIS and NPIC went to the Directorate of Science and Technology. Moving FBIS and NPIC to DDS&T, in fact, continued a process begun in 1962.

John McCone, who became DCI in 1961, created the *Directorate of Science and Technology (DDS&T)* in 1963, in response to new opportunities for technical collection and to certain problems that the CIA had been experiencing. The rapid developments in space technology and electronics, coupled with the Bay of Pigs failure and the critical role of aerial reconnaissance in the Cuban missile crisis, caused McCone to seek to modernize the CIA and change its cloak-and-dagger image, which he considered out of date. Even so, he had difficulty in achieving the reorganization.

In 1961, scientific and technical intelligence operations were scattered among the three Directorates. The reconnaissance component had been transferred to the DDP under the title Development Projects Division (DPD); in the DDI, the Office of Scientific Intelligence conducted basic scientific and technological research; the Technical Services Division of the DDP engaged in research and development to provide operational support for clandestine activities; and the Office of ELINT [electronics intelligence] in the DDP was responsible for electronic intercepts. Organizing an independent directorate meant wresting manpower and resources from existing components. The resistance was considerable, and a year and a half passed between the first attempt at creating the directorate and its actual establishment.[31]

Not only did McCone build the DDS&T with parts taken from the DDI and the DDP; the new directorate also enjoyed a more open relationship with elements outside of the Agency. While the DDS&T remained relatively small (approximately thirteen hundred persons in 1974), it supplemented its workforce through external contracts, engaging the resources of the scientific and industrial community. The DDS&T's essentially overt responsibilities included both intelligence and operations, paralleling in a sense the distinction between pure and applied science. Diverse in its functions during its early days, the key offices of DDS&T were those (see figure 17–2) that developed and even operated new technical collection systems.

One of these was the *Office of Research and Development (R&D)*. Even before the creation of the S&T directorate, while still part of the DDP, the engineers and scientists of R&D were responsible for major successes in inventing new machines for collecting intelligence. Beginning in 1954, under the direction of Dulles's special assistant (later DDP), Richard Bissell, and in collaboration with Lockheed Aircraft Corporation, the CIA built the prototype of the U-2 airplane at the so-called Skonk Works (à la Li'l Abner), an isolated facility in the California desert. This gave a CIA the lead in overhead reconnaissance; soon even that was topped by the A-11 (SR-71), which could fly higher than the U-2's eighty thousand feet and exceed a speed three times that of sound, and next by space satellites. R&D also developed "other technical espionage techniques, such as over-the-horizon radars, 'stationary' satellites, and various other electronic information-gathering devices."[32]

This activity was eventually formalized within DDS&T by the offices of *Development Projects* and *Special Activities.* Development Projects involved building prototypes of technical collection systems, and Special Activities exercised operational control over particular systems (as in the case of the U-2 earlier).

Generally, however, despite McCone's effort to strengthen the CIA's role in technical collection, the Agency was no match for the Pentagon. Whereas the DOD was spending over $4 billion annually in the early 1970s on technical collection and employed tens of thousands of people, the CIA's annual budget for technical programs during the same period amounted to only $150 million, and the DDS&T employed fifteen hundred people.[33] More than a decade later, the DS&T was still lean but better focused—the offices of Development Projects and Special Activities being replaced by the *Office of Development and Engineering* (figure 17-4); its job, as it described itself, was "to identify, develop, and apply technology to promote the collection, analysis, and dissemination of intelligence."

Just as the Directorate of Science and Technology was outclassed by the Pentagon, Intelligence was eclipsed by Operations within the CIA itself. After twenty-five years of experience, the clandestine side accounted for about two-thirds of the CIA's budget and personnel.

> Out of the agency's career work force of roughly 16,500 people [in 1974] and yearly budget of about $750 million, 11,000 personnel and roughly $550 million are earmarked for the Clandestine Services

and those activities of the Directorate of Management and Services
. . . which contribute to covert activities. Only about 20 percent of
the CIA's career employees (spending less than 10 percent of the
budget) work on intelligence analysis and information processing.[34]

In reviewing the work of the Intelligence and S&T directorates,
it is difficult to believe that they do not constitute the mainstream
of the CIA. Certainly, Intelligence has created the mechanism for
avoiding another Pearl Harbor. Yet examining the development of
the CIA's clandestine side reveals the true meaning of the figures
comparing Intelligence and Operations above. The most recent
literature on this topic demonstrates that more personnel and funds
continue to be devoted to clandestine operations than to intelligence. In the mid-1980s, writing about who gets ahead at the
CIA, Glenn P. Hastedt found that in two areas of the CIA's motivation system, "the nature of the training program" and "the
skills, roles, and career paths being emphasized," "high-quality
intelligence is not being emphasized in either area."[35]

Intelligence is like the piano player in the brothel. It adds a
touch of class to the place, but had nothing to do with what is going
on upstairs.

18

The Clandestine CIA

A s complex and expert as the CIA became in producing intelligence, having assembled an impressive array of research analysts and specialists, the intelligence side of the Agency was not where the action was. For most of the first thirty years, Clandestine Services was the glamour side of the Agency, as well as its dominant force. The CIA, indeed, became an integral part of American foreign policy by serving as its "invisible arm." Although, as Lyman Kirkpatrick wrote, "throughout history . . . intelligence organizations have attempted to obtain secrets, influence political developments, or conduct insurgency on foreign soil,"[1] it was not until the CIA came into existence that the United States really had the capability to perform these functions in peacetime. The combination of the cold war, wherein the United States perceived covert intervention as necessary, and the personality of Allen Dulles, the "quintessential case officer" sitting in the director's chair, enhanced its clandestine capabilities and made them central to the mission of the CIA.

Dulles, according to David Wise and Thomas Ross, placed his "personal stamp" on the CIA more than anyone else.[2] He made the Directorate of Plans "preeminent" within the CIA: "Rather than functioning in a strict support role to the State and Defense Departments, [through Dulles's buildup of the DDP] the CIA assumed the initiative in defining the ways covert operations could advance U.S. policy objectives and in determining what kinds of operations were suited to particular policy needs."[3] Dulles's success was facilitated tremendously by the fact that his older brother, John Foster, was the secretary of state. The Dulles brothers constituted an extraordinary team, with John Foster taking the "high road" and Allen, as he once stated on "Meet the Press," able "to fight fire with fire."[4] Such a capability had grave implications in the light of the nature of the opposition, as Dulles assessed it:

> In the Soviet Union, we are faced with an antagonist who has raised the art of espionage to an unprecedented height, while developing the collateral techniques of subversion, deception, and penetration into a formidable political instrument of attack. . . .
>
> [The KGB] is an instrument for subversion, manipulation and violence, for secret intervention in the affairs of other countries.
>
> [The Soviet intelligence officer] is blindly and unquestioningly dedicated to the cause. . . . He has been fully indoctrinated in the political and philosophical beliefs of communism and in the basic "morality" which proceeds from those beliefs. This morality holds that the ends alone count, and that any means that achieve them are justified.[5]

Any comparison of the CIA with the KGB (Komitet Gosudarstvennoy Bezopasnosti) may seem outrageous. But "fighting fire with fire," as explained by General James H. "Jimmy" Doolittle, seems to have meant just that. Doolittle, who at the behest of President Eisenhower headed a secret NSC "Special Study Group on Covert Activities," reported on September 30, 1954, that "there are no rules in such a game. Hitherto accepted norms of human conduct do not apply."

> If the United States is to survive, long-standing American concepts of "fair play" must be reconsidered. We must develop effective espionage and counter-espionage services and must learn to subvert, sabotage and destroy our enemies by more clever, more sophisticated, and more effective methods than those used against us. It may become necessary that the American people be made acquainted with, understand and support this fundamentally repugnant philosophy.[6]

According to authors Stephen Ambrose and John Prados, Eisenhower shared this viewpoint and became "intimately involved" in covert operations.[7] "He intended to fight the Communists just as he had fought the Nazis, on every battlefront, with every available weapon."[8] Thus, while Allen Dulles placed his "personal stamp" on the CIA, President Eisenhower has been described as the "hidden hand." He established the 5412 Group, the first formal mechanism at the policy level for managing covert operations.

> At the strategic nuclear level, Eisenhower did his best to resist a stampeding arms race and avoid war with the Soviet Union. But, as the man who institutionalized covert operations, Eisenhower does not appear the moderate, even liberal, Republican who seems to be emerging from historical reappraisal.[9]

To appreciate these developments and to follow the unfolding of events in the remaining chapters, it is essential to understand the secret structure that Eisenhower and Allen Dulles built.

The chart in figure 18–1, showing the organization of the *Directorate of Operations (DDO)* or *Clandestine Services* in 1973, is one of the few depictions of the clandestine CIA available to outsiders. It is essentially the same organization that functioned as the *Directorate of Plans (DDP)* from 1952 to 1972[10]; nor in its basic features is it very different from the DO today.[11]

Clandestine Services divides its labor into the three top-tier staffs shown: Foreign Intelligence, Counterintelligence, and Covert Action. These staffs support the area divisions that administer the CIA stations and bases in the field. They are supplemented by certain headquarters technical divisions that also render overall assistance to the area divisions and field stations.

The task of *Foreign Intelligence (FI)* is the clandestine collection of intelligence, "obtaining secrets" in the traditional way, by building spy nets and managing agents. Because the Soviet Union has been a closed society, constituting a vast "denied area," FI has not had a great deal of success there. This has led to the machine "taking over"; that is, to reliance upon technical collection.

But the machine could not replace the human operative in *Counterintelligence (CI)*, although CI has remained small, specialized, and mysterious. CI is the stuff of James Bond novels, involving countermeasures (a security function) against a rival nation's spies and dirty tricksters achieved, in part, by penetrating its intelligence service (counterespionage).[12] CI services are on the front

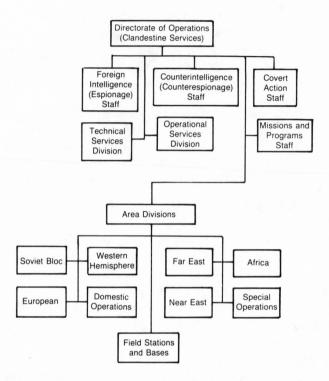

Source: Victor Marchetti and John D. Marks, *The CIA and the Cult of Intelligence* (New York: Alfred A. Knopf, 1974), p. 69. Reprinted with permission.

Figure 18-1. *CIA, Directorate of Operations, 1973*

lines. In confronting the Soviets, CI, unlike FI, is not hamstrung by the tight security within the USSR, because *outside* the Soviet Union KGB officers are "the most accessible and least supervised of all Soviet citizens . . . [and], therefore, potentially the most recruitable."[13] Among the few publicized CI cases are the controversial defections of Soviet intelligence officers Oleg Penkovsky and Vitaly Yurchenko, incidents that conjure images of, in Ladislav Farago's phrase, "the game of the foxes."

For a long time, the CI staff ran counterintelligence at the CIA. This paralleled the career of James Angleton, the chief of Counterintelligence from 1954 to 1974. Angleton began with X-2 in Italy in

World War II, as described so well by Robin Winks in *Cloak and Gown* (1987). A mysterious, almost sinister figure, maintaining "deep cover," Angleton exemplified CI's passion for secrecy and compartmentalization. He created an organization within an organization, which ultimately cost him his job in the fallout after Watergate, when passion for secrecy fell on hard times. Angleton "retired" in December 1974 in sharp disagreement with DCI William Colby's new approach: "emphasizing a diffusion of CI responsibilities throughout the Operations Directorate."[14] Ten years later, the number of Americans arrested for spying suggests that Angleton was doing something right.

Since CI was small by choice and FI was losing out to machines, the CIA may have emphasized *Covert Action (CA)* in order to survive.[15] Actually, the opportunity to do so was clear; American policymakers adopted covert action as an essential weapon in the struggle against communism. The United States, perceiving the need to influence the course of events without appearing to do so, intervened in other countries' affairs using methods that were "concealed, secret, disguised, and nonattributable."[16] According to Richard Bissell, the DDP from 1958 to 1962 (as quoted by Marchetti and Marks), such methods or tactics took the following forms:

1. political advice and counsel;

2. subsidies to an individual;

3. financial support and "technical assistance" to political parties;

4. support of private organizations, including labor unions, business firms, cooperatives, etc.;

5. covert propaganda;

6. "private" training of individuals and exchange of persons;

7. economic operations;

8. paramilitary [or] political action operations designed to overthrow or to support a regime.[17]

These various tactics, running the gamut from bribing a politician ("subsidies to an individual") to adulterating a shipment of Cuban sugar ("economic operations"), will be examined in subsequent chapters in connection with specific episodes and events. It is helpful to understand here that the CA staff, like CI, conducted operations in the field while it also served as an "advisory and coordinating" body for the dirty tricks performed by the geographic divisions.[18]

Supporting these three key staffs of Clandestine Services are the *Missions and Programs Staff,* which handles most of the paperwork, preparing budgets and working out administrative details; the *Operational Services Division,* which has responsibility for providing the "big stuff"—planes, tanks, and bazookas—and for setting up complex "cover" arrangements; and the *Technical Services Division (TSD),* which develops and provides the "tools of the trade," as well as having on call certain specialists, such as safecrackers and experts in "flaps and seals" (mail opening).[19]

The TSD maintains an inventory of spy gadgetry and paraphernalia, including cameras, "bugs," special weaponry and explosives, and disguises. It was the TSD that furnished White House "plumber" E. Howard Hunt with a miniature camera concealed in a tobacco pouch, a voice-distorting device, and a red wig to aid him in investigating "leaks" in 1971 in connection with the activities of ITT lobbyist Dita Beard. In the same year, after the Plumbers "cased" the office of Dr. Lewis J. Fielding, the psychiatrist of Daniel Ellsberg (who leaked the Pentagon Papers), it was the TSD that processed the photographs they took in anticipation of the break-in. The TSD provided the bulk of the equipment used in clandestine operations and other episodes from the 1950s to the 1970s. In the continual reorganizing within the CIA, the TSD was transferred to the Directorate of Science and Technology in 1973 and renamed the Office of Technical Service (see figure 17–4).

Beneath the staff level are the *Area Divisions,* which are in charge of clandestine operations in the field (see figure 18–1). Responsibility is divided along geographical lines, but the *Domestic Operations (DOD), International Organizations (IOD)* (not shown in figure 18–1), and *Special Operations (SOD)* divisions require further explanation. Although the CIA has no domestic surveillance or internal security functions and may not engage in domestic operations, it has secretly used private American citizens and residents and private and public U.S. institutions and organizations in carrying out its foreign intelligence mission. In time, Domestic Operations became one of the most controversial aspects of CIA activity, particularly when it seemed to intrude upon the free functioning of American affairs and institutions.

Always cloaked in the tightest secrecy, the DOD's covert use of academic and voluntary organizations, publishing firms, and refugee centers nonetheless came to light during the U.S. Senate select committee investigation of intelligence activities in 1975 and 1976. (*Ramparts* magazine had already exposed some of these activities in 1967; see chapter 19.) Its operations had included hiring the resources of Michigan State University between 1955 and 1959 to conduct a police-training program in South Vietnam: "The agency paid $25 million to the university for its service, and five CIA operators were concealed in the program's staff."[20] More tricky, it paid subsidies to respected firms, such as Frederick A. Praeger, a New York and London publisher, in the period before 1967 for the publication of books by favored scholars and foreign affairs specialists, either witting or unwitting, on the premise that "books [are] the most important weapon of strategic (long-range) propaganda."[21] And DOD case officers collaborated with émigré and refugee groups in certain American cities—Cubans in Miami and various Eastern Europeans in Chicago and New York—to carry out clandestine operations abroad.

In much the same way, the International Organizations Division used private international organizations—a number of them based in the United States—as instruments of covert action in foreign policy. These organizations, representing such diverse interests as students and youth, labor unions, community development, health care, and freedom of the press and human rights, were rarely aware of CIA sponsorship. In fact, many of them were part of the non-Communist Left and strongly opposed certain foreign governments that were considered U.S. allies at the time. The contradiction between official U.S. foreign policy and the one being carried out by the IOD caused consternation and controversy when the American public became aware of it in the mid-1960s.

The IOD provided funding to organizations that were out-spoken in their criticism of U.S. foreign policy and that would have been outraged to know that they were receiving CIA support (although in some cases insiders knew what was going on). In order to conceal its involvement, the IOD devised the "pass-through," a means of channeling money through several conduits before it reached the intended beneficiary. The CIA would create a phony foundation that was little more than a post office box; it would con-tribute funds for a particular purpose to a legitimate foundation that was known to support certain causes and to have the necessary connections; the legitimate foundation finally passed the money to the organizations that the CIA wanted to favor in the first place.

Since the IOD seemed to be fomenting change in countries where the United States was officially supporting the status quo, the purported split between "DDI liberalism" and "DDP/DDO conservativism" was not really that clean. From 1950 to 1954, the chief of the IOD was Tom Braden, a former OSS operative and liberal journalist. (Thirty years later, Braden sat "on the left" in the Cable News Network program *Crossfire*.) His successor for the rest of the 1950s and into the 1960s was Cord Meyer, who had lost an eye in World War II combat and came out of the war dedicated to the cause of world federalism. Ray Cline, who became DDI in 1961, had earlier been station chief in Taiwan.

But there was less doubt about where the Special Operations Division stood politically.

> By definition, special ops are violent and brutal; most clandestine operators prefer more refined techniques. The CIA professional is a flimflam artist, involved in the creative challenge of plotting and orchestrating a clandestine campaign without resorting to violence. In such nonparamilitary covert action, the operator tends to keep his hands unbloodied, and his crimes are of the white-collar variety—conspiracy, bribery, corruption. His fail-ure or exposure is normally punished only with expulsion from the country where he is operating. He is, in the end, merely engaging in a "gentleman's" game. The paramilitary operator on the contrary, is a gangster who deals in force, in terror, in vio-lence. Failure can mean death—if not to the operator himself, then to the agents he has recruited. The SOD man wages war,

albeit on a small and secret level, but none of the rules of warfare apply. His is a breed apart; in the CIA, special ops types are sometimes referred to as the "animals" of the agency.[22]

Special Operations engaged in the most direct and aggressive form of intervention—military action designed to overthrow a regime or prop it up. It helped President Joseph Mobutu put down a rebellion in the Congo in 1964 and, during most of the 1960s and early 1970s, conducted a "secret" war in Laos, equipping and maintaining an army of over thirty thousand men at an annual cost of approximately $500 million.[23] SOD operatives trained for clandestine warfare at Camp Peary, near Williamsburg, Virginia (dubbed The Farm by CIA insiders). Calling Camp Peary "the CIA's West Point," Marchetti and Marks described the training as "oriented toward such paramilitary activities as infiltration/exfiltration, demolitions, and nighttime parachute jumps."[24]

To carry out special operations and other covert actions, Clandestine Services created organizations outside the Agency, known as *proprietaries*. These seemingly private commercial or nonprofit entities were wholly owned and managed by the CIA for facilitating and providing cover for clandestine operations. There were two types of proprietaries. Operating companies actually served the general public and even generated income; nonoperating companies appeared to be doing business but actually performed services exclusively for the CIA.[25] The proprietaries do not appear on the chart in figure 18–1 but could occupy a disconnected box floating next to "Field Stations and Bases." According to Marchetti and Marks, CIA officers referred to proprietaries as "Delaware corporations," since the Agency took advantage of the "lenient" laws of incorporation in that state.[26]

The CIA's best-known proprietaries were Radio Free Europe and Radio Liberty, both established in the early 1950s. The corporate structures of these two stations served as something of a prototype for other agency proprietaries. Each functioned under the cover provided by a board of directors made up of prominent Americans, who in the case of RFE incorporated as the National Committee for a Free Europe and in the case of RL as the American Committee for Liberation. But CIA officers in the key man-

agement positions at the stations made all the important decisions regarding the programming and operations of the stations.[27]

Unsuspecting Americans responded to public appeals and contributed money for the work of Radio Free Europe—"broadcasting
the truth to the people of Eastern Europe"—but the truth is that
RFE did not need a dime of their money. The CIA covered 95 percent of the radio station's expenses.

Another well-known company that is suspected of being a proprietary (at least until the mid-1960s) is the International Armaments Corporation (Interarmco), with headquarters on the banks
of the Potomac in Alexandria, Virginia. Founded in 1953 by
Samuel Cummings, a former CIA operative, Interarmco was the
subject of two feature stories by the *Washington Post,* whose headlines told a lot: "Need a Weapon? Visit Interarmco. . . . Your
Friendly Neighborhood Merchant of Death" (October 31, 1965);
and " 'Old' Weapons Turned to Gold by Ex-CIA Man" (January
16, 1966). In the first story, the *Post* noted that the Russians had
denounced Interarmco as an "arm" of the CIA and observed,
"Regardless of the truth or falsity of that, both sides in the cold war
obviously must use a variety of means in their giant chess game of
limited arming of friends and nonfriends to promote larger goals."

There was never any confusion, however, about the status of
the CIA's air proprietaries. The CIA had absolute control over a
number of "airlines" from the 1950s to the mid-1970s. These provided logistical support and air power for clandestine operations
worldwide. Beginning with Civil Air Transport (CAT), which
operated out of Taiwan and was organized as a Delaware corporation in 1950, the CIA expanded its holdings to include Air America
(which operated in Southeast Asia and grew huge with the American involvement in Vietnam), Air Asia (a major repair and maintenance facility based on Taiwan), Southern Air Transport (SAT,
acquired in 1963, a Miami-based carrier for Latin American operations), and Intermountain Aviation (a parking, repair, and maintenance facility and "charter service" operating from a private air-
field near Tucson, Arizona).

These proprietaries were in some cases highly profitable. In
time, this led legitimate carriers to complain of unfair competition,

and the issue of "back-door" funding of covert operations was raised. During the 1960s, for example, the CIA's airlines converted from propeller to jet aircraft more readily than commercial operators did and had on hand a large number of personnel, including well-paid pilots: "At its peak, Air America, the Agency's largest proprietary, had total assets of some $50 million and directly employed more than 5,600 individuals (the total number of employees for the Air America complex was in excess of 8,000)."[28] Air Asia, which operated repair and maintenance shops on Taiwan and serviced U.S. Air Force planes under contract, employed another eight thousand people, particularly during the Vietnam conflict.

Although the CIA continues to own proprietaries for covert action, it had divested itself of most of its air proprietaries by 1975. (Or so it would seem; SAT, supposedly sold off in 1973, still figured prominently in the secret airlift of arms and supplies to the Nicaraguan contras in the mid-1980s.) One reason for disposing of the airlines was their very success. "Size was a problem and made it 'inevitable that cover would not last.'"[29] Apparently their success stemmed from the entrepreneurial skills of the CIA man in charge, George Doole. Doole, taking his cue from the wheeler-dealers of a bygone era, organized a holding company, the Pacific Corporation, to control an "empire" in the Far East that was larger than the CIA itself.

> Doole was known to his colleagues in the agency as a superb businessman. He had a talent for expanding his airlines and for making them, functionally if not formally, into profit-making concerns. In fact, his proprietaries proved something of an embarrassment to the agency because of their profitability. While revenues never quite covered all the costs to the CIA of the original capital investment, the huge contracts with U.S. government agencies resulting from the war in Indochina made the Pacific Corporation's holdings (CAT, Air America, and Air Asia) largely self-sufficient during the 1960s. Consequently, the CIA was largely spared having to pay in any new money for specific projects.[30]

But their size and profitability were not the only problems of the air proprietaries. Allegations were persistently made that they

(Air America, in particular) engaged in drug trafficking as part of a CIA policy "to make profits which could be used to fund operations."[31] The Church Committee, investigating these charges, concluded that they were untrue, although it conceded that CIA planes, as private charters, may have been unwitting instruments in the widespread heroin trade in Southeast Asia. Similarly, over a decade later, rumors circulated that SAT planes involved in the secret arms shipments to the contras were also involved in drug smuggling; again, it was suggested that because covert operations can bypass law enforcement officials, they may be preyed upon by the company they keep.

Although the proprietaries have been treated here as components of the Directorate of Operations, it is quite likely that they also made up part of the *Directorate of Support (DDS)*, which was called the Directorate of Administration (DDA) after 1975. For example, Marchetti and Marks affirm that Doole's Pacific Corporation was "formally" located within the DDS. They claim, furthermore, that the DDS was the "slave" of Clandestine Services. Accordingly, though the support directorate (see figures 17–2 and 17–4) performs administrative services for the entire Agency, "most of its budget and personnel is devoted to assisting the Clandestine Services in carrying out covert operations."[32]

> Support functions are often vital for successful conduct of covert operations, and a good support officer, like a good supply sergeant in an army, is indispensable to a CIA station or base. Once a station chief has found the right support officer, one who can provide everything from housekeeping to operational support, the two will often form a professional alliance and stay together as they move from post to post during their careers. In some instances the senior support officer may even serve as the *de facto* second-in-command because of his close relationship with the chief.[33]

The DDS/DDA thus exhibits the same split personality as the CIA as a whole; its visible side displays the expected, and its hidden side conceals a deep involvement in Operations. With this in mind, and referring to figures 17–2 and 17–4, the components of DDS/DDA may be surveyed.

The *Office of Finance* is responsible for budgetary and accounting procedures Agencywide. But in support of covert action, it can "launder" money, manage secret bank accounts, and engage in black-market operations to acquire foreign currencies.

The *Office of Security* performs security functions: it physically protects the workspace and is responsible for clearance of CIA personnel at all locations (headquarters, field stations, and bases). It assigns polygraph operators where CIA case officers request them to "clear" foreign agents and contract personnel for participation in espionage and covert action.

The *Office of Training* provides ongoing programs for training in everything from clerical skills to tradecraft, but its principal effort has been its junior-officer training program, which has been publicized by Patrick McGarvey and Philip Agee. The eight-month training program was characterized by McGarvey as "an admixture of common sense, insanity, old-time religion, and some of the weirdest lectures you can imagine." The stress upon the importance of intelligence was so intense, he related, "that we became total loyalists. . . . Because of my indoctrination, I still get a visceral twinge [ten years later]—and have qualms of conscience about writing this book."[34] Agee's *Diary* left nothing to the imagination: he described an orientation program designed to acquaint junior officer trainees with the mission and organization of the CIA and rendered a thorough account of the paramilitary training at ISOLATION, which was then the cryptonym for Camp Peary in Virginia.

The *Office of Logistics* assigns space and provides office furniture and equipment at headquarters. It provides the same service in the field while maintaining cover—a demanding job. Its tasks of transporting goods and personnel abroad and providing secure living quarters involve it intimately with Clandestine Services. When unfriendly persons disclosed the identity and residence of Richard Welch, the CIA station chief in Athens, it contributed to his murder in 1975. Given the evidence that Logistics is responsible for warehousing and transporting Agency weapons and "esoteric clandestine matériel,"[35] it is reasonable to conclude that it operates through proprietaries like the Pacific Corporation, if not exercising actual jurisdiction over them, and is linked closely to the Technical

Services and Operational Services divisions in the Operations or Science and Technology directorates.

The *Office of Communications* "maintains facilities for secret communications between CIA headquarters and the hundreds of stations and bases overseas."[36] Within Langley itself, it is responsible for installing and managing a network of secure internal telephones and information systems.

The *Office of Medical Services* handles medical emergencies (having an operating room at the Langley headquarters) and in more normal situations provides its employees with lists of "cleared" doctors, dentists, and specialists, including psychiatrists. The nature and extent of medical services and benefits are part of what has been called "the Agency culture." During routine surgery or dental work, when an employee may be anesthetized and hence become a potential security risk, the Agency is there literally to hold the patient's hand. If an employee requires psychiatric treatment—mental breakdowns are not uncommon in the stressful atmosphere of intelligence work—such care is monitored and special facilities are made available. The Agency provides medical insurance and benefits, since security considerations proscribe the use of such private plans as Blue Cross/Blue Shield. One of the major proprietaries that the Agency maintained for a time was its so-called insurance complex, which provided not only health insurance but all types of accident and liability coverage for persons who were "uninsurable" because of cover or hazardous activities.[37]

The *Office of Personnel* provides services by which the Agency "takes care of its own." Even spies and dirty tricksters accumulate annual and sick leave and have to be evaluated for promotions and salary increments. But the usual personnel tasks of recruitment, record keeping, career development, and activities and services go well beyond the ordinary at the CIA. The CIA does not operate under civil service regulations, but its relationship to the people in its service is special, to say the least. McGarvey entitled one chapter in *C.I.A.: The Myth and the Madness,* "I Owe My Soul to the Company Store," to demonstrate the pervasive role that the CIA plays in the lives of its employees.

Personnel provides or arranges services ranging from car loans and home mortgages to life insurance and funerals. On their own,

CIA employees may have difficulty even applying for something as simple as a library card, because information on their employer is restricted—even the size of the CIA is classified information. Personnel organizes social and recreational activities, including bowling leagues, tennis and golf tournaments, and interest groups of every kind, so that employees may truly relax and not have to answer the question, "Where do you work?" The CIA, as a great support group, has tolerant views about drinking ("an occupational hazard") and about the "problems" that can develop as a result of performing a pressure-cooker job under conditions of tight security and imposed anonymity. It is clear that within the CIA, loyalty is a two-way street.[38]

This may explain the response of Watergate burglar James McCord to efforts to blame "The Company" for Watergate. A nineteen-year veteran of the CIA, McCord warned the White House to cease or else, and he declared, "Every tree in the forest will fall. It will be a scorched desert."[39] Such esprit de corps is good for security because contented employees are less apt to defect; but McCord's attitude also demonstrates the degree to which the CIA spins a cocoon around itself and its employees. The clandestine CIA, in particular, flourished in the cold war atmosphere but tended to lose perspective in going about its business.

In its first fifteen years, mostly under the influence of Allen Dulles, the CIA developed both by choice and by circumstance. It abandoned the Pearl Harbor watch to take a more active role as the covert arm of U.S. foreign policy. It became America's secret cold war weapon for combating communism, using covert action to influence events in other countries, going beyond diplomacy but avoiding open intervention and the criticism it would have drawn. As Allen Dulles expressed it, "Where there begins to be evidence that a country is slipping and a Communist takeover is threatened . . . we can't wait for an engraved invitation to come and give aid."[40] Under his stewardship, the CIA became most adept at rendering "aid" uninvited.

19

The New Interventionism

The High Contracting Parties declare inadmissible the intervention of any one of them, directly or indirectly, and for whatever reason, in the internal or external affairs of any other of the Parties.

Additional Protocol Relative to Non-Intervention,
Buenos Aires, December 23, 1936

. . . to establish conditions under which justice and respect for the obligations arising from treaties and other sources of international law can be maintained, . . .
to develop friendly relations among nations based on respect for the principle of equal rights and self-determination of peoples, . . .
The Organization is based on the principle of the sovereign equality of all its members.

Charter of the United Nations,
San Francisco, June 26, 1945

We believe that all peoples who are prepared for self-government should be permitted to choose their own form of government by their own freely expressed choice, without interference from any foreign source.

President Harry S Truman,
New York, October 27, 1945

W henever the political situation in the Caribbean region appeared unstable during the first three decades of the twentieth century, the U.S. response was "send in the marines" and restore order. Its use of the "big stick" engendered a great deal of ill will toward the United States in the Caribbean and Latin America. This caused the United States in time to subscribe to the principle of nonintervention and promote the broader goal of the good neighbor. It took another step away from "gunboat diplomacy" during World War II, when it condemned, among other things, the position of the Axis powers that treaties are "mere scraps of paper." This inclination to take a legalistic-moralistic approach to international relations did not endure, however, because the United States and the Soviet Union ended World War II as serious rivals, not as partners.

The United States and the Soviet Union both engaged in military intervention of varying kinds after the war. American forces continued to occupy former enemy territories in Germany, Japan, Taiwan, and Korea, and the United States established military bases abroad as it implemented such policies as the Truman Doctrine (which provided economic and military aid to Greece and Turkey), the Marshall Plan, and NATO. The Red Army, too, occupied former enemy territory, as well as formerly German-occupied territories in Central and Eastern Europe. Although the political division of postwar Europe generally followed a line that was determined by the military presence of the rival powers, the United States contended that whereas its forces were serving to defend democracy, the Red Army was violating the Yalta "free elections" pledge. American leaders observed, furthermore, that the Soviets had effectively used local Communist parties to seize control. They concluded that such groups could potentially serve the same purpose in other areas of the world, even without the Red Army, and that the United States had to develop a strategy to face that challenge.

In this political climate, where interventionism itself was an issue, Secretary of War Robert Patterson may have been the first to recommend that the United States take covert action as a means of counteracting the Soviet threat. The CIA, although created essentially to coordinate intelligence, got the assignment because of its operational capability and its authorization to perform "other functions."

At first, where the Red Army occupied Eastern Europe, the United States contemplated developing OSS-style resistance movements. But the odds against success were too great. Efforts to aid partisan groups in the Baltic states (1948–56), the Ukraine (1949–54), and Albania (1949–54) were terribly tragic.[1] In Lithuania, assistance came too late to be of any use, and in the Ukraine, the "resistance had no hope of winning unless America was prepared to go to war on its behalf. Since America was not prepared to go to war, America was in effect encouraging Ukrainians to go to their deaths."[2] In Albania, Kim Philby betrayed the U.S.-British infiltration teams even before they left their base in Malta, resulting in the ambushing and killing of many brave men.[3] Yet if Philby was a monster of sorts, the CIA's Eastern European programs themselves had particularly malodorous features. Frank Wisner, who was in charge of the Office of Policy Coordination (the forerunner of the DDP), ran the programs with the collaboration of General Reinhard Gehlen. Gehlen was a German officer who had been responsible for Soviet intelligence during the war; he had planned his own capture by American forces in the closing days of the war and had brought his files with him. Gehlen aided Wisner in assembling "a cadre of German specialists on the Soviets [but] without regard for their pasts; some of his best experts were in fact former Nazis. This and similar Army connections with Nazis would prove embarrassing for the United States many years later."[4]

Conducting guerrilla operations behind the iron curtain was infeasible, and the situation in Western Europe was improving in any case through conventional diplomacy. So Clandestine Services shifted its attention to parts of the globe where there was unrest. Events in China and Korea helped focus attention beyond Europe and broadened the cold war to the world arena. Some foreign affairs specialists questioned whether every coup or insurgency in Asia or Latin America was Moscow-inspired, but the American president did not have to worry about public debate in using his new secret weapon. Employing covert action, the CIA replaced the marines as the instrument of "Yankee interventionism."

The chart in figure 19-1 lists the places where the CIA has intervened since its beginning. It is not exhaustive and has been compiled exclusively from published sources and public documents, but it serves to indicate the extent of the "new interventionism" and to identify the various covert action tactics used.

In the rich variety and broad extent of its deployment, covert action produced a new American personality: the "swashbucklers of secret wars," such as Edward Lansdale, Kermit "Kim" Roosevelt, John Peurifoy, Cord Meyer, William Colby, and Oliver North. Though there have been many others, these persons are

Baltic states	1948–54
the Ukraine	1948–54
Albania	1949–54
the Philippines	1949–53
Korea	1950
Vietnam	1954; 1955; 1963
China/Taiwan	1951–54; 1967
Burma	1952–61
Tibet	1959–69
Thailand	1960–73
Laos	1962–71
Indonesia	1958
Iran	1953
Guatemala	1954
Costa Rica	1955; 1959–61
Hungary	1956
Cambodia	1958–59
the Dominican Republic	1960–61
Cuba	1960–65
British Guiana (Guyana)	1963–64
Chile	1962–73
Ecuador	1960–63
Uruguay	1964–66
Mexico	1967–68
Bolivia	1967
the Congo/Zaire	1964
Ghana	1966
Angola	1965/1975
West Germany	1963
the United States	1952–67
Iraq (Kurds)	1972–75
Afghanistan	1979–89
Libya	1981/1984
El Salvador	1980
Nicaragua	1981–87

Figure 19–1. *CIA Covert Operations*

associated with some of the CIA's most sensational episodes. Marchetti and Marks suggested that Lansdale's work was the "prototype" for CIA covert operations during the 1950s: "His exploits under agency auspices, first in the Philippines and then in Vietnam, became so well known that he served as the model for characters in two best-selling novels, *The Ugly American* by William J. Lederer and Eugene Burdick, and *The Quiet American* by Graham

Greene. In the former, he was a heroic figure; in the latter, a bumbling fool."[5]

In the list of covert operations, Lansdale figured in the very first episode outside Europe, which occurred in the Philippines in 1949. Lansdale, an air force colonel, assisted Philippine leader Ramón Magsaysay in putting down the rebellion of the Communist Hukbalahaps, or "Huks." He was one of the earliest advocates of counterinsurgency warfare, or the use of guerrilla tactics to defeat guerrillas. Lansdale's mission enabled Magsaysay to win popular support by providing effective propaganda and by secretly providing funding for economic and social reforms. It ended when Magsaysay was elected president in 1953.

Lansdale's success in the Philippines inspired President Eisenhower to have him try the same tactics in Vietnam. Although Eisenhower warned against getting involved in a "land war" in Asia, the CIA's proprietary airline CAT airlifted supplies to the beleaguered French at Dien Bien Phu in 1954. After the French were defeated and Indochina was divided in compliance with the Geneva Accords, the Eisenhower administration concentrated on South Vietnam as the place to stop "the dominoes from falling." Lansdale gave his support to Ngo Dinh Diem, an anti-Communist leader who had also opposed the French and Japanese, and engineered his election to the presidency in 1955. But Diem was no Magsaysay. He and his brother, Ngo Dihn Nhu, proved to be corrupt and repressive. This led to Lansdale's departure and created in time a made-to-order situation for the Communist Viet Cong and the North. Moreover, the usually astute Lansdale had intervened in favor of a Roman Catholic in a predominantly Buddhist nation. On November 1, 1963, as U.S. involvement in Vietnam was deepening, Diem and his brother were overthrown and subsequently assassinated. The CIA had put Diem in power and had now removed him after secretly conspiring with a group of army generals.

Elsewhere in the Far East, the CIA was similarly energetic and achieved similarly mixed results. It maintained one of its largest stations on Taiwan and cooperated with Chiang Kai-shek's Nationalist government in a variety of covert actions against the People's Republic of China. The China station was so large and its influence so strong that it did not even need the immunity provided by the U.S. embassy but used instead the thinly veiled cover of a "private" company, Western Enterprises, Inc. In its "secret" war against Communist China, the CIA engaged in paramilitary and psychological operations, including commando and penetration raids, airdrops of supplies to guerrillas, ferret missions, and propaganda via radio and balloons. Lansdale reported in 1961 that "during the past ten years," CAT had made "more than 200 overflights of Mainland China and Tibet."[6]

In 1952, on one of these missions, John Downey and Richard Fecteau were shot down. After delaying for two years, the Communist Chinese announced the capture of these "special agents of the CIA" and claimed that "all told, [they] had killed 106 American and Chinese agents parachuted into China between 1951 and 1954 and had captured 124 others." They added that "these agents were trained in 'secret codes, invisible writing, secret messages, telephone tapping, forging documents, psychological warfare, guerrilla tactics and demolition.' "[7] The CIA denied the charges and disavowed any connection with Downey and Fecteau, who received long jail terms. Fecteau was released in December 1971 and Downey in March 1973, in the context of improved Sino-American relations.[8]

But before relations improved, the CIA developed a significant paramilitary capability in the Far East: "By 1953, the elements of that capability were 'in place'—aircraft, amphibious craft, and an experienced group of personnel. For the next quarter century paramilitary activities remained the major CIA covert activity in the Far East."[9] Most of the buildup took place on the China station, particularly during the Korean War, as part of an effort to keep Chicom (Chinese Communist) forces pinned down in the south and to prevent Chicom intervention on the side of the enemy.

Later, while the United States was involved in Vietnam and Saigon was a center of CIA paramilitary operations, the China station tried a different kind of initiative against mainland China to keep its forces at home. In "high-tech" 1967, the CIA's covert operatives in Taiwan used an old-fashioned technique, launching balloons that would float westward carrying propaganda leaflets and materials. The moment seemed propitious for psychological warfare because China was in a tumult as a result of the Cultural Revolution and the violent behavior of the Red Guards.

> Almost immediately after it began, the balloon project was a success. The CIA's China watchers soon saw evidence of increased resistance to the Red Guards in the southern provinces. . . . [Within] weeks, refugees and travelers from the mainland began arriving in Hong Kong with copies of the leaflets and pamphlets that the agency's propagandists had manufactured—a clear indication of the credence being given the false literature by the Chinese masses.[10]

But not all the covert actions against Communist China originated in Taiwan. Clandestine Services maintained about twelve thousand Chinat (Chinese Nationalist) troops across the border in Burma. These forces, from Yunnan province, had fled south into Burma in 1949 and were supposedly awaiting removal to Taiwan. But the Burmese government felt that the Chinat forces posed an internal threat, and to avoid provoking a war with China, it wanted them out. William J. Sebald, the American ambassador (1952–54), apparently tried to help. But the CIA's clandestine operators connived to keep the Chinat troops there as leverage against both Beijing (then Peking) and Rangoon, thereby working at cross-purposes with the State Department and keeping even DDI Robert Amory in the dark.[11] The Chinat troops were not actually expelled until January 1961. This was the first of many episodes of covert action that contradicted U.S. diplomacy, when the right hand did not know what the left hand was doing. Ultimately, the CIA got little for its efforts; the Nationalist troops made only "occasional raids" into China, preferring instead to engage "in their principal pastime of trafficking in opium."[12]

Undaunted, CIA case officers engaged in a similar project in Tibet. In 1959, when the Dalai Lama fled into exile, the CIA sought to make him the focus of resistance and established a secret base for Tibetan operations in northeastern India. Diplomatically, the United States sponsored the deposed leader on "a tour of friendly Asian and European capitals" and an appearance before the United Nations, while covertly the CIA began preparing his troops—"fearsome Khamba horsemen"—for penetration raids into Tibet.[13] Intermountain Aviation airlifted the tribesmen to Camp Hale in the Colorado Rockies for special exercises in a simulated setting. In the actual Tibet operations, the CAT initially flew air support, but the distance from Taiwan to Tibet proved too great, causing the Agency to establish a new "airline" in Katmandu, Nepal, "the CIA's most out-of-the-way proprietary."[14]

> Although the CIA officers led their Tibetan trainees to believe that they were being readied for the reconquering of their homeland, even within the agency few saw any real chance that this could happen. Some of the covert operators who worked directly with the Tibetans, however, eventually came to believe their own persuasive propaganda. Years later, they would flush with anger and frustration describing how they and their Tibetans had been undone by the bureaucrats back in Washington. Several of them would turn for solace to the Tibetan prayers which they had learned during their years with the Dalai Lama.[15]

Aside from sporadic raids into Tibet that were designed to keep alive the "impossible dream," the effort languished. In 1964, a minor revolt did occur inside Tibet, but the Dalai Lama's troops were unable to exploit the situation, revealing that they were a nuisance at best. Old assets die hard, however, and the CIA did not abandon the project until the end of the 1960s.

Paralleling the Tibet project, the CIA also intervened in Laos. Though it had previously been engaged in covert action there, the CIA assumed exclusive responsibility for U.S. paramilitary operations in Laos in the wake of the Geneva agreements of 1962, which "neutralized" the country and ordered all foreign troops to leave. William Colby (one of the Agency's "swashbucklers"; see chapter 22) organized L'Armée Clandestine with only about forty or fifty case officers. He successfully ran what eventually became "the largest [U.S.] paramilitary effort in post-war history"[16]; the "secret war" in Laos cost the American people $500 million annually. Colby recruited thirty thousand Meo and other Lao tribesmen for the CIA's "private army," and he and his officers and agents "directed—and on occasion participated in—the battles against the Pathet Lao, in bombing operations by the CIA's proprietary company Air America, and in commando-type raids into China and North Vietnam, well before Congress had passed the Gulf of Tonkin Resolution."[17] Among Colby's officers, Anthony Poshepny ("Tony Po," as he called himself) became a legend in his time. "Solidly cast in the CIA 'cowboy' mold," Tony Po "reportedly suffered more than a dozen wounds in assorted firefights."[18]

The escalation of the Vietnam War caused the CIA to transfer most of its South Vietnam paramilitary operations to the Department of Defense at the end of 1963, but the Agency retained responsibility for Laos until 1971. According to Marchetti and Marks, many CIA career officers lost heart in the Agency's Laotian and Vietnamese programs, "not because they objected to the Indochina wars (few did), but because the programs consisted for the most part of huge, unwieldy, semi-overt paramilitary operations lacking the sophistication and secrecy that most of the agency's operators preferred."[19] While nonattribution was always hard to maintain, the CIA was clearly not immune to the general disillusionment of Vietnam.

Because the CIA engaged in a number of covert actions almost simultaneously, it is difficult to establish an orderly sequence of the events. For example, while it was conducting secret warfare in Tibet and Laos and its proprietary Air America was flying air support for L'Armée Clandestine from bases in Thailand,[20] the CIA was also intervening in Indonesia. The Tibetan and Laotian operations dragged on for over a decade and the intense support activity from Thailand extended over the same period, but the Indonesian project lasted less than six months. The CIA apparently did not learn from such mistakes, probably because the cloak of secrecy that the new interventionism required covered up failure as well. Clandestine Services suffered a private humiliation in Indonesia in 1958, but it was subjected to no real public embarrassment.

During the cold war, the United States distrusted "neutralist," "third position," or "nonaligned" foreign leaders like Nehru of India, Nasser of Egypt, Perón of Argentina, and Sukarno of Indonesia. It looked upon the generally nationalistic and anticolonial positions of these leaders as not neutral at all but dangerously leftist and a threat to the peace and security of the "free world." So when a group of Sumatran leaders rebelled against Sukarno in February 1958, accusing him of trying to establish a dictatorship and of collaborating with the Communists, the United States took the initiative to help the rebellion.

Publicly, the United States denied any involvement in the uprising. But secretly, the CIA furnished the rebels with arms, aircraft, and pilots. Sukarno charged the United States with intervention and warned against "[playing] with fire in Indonesia," while Secretary of State John Foster Dulles repeatedly insisted that the United States had not departed from the "high standard" of international law and President Eisenhower gave assurances that "our policy is one of careful neutrality and proper deportment all the way through so as not to be taking sides where it is not of our business."[21] These assurances ceased abruptly on May 18, when Allen Pope, a CAT pilot flying a B-26 bomber, was shot down and captured during a raid over the Moluccas. The fragile operation was exposed immediately. To get its pilot back and "cut its losses," the United States abandoned the rebels and made quick concessions to Sukarno. It approved the sale to Indonesia of thirty-seven thousand tons of rice in local currency, and it permitted $1 million in arms and related equipment to be shipped to Indonesia—materiel that had been embargoed since the beginning of the rebellion. Commenting upon this "ignominious failure," Ray Cline wrote that it provided a lesson, but one that was "not clearly perceived" at the time.

> The weak point in covert paramilitary action is that a single misfortune that reveals the CIA's connection makes it necessary for the United States either to abandon the cause completely or convert to a policy of overt military intervention. Because such paramilitary operations are generally kept secret for political reasons, when the CIA's cover is blown the usual U.S. response is to withdraw, leaving behind the friendly elements who had entrusted their lives to the U.S. enterprise.[22]

The CIA apparently learned this lesson slowly. Probably because, in the meantime, in other parts of the world, other Agency swashbucklers enjoyed spectacular "successes."

The principal episode that made Allen Dulles "giddy with success" and that provided justification for the new interventionism was Iran 1953. The CIA operated through Theodore Roosevelt's grandson, Kermit "Kim" Roosevelt, to promote a coup that ousted Premier Mohammed Mossadegh and restored Shah Mohammed Reza Pahlevi. Mossadegh, another of those "unreliable" nationalists, seemed too friendly to the Communists and hostile toward the West. Though Americans were generally amused by Mossadegh's behavior—he wept in public and frequently governed from a sickbed—he was a formidable personality. He nationalized Iranian oil in 1951 and caused *Time* magazine to name him its "man of the year." But the Tudeh (Communist) party had controversial influence, and the oil nationalization caused economic distress. The CIA, sensing that Mossadegh's authority might be slipping and aware that the monarchy still enjoyed legitimacy, sent Roosevelt to Iran to organize popular opposition to Mossadegh and rally army units loyal to the shah. Roosevelt was an OSS veteran in the Rooseveltian tradition of the "strenuous life" and an experienced Middle East operator. Roosevelt was aided by H. Norman Schwarzkopf, another Iranian "old hand," who had helped train Iranian police forces in the 1940s.[23] (The listeners of "Gang Busters," a popular radio program of the 1930s knew him as Chief Norman Schwarzkopf of the New Jersey State Police.)

From a basement room in Teheran and with "a suitcase full of money,"[24] Roosevelt worked with case officers of the CIA's embassy station and a number of local agents to encourage General Fazollah Zahedi to challenge Mossadegh for the premiership. Zahedi, a colorful and somewhat besotted figure, had been minister of interior but had resigned over the issue of Tudeh influence. Roosevelt's agents precipitated a crisis by having the shah dismiss Mossadegh and organized street demonstrations when the premier resisted. Zahedi secured the backing of key army commanders. Mossadegh held out for about a week, forcing the shah to flee to Rome, but the shah's flight was only for effect, and he returned in triumph as the street mobs and army turned the tide. The Iranian operation was heady stuff for the CIA, but it worked because the conditions were right and required only a stiffening of the shah's backbone. Even so, its success was flawed by its very secrecy, wherein complex issues about the Iranian revolution were not debated seriously.

This was also true of the CIA intervention in Guatemala in 1954; its operational success treated only the symptoms but left fundamental issues unresolved and fueled resentment toward the United States that undid the era of the good neighbor. The Guatemalan Revolution of 1944 had begun as a reaction against thirteen years of misrule by the dictator Jorge Ubico. But both John Foster and Allen Dulles were convinced that the Communists had seized control, especially on the election of Major Jacobo Arbenz as president in 1950. But it was middle-class professionals and junior officers of the army who had made the revolution, and they were not particularly radical. The revolution's first president, Juan José Arévalo, was faced with the basic challenge of survival and was far from able to implement reforms or make changes in Guatemala's long-neglected economic and social problems. Nonetheless, the country was in an effervescent situation, and Guatemala became a magnet for revolutionary politics, as well as for refugees from tyranny in a region dominated by tyrants. Among the exiles were a number of Communists who adapted well to the rhetoric of the revolution—especially the bashing of the oligarchy and the major foreign enterprise, the United Fruit Company.

The revolution did veer sharply to the left under Arbenz, facilitated in part by the murder of his political rival, moderate leader Major Francisco Arana, in 1949. (Although Arbenz was the chief beneficiary of Arana's death, Arana may have actually been the victim of a group of exile adventurers, the so-called Caribbean Legion, who had been using Guatemala as a staging area for armed attacks against the principal dictators of the region, Anastasio Somoza of Nicaragua and Rafael Trujillo of the Dominican Republic.) Under Arbenz, Guatemala was one of the few Latin American countries to circulate the Stockholm ''peace'' petition in 1953 (with Picasso's doves) and to show a propaganda film prepared by the Red Chinese that accused the United States of waging bacteriological warfare in Korea. The governments of Costa Rica, Nicaragua, and Panama expelled Guatemalan diplomats for ''subversive activities'' in those countries, and Honduras complained that Guatemala had encouraged and supported a paralyzing strike in the North Coast banana regions in 1954. The U.S. State

Department documented these and additional grievances in a White Paper entitled "Intervention of International Communism in Guatemala," and NBC television aired a "white paper" of its own charging that the Arbenz government censored the press and suppressed political opposition. Guatemala, in turn, alleged that John Foster Dulles was more concerned about the expropriation of 230,000 acres of United Fruit Company land than about international communism.

In what may have been a one-time-only phenomenon, the CIA and the State Department collaborated in the Guatemalan intervention hand in glove; as James Reston described it in the *New York Times* (June 20, 1954), "With the Dulles Brothers in Darkest Guatemala." Besides the obvious link between John Foster and Allen Dulles, the number-two official of the State Department, the undersecretary, was now former DCI "Beedle" Smith, and the U.S. ambassador to Guatemala, John "Smiling Jack" Peurifoy, was "picked off the beach" for the job by Frank Wisner of the CIA.[25] Peurifoy had already served in a similar diplomat/covert action capacity in Greece. (He later served as ambassador to Thailand, where he was killed in a suspicious automobile accident.)

In March 1954, at the Tenth Inter-American Conference in Caracas, the secretary of state secured a resolution affirming that the establishment of a Communist government in the Americas constituted a threat to hemispheric peace and security and justified appropriate defensive measures. Over the following months, the United States extended military assistance to Honduras and Nicaragua, whose governments were hostile to Arbenz and favored his overthrow. The CIA recruited Colonel Carlos Castillo Armas, a former associate of Arana, as its point man and assisted him in organizing a small army in next-door Honduras for the invasion of Guatemala. The opportunity to act arose in May, when the Guatemalan government received a shipment of two thousand tons of arms from behind the iron curtain. Arbenz pointed out that the United States had refused to sell arms to his government but that it supplied weapons to rival nations in the region. But President Eisenhower, convinced that Guatemala was in the Communist camp, gave the operation the green light, and Castillo Armas attacked on June 18.

The Guatemalan invasion did not cause much of a fight; Castillo's tiny force encountered little resistance. But it refused to penetrate more than a few miles into the country, apparently expecting to provoke a popular uprising. CIA aircraft—World War II–vintage P-47 Thunderbolts—buzzed Guatemala City in terroristic raids, earning the sobriquet *sulfato,* a Guatemalan term for laxative.[26] The main action took place in the capital city, where Peurifoy conspired with Lieutenant Colonel José Luis Cruz Salazar to keep the army in the barracks and thereby passive in the conflict. The army was the key to success. Having supported the revolution in 1944, it had subsequently maintained its independence—a lesson not lost on Communist leaders in the Caribbean. Arbenz, lacking army support and further weakened by Communist demands to "arm the workers," capitulated on June 27 and fled to Mexico. Peurifoy still had his hands full with competing factions, but Castillo, as the head of the "liberation army," emerged as Guatemala's next president.[27] He governed for three years before being assassinated, but he left unattended the essential causes of the Guatemalan Revolution.

The CIA intervention in Guatemala stirred up a great deal of ill will toward the United States in Latin America. Even moderate, pro–United States leaders in the region, who had shunned the Arbenz regime, now complained about a Yankee double standard that used "free world" rhetoric against communism but that ignored the transgressions of right-wing tyrants. President José Figueres of Costa Rica, for one, urged the United States to stop arming dictators and to fight communism by eradicating poverty and injustice in Latin America. His urgings led to his becoming involved with the CIA as a target of intervention himself and, then, as an "agent of influence."

In the mid-1950s, Figueres was one of the Caribbean's few progressive leaders to hold office. He condemned the region's dictators and permitted political exiles to engage in conspiratorial activities on Costa Rican soil. Figueres's policy riled Nicaragua's Somoza, who, encouraged by the events in Guatemala, decided it was time to get rid of his annoying neighbor. Citing evidence that Figueres had abetted an assassination attempt against him in April 1954, Somoza helped Figueres's enemies launch an invasion of Costa Rica from Nicaragua in January 1955. Figueres had played a dangerous game, but he had also abolished the Costa Rican army, which forced him to appeal to the Organization of American States to protect his country from Somoza's aggression. The OAS, with the concurrence of the U.S. representative, ordered a cease-fire and sent a delegation to Costa Rica for an on-site investigation.

At that point, Somoza realized that he had to act quickly. He called in his IOU from the CIA. He had permitted the CIA to use Las Mercedes Airport, outside Managua, as a base for its P-47s during the Guatemalan intervention. Now he wanted the planes that were parked there to help him in his feud with Figueres. On January 15, three days after the OAS action, a P-47 Thunderbolt violated Costa Rican airspace and bombed and strafed a number of Costa Rican towns. Figueres, alarmed by this escalation, pointed out that Costa Rica had no defense against "modern weapons" of this kind and again appealed to the OAS. The council of the organization immediately authorized the United States to sell four F-51 Mustang fighters to Costa Rica for a dollar apiece. The State Department, responding to pressure from certain U.S. congressmen and sensing an opportunity to improve America's image in Latin America after Guatemala, came to the rescue and preserved the Caribbean's "lone democrat." Its gesture ended the "invasion," and the State Department scored one over the CIA.[28]

But the roles were soon reversed. Within the State Department, Assistant Secretary of State for Inter-American Affairs Henry F. Holland considered Figueres a "troublemaker." He rebuked him for his interventionism and refused to take seriously his warning of "reform now, or revolution later." Meanwhile, the CIA acting covertly hedged its bets when Latin American dictators started to slip toward the end of the 1950s and after the rise of Fidel Castro. Cord Meyer, chief of the DDP's International Organizations Division, was already intervening in behalf of the non-Communist left and extended CIA support to Figueres in the wake of the so-called Nixon riots in the spring of 1958.

Americans were shocked by that series of hostile demonstrations during Nixon's "goodwill" tour of Latin America. They climaxed in May in Caracas, where a mob stoned and spat upon the vice president's motorcade and threatened his life. At the invitation of Representative Charles Porter of Oregon, Figueres (at the time, just out of office) came to Washington to explain what had caused these events. "People cannot spit on a foreign policy," Figueres told a House committee, "which is what they meant to do." Figueres insisted that Latin America supported the United States in the cold war, but he asked, "If you talk human dignity to Russia, why do you hesitate so much to talk human dignity to the Dominican Republic?"[29] He testified that the United States must change its policy in Latin America and that it could not sacrifice human rights for "investments."

But the best that Figueres could do was to induce the CIA to help Latin America's liberals secretly. The CIA gave him money to publish a political journal, *Combate,* and to sponsor the founding meeting of the Institute of Political Education in Costa Rica in November 1959. The institute was organized as a training school and a center for political collaboration for political parties of the democratic left, principally from Costa Rica, Cuba (in exile), the Dominican Republic (in exile), Guatemala, Honduras, Nicaragua (in exile), Panama, Peru, and Venezuela. The CIA concealed its role from most of the participants except Figueres. Its funds passed first to a shell foundation, then to the Kaplan Fund of New York, next to the Institute for International Labor Research (IILR) located in New York, and finally to San José. Socialist leader Norman Thomas headed the IILR. After the CIA connection was revealed, Thomas maintained that he had been unaware of it, but the IILR's treasurer, Sacha Volman, who also became treasurer of the institute in San José, was a CIA agent. The CIA used Volman to monitor the institute, and Meyer collaborated directly with Figueres.

Meyer came to San José sometime in the summer of 1960. He and Figueres created the Inter-American Democratic Social Movement (INADESMO), which was nothing more than a front. A flier describing the idealistic purpose of INADESMO (figure 19-2a) carried the same post office box as Figueres's personal letterhead (figure 19-2b). The INADESMO setup enabled Meyer to disperse funds more directly, without having to bother with conduits or the accounting procedures of the institute. For example, INADESMO contributed $10,000 to help finance the First Conference of Popular Parties of Latin America in Lima, Peru, in August 1960.

I N A D E S M O

P. O. Box 4484
San José, Costa Rica, C. A.

ABOUT INADESMO

The Inter-American Democratic Social Movement
(INADESMO) is an effort to help integrate the popular political parties, and the labor and student groups that are
fighting the democratic battle in Latin America.

Traditionally these forces have been isolated,
starved by the local oligarchies and dictatorships, and denied international recognition. Yet, the Battle of the Hem
isphere can only be won for democracy by these popular move
ments.

INADESMO receives contributions from individuals
and organizations who will not attach any strings, other than
the upholding of the Western democratic system and the princi
ples of social justice.

INADESMO is coordinated with the groups of both
Americas, that operate the Institute of Political Education
in San José, Costa Rica, and that publish the magazine COMBA-
TE.

There is a great field of democratic and social
activity in Latin America where help is needed. Costs are
negligible by comparison to results. The main effort is made
enthusiastically by Latin Americans.

Other ideologies and cultures carry on well supplied movements, internationally integrated. Why should the
democratic groups be weakened by fragmentation and poverty?

Figure 19–2a. *Flier describing INADESMO*

JOSE FIGUERES

APARTADO 4484

SAN JOSE, COSTA RICA, A. C.

Figure 19–2b. *Personal Letterhead of José Figueres*

The following May, Meyer returned to San José for a more urgent purpose. In the wake of the Bay of Pigs failure, he provided Figueres with INADESMO funds to sponsor a meeting at his farm (May 12–20) between the leaders of the principal Dominican exile movements, Juan Bosch and Horacio Ornes. With Figueres as sponsor, Bosch and Ornes agreed to form a coalition government in anticipation of the overthrow of dictator Rafael Trujillo. As the United States moved to rally the hemisphere against Fidel Castro, Trujillo had become expendable, because the United States needed to demonstrate that it opposed all dictators, not just those on the left.

For over a year, the CIA had been in contact also with dissidents inside the Dominican Republic who argued that assassination was the only certain way to remove Trujillo. The CIA station in Ciudad Trujillo (now Santo Domingo) had encouraged the dissidents and actually delivered to them three pistols and three carbines "attendant to their projected efforts to *neutralize* Trujillo."[30] Because the Bay of Pigs failure created an uncertain situation, the United States tried to put the brakes on this operation and refused to pass along additional weapons to the dissidents which the Dominican station already had, specifically M-3 machine guns. The National Security Council, meeting on May 5, "noted the President's view that the United States should not initiate the overthrow of Trujillo before [knowing] what government would succeed him."[31]

On May 30, Trujillo was ambushed and assassinated. The same "action group" with whom the CIA had been in contact and to whom it had delivered pistols and carbines carried out the attack. According to the 1975 report of the Church Committee, there was "no direct evidence" that CIA weapons had been used in the assassination,[32] and the effect of the Bosch–Ornes pact upon the events that transpired remains a matter for speculation. Nonetheless, the CIA described its role in "changing" the government of the Dominican Republic "as a 'success' in that it assisted in moving the Dominican Republic from a totalitarian dictatorship to a Western-style democracy."[33] Bosch himself was elected president of the Dominican Republic. Sacha Volman followed him there, establishing a new "research and publication center" and taking with him the CIA funding that used to go to Figueres in Costa Rica. Though one cannot prove that there was a coordinated link between the external and internal opposition groups, Meyer was in a position to know what both elements were doing. In March 1962, Meyer's IOD was merged with the Covert Action staff, and Meyer became chief of the new and enlarged unit.[34]

In this review of Meyer's activities in Costa Rica and the Dominican Republic, there have been repeated references to Fidel Castro and the Cuban Revolution. In fact, most of the CIA's clandestine operations in Latin America during the 1960s occurred in the context of Cuban developments. (For direct covert actions against Cuba, see chapter 20.)

Elsewhere in the hemisphere, too, CIA actions had the objective, "No more Cubas." In British Guiana (which became independent Guyana in 1966), the CIA worked through its assets in the international trade union movement to topple the pro-Communist government of Prime Minister Cheddi Jagan. In the early 1960s, Jagan had made friendly overtures toward Castro and had chosen to make the labor unions a factor in his bid for absolute power. In 1963 and 1964, the American Federation of Labor (AFL) and its international allies, the Inter-American Regional Labor Organization (ORIT) and the International Confederation of Free Trade Unions (ICFTU), helped stage an eighty-day general strike that prevented Jagan's takeover of the unions and led to his eventual political defeat.

Tom Braden later revealed that when he was head of the IOD, he had passed money to American labor leaders to fight Communist labor unions in Italy and Germany. Columnist Drew Pearson wrote, "Jay Lovestone, sometimes called [AFL-CIO president George] Meany's minister of foreign affairs . . . takes orders from Cord Meyer [Braden's successor] of the CIA."[35] Lovestone, who was appointed executive secretary of the AFL Free Trade Union Committee after World War II and a dedicated cold warrior, needed little prodding from Braden and Meyer in opposing Communist influence in the international labor movement. At about the time that Meyer took charge of expanded operations in international organizations as chief of the Covert Action staff, Lovestone helped create the American Institute of Free Labor Development

(AIFLD) for the purpose of training labor leaders in Latin America in labor organizing techniques and tactics. The AIFLD was one of several AFL-CIO entities that received covert funding from the CIA; Philip Agee alleged that its collaboration with CIA stations abroad was extremely close, amounting to a "country-team effort."[36]

In the British Guiana case, Jagan accused the AIFLD of intervening in the general strike and denounced its executive director, Serafino Romualdi. Romualdi, the AFL's long-time "roving ambassador" in Latin America, did not deny the charge but showed only nonchalance: "I simply put at the disposal of the strike committee the services of six graduates of [AIFLD], . . . who were working as interns with various local unions. They performed so well that one of them, David Persaud, later was elected President of the BGTUC [British Guiana Trade Union Congress]."[37] In reality, the operation had not been simple. The strike became very violent and had taken a toll of 160 lives and required huge sums of money to sustain. Jagan insisted that there were eleven, not six, AIFLD graduates active in the strike, and one critic claimed there were "more visitors to that tiny country in the name of 'labor solidarity' in 18 months than in the previous 18 years."[38] Romualdi charged that Cuba and Russia had acted as "strikebreakers" by shipping food and fuel to Jagan, but, in the end, before British Guiana became independent, Jagan was out as premier.

Jagan's defeat paralleled another CIA initiative, at the other end of South America in Chile. The CIA's intervention in Chile began in 1962, with a $50,000 covert contribution to the Christian Democratic party; it lasted through 1970–73, when it made an $8 million expenditure to oppose the government of Salvador Allende (see figure 19–3a). Chile, a nation with a democratic tradition and chronic economic ills, troubled the United States because its leftist political parties appeared to be capable of achieving electoral victory. During the period 1962–69, the United States provided Chile with more than a billion dollars in direct, overt economic assistance to improve economic and social conditions. During the same period, the CIA acted covertly to strengthen the Christian Democratic party as the most viable reformist movement. It expended

EXHIBIT 6

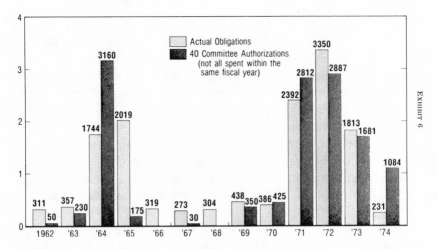

Figure 19–3a. *Annual Covert Action Expenditures and "40" Committee Approvals in Chile, 1962–74 (in thousands of dollars)*

TECHNIQUES OF COVERT ACTION

Expenditures in Chile, 1963 - 1973 (to nearest $100,000)

HEARINGS EXHIBITS

EXHIBIT 1

Techniques

Propaganda for Elections and Other Support for Political Parties $8,000,000

Producing and Disseminating Propaganda and Supporting Mass Media $4,300,000

Influencing Chilean Institutions: (labor, students, peasants, women) and Supporting Private Sector Organizations . . $ 900,000

Promoting Military Coup d'Etat . . . Less than $ 200,000

Source: U.S. Senate, Select Committee to Study Governmental Operations. Hearings. *Intelligence Activities—Volume 7: Covert Action.* 94th Cong., 1st sess., 1975.

Figure 19–3b. *Techniques and Costs of Covert Action in Chile, 1963–73*

$2.6 million in 1964 alone to ensure the election of Eduardo Frei as president. While Frei was president, it spent an additional $2 million in covert activities, including spreading propaganda (both "black" and "white"), subsidizing friendly media organizations, infiltrating Chilean institutions and groups, and supporting private organizations[39] (see figure 19–3b).

These activities notwithstanding, Salvador Allende, the candidate of Popular Unity (a coalition of political parties dominated by the Marxist left), emerged as the front-runner for the 1970 elections. The CIA worked desperately to prevent his election with a "spoiling" operation, trying to divide the Popular Unity coalition and launching a "scare campaign, . . . [equating] an Allende victory with violence and Stalinist repression."[40] In the election on September 4, 1970, the CIA's campaign succeeded only partially, limiting Allende to receiving only a plurality among the three candidates and thereby requiring Congress to choose between the two top vote-getters. At this point, President Nixon took charge. He told CIA director Richard Helms that Allende was unacceptable and instructed the CIA "to play a direct role in organizing a military "*coup d'état* in Chile to prevent Allende's accession to the Presidency."[41]

Responding to Nixon's strong antagonism toward Allende, the U.S. intervention followed two tracks: Track I consisted of using virtually all covert action techniques to influence events; Track II consisted of contacting the Chilean military to promote a coup. Neither track prevented the eventual election of Allende, but the dissension and turmoil that they created continued into the three years of his government. Most of the Track I activities, including a $250,000 slush fund for bribing Chilean congressmen, were directed toward the so-called Frei reelection gambit. President Frei had not been a candidate in 1970 because the Chilean constitution did not permit a president to run for reelection. The CIA's plan called for the congress to choose Jorge Alessandri (the second-place finisher), who would immediately resign, requiring a special election in which Frei could participate since technically he was not succeeding himself. Track I failed because President Frei refused to violate the spirit of the constitution.

Similarly, Track II failed because the commander in chief of the army, General Rene Schneider, opposed a military coup, insisting that the constitutional process be respected.

As a result of his strong constitution stand, the removal of General Schneider became a necessary ingredient in the coup plans of all the Chilean conspirators. Unable to have General Schneider retired or reassigned, the conspirators decided to kidnap him. An unsuccessful abduction attempt was made on October 19, 1970, by a group of Chilean military officers whom the CIA was actively supporting. A second kidnap attempt was made the following day, again unsuccessfully. In the early morning hours of October 22, 1970, machine guns and ammunition were passed by the CIA to the group that had failed on October 19. That same day General Schneider was mortally wounded in an attempted kidnap on his way to work. The attempted kidnap and the shooting were apparently conducted by conspirators other than those to whom the CIA had provided weapons earlier in the day.[42]

These bizarre and terribly bungled events put an end to Track II, but they still had the effect of removing an obstacle from the military and making it easier to try again.

When the Chilean Congress confirmed Allende as president on October 24 (two days after the assassination of Schneider), President Nixon assumed a "cool but correct" public posture. But the United States continued its covert intervention. During Allende's presidency, the CIA spent over $6 million on covert activities, including a total of $1,665,000 to support *El Mercurio,* the major Santiago newspaper. The principal goal of the campaign to "destabilize" the Allende government was to create the conditions for a military coup. CIA money was passed for propaganda tactics and to encourage various labor and special interest groups to resist; it also went to a particularly strident right-wing paramilitary group, Patria y Libertad, which engaged in highly provocative, even violent actions. Along with its diplomatic and clandestine efforts, the United States put an economic squeeze on the Allende regime, both covertly and overtly. According to Helms, President Nixon intended to "make the economy scream." U.S. ambassador Edward Korry made clear that "not a nut or bolt would be allowed to reach Chile under Allende."[43] Especially disturbing, the CIA and certain U.S. multinational companies with economic interests in Chile (particularly International Telephone and Telegraph) cooperated in covert action. ITT contributed large sums to the Alessandri campaign, and during the Allende presidency, it channeled money to *El Mercurio* and conferred with CIA officials about various plans for "economic warfare" against Allende.[44]

Although the CIA denied any direct involvement in the military coup that overthrew Allende on September 11, 1973, it had clearly expended great energy and resources to create the climate and conditions necessary for it to happen. Moreover, the CIA had contact with the military conspirators virtually up to the time they acted. It insisted that this contact had been for intelligence-gathering only, but in fact, it "included activity [that] went beyond the mere collection of information."[45] The CIA's covert action in Chile was continuous, diverse, and extensive. It was apparently also excessive in terms of U.S. interests. In a "threat assessment" made by the intelligence community shortly after the September 4 election, the Interdepartmental Group for Inter-American Affairs (consisting of representatives of CIA, State, Defense, and the White House) concluded

> that the United States had no vital interests within Chile, the world military balance of power would not be significantly altered by an Allende regime, and an Allende victory in Chile would not pose any likely threat to the peace of the region. The Group noted, however, that an Allende victory would threaten hemispheric cohesion and would represent a psychological setback to the U.S. as well as a definite advance for the Marxist idea.[46]

Not only did Nixon disregard the intelligence analysts in fixing the level of covert intervention in Chile, he instructed that Track II was to proceed—without informing the U.S. ambassador in Santiago, the State Department, or any "40" Committee member except National Security Adviser Henry Kissinger: "The President and his senior advisors thus denied themselves the Government's major sources of counsel about Chilean politics."[47]

Finally, the American intervention in Chile resulted in the installation of a repressive military regime. The 1975 Church Committee could not have foreseen how long the regime of Augusto Pinochet would last, but even so, its report reached a particularly thought-provoking conclusion about the use of covert action:

> The Chilean institutions that the United States most favored may have been discredited within their own societies by the fact of their covert support. In Latin America particularly, even the suspicion of CIA support may be the kiss of death. It would be the final irony of a decade of covert action in Chile if that action destroyed the credibility of the Chilean Christian Democrats.[48]

The sorts of activities that constituted the Chilean intervention were also described by Philip Agee in the places where he was posted: Ecuador (1960–63), Uruguay (1964–66), and Mexico (1967–68). None of Agee's activities produced sensational developments, such as those in British Guiana or Chile, but in some respects they are more striking because of their very pervasiveness. In citing the CIA station requirements, or Related Missions Directive, for Ecuador (pages 108–9 of his book) and for Uruguay (pages 343–45), Agee showed that virtually no facet of political life in those countries was exempt from CIA meddling. The Agee book is unrelentingly critical of the CIA and may actually be a product of Soviet intelligence in its detail. But it has been refuted essentially only on these grounds and is therefore useful in tracing the day-to-day, nitty-gritty work of a CIA case officer, when Agee was one.

Agee himself claims that this activity caused him to become disillusioned. In a purported draft letter of resignation, he affirmed that U.S. reformist policies in Latin America would not overcome "the injustices forced by small ruling minorities on the mass of the people" and that socialism was "the only real alternative to injustice in Latin America." Agee then charged that CIA operations perpetuated these "injustices":

Our training and support for police and military forces, particularly the intelligence services, combined with other U.S. support through military assistance missions and Public Safety programs, give the ruling minorities ever stronger tools to keep themselves in power and to retain their disproportionate share of the national income. Our operations to penetrate and suppress the extreme left also serve to strengthen the ruling minorities by eliminating the main danger to their power.[49]

Somewhere along the way, Agee, a graduate of Notre Dame University (like Eduardo Frei), converted to Marxism and quit the CIA after twelve years of service. He wrote a harmful book, but one can ignore neither the information he provided about the new interventionism nor the questions he raised.

Agee also commented about the 1967 CIA intervention in Bolivia concerning the tracking and capture of revolutionary Ernesto "Che" Guevara. This story has been discussed extensively, and the controversy surrounding Guevara's death— particularly the charges of CIA complicity—weighed heavily upon the CIA and contributed to the general deterioration of its image toward the end of the 1960s. Revelations about other covert action in the Congo (1964) and Angola (1965) also raised an outcry, and an espionage trial in West Germany in 1963 disclosed the relationship between the CIA and General Reinhard Gehlen, who had risen to head of West German intelligence, creating more embarrassment.[50] Most of these episodes are variations of themes already discussed. But the case of CIA intervention in the United States itself, uncovered by Congressman Wright Patman in 1964 and exposed by *Ramparts* magazine in February 1967, was a wholly different tune.

The CIA funded certain nongovernmental organizations within the United States in order to promote its foreign policy objectives. The organization whose disclosure was most important and that unraveled most of the rest was the National Student Association (NSA). The CIA financed the international activities of the NSA from 1952 to 1967. Cord Meyer, who had directed the CIA's covert funding of the NSA, rejected the notion that the program was interventionist, writing "the CIA relationship with the NSA during a fifteen-year period of discreet cooperation . . . was based on a shared commitment to a common purpose. The NSA leadership wanted to cooperate with democratic and representative university student groups abroad and to oppose the attempt of the Communists to dominate the international student community. The Agency shared that objective and was prepared to help them achieve what they had already decided to do.''[51] The students had been denied open support by the State Department and Congress because ''they were considered too far to the left in the general climate of McCarthyism and anti-intellectualism of the 1950s.''[52] They had then turned to the CIA and accepted its secret funding. Under the arrangement, ''CIA funds would support only the international division of the National Student Association; only the NSA President and the International Affairs Vice President would be witting of the CIA connection. Each year, after the election of new student leaders, the CIA held a secret briefing for the new officers, and elicited from them a secrecy agreement.''[53]

Despite the seeming ''blank check'' relationship between the CIA and the NSA, the Agency in fact made ''operational use'' of individual students. Students attending world youth congresses were asked to report on ''Soviet and Third World personalities'' and to observe ''Soviet security practices.'' In 1957, a U.S. student delegate to the Sixth World Youth Festival in Moscow ''was instructed to report on Soviet counterintelligence measures and to purchase a piece of Soviet-manufactured equipment.''[54] Besides these actions pertaining to the international sphere, the CIA intruded upon the functioning of NSA itself by influencing the selection of officers, spotting sympathetic leaders and promoting their candidacies.[55] It was this latter aspect that created the greatest furor.

Immediately after the publication of the *Ramparts* article about the NSA, the *New York Times* and the *Washington Post* published lists of private American organizations and foundations that had received CIA secret funding. The presence of educational and private voluntary organizations, labor unions, elements of the media, and religious groups on the list aroused grave concerns about the effects of CIA operations upon the ''independence and integrity" of American institutions. To head off a congressional investigation, President Lyndon Johnson instructed Undersecretary of State Nicholas Katzenbach to organize a committee that consisted of Secretary of Health, Education, and Welfare John Gardner and CIA director Helms to look into "the relationship between the CIA and 'U.S. educational and private voluntary organizations which operate abroad.'" Even with Helms as a member and its limited mandate, the committee quickly recommended an end to providing "covert financial assistance or support, direct or indirect, to any of the nation's educational or private voluntary organizations."[56]

The timely action of the Katzenbach Committee allayed the so-called *Ramparts* flap but did not really end the CIA's practice of covert funding of private organizations. Nor, in the 1975 opinion of the Church Committee, did it cause the CIA to rethink "where boundaries ought to be drawn in a free society." It merely created "a different ballgame" in which the CIA tried to be more careful in conducting these operations so as not to get caught.[57] To some organizations, with whom the CIA had terminated its relationship, it paid out "surge funding"—a kind of severance pay—that kept the organization in business for a few more years. Radio Free Europe and Radio Liberty, for example, received major advances to continue broadcasting until they "went public"; the U.S. Congress assumed the financial costs several years later.

Though the CIA probably profited from the mistakes it made in its relationship with private American institutions, it did not profit from its mistakes in most other covert operations. Secrecy, the "necessary ingredient," seemed to exact an excessive price. It made it difficult to learn from experience, and it made it easy for covert operators to minimize failure or cover it up completely. Secrecy prevented counsel, much less public debate. Serious operations were undertaken without studying the issues and possible effects. Most of the covert action took place in the Third World, where Clandestine Services expanded, but even operational "successes" turned sour in the long run. Was it desirable to trade Mossadegh for the Ayatollah Khomeini? Ten years after the overthrow of Arbenz in Guatemala, Wise and Ross wrote, "The yoke of Communism had been thrown off but in its place there remained the yoke of poverty and an indifferent oligarchy. The abysmal conditions that led to Arbenz in the first place were as apparent as ever.''[58] And one shudders at what the Chileans may do or say when they get their freedom back.

Beyond these considerations are the constitutional issues of the formulation and conduct of foreign policy and of respect for international treaties. There are also ethical and moral questions; assassination has been alluded to as a covert action technique. These matters have only been touched upon lightly so far. In order to treat them more thoroughly, the case of Cuba provides rich detail.

20
Cuba

I n the development of U.S. foreign intelligence after World War II, American relations with Cuba are particularly important because intense effort was involved and a full range of actions was taken. The Cuban case contains examples of both Operations and Intelligence; the Bay of Pigs and the missile crisis represent the perigee and apogee, respectively, of postwar U.S. intelligence. Other dirty tricks that the CIA committed in Cuba did not have the tragic dimensions of the Bay of Pigs, but they still brought covert action to another new low.

Behind all this activity was the Cuban Revolution and Fidel Castro's assumption of power. Castro's struggle against the dictator Fulgencio Batista took place at a moment that was opportune for him, from the standpoint of U.S. Latin American policy. The fall from power of Latin American dictators in the mid-1950s was causing the United States to reassess its policy in the region. It now tended to cut back its military assistance and to take a more tolerant view of political unrest. But Castro was more than the United States had bargained for, and the Eisenhower administration decided that his brand of revolution was unacceptable and had to be eliminated before it spread to the rest of the hemisphere. Many Cubans became disillusioned, too, believing that Castro had promised one revolution and delivered another. Tens of thousands fled the island and sought refuge in the United States. The idea of helping them return home to overthrow Castro occurred to some Americans very early.

In mid-April 1959, barely four months after his triumphal entry into Havana, Castro visited the United States at the invitation of the American Society of Newspaper Editors. He had a great time; he appeared on "Meet the Press" and turned up on Steve Douglas's WWDC radio talk show from the Peiking Restaurant after spending a lively evening rapping with Georgetown University students at the Rathskeller. The only high-ranking U.S. official whom he met was Vice President Richard Nixon. Eisenhower was golfing in Georgia, and John Foster Dulles, stricken with cancer, had resigned his post on April 15. After meeting with Castro, Nixon was convinced that the bearded leader was a Communist and became, as he stated in *Six Crises,* "the strongest and most persistent advocate" of the need to take action to get rid of him.

Almost a year later, U.S.-Cuban relations were in a shambles and Castro was quite literally embracing Nikita Khrushchev. On March 17, 1960, Eisenhower authorized Allen Dulles to prepare a Cuban exile force for possible covert military action against Castro. Dulles placed the deputy director for plans, Richard Bissell, in charge of the project.

Bissell moved quickly. He recruited and trained a secret force of Cuban exiles to liberate the Cuban homeland—or at least that is how the operation was conceived and presented. The CIA, after assuming responsibility for interventionism, lost sight of William Donovan's original concept of Operations as the *unconventional* part of conventional warfare. The CIA had gotten away with it in Guatemala, but that success was a distraction from the standpoint of expectations and the planning of the Cuban invasion. Bissell brought in many CIA veterans from the Guatemalan affair as case officers for the Cuban project. Miami served as the focal point for the operation, but to avoid breaking U.S. laws, the CIA trained the Cuban brigade in Guatemala (with the consent of President Miguel Ydígoras Fuentes) and established air operations at Puerto Cabezas, Nicaragua (in cahoots with National Guard chief Anastasio Somoza Debayle).

The Cuban Expeditionary Force—Brigade 2506—took its name from the ID number of a recruit who had been killed in a training accident. The force numbered 1,543 men, but in a minor deception, it started counting at 2,500 so that it would appear stronger than it actually was. The men in the force were trained on Roberto Alejos's coffee *finca* near Retalhuleu, Guatemala, under the supervision of U.S. military personnel—who had been "sheep-dipped" (under civilian cover) for the purpose—and such CIA personnel as E. Howard Hunt and "Frank Bender" (Gerry Droller). For air support, the CIA gathered twenty-four B-26 Marauder medium bombers at its Puerto Cabezas air field and enlisted General George Reid Doster and numerous officers of the Alabama Air National Guard as pilot instructors of the Cubans.[1] It had chosen B-26s because there were six in Castro's air force, and it had recruited the Alabama ANG because it was one of the few units still flying the Marauder. The CIA also assembled a small fleet for the amphibious operation, acquiring two landing craft infantry and chartering five steamers of the García Line (with the full cooperation of the Cuban owners); but when the time came, it was U.S. Navy destroyers and the carrier *Essex* that escorted the invasion force to Cuban waters.

While these preparations were under way, Bissell tried to maintain absolute secrecy. He and Dulles kept even DDI Robert Amory uninformed, so that Intelligence contributed very little to the Cuban project. Dulles instead relied upon the reporting of field operatives, who self-servingly supported a basic premise of the invasion—that the climate in Cuba was such that the landings would spark popular resistance against Castro. (If the Intelligence analysts had been asked, they would have disagreed and might have cited the fate of Narciso López more than a hundred years before.[2])

The Eisenhower administration was thus contemplating taking a major foreign policy action without consultation or free debate. (The general had fought a war that had been justified on the basis that dictatorships were evil because they could act secretly to commit aggression.) In comparison to later congressional oversight, 1960–61 were the dark ages.

The closest the American people came to having a public debate about whether the United States should support Cuban exiles to overthrow Castro had occurred during the 1960 presidential campaign, and even that had been deceptive. Presidential candidate John F. Kennedy had complained in a press release on October 20, 1960, that the United States was not doing enough to help Cuban "fighters for freedom." During a televised debate the next evening, Kennedy's opponent, Vice President Richard Nixon (who was privy to the CIA operation) called Kennedy's statement "dangerously irresponsible" and said that if the United States supported a revolution in Cuba, "right off the bat," it would violate five inter-American treaties plus the UN Charter.[3] Angry because he believed that Kennedy had been briefed about the Cuban project and was *really* acting irresponsibly, Nixon later explained that he had felt he had to "go to the other extreme" in order to protect the project from being compromised. The effect of such an intrusion of U.S. foreign intelligence on the American political process is a matter for speculation. But ironically, Nixon, who had concealed his hard-line position and publicly taken the moral high ground, lost the election.

In another, more deliberate move, the principal Cuban exile organization (which was financed by the CIA) distributed propaganda in the United States that was designed to win support for the U.S. government's covert foreign policy. The Democratic Revolutionary Front (FRD) was a coalition of Cuban exile groups organized by the CIA and headed by José Miró Cardona to oppose Castro and take over provisionally as a successor government. It began issuing the *Cuban Newsletter* in the fall of 1960. (This activity should not be confused with Radio Swan, the clandestine radio station that CIA case officer David Atlee Phillips operated from Swan Island, off the coast of Honduras, under the cover of the Gibraltar Steamship Corporation—a CIA proprietary. Radio Swan, which was characterized by Castro as "a cage of hysterical parrots,"[4] broadcast to Cuba in Spanish as part of a modest psychwar effort.) The newsletter appeared in an English version (figure 20–1a). Making use of various mailing lists, it was sent to persons and organizations within the United States. Figure 20–1b is a reproduction of an envelope that contained a copy of the *Cuban Newsletter;* it was mailed to "DEAN, BOWLING GREEN STATE UN" and was forwarded internally to "Dr. [Kenneth] McFall, V. President." He in turn sent it to the present author, who was then an assistant professor specializing in Latin American history at Bowling Green. The CIA's covert operators viewed such activity as essential for establishing the legitimacy of the FRD, but it could not avoid influencing American public opinion and, hence, affecting the free interplay of the U.S. political system.

In a more conventional propaganda move, the State Department prepared American and international public opinion for what was to come. As D-Day approached, the inevitable diplomatic White Paper appeared (figure 20-2), written by Arthur M. Schlesinger, Jr., who was then a special assistant to President Kennedy. The brief thirty-page pamphlet attacked Castro for "The Betrayal of the Cuban Revolution," "The Establishment of the Communist Bridgehead," and "The Delivery of the Revolution to the Sino-Soviet Bloc." When a White Paper is published, it is only a matter of time before the other shoe falls. It is difficult to believe that DDI Amory and his analysts were as uninformed as has been said, given the known significance of White Papers and the fact that the exile plans to invade Cuba had become an open secret as early as February 1961.

The fact that the Cuban project had started in the Eisenhower administration and ended in Kennedy's contributed to its failure, helped by the cloak of secrecy. During its year of preparation, the project had changed in character. From a plan to infiltrate a relatively small force that would conduct protracted guerrilla warfare in the mountains, it grew to a plan for a World War II–style amphibious assault that would defeat Castro quickly, probably in combination with internal resistance and uprisings. By the time Kennedy took office, he objected to the plan as it then stood as "too spectacular," seeming to resemble Normandy and D-Day. He permitted the preparations to continue, but he wanted something "less noisy, . . . minimal."[5] Kennedy, the last to be persuaded, gave his final okay on April 16, but no one had made it clear to him what the imperatives of the operation were. Only Bissell had the full picture, and he was not forthcoming because he feared what the new president might do. Even after the landing site was changed from Trinidad, on the south-central coast, to the more "quiet" Zapata swamp on the Bay of Pigs, no adviser got through to the president that the invasion force was too large to remain secret (that is, holding too rigidly to nonattribution could imperil the operation) and that control of the air was "absolutely vital to success."[6]

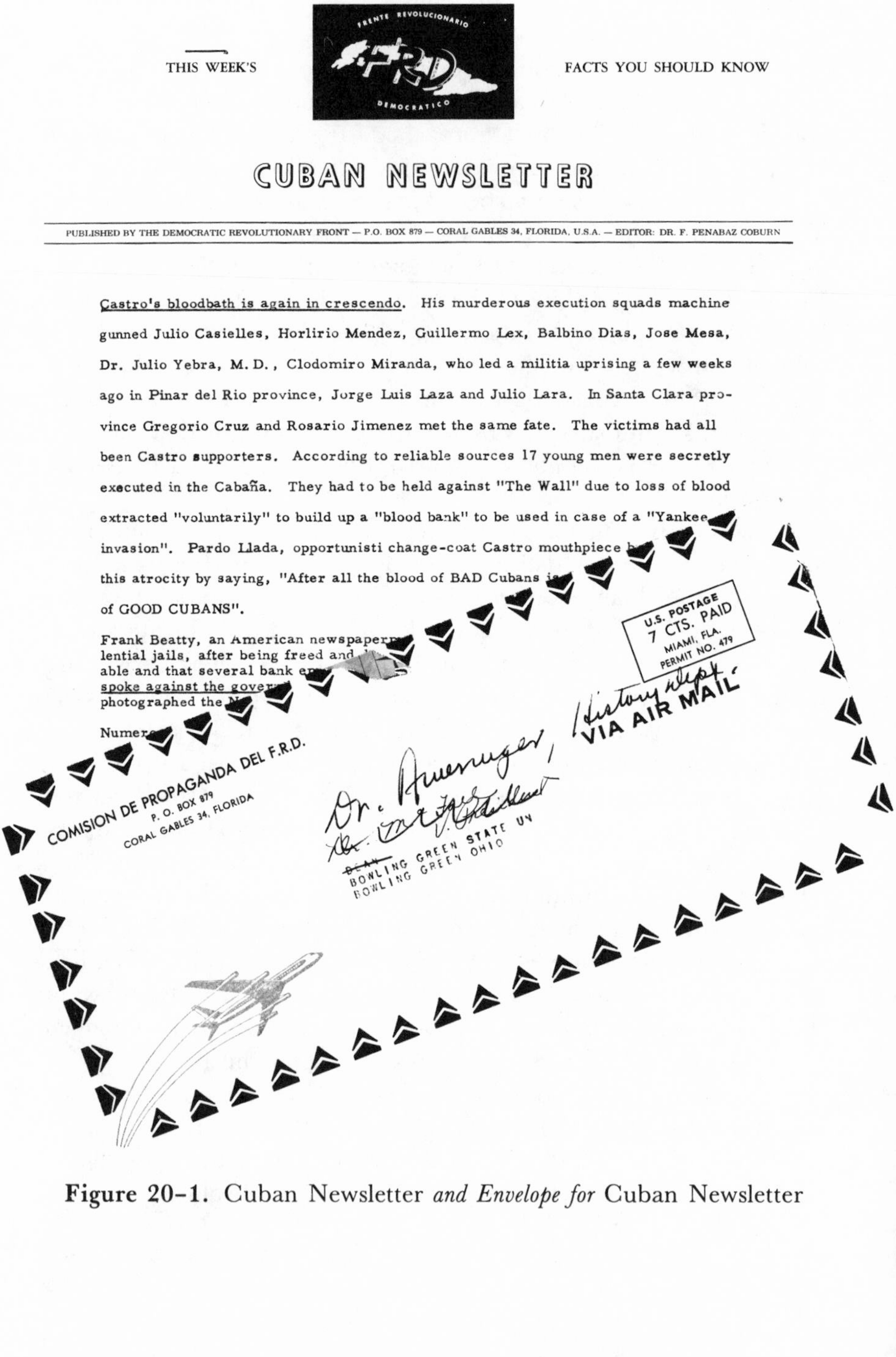

THIS WEEK'S — FRENTE REVOLUCIONARIO FRD DEMOCRATICO — FACTS YOU SHOULD KNOW

CUBAN NEWSLETTER

PUBLISHED BY THE DEMOCRATIC REVOLUTIONARY FRONT — P.O. BOX 879 — CORAL GABLES 34, FLORIDA, U.S.A. — EDITOR: DR. F. PENABAZ COBURN

Castro's bloodbath is again in crescendo. His murderous execution squads machine gunned Julio Casielles, Horlirio Mendez, Guillermo Lex, Balbino Dias, Jose Mesa, Dr. Julio Yebra, M. D., Clodomiro Miranda, who led a militia uprising a few weeks ago in Pinar del Rio province, Jorge Luis Laza and Julio Lara. In Santa Clara province Gregorio Cruz and Rosario Jimenez met the same fate. The victims had all been Castro supporters. According to reliable sources 17 young men were secretly executed in the Cabaña. They had to be held against "The Wall" due to loss of blood extracted "voluntarily" to build up a "blood bank" to be used in case of a "Yankee invasion". Pardo Llada, opportunisti change-coat Castro mouthpiece b this atrocity by saying, "After all the blood of BAD Cubans i of GOOD CUBANS".

Frank Beatty, an American newspaper
lential jails, after being freed and
able and that several bank e
spoke against the gove
photographed the N

Numer

COMISION DE PROPAGANDA DEL F.R.D.
P. O. BOX 879
CORAL GABLES 34, FLORIDA
U.S. POSTAGE
7 CTS. PAID
MIAMI, FLA.
PERMIT NO. 479
VIA AIR MAIL
Dr. Auernuger, History Dept.
BOWLING GREEN STATE UN
BOWLING GREEN OHIO

Figure 20–1. Cuban Newsletter *and Envelope for* Cuban Newsletter

CUBA

DEPARTMENT OF STATE

Contents

Figure 20-2. *U.S. State Department White Paper on Cuba, April 1961*

If the president acted on the basis of incomplete or misleading information, there was also no agreement among his top advisers on the nature of the Bay of Pigs operation. When Allen Dulles later testified before the Board of Inquiry on the Bay of Pigs (chaired by General Maxwell D. Taylor), he was asked to explain the objective of the operation. Dulles replied, "Get a beachhead, hold it, and then build it up."[7] In response to the same question, General David M. Shoup (the commandant of the U.S. Marine Corps and a member of the Joint Chiefs of Staff) stated, "The mission was to get some well-trained military people into Cuba, who could gather into their fold and equip all the people that were just waiting for a chance to get at Castro, then these military people could develop a real military organization and increase their strength to the extent that the whole Castro regime would fall apart."

Question: The success of this operation was wholly dependent upon popular support?
General Shoup: Absolutely. Ultimate success.
Statement: Not only ultimate success, but any success really.
Question: Who gave you this information on the uprisings?
General Shoup: I don't know. I suppose it was CIA. Well, it's obvious we wouldn't be taking 30,000 additional rifles if we didn't think there was going to be somebody to use them. I don't think any military man would ever think that this force could overthrow Castro without support. They could never expect anything but annihilation.[8]

Even with this understood, General Shoup reiterated that air superiority was absolutely vital, "or you are not going to be able to get ashore."

Secretary of State Dean Rusk agreed with General Shoup that a popular uprising was "utterly essential" for success and viewed the invasion as a "shock" to spark uprisings.

The impression existed that 1,200 highly-trained men expected to get ashore and run into some militia units and beat the hell out of them. This would be the kind of a bloody nose that would get things moving. The feeling was that there would be no fighting on the beach. It seemed that this area was virtually empty. There was a good chance the invasion force could get well ashore without being discovered.[9]

Bissell, who helped create many of these impressions, testified that he had hoped to hold the beachhead area "for a period of several weeks," for which "we would have had to assume that we would have knocked out Castro's air force."[10]

If the Americans did not have a clear idea about the purpose of the operation, the Cubans in Miami and Guatemala were totally confused. The June 1963 cover of *Esquire* magazine parodied the famous Uncle Sam recruiting poster, bearing the caption, "The C.I.A. Wants YOU. Join Up For the March Through Havana." The accompanying story, written by Terry Southern, purported to be an interview with a "hipster-mercenary" who had "signed up at $250 a month for the big parade through Havana bla-bla-bla and wound up in Guatemala with the CIA.

> . . . But I guess the main thing was these cats at the recruiting station, giving this big spiel about "bla-bla-bla the American Government, the C.I.A., the U.S. Army," and so on. I mean the picture they were painting had *battleships* in it, Dad—you know, rockets against pitchforks. Well man, I mean how could we lose? Cuba versus America—are you kidding?
>
> *So it was pretty obvious even then that it was an American project?*
>
> Well *of course*, man—that was the whole pitch. You don't think they could have got these guys in there any other way, do you? I mean most of *these* guys were just sort of tired, middle-aged businessmen, or young hustlers . . . *they* weren't going to do anything, anybody could see that. It was like they were recruiting for the *parade*, you know, to march through Havana—and these guys were joining up to be *in* the parade, that's all. . . . There were some of these C.I.A. faces running around, trying to make a cloak-and-dagger scene out of it, but that was just sort of a *game* with them. I mean everybody in Miami knew about the recruiting.[11]

Though the above account may be an exaggeration, the Cubans never lost faith that the United States would "come to their assistance, if necessary."[12] Actually, the Cuban exile Brigade performed very well, inflicting heavy casualties upon Castro's forces. They might even have had a chance, except that an old British-made Sea Fury torpedo-bomber sunk the *Rio Escondido,* one of the García Line ships laden with "ten days' supply of ammunition."[13] The plan to knock out Castro's "air force" had gone awry.

According to the plan, the B-26 bombers were to carry out air raids against Cuba, but disguising the fact that they came from outside, they were to pretend to be defectors. To establish the "defector" story, six B-26s from Puerto Cabezas raided Cuban air bases on Saturday, April 15, two days before the invasion. Mario Zúniga, a CIA pilot pretending to be one of the raiders, flew his B-26 to Key West and announced his defection, but his story did not hold. This severely embarrassed UN ambassador Adlai Stevenson, who was made an unwitting participant in the cover, and it caused President Kennedy to order an eleventh-hour cancellation of a second air strike set for D-Day, April 17, 1961. At that moment, it was Bissell's responsibility—and he had the opportunity—to level with President Kennedy and tell him that "going guerrilla" was not in the picture, that they were putting fourteen hundred men ashore as a "cadre" to arm and train the resistance, that they would offload thirty thousand rifles and other equipment, and that control of the air was critical. They would have to have time to establish the beachhead and to bring in Miró Cardona and the other leaders of the FRD to form a provisional government, thereby creating the conditions for the United States to intervene openly.

Granted that the wisdom of the undertaking was questionable and granted that it might have failed in any event, Kennedy's decision to cancel the second or D-Day air strike was fatal to the operation. On the day of the invasion, as the men on the beaches fought like demons to avoid disaster, Admiral Arleigh Burke argued that it was not too late to send in just two jets from the carrier *Essex* to "shoot down the enemy aircraft"—or at least bring in a destroyer to knock "the hell out of Castro's tanks." But Kennedy would not undo the damage and "got angry":

> "Burke, I don't want the United States involved in this," he said sharply.
>
> Burke, feeling he had "never been so distressed," raised his voice. He wanted to be "as forceful as I could be in talking to the President." He said, "Hell, Mr. President, but we *are* involved!"[14]

By refusing to revert to the old interventionism, Kennedy discovered the limitations of the new. The Bay of Pigs demonstrated that there was an inverse relationship between the requirements of military victory and the need to preserve plausible denial (nonattribution).

Because of this reality, the Taylor Board concluded, "Operational restrictions designed to protect [the] covert character [of the operation] should have been accepted only if they did not impair the chance of success."[15] Lest the board appear to be criticizing the president, it affirmed that he had not been briefed sufficiently to be forewarned of the "probable military consequences" of his decision. Moreover, it observed, the JCS "individually, . . . had differing understandings of important features of the operation."[16] This unrealistic attempt to deceive outsiders contributed to failure, and excessive secrecy within the executive branch crippled the operation further. General Shoup, when asked if he felt he had "absolute and complete knowledge" about the operation, replied, "Absolutely not."[17]

The Directorate of Plans got so caught up in the secret preparations for the invasion that it neglected its own covert action function: to soften up Castro and organize the Cuban resistance. In Operation Torch in North Africa, OSS agents and personnel had literally met the invasion force on the beach and run interference. The CIA's secret preinvasion reports about "agent, guerrilla, and dissident assets" (which it gave the Taylor Board) estimated that "from 2,500 to 3,000 persons supported by 20,000 sympathizers were actively engaged in resistance in Cuba."[18] But the operation collapsed too quickly to determine if these assets were actually in place. Plans were made for leaflet drops on D-Day, and E. Howard Hunt and David Phillips announced excitedly over Radio Swan, "Alert! Alert! Look well at the rainbow. The fish will rise very soon. Chico is in the house. Visit him. . . . The fish is red." This message, although described as "jibberish" and designed to sow confusion and cause panic,[19] may actually have been open code to the underground. (Except to salve wounded pride, there was no purpose in clarifying the issue of the existence or nonexistence of a Cuban resistance afterward; if an underground really did exist, saying so would only have caused Castro to start a witch-hunt.)

From every perspective, the Bay of Pigs was a dismal event. A large number of Cubans on both sides got killed, along with four Alabama ANG pilots. The United States received a "bloody nose" in taking a foreign policy action that significantly excluded the institutions and persons normally involved in the decision-making process, including the president. (The only member of Congress to get seriously involved was Senator J. William Fulbright of Arkansas, and that was only because he wrote a memo objecting to a Cuban invasion in the context of reports that had appeared in the *New York Times*.) After a discreet delay, President Kennedy replaced Dulles, Bissell, and Amory with John McCone, Richard Helms, and Ray Cline, respectively.

McCone, an industrialist and a businessman, emphasized intelligence collection as director of the CIA. He believed that the Bay of Pigs had discredited the cloak and dagger and that the CIA had lost its edge because it lagged in applying technology to intelligence. He concentrated upon creating the Directorate of Science and Technology. Though the CIA could not catch up to the Department of Defense in technical collection, McCone's work in this regard paid off in the fall 1962 Cuban missile crisis.

The Cuban missile crisis was one of the Intelligence Community's best moments. It was then that U.S. foreign intelligence performed largely as it was intended to perform. American intelligence might possibly have predicted better or have discovered the missile sites a bit earlier; but it was still as if intelligence had caught the Japanese strike force in the North Pacific well out of range of Pearl Harbor. Nor did the intelligence apparatus intrude upon the decision-making process. It collected the information and let the policymakers decide what to do.

Throughout the summer of 1962, there were all sorts of rumors that the Russians were up to something in Cuba. U.S. intelligence reports estimated that twenty Soviet cargo ships arrived in Cuba in August alone and that there were three thousand to five thousand Soviet technicians on Cuban soil. Senator Kenneth Keating of New York, citing refugee reports, claimed that the Russians were putting offensive missiles in Cuba. He attacked the Kennedy administration for its "do-nothing policy." The Russians, at the same time, were engaged in deception. Khrushchev, Anatoly

Dobrynin (the Soviet ambassador to the United States), and Foreign Minister Andrei Gromyko emphatically denied up to the time of discovery—and beyond—that the Soviet Union had any intention to install offensive weapons in Cuba.

Amid various "signals" and "noise," however, the intelligence community as a whole doubted that the Soviets would put nuclear-tipped ballistic missiles in Cuba. It expressed this opinion in a general intelligence estimate in August and followed it up more conclusively with the famous special national intelligence estimate of September 19, 1962. Lacking "hard" evidence of Soviet missiles in Cuba at the time, the SNIE relied on previous Russian behavior. The USSR had "never given offensive missiles to other nations" nor "displayed a willingness to proceed with ventures that would so clearly and significantly raise the level of risk in U.S.–Soviet relations." [20]

The CIA's latest technique of "crateology"—determining the contents of crates by their configuration and construction and the port and time of embarkation [21]—apparently confirmed that there were no Russian rockets in Cuba. But DCI McCone was troubled. He explained later that he could not understand the reason for the presence of surface-to-air missile sites in Cuba, except to destroy high-altitude reconnaissance aircraft, or U-2s. [22] Moreover, on September 20, a CIA agent in Cuba had reported seeing a missile part being transported on a highway (the basis of the novel and movie, "Topaz"). McCone did not impose his "intuition" on the intelligence community but persuaded the president to authorize increased flights by U-2s over Cuba. To avoid controversy in case of a shoot-down, the air force flew the missions, not the CIA.

On October 14, after weather delays, "Bingo!" A U-2 brought back pictures that revealed to photo-interpreters the preparation of medium-range and intermediate-range ballistic missile sites in Cuba. On the morning of the sixteenth, after thorough analysis, the CIA briefed the president and his top advisers as described by Robert Kennedy:

> Experts arrived with their charts and their pointers and told us
> that if we looked carefully, we could see there was a missile base
> being constructed in a field near San Cristobal, Cuba. I, for one,

had to take their word for it. I examined the pictures carefully, and what I saw appeared to be no more than the clearing of a field for a farm or the basement of a house. I was relieved to hear later that this was the same reaction of virtually everyone at the meeting, including President Kennedy. Even a few days later, when more work had taken place on the site, he remarked that it looked like a football field.[23]

What looked like a "farm clearing" or a "football field" was the beginning of the "thirteen days" that "brought the world to the abyss of nuclear destruction and the end of mankind."[24] The intelligence community, particularly the CIA, presented irrefutable evidence in time for deliberate discussion and thereby contributed enormously to avoiding a possible nuclear holocaust.

President Kennedy constituted his principal advisers as the Executive Committee of the National Security Council, or ExComm, which agonized over various ways of reacting to the Soviet missiles in Cuba, "all the way from knocking them out to letting them be." ExComm consulted with McCone and the intelligence chiefs from Defense and State throughout the deliberations, and at least two SNIEs were prepared to assess the feasibility of certain actions and estimate probable Soviet responses. But intelligence proved most effective in playing an objective and passive role. Kennedy was irked over the IC's failure to read Soviet intentions (though even to date no one has produced satisfactory evidence that the Russians actually placed nuclear *warheads* in Cuba). But he viewed the CIA in a more favorable light because of McCone's leadership and persistence. On October 28, Khrushchev agreed to withdraw the missiles from Cuba, facilitated by Kennedy's relatively temperate decision to establish a naval blockade; the president sent a portrait photo to the CIA, autographed "with esteem."[25]

If Kennedy had known what the CIA had really been up to in Cuba, he might have used a different word. The missile crisis redeemed the CIA after the Bay of Pigs disaster, but it had been engaged in a series of dirty tricks against Fidel Castro that, when revealed, seriously damaged its reputation once again. The CIA's obsession with Castro went beyond the Bay of Pigs operation. Even as the Cuban invasion was being planned, the CIA's Clandestine Services was considering ways of removing Castro personally, in the hope of avoiding wider bloodshed. The schemes ran the gamut from "screwball" pranks to murder.

The CIA's first target was Castro's "charisma." During the summer of 1960, the Technical Services Division prepared a number of substances that were designed to destroy Castro's image. These included various hallucinogens, such as LSD, which were to be administered to Castro before a public appearance or speech and cause him to become disoriented. The TSD tested various ways that Castro could ingest the drugs unwittingly, such as using an aerosol spray or doctoring his cigars. Not succeeding in this, the TSD turned next to Castro's beard, a major element of the Cuban leader's appeal: the TSD would dust Castro's shoes with thallium salts, a powerful depilatory "that would cause his beard to fall out."

> The depilatory was to be administered during a trip outside Cuba, when it was anticipated Castro would leave his shoes outside the door of his hotel room to be shined[!]. TSD procured the chemical and tested it on animals, but apparently abandoned the scheme because Castro cancelled his trip.[26]

The CIA also lost interest in these schemes because DDP Bissell had something more lethal in mind. In August 1960, Bissell in effect "put out a contract" on Castro and employed criminal elements, including the so-called Mafia or Cosa Nostra. As outrageous as it is, the idea made sense in that underworld gambling syndicates had been hurt by Castro's closing of the casinos in Havana. (The opening scene of "Godfather II" depicting New Year's Eve 1959 in Havana is not far from actual events.) The CIA used Robert Maheu, a former FBI agent and private detective, as a go-between and offered underworld figure John Rosselli $150,000 for the "removal" of Castro. Almost every aspect of the Castro assassination plot is bizarre; even the legendary Howard Hughes appears to have been on the fringes of it. Hughes was an important client of Maheu; Maheu wanted to retain Hughes as a client but felt he "owed it" to the Agency to help out. He told Hughes in November 1960 that he was engaged in a project "on behalf of the United States Government, that it included plans to dispose of Mr. Castro in connection with a pending invasion."[27]

Not even Terry Southern could have exaggerated this episode of high-jinks and high rollers, which was at the same time a deadly business. During September 1960, Maheu met and talked with Rosselli in the plushest spots coast-to-coast, successively at the Brown Derby Restaurant in Beverly Hills, the Plaza Hotel in New York, and the Fountainebleau in Miami. Rosselli sought assurances that he was really being asked to get rid of Castro for the U.S. government; Maheu arranged a meeting for him with his case officer, James O'Connell, the chief of the Operational Support Division of the Office of Security. After being wined and dined, Rosselli finally agreed to take the job because "he felt that he had an obligation to his government." In mid-October in Miami, Rosselli introduced Maheu and O'Connell to "Sam Gold" and "Joe," whom he said he planned to use in the operation as a "back-up man" and "courier to Cuba," respectively. According to O'Connell,

> he learned the true identities of his associates one morning when Maheu called and asked him to examine the "Parade" supplement to the *Miami Times*. An article on the Attorney General's ten-most-wanted criminals list revealed that "Sam Gold" was Momo Salvatore Giancana, a Chicago-based gangster, and "Joe" was Santos Trafficante, the Cosa Nostra chieftain in Cuba.[28]

As these events transpired, an even more ludicrous sideshow was taking place. Sam Giancana suspected that his woman friend in Las Vegas (singer Phyllis McGuire of the McGuire Sisters) was having an affair with another entertainer (comedian Dan Rowan of *Laugh-In* fame). He wanted to fly there to check it out. To keep Giancana in Miami so as not to disrupt the project, Maheu secured O'Connell's approval to tap Rowan's phone and hired Arthur Balletti, a wiretap specialist, to install the "bug." While he was working in Rowan's hotel room in Las Vegas, Balletti took a lunch break and left his equipment unattended. A maid discovered it and called the police. Balletti first called Maheu, "tying [him] into this thing up to his ear," although Rosselli eventually arranged Balletti's bail. O'Connell described the incident as a "Keystone Comedy act," but it also had the effect of alerting the FBI and J. Edgar Hoover, with important consequences later on.[29]

Despite these distractions, Giancana and Rosselli devised a plan to assassinate Castro by having him poisoned. They were in touch with a Cuban exile leader who had a contact inside Cuba working in a restaurant where Castro often dined. This gave him access to Castro's food and drink. Rosselli asked the CIA to prepare "something 'nice and clean, without getting into any kind of out and out ambushing,' preferably a poison that would disappear without a trace."[30] The TSD prepared a batch of pills containing botulinum toxin, which " 'did the job expected of them' when tested on monkeys." Maheu, according to one version, passed the pills to Rosselli and his Cuban agent outside the Boom Boom Room of the Fountainebleau Hotel around March 12, 1961. The date is fairly definite because the whole team had gathered in Miami to see the third Patterson–Johansson heavyweight title fight. After delivering the poison pills, Giancana reportedly told a confederate, "Maheu's conning the hell out of the CIA."[31]

Whether it was a con or not, the Rosselli operation set in motion at least one assassination attempt against Castro in the weeks before the Bay of Pigs. The attempt was stillborn, either because Castro stopped going to the restaurant where the poison was to be administered, or because there was confusion about sending the "go signal," which never came. But O'Connell definitely passed the poison pills, along with a $10,000 cash advance. The Cuban agent subsequently returned the pills and the money.[32]

After the Bay of Pigs and the personnel turnover, the CIA maintained its contract with Rosselli, but it asked him to drop Maheu and Giancana as "untrustworthy." William Harvey was now serving as case officer, and Rosselli planned at least two assassination attempts during 1962. He received more poison pills and a U-Haul truckload of "explosives, detonators, rifles, handguns, radios, and boat radar costing about $5,000." Harvey was in charge of developing a general CIA program "for disabling foreign leaders" known as Executive Action (code name ZR/RIFLE); he became convinced that Rosselli "wasn't getting anywhere," and the two parted company on friendly terms in February 1963.[33]

Though Rosselli remarked later that it was Trafficante who had pulled the "scam," who had "sat on it" and "never did nothing,"[34] he apparently played it straight with the CIA. Agency officers believed that he was motivated by "patriotism" and noted that he "never took a nickel" for his services. More likely, he was seeking to create a situation for himself that would enable him to avoid prosecution or deportation. But he did not anticipate becoming involved in a Senate investigation of intelligence activities years later. In August 1976, his dismembered body was found in an oil drum floating in Biscayne Bay. Just the year before, in June, Sam Giancana, already gravely ill, was executed gangland-style in the kitchen of his home in Chicago.

The termination of Rosselli's contract did not end the CIA's efforts to assassinate Castro. In early 1963, Desmond Fitzgerald, who had replaced Harvey as chief of covert operations against Cuba (then called Task Force W and soon after, the Special Affairs staff), proposed two assassination schemes. Castro had a passion for scuba diving, so Fitzgerald first considered booby-trapping an "exotic" seashell. When that appeared unworkable, he considered having James Donovan (at the time involved in negotiations for the ransom and release of the Bay of Pigs prisoners) give Castro a diving suit treated with a deadly substance. The TSD actually procured a diving suit and laced it with Madura foot, a fungus that causes a skin disease, and contaminated the breathing apparatus with a tubercule bacillus. DDP Helms described the plan as "cock-eyed" and affirmed that the suit "never left the laboratory."[35]

In a more serious plan, Fitzgerald encouraged Rolando Cubela—one of the "majors" of the Cuban Revolution, who had been cooperating with the CIA since early 1961—to consider "eliminating" Castro as part of a possible coup attempt. Cubela (who was given the cryptonym AM/LASH) was disappointed in Castro's leadership and wanted to defect, but the CIA convinced him that he could do more for "a new Cuba" by remaining in a position of influence and working from within. During 1963, Fitzgerald met several times with Cubela, usually in Paris, and pledged U.S. support in any attempt to overthrow Castro. Cubela requested a high-powered rifle with a telescopic sight for killing Castro, but Fitzgerald wanted him to try a different technique and offered him "a ball-point pen rigged with a hypodermic needle . . . so fine that the victim would not notice its insertion."

On November 22, 1963, Fitzgerald . . . met with AM/LASH and offered him the poison pen, recommending that he use

Blackleaf-40, a deadly poison which is commercially available. [According to the IG's report of the incident], "it is likely that at the very moment President Kennedy was shot, a CIA officer was meeting with a Cuban agent . . . and giving him an assassination device for use against Castro."[36]

Even after the tragic murder of the American president (claims linking it to the Castro assassination plots are unsubstantiated), the CIA persisted in its efforts to get rid of Castro, at least until the middle of 1965. Kennedy's assassination apparently caused the CIA to move more gingerly, but it maintained its relationship with Cubela, and twice during 1964, in March and June, it directly gave him arms. Later in the year it used Manuel Artime, an anti-Castro leader in exile, to pass silenced weapons and grenades to him. The Church Committee reported in 1975 that the CIA ended its collaboration with AM/LASH in June 1965, supposedly because of his public boasting about his intention to kill Castro. But Cubela was arrested in Cuba in connection with an assassination plot in March 1966 and sentenced to thirty years' imprisonment.

When these attempts against the life of Fidel Castro became part of the public record in the mid-1970s, the U.S. Congress acted to outlaw assassination as an instrument of U.S. foreign policy. The CIA's reputation plummeted again, along with the morale of its clandestine operators, who regarded themselves as honorable public servants and resented being called irresponsible "cowboys." But having performed as professionals, they could not avoid the blame, because an inherent feature of covert action is nonattribution, the disconnecting of lines of authority and accountability. The Congress failed to determine who had authorized the CIA to attempt murder, and thereby it dealt with the effects of the abuse of authority, not with the cause. As long as covert action was a legitimate tool of U.S. foreign policy, there could be no effective way to control it without resolving the issue of accountability.

There is no question that the DDPs Bissell and Helms were responsible for the assassination plots and knew most of the details, including the use of underworld figures. According to Bissell, Allen Dulles also knew about and authorized the first plot against Castro involving the Mafia.[37] McCone, however, denied having any knowledge of assassination plots that occurred during his tenure. In August 1963, when the *Chicago Sun Times* had published an article dealing with Giancana and the CIA, Helms had prepared a memo for McCone informing him of underworld ties. McCone read the memo and said, "Well, this did not happen during my tenure." Helms did not tell McCone that the activity had been resumed, nor did McCone, as Helms put it, "[tell me] not to assassinate Castro."[38] According to another person who was present at this briefing, McCone was "perfectly aware" of what Helms was trying to say to him and McCone never said that "we absolutely could not have this activity going on in the future."[39]

Such talking in riddles is at the heart of the matter—that is, presidential responsibility, and specifically the role played by Presidents Eisenhower, Kennedy, and Johnson in the Castro assassination plots. According to Thomas Powers, Helms's biographer, "no one in CIA doubted for a minute that Eisenhower and Kennedy 'jolly well knew.'" But those directly involved, such as Helms, became distraught when the Church Committee kept returning to the question of authority: Helms "was being as clear as he could: the Kennedys wanted Castro out of there, the CIA did not go off on its own in these matters, the Agency was only doing its job. What more could he say: Senator, how can you be so goddamned dumb? *This isn't the kind of thing you put in writing.*"[40] But that was precisely the point of the questioning. Because of the use of "plausible denial" to reinforce nonattribution in covert operations, only a Richard Helms *could* state what had not been put in writing:

> "Plausible denial" has shaped the processes for approving and evaluating covert operations. For example, the 40 Committee and its predecessor, the Special Group, have served as "circuit breakers" for Presidents, thus avoiding consideration of covert action by the Oval office.
>
> "Plausible denial" can also lead to the use of euphemism and circumlocution, which are designed to allow the President and other senior officials to deny knowledge of an operation should it be disclosed. The converse may also occur; a President could communicate his desire for a sensitive operation in an indirect, circumlocutious manner. An additional possibility is that a President may, in fact, not be fully and accurately informed about a sensitive operation because he failed to receive the "cir-

cumlocutious" message. The evidence . . . reveals that serious problems of assessing intent and ensuring both control and accountability may result from the use of "plausible denial." [41]

The Church Committee did not find out much about Eisenhower's role in the plotting against Castro, but it did learn a great deal about plausible denial from the case of Eisenhower and Patrice Lumumba of the Republic of the Congo (now Zaire). During an NSC meeting on August 18, 1960, Eisenhower apparently made a strong statement about Lumumba, and Robert Johnson, an NSC staffer, affirmed that it "came across to me as an order for the assassination of Lumumba." [42] Acting Secretary of State C. Douglas Dillon, also present at the meeting, did not think the statement was "a direct order to have an assassination," but he conceded that it was "perfectly possible" that Allen Dulles "would have translated such strong Presidential language about 'getting rid of' Lumumba into authorization for an assassination effort."

Dulles obviously did get the message and conveyed the president's "extremely strong feelings on the necessity for very straightforward action" to a meeting of the Special Group (or 5412 Group, the NSC committee responsible for approving "high-risk" covert operations) on August 25. He secured agreement "that planning for the Congo would not necessarily rule out 'consideration' of any particular kind of activity which might contribute to getting rid of Lumumba." The very next day, Dulles personally sent a cable to the station chief in Leopoldville (now Kinshasa) declaring that Lumumba's "removal must be an urgent and prime objective. . . . A high priority of our covert action." [43]

The incident demonstrates that a president has to be careful what he says in front of his DCI. But Bissell, in a later commentary, said that things had not happened by accident but that matters such as assassination would be discussed only in a "circumlocutious manner." He referred to the Special Group meeting of August 25 as a "prime example."

When you use the language that no particular means were ruled out, that is obviously what it meant, and it meant that to everybody in the room. . . . Meant that if it had to be assassination, that that was a permissible means.

You don't use language of that kind except to mean in effect, the Director is being told, get rid of the guy, and if you have to use extreme means up to and including assassination, go ahead.[44]

Moreover, Bissell told the Church Committee that Dulles's August 26 cable "signaled to him" that there was presidential authorization to assassinate Lumumba. In his testimony, he elaborated:

Q: Did Mr. Dulles tell you that President Eisenhower wanted Lumumba killed?
Mr. Bissell: I am sure he didn't.
Q: Did he ever tell you even circumlocutiously through this kind of cable?
Mr. Bissell: Yes, I think his cable says it in effect.[45]

After spending weeks on this problem, the Church Committee, in some circumlocutious language of its own, concluded:

The chain of events revealed by the documents and testimony is strong enough to permit a reasonable inference that the plot to assassinate Lumumba was authorized by President Eisenhower. Nevertheless, there is enough countervailing testimony by Eisenhower Administration officials and enough ambiguity and lack of clarity in the records of high-level policy meetings to preclude the Committee from making a finding that the President intended an assassination effort against Lumumba.[46]

There appeared to be stronger evidence that President Kennedy had knowledge (implying tacit consent?) of assassination plots against Castro, but the Church Committee again showed reluctance to make a finding that implicated, as it said, "Presidents who are not able to speak for themselves."[47]

During the Kennedy administration, there were two other major covert action programs that were closely related to the Castro assassination plots. The first of these, inaugurated in 1961, was the Executive Action program, whose purposes included developing a "capability to perform assassinations." Bissell placed William Harvey, Rosselli's case officer, in charge. Bissell claimed that the "generalized" capability was never used, but Harvey did brief McGeorge Bundy, President Kennedy's adviser for national security affairs, about the project. Harvey related that Bundy "gave no instruction," but neither did he offer "any impediment."[48] Thus, although Bundy may not have been told about actual assassination efforts, he did learn that the CIA had assassination in its bag of tricks—from an officer who was actually running such an operation.

The second program was Operation Mongoose, an intense covert action program created to overthrow Castro, that lasted from November 1961 to November 1962. President Kennedy, having been humiliated by the Bay of Pigs and upset with the CIA, assigned Mongoose not to the CIA but to the NSC's Special Group—actually, the Special Group–Augmented, to include Attorney General Robert Kennedy—and appointed General Edward Lansdale as coordinator. Lansdale advocated carrying out an elaborate program of subversion and resistance-building over time, in which the Cuban people, not the Americans, might overthrow Castro. The CIA assigned Task Force W to work with him, headed by Executive Action officer William Harvey.

Not only did the Kennedys not give Mongoose to the CIA; they personally scolded Bissell and exerted heavy pressure on him, "chewing him out" in the Cabinet Room of the White House "for, as he put it, sitting on his ass and not doing anything about getting rid of Castro and the Castro regime."[49] Subsequently, on May 7, 1962, when the question of dropping the Las Vegas wiretap case (on Dan Rowan's phone, October 30, 1960) arose, CIA general counsel Lawrence Houston thoroughly briefed Attorney General Kennedy about the use of Sam Giancana and other Mafia figures in the plot to assassinate Castro. Houston, hoping to avoid a prosecution, later related that Kennedy was "mad"—but not about the attempts to kill Castro, only angry with the CIA for getting involved with the Mafia.[50] Although Robert Kennedy was not told that contact with Rosselli had been resumed (nor, presumably, about AM/LASH), given the climate the Kennedys were creating, it was, as Thomas Powers suggested, "a case of the dog that didn't bark."[51]

In the unlikely event that Robert Kennedy did not tell his brother that the CIA had been plotting Castro's death, the president had an opportunity to learn it from at least one other source. The Las Vegas wiretap case had made FBI director Hoover privy to knowledge of the CIA's use of the Mafia against Castro. During the course of his own investigation, Hoover discovered that a close friend of the president's maintained a similar relationship with Giancana and Rosselli. The Church Committee delicately referred to this person as "the President's friend"; she was Judith Campbell Exner, whom Kennedy had met in Las Vegas in March 1960, when he was a senator, and with whom he had frequent contact through mid-1962. Hoover, alarmed that Exner was also associating with "hoodlums," brought this matter to the president's attention at a private luncheon on March 22, 1962.

> There is no record of what transpired at that luncheon. According to the White House logs, the last telephone contact between the White House and the President's friend occurred a few hours after the luncheon.
>
> The fact that the President and Hoover had a luncheon at which one topic was presumably that the President's friend was also a friend of Giancana and Rosselli raises several possibilities. The first is, assuming that Hoover did in fact receive a summary of FBI information relating to Giancana prior to his luncheon with the President, whether that summary reminded the Director that Giancana had been involved in a CIA operation against Cuba that included "dirty business" and further indicated that Giancana had talked about an assassination attempt against Castro. A second is whether Hoover would then have taken the luncheon as an opportunity to fulfill his duty to bring this information to the President's attention. What actually transpired at that luncheon may never be known, as both participants are dead and the FBI files contain no records relating to it.[52]

Though the matter of presidential authorization remains elusive, the fact that a Senate investigating committee and the FBI director ended up boudoir-peeping in this case reveals much about the nature and problem of covert action in American society.

There is no evidence that Kennedy's successor, Lyndon Johnson, had any direct knowledge of assassination plots before becoming president. He told writer Leo Janis that, when he took office, he discovered that "we had been operating a damned Murder, Inc., in the Caribbean."[53] Despite the terrible innuendos made about Johnson and the presidential succession (of which *MacBird* is an extreme case), the CIA sounded out the new president and learned that "he wanted no part of assassination." Those involved in AM/LASH permitted it to lapse "when it was probably clear they did not have the President's sanction."[54] At that point, Richard Helms, who was now deputy DCI, had his eye on the top spot and undoubtedly wanted to avoid making any mistakes.

In March 1967, Drew Pearson published a column that charged that the CIA had been involved with the Mafia in attempts to kill Castro. (Rosselli, desperately trying to avoid deportation, had leaked the story.) Johnson ordered Helms—who had been DCI since June 1966—to look into the matter. Helms briefed the president the following May, informing him of the CIA's use of underworld figures. But when the Church Committee asked Helms if he told Johnson that the assassination plots had continued into his presidency, Helms replied, "I just can't answer that, I just don't know. I can't recall having done so." By way of further explanation, Helms added that he did not regard AM/LASH as a simple assassination plot.[55]

The Church Committee's evidence on the matter of presidential authority and the Castro assassination plots leads to the conclusion that either Presidents Eisenhower and Kennedy abused their authority and deceived the American people about it, or that the control system was so wired with ambiguity, euphemism, and circumlocution that the CIA believed it had the authorization to act when it did not. Both circumstances depended upon the existence of a secret apparatus with a capability for extraordinary deeds, and either would have constituted a breakdown of the democratic process. The combination of covert action and plausible denial was creating a crisis of government whose existence became apparent only when a blunder occurred. But even then it was perceived merely as a matter of ineptitude: Fidel Castro, after all, survived everything the CIA threw at him—including poisoned cigars, exploding sea shells, and the Mafia—but a lone gunman murdered the American president.

The decline or fall from grace of U.S. foreign intelligence, and especially of the CIA, is usually dated from the Bay of Pigs covert action. But something was going haywire overall: there was a series of tragic blunders in the 1960s that involved other intelligence agencies and functions as well. These events added to the discord of that decade, but they were not directly related to the issues of the times. Rather, they stemmed from operational deficiencies having to do with bureaucracy and technology. Ironically, the problems of governmental secrecy and accountability came to the surface not when covert action was abused but when technical collection, with its emphasis upon machines, broke down.

21
Of Machines and Follies

I f the United States had a KH-11 reconnaissance satellite in December 1941, the Japanese attack force would have been detected long before it got within striking distance of Pearl Harbor. Technical intelligence (TECHINT) became an obsession of the intelligence community during the cold war era, which is not surprising considering the geographical expanse of the Soviet Union and its status as one vast "denied area." The very speed, range, and destructiveness of modern weapons systems created an imperative to prevent surprise and led to the application of science to information-gathering, with astounding results.

The United States developed machines that could detect, identify, and monitor targets, using sensors that could feel, hear, see, and smell. President Eisenhower's Technological Capabilities Panel, created in 1954 and headed by MIT president James Killian and Edwin Land of the Polaroid Corporation, inspired the intelligence community to sponsor research and development by science and industry that produced an incredible array of *black boxes*—that is, inanimate technical methods of spying.[1] In 1971, when the CIA's William Colby returned from Vietnam, he was briefed before taking a new assignment. His reaction indicates the extent and swiftness of the achievement.

I went on a tour of the aero-space-technology factories on the West Coast and there had my eyes opened to the veritable science-fiction world of space systems, radar, electronic sensors, infrared photography, and the ubiquitous computer, all able to gather intelligence from high in the sky to deep in the ocean with

astounding accuracy and precision. I found that when this information was processed it produced exquisitely detailed reports of
secret test centers and experiments deep in Asia; of truck parks
and barracks for armored divisions in Eastern Europe, permitting a stunningly accurate reading of foreign military forces.[2]

If Colby had made the same tour fifteen years later, his eyes would
have opened even wider. As William Burrows wrote in 1986,

> To be sure, the technical intelligence systems are extraordinary,
> whether they are low-orbiting satellites that silently record images
> of events with remarkable clarity and relay them even as the
> action itself is occurring [real-time intelligence], or whether they
> are other spacecraft, some parked a tenth of the way to the moon,
> that point their mechanical ears in directions allowing them to
> listen to and pass on a crescendo of military and civilian commu-
> nication signals and even eavesdrop on conversations taking
> place deep within the walls of the Kremlin.[3]

From the first U-2s of the late 1950s to the reconnaissance satellites of the 1980s, American scientists have developed imaging systems capable of taking advantage of the improved performance of
each new generation of *platforms*. From cameras that "could differ-
entiate between objects the size of a basketball . . . at a distance
of more than thirteen miles," it developed computer-enhanced
imagery that could produce close-up photographs of Soviet military and industrial installations from a height of 504 miles.[4] DCI
Stansfield Turner (March 1977–January 1981) once boasted that
satellite photos taken from 150 miles up could show whether graz-
ing cattle were Guernseys or Herefords. Experts even designed
infrared cameras that could take overhead pictures of objects that
were no longer there—reproducing, for example, "shadows" of
the wing tanks of parked aircraft long gone (since gasoline radiates
heat) and radar "cameras" that could "see" through clouds.

The eavesdropping devices were just as spectacular. Signals
intelligence (SIGINT) was the first form of technical intelligence,
composed of communications intelligence (COMINT), electronic
intelligence (ELINT), telemetry intelligence (TELINT), and other
forms of intelligence based on intercepting electromagnetic

emissions. In the mid-1950s, the National Security Agency, which was in charge of the U.S. SIGINT effort, began implementing the Intercept Deployment Plan, which called for the establishment of over four thousand "ears," or intercept stations, worldwide. An intercept station may be "little more than a radio receiver" and as simple as "a vaultlike van on the back of an Army truck," or it may be a massive installation that accommodates a network of Wullenweber antennas, "each capable of holding three football fields, end to end."

> Typical of the large, Wullenweber-type stations is the Naval Security Group Activity at Edzell, Scotland. . . . The 490-acre station takes its name from the village of Edzell, about three miles away. . . .
>
> At first sight the antenna appears to resemble either a frightening prison out of a Kafka-esque nightmare or possibly a leftover set from the latest sci-fi thriller.
>
> Actually, the antenna is more a twentieth-century Stonehenge. The forty-acre Wullenweber site consists of a two-story, boxlike cement operations building surrounded by four concentric circles of poles and wires almost a thousand feet in diameter and from eight feet to over a hundred feet in height.
>
> Also known as a circularly disposed antenna array (CDAA), the system is designed to locate and intercept signals ranging from the low-band, such as submarine traffic, to the high-band, such as radio-telephone. Because of its omnidirectional design, the system is capable of plucking the signal from the sky regardless of its origin.[5]

In addition to operating ground stations, the NSA also sent various platforms (aircraft and satellites) aloft, loaded with electronic sensors (black boxes). These sensors were a great deal more than radio receivers. NSA undertook "ferret" missions to map radar sites. Initially, manned aircraft had been used to fly along and toward the borders of the Soviet Union and other target countries to induce them to "turn on" their radar. Eventually, satellites capable of achieving polar orbits three hundred miles high were substituted. "In one day," as a ferret satellite (the size of an oil drum) "orbits north to south and the earth rotates east to west, [it] would come within receiving range of virtually all radars and high-frequency transmitters in the world."[6] Even more awesome was the satellite code-named Rhyolite. First launched in 1973, it could intercept signals in the microwave frequencies from its geosynchronous orbit (that is, "parked" over a single spot on earth) 22,300 miles in space.

> Each [Rhyolite] carried a battery of antennas capable of sucking foreign microwave signals from out of space like a vacuum cleaner picking up specks of dust from a carpet: American intelligence agents could monitor Communist microwave radio and long-distance telephone traffic over much of the European landmass, eavesdropping on a Soviet commissar in Moscow talking to his mistress in Yalta or on a general talking to his lieutenants across the great continent.[7]

From outer space to the ocean depths, little escapes the black boxes of American TECHINT. A string of huge tanks lines the ocean floor between North Cape, Norway, and Bear Island in the Barents Sea. Each contains clusters of hydrophones tuned to different frequencies, and they are linked by deeply buried cable, in order to monitor the passage of Soviet submarines to and from their base at Polyarnyy, near Murmansk.[8] Back on land, sensors like the arrays of seismometers and seismographs installed by the Air Force Technical Applications Center near Lawton, Oklahoma, detect vibrations from underground and underwater nuclear explosions anywhere in the world. Set up in 1960, this surveillance system "can serve two masters at the same time: arms control and military intelligence."[9] The gadgets may take smaller, though no less imaginative, forms, from various types of bugs and wiretaps to a device that can aim a laser beam "at a closed window from outside, [in order] to pick up the vibrations of the sound waves caused by a conversation inside the room."[10]

Though communications intelligence established TECHINT, the U-2 airplane best symbolizes the post-World War II generation of spy machines. The CIA's Richard Bissell and Lockheed's Clarence L. "Kelly" Johnson developed the U-2 and sent it on its maiden flight over the Soviet Union on the Fourth of July 1956. From that time to the shootdown of a U-2 near Sverdlovsk on May 1, 1960, the so-called Black Lady of Espionage completed twenty "deep penetration missions" over the Soviet Union.[11] From an altitude of 80,000 feet (fifteen miles plus), the U-2's cameras could pick out the white stripes in a parking lot below and produce photographs "[covering] terrain up to 125 miles wide over the course of a 2,600-mile-long flight."[12] In addition to its imaging systems, the U-2 "sprouted" specialized antennas for signals intercept and "sniffers" for detecting radioactivity in the atmosphere that resulted from nuclear explosions.[13]

Sooner or later someone was going to shoot down a U-2, so Kelly Johnson designed the SR-71, which could fly higher (125,000 feet) and faster (four times the speed of sound, or 2,600 mph). Although it looked like a hooded cobra, the SR-71 was nicknamed Blackbird because of its sooty-black exterior (so designed for "stealth" or radar evasion). The SR-71, too, carried a variety of black boxes for PHOTINT (photographic intelligence), ELINT, and COMINT: "An SR-71 tearing along the coast of Sakhalin Island . . . can photograph air bases, missile sites, and port facilities (including berthed submarines) while simultaneously eavesdropping on Soviet communication traffic and ferreting radar."[14]

Even this spectacular aircraft was surpassed in the mid-1960s by the orbiters. Of these, the imaging satellites (code-named Keyhole, or KH) were awesome examples. The KH-9 series Big Bird—twelve-ton giants launched for the first time in 1971—monitored Soviet missile programs with incredible precision for more than a decade from a relatively safe distance of over a hundred miles.

> During the summer of 1974, a KH-9 discovered that the Russians were trying to conceal construction of what appeared to be new missile silos. That winter, another of the spacecraft recorded the first deployment of SS-18s. In the following months, KH-9 inventoried ten SS-17s, an equal number of SS-18s, and fifty SS-19s, all of them deployed. Big Birds also participated in the discovery and subsequent monitoring of an important new ballistic missile being tested: the mobile SS-20 IRBM.[15]

Satellites did not completely replace the U-2s, the SR-71s, or even the reconnaissance versions of such old reliables as Goonies (EC-47), Connies (EC-121), and Boeing 707s (RC-135), because of their predictability (in fixed orbits) and their inability to perform certain specialized functions. A certain redundancy is intentionally built into technical collection—so as not to miss anything, for purposes of cross-referencing and verification, and for backup. But satellites are very expensive. The National Reconnaissance Office, the air force "component" that launches the spy satellites and does the housekeeping ("any or all of the scores of operations that must be done to keep a satellite in orbit and performing its mission "),[16] has a budget that is probably second only to that of the NSA in the intelligence community. In 1974, Marchetti and Marks cited a figure of $1.5 billion; just over ten years later, William Burrows put it at "close to $5 billion." Because of its high cost and its duplications, TECHINT has not escaped criticism, for all its miracles.

One major criticism is that it provides too much of a good thing. TECHINT's black boxes can collect a tremendous volume of raw intelligence. According to one analyst, an astro-physicist, "The information coming down from these things [reconnaissance satellites] is just going to choke you. . . . It gets awful real fast. You can't buy big enough computers to process it. You can't buy enough programmers to write the codes or to look at the results to interpret them. At some point you just get saturated . . . and that defeats your whole purpose."[17] Regardless, as Patrick McGarvey has noted, "Our almost limitless ability to collect information has prompted only a few to question the utility of the information that is collected. . . . The results are frightening. More and more information of less and less value is collected. The worthless items are stored, against a slim hope that their value will increase when more technology affords meaning to them."[18]

This situation, McGarvey added, is exacerbated by the "Pearl Harbor syndrome." Every "tidbit" is forwarded speedily to Washington so that no piece of the puzzle will be overlooked. In addition, says McGarvey, the "Church of What's Happening Now syndrome" means that everbody wants to have "the latest." This results in the broadest dissemination possible and adds to the flow of paper already overloading the system.[19] "In intelligence," McGarvey affirmed, "technology has allied itself with bureaucracy, and together they ride roughshod over reason and logic."[20]

McGarvey believed, in fact, that technology had come to dominate intelligence, that it was "the tail wagging the dog." Writing in 1972, he cited Henry Howe Ransom's observation that in intelligence work the social scientist was being displaced "by the electronics expert, the physical scientist and the specialist in technical means of collecting and collating and interpreting data." McGarvey "checked it out" and discovered that at the Defense Intelligence Agency, where he worked, "the proportion of high grades [top jobs] [was] three times as high on the technical side as on the production side.

> Careerwise, the production analyst—the guy who interprets and reports on the "data" collected by technical intelligence—has been left behind. His colleagues on the technical side, who theoretically exist to support his efforts, outrank him and thus effectively control the direction of intelligence collection. The technocrats reign supreme.[21]

McGarvey's conclusion, written while Richard Nixon was president, remained valid during the presidency of Ronald Reagan. But it was compounded by the fact that "the torrent of data generated by technical systems" had continued to pile up in the years between.[22] The United States sought "only to collect all available facts," without determining "which facts [were] more significant and what they might mean."[23] " 'Everyone tasks,' " the complaint persists, but "no one does the 'quality job' of authoritatively prioritizing."[24]

Closely related to this problem is the problem of risk assessment. The technocrats assumed management positions but concentrated upon hardware; as they did, the possibility of a political blunder became real. Gadgets used to collect useless information might also be sent to the wrong place at the wrong time. This happened a number of times in the 1960s, resulting in crises that almost caused exactly what the spy machines were designed to prevent: war.

The shootdown of a U-2 over the Soviet Union was inevitable. But that the plane was shot down while flying over the Soviet Union in May 1960, on the eve of a "summit conference" among the leaders of France, Russia, the United Kingdom, and the

United States, was inexplicable. Being caught while spying is always embarrassing; under these circumstances, it was humiliating. At first, the United States and President Eisenhower lied about the nature and the mission of the aircraft. But when the Soviets displayed the wreckage of the U-2 and its live pilot, Francis Gary Powers, further denials were impossible. U-2 pilots had been provided with means for committing suicide and were instructed to activate the destruct mechanism (with a seventy-second delay) before ejecting from a stricken craft. Powers had done neither; U-2 pilots had an ugly suspicion that there was actually no delay at all in the "destruct" switch: "once they flipped [it], the [explosive charge] would obliterate not only the equipment but them too."[25]

With Powers in Soviet custody, President Eisenhower reversed himself and took personal responsibility for the flights. He now insisted that they were necessary and even indicated that they would continue. The United States actually stopped U-2 flights over the Soviet Union after the shootdown, but Soviet premier Nikita Khrushchev exploited the incident. He threatened to retaliate against neighboring countries that based the U.S. spy plane, demanded an apology from the American president, and caused the Paris summit to collapse. U.S. foreign intelligence had emerged from the background and seriously compromised American foreign policy.

Even more tragic—from the standpoint of the loss of life—was the attack upon the USS *Liberty* in June 1967. The *Liberty* was a World War II Liberty ship that the NSA and the navy had taken out of mothballs and converted into a seagoing intercept station. Commissioned in late 1964, the *Liberty* usually patrolled the west coast of Africa. But in May 1967, the ship was ordered to the eastern Mediterranean, in anticipation of the Arab-Israeli Six-Day War. On June 8 occurred what was later described as "one of the most incredible failures of communications in the history of the Department of Defense." "Hearability studies" had established that the waters just east of Crete were the ideal location for Middle East intercept.[26] But the *Liberty* was sailing thirteen nautical miles off the coast of Egypt's Sinai Peninsula—instead of off the eastern end of Crete. It came under attack by Israeli jets and P-T boats;

thirty-four American sailors were killed and more than a hundred others wounded.

Israel apologized for the attack and insisted that it was accidental, but circumstances supported the view that it was deliberate. The Joint Chiefs of Staff, outraged by what the ship and its crew had been through, "proposed a quick retaliatory air strike on the Israeli naval base which launched the attack."[27] But such an action would sharply contradict American policy in the Middle East—as, indeed, the *Liberty's* presence off Sinai had contradicted U.S. policy. According to Frank Raven, the NSA official in charge of the intercept program, the navy had put the ship in harm's way in order to listen to low-level or tactical traffic that nobody "gave a damn about." "There was nothing to be gained by having her in there that close," he stated, "nothing she couldn't do where we wanted her. . . . She could do everything that the national requirement called for [from the coast of Crete.]"[28]

Nevertheless, just a short time later, another U.S. spy ship sailed into troubled waters and precipitated another crisis. In January 1968, North Korean patrol boats seized the USS *Pueblo,* a navy SIGINT vessel that had been eavesdropping off the east coat of Korea. The United States claimed that its ship was in international waters when attacked and boarded, and it was incensed by the spectacle of a U.S. Navy captain and crew being paraded in the port of Wonsan as "pirates." It contemplated taking armed retaliatory action. Once again, a TECHINT platform had caused a war scare. Yet according to McGarvey, "The *Pueblo* was totally unnecessary from an intelligence point of view."[29] Even with the principle of redundancy, duplicate stations capable of covering the *Pueblo's* targets already existed in South Korea and Japan. But the Navy had been fighting with the NSA for control over SIGINT vessels and, getting the *Pueblo* for its own, had "had a new ship to play with."[30]

The *Pueblo* debacle finally provoked a public debate about U.S. reconnaissance missions and the risks involved. Among the critics, McGarvey disputed the navy's claim that it evaluated the risks of reconnaissance missions carefully. That assertion was a "polite fiction," he wrote, and added that TECHINT was "out of control."

"The sheer amount of paper in the system," McGarvey said, made it impossible for anyone to know what was going on, from the "recon" officer (a navy lieutenant in Japan) who had plotted the *Pueblo's* course, to the chiefs in Washington who "signed off" on the mission. The navy lieutenant, overwhelmed by the glut of "paper" and constrained by "need to know," "was not tuned into the political and diplomatic realities surrounding North Korea at the time." As a result, he had ignored at least two vital criteria in making his risk assessment: "the political climate" and the "sensitivity of the target country." Because the *Pueblo* was to sail in international waters, he had assessed the risk as "minimal."[31] According to McGarvey, the chiefs up the line rarely questioned a "minimal risk" evaluation, and besides, there were "close to four hundred" reconnaissance missions scheduled for January 1968.

> When all of the individual proposals finally filter into Washington from military commands around the world, they are compiled into one large monthly reconnaissance schedule. It normally runs about the thickness of a Washington phone book. Once assembled, it is sent around the intelligence community for coordination and approval. The speed with which the January, 1968, recon schedule containing the ill-fated *Pueblo* mission was approved by all of official Washington—three days—bears moot testimony to the "careful scrutiny" allegedly given the missions.[32]

McGarvey based his criticisms upon his experience as an employee of the CIA and the DIA. Two official government studies corroborated much of what he said. The President's Blue Ribbon Panel on Defense, July 1, 1970, chaired by Gilbert W. Fitzhugh (the Fitzhugh Report), concluded that "intelligence activities are spread throughout the Department of Defense with little or no effective coordination; . . . There is a large imbalance in the allocation of resources, which causes more information to be collected than can ever be processed or used; [and] . . . Collection efforts are driven by advances in sensor technology, not by requirements filtering down from consumers of the [IC's] products."[33] In March 1971, James Schlesinger—then OMB director and later

DCI (February–July 1973)—made a similar finding in "A Review of the Intelligence Community" (the Schlesinger Report). He declared that too much was being collected by "ever more sophisticated technical collection systems." Such systems, he believed, "had led to 'gross redundancies' in [intelligence] operations."[34]

The fallout from the *Pueblo* affair caused the navy and the NSA to decommission their SIGINT "fleet" and sell it "for scrap"[35] (although a navy EC-121 was shot down off the coast of North Korea in April 1969). As the Fitzhugh Report had recommended, the office of assistant secretary of defense for intelligence (ASD/I) was created to centralize the DOD's intelligence budget and thereby to bring technical collection programs under control. Even so, the situation did not improve significantly. According to Roy Godson, coordinator of the Consortium for the Study of Intelligence, "the United States is now [1987] not photographing, listening, and processing data pertaining to everything," but there are collection "models" or patterns that persist.

> The model and intelligence collection budget are now being set by collection managers, more or less on their own, according to implicit rather than explicit choices. These are based on the often unconscious intellectual habits of the collectors, the inevitable bureaucratic battles over resoursces, and what collection managers believe their capabilities might allow them to learn.[36]

The *Pueblo* affair may have ultimately impelled, rather than curtailed, the collection of unreadable foreign cipher traffic. One NSA official, referring to the "boxcars and warehouses" full of "not-yet 'broken' Soviet and Chinese messages" stored at NSA's Fort Meade headquarters, expressed the hope that "maybe we'll get a break sometime, like the *Pueblo*."

> [When captured,] much of the *Pueblo's* cryptological machinery was seized intact . . . and probably turned over to the Soviets. While these machines were not associated with the highest-grade U.S. military or diplomatic systems, the Soviets would have been able to use them to read messages previously sent through certain American military channels and intercepted and stored by the Soviets.[37]

With the advent of reconnaissance satellites, technical collection programs tended to become involved less in international incidents (although the expense and volume of paper continued to grow). Occasionally, a spy satellite survived reentry and fell to earth, causing sensational headlines. Such was the case of the Soviet Cosmos satellite that crashed in the Canadian wilderness in January 1978, and another that splashed into the Indian Ocean five years later.

The controversy over U.S. ferret missions was rekindled in September 1983, when a Korean Jumbo jet, KAL flight 007, was shot down off Sakhalin Island "soon after it had passed through forbidden airspace near the Soviet naval base at Petropavlovsk,"[38] killing all 269 passengers aboard. Though one recoils from the charge that the United States would jeopardize the lives of innocent passengers on a commercial flight for intelligence purposes, nonetheless the fact that ferret missions actually were undertaken created the circumstances in which an aircraft that strayed into Soviet airspace might be attacked. Moreover, an RC-135S—a specialized U.S. reconnaissance plane (code-named Cobra Ball) that routinely flew the Bering Sea to "collect intelligence on ballistic missile testing, including telemetry"—had been in the "immediate vicinity" of KAL 007 on that fateful evening.[39]

Additionally, TECHINT caused the embassy "bugging war" of 1987. The Russians managed to obtain Mount Alto as the site for its new embassy. Mount Alto is one of the highest points in the District of Columbia; described as "electronically quiet," it would enable Soviet radios to pick up signals from the White House, the State Department, and the Pentagon. On the other hand, while the United States was constructing its new embassy in Moscow (with Russian workers), it discovered that the walls literally "had ears," rendering it useless and causing U.S. officials to consider demolishing it. As this is being written, both multimillion-dollar structures stand vacant—an "odd couple" in a TECHINT standoff.

These recent episodes did not produce the same clamor for reform as the U-2, the *Liberty,* and the *Pueblo* affairs of the 1960s. In the 1980s, TECHINT went "high tech," promoting an "explosion" of activity on the part of military intelligence especially.[40]

This explosion was fueled by an enhanced DOD budget and was linked to popular programs such as arms limitation verification, early warning systems (like SPADATS, or Space Detection and Tracking System), and the Strategic Defense Initiative (SDI, or "Star Wars"). But the events of the 1960s had occurred in the context of the Vietnam War, a time of frustration and turmoil. To understand the force of that clamor for reform, it is necessary to examine U.S. foreign intelligence during the Vietnam era in detail.

22

Vietnam:
Foreign and Domestic

According to Lyman Kirkpatrick, former inspector general of the CIA, the Vietnam War was "the largest intelligence effort by the U.S. government in any one area since the Second World War."[1] It was also a setback for American intelligence, as a negative public attitude toward the intelligence community focused especially upon the CIA. The slide that began with the Bay of Pigs continued when CIA intervention in the regime of Ngo Dinh Diem was revealed and certain paramilitary and counterterror programs were carried out in Southeast Asia. Allegations of CIA black-market operations, money laundering, and even drug trafficking to finance covert operations exacerbated the situation. Beyond this, the perception existed that U.S. intelligence did not perform well in Vietnam and had very little influence upon policymakers in Washington, despite America's highly sophisticated intelligence capability. Finally, amid the turmoil that the war in Vietnam engendered within the United States, controversy arose over the activities of U.S. intelligence agencies and the rights of Americans.

As the commitment of U.S. military forces to Vietnam increased, the intelligence components of the Department of Defense assumed most of the responsibility for operational and technical intelligence (COMINT, ELINT, and so on), as well as for paramilitary and counterinsurgency action. The CIA continued throughout the 1960s to conduct the "secret war" in Laos (see chapter 19), and its proprietaries (Air America, especially) provided general support for "unconventional warfare" in the region. The CIA's Saigon station had the responsibility for conducting espionage, but its nets readily combined covert action with spying. While the war raged, the CIA intervened in the internal affairs of America's own ally, the Republic of Vietnam, seeking to influence the political situation and propping up or tearing down the government in power, frequently without the knowledge of U.S. diplomatic representatives.

William Colby insisted that "we were . . . all FI [Foreign Intelligence/espionage] here,"[2] but Frank Snepp depicted the Saigon station differently. He declared that "we neglected our primary job—gathering intelligence . . . dabbling increasingly in other millponds."

> . . . The Station in Vietnam gradually expanded in the mid-sixties to over 600 assorted bodies, including secretaries, intelligence analysts and spy handlers. . . . It was the largest concentration of CIA personnel anywhere in the world outside agency headquarters in Virginia. . . .
> In pursuit of this goal [strengthening the government of Nguyen Van Thieu after 1968], we had bought, bribed and sold so many South Vietnamese military and political figures that our spies and collaborators inside the government were mere extensions of ourselves.[3]

The Saigon station intervened pervasively in Vietnamese affairs, either through liaison (that is, in cooperation with Vietnamese intelligence and security services) or through unilateral operations (developing its own nets). So pervasive was its intervention, in fact, that it frequently worked at cross-purposes with itself. For example, seeking "sterile" currency for its clandestine operations, the CIA purchased Vietnamese piasters on the black market. A "normal" practice of tradecraft, this contributed to the very corruption it was seeking to eliminate in South Vietnam.

Tainted by the company it kept, the CIA also damaged its reputation by collaborating with the Meo tribesmen of Laos, who "for generations" had trafficked in opium: "Opium was as much a part of the agricultural infrastructure of [Southeast Asia] as was rice, one suitable for the hills, the other for the valleys."[4] The CIA imposed "strict anti-contraband regulations" upon Air America, but it could not shake the charge that its air proprietaries engaged in drug smuggling, either to generate profits to finance covert operations or to secure the cooperation of the Meo chiefs.[5] In 1972, Alfred McCoy, author of *The Politics of Heroin in Southeast Asia,* charged that CIA operations in the Golden Triangle region (where Burma, Laos, and Thailand meet), which produces "70 percent of the world's illicit opium supply," helped create "a generation of junkies."[6]

Reacting to this allegation, the CIA inspector general undertook an "Investigation of the Drug Situation in Southeast Asia." The investigators gave Air America pilots "a clean bill of health," one of whom proclaimed,

> You get me a contract to defoliate the poppy fields in Burma, and I'll take off right now and destroy them. I have a friend whose son is hooked on drugs, and I too have teenage children. It scares the hell out of me as much as it does you and the rest of the people in the States.[7]

The Church Committee concurred: "the CIA air proprietaries," it reported, "did not participate in illicit drug trafficking."[8]

Nonetheless, the accusation developed a life of its own and was fueled by related charges that the CIA had committed atrocities in Vietnam in carrying out its counterterror programs. President Johnson wanted the CIA to play a larger role in Vietnam. In the mid-1960s, under pressure from him, the Agency developed the counterterror (CT) program, designed to achieve pacification in South Vietnam by "rooting out" the Viet Cong. Chosen because of its experience in clandestine operations, the CIA was actually cast in an unfamiliar role—not Donovan's concept of *resistance* activity in support of conventional forces, but an internal security or secret police activity. In what was described as a unilateral operation, "CIA representatives recruited, organized, supplied, and directly paid CT teams, whose function was to use Vietcong techniques of terror—assassinations, abuses, kidnappings and intimidation—against the Vietcong leadership."[9] In 1968, William Colby took charge of the program; he dropped the "terror" designation and attempted to make reforms, but much of the damage had already been done.

Colby named the new effort Phoenix and set out to detect and destroy the Viet Cong infrastructure. The operation achieved notoriety and was accused of using torture and was charged with twenty thousand murders, but Colby claimed that, far from committing atrocities, Phoenix attempted to create "an atmosphere of law and decency" in the midst of a very dirty war: "Abuses, unquestionably, did take place but the full truth is that Phoenix went far to eliminate them as an accepted aspect of the war."[10] Whereas CT teams had formerly rounded up suspects indiscriminately and held them incommunicado in interrogation centers, Colby claimed that he established humane standards for processing and questioning prisoners. "The word 'Phoenix' became a shorthand for all the negative aspects of the war," Colby complained—but he himself was the victim of his own clandestinity. As the American people became increasingly aware of covert operations, they learned about them mainly from critics such as Victor Marchetti:

> Thus, a William Colby can, with no legal or ethical conflict, propose programs to end corruption in Vietnam while at the same time condoning the CIA's dubious money practices. And extending the concept of the agency's immunity to law and morals, a Colby can devise and direct terror tactics, secret wars, and the like, all in the name of democracy. This is the clandestine mentality: a separation of personal morality and conduct from actions, no matter how debased, which are taken in the name of the United States government and, more specifically, the Central Intelligence Agency.[11]

Marchetti had all the advantages in exposing the secret world of Colby, to the point that whatever Colby said or did only dug his hole deeper. Insisting, for example, that neither he nor Phoenix was CIA during 1968–71, Colby generated disbelief when he "rejoined" the CIA in mid-1971 as its number-three executive officer.

> So I left CIA—really [in 1968]. I took leave without pay, so my name would remain on the Agency roll, allowing me to come back some day, and I went through all the procedures to be hired by the Agency for International Development and be assigned by it to CORDS [Civilian Operations and Revolutionary Develop-

ment Staff, the "hybrid" agency responsible for American and Vietnamese pacification efforts] in Saigon. This is a point worth underscoring in the light of misunderstandings later that the CORDS pacification program was some kind of cover for CIA. In fact, it was primarily a joint AID-military effort; they furnished most of the funds and people involved, supplemented by a few from the Foreign Service, CIA, and USIA.[12]

Owing to his daughter's illness, Colby returned to Washington in mid-1971 but, he explained, the "Foreign Service establishment" would not accept "an ex-CIA type" in a high-level State Department position. So he then turned to his "first love and old employer, the CIA." "Helms [then DCI] welcomed me back with that sense of concern for a veteran member of CIA's clandestine services team that characterized him, and with sincere thanks for the way I had gone off to Vietnam three and a half years before."[13] Whether this was true did not matter; the 1960s "credibility gap" affected American intelligence and foreshadowed the crisis of confidence of the 1970s.

Criticism of CIA operations in Vietnam was accompanied by the assumption that Intelligence did not do a very good job of helping policymakers avoid mistakes in Vietnam. Critics of American involvement in Vietnam argued that U.S. intelligence had failed to provide adequate analysis and information on several key issues: the unpopularity of the Diem regime, the indigenous nature of the Viet Cong insurrection, the effect of bombing on the North, and the escalation of the war effort through ever-increasing numbers of U.S. ground forces. As it turned out, the critics were wrong. There had been adequate intelligence about these issues—but it had little influence upon policy.

In 1971, the release of the Pentagon Papers by Daniel Ellsberg showed that the intelligence community had warned repeatedly against U.S. intervention in Southeast Asia and had opposed most of the key decisions relating to the conduct of the war. "The Pentagon Papers" was the popular designation for the seven-thousand-page, forty-seven-volume *History of U.S. Decision-Making Process on Vietnam Policy,* a study of "the history of United States involvement in Vietnam from World War II to the present." It was prepared at the initiative of Secretary of Defense Robert McNamara starting

in 1967. Based on National Intelligence Estimates and other classified documents, the McNamara study revealed that the intelligence
community had advised against intervention in Vietnam from the
beginning and, after being ignored, "was consistently skeptical
about the efficacy of the measures attempted to end the conflict in
Vietnam and pessimistic about the results." [14] In 1954, an NIE
affirmed,

> Although it is possible that the French and Vietnamese, even
> with firm support from the U.S. and other powers, may be able
> to establish a strong regime in South Vietnam, we believe that
> the chances for this development are poor and moreover, that the
> situation is more likely to continue to deteriorate progressively
> over the next year. [15]

In 1964, after the United States decided to intervene and in the
face of increased guerrilla activity in the South, various policymakers proposed bombing the North to force Hanoi to stop aiding
the Viet Cong. But the intelligence community objected, explaining
that Communist strength in the South was "indigenous": "This
was to remain the key difference between the Intelligence Community and the policy-makers: the former skeptical about bombing
breaking the will of the North; the latter convinced it would force
concessions." [16] In mid-1965, the objective of the air raids changed
from breaking the will of Hanoi to cutting the supply lines to the
South. The Defense Intelligence Agency reported,

> The air strikes do not appear to have altered Hanoi's determina-
> tion to continue supporting the war in Vietnam.
>   The idea that destroying, or threatening to destroy, North
> Vietnam's industry would pressure Hanoi into calling it quits,
> seems, in retrospect, a colossal misjudgment. [17]

And so it seemed to go. Even in January 1966, when Secretary
McNamara recommended increasing the number of American
forces in Vietnam to more than 400,000, he knew, according to an
intelligence estimate the preceding month, that such deployments
would "not guarantee success":

Even though the Communists will continue to suffer heavily from [Vietnam] and U.S. ground and air action, we expect them, upon learning of any U.S. intentions to augment its forces, to boost their own commitment and to test U.S. capabilities and will to persevere at higher level of conflict and casualties.[18]

Six months earlier, DCI John McCone (1961–65) expressed a similar view in a secret memorandum: "ground force operations, . . . in all probability, will have limited effectiveness against guerrillas, although admittedly will restrain some VC advances. However, we can expect requirements for an ever-increasing commitment of U.S. personnel without materially improving the chances for victory."[19]

Vietnam clearly demonstrated the limitations of intelligence. Intelligence, no matter how good, is useless if it is ignored. Lyman Kirkpatrick suggested that it was ignored for political and technical reasons. Politically, John Foster Dulles decided to intervene because he viewed the Geneva accords as an invitation to the Communists to take over Southeast Asia: "The Republicans had accused the Democrats of 'losing China,' and now [1954], in their turn, they didn't want to lose Indochina."[20] Technically, it was ignored because, judging from the number of documents contained in the Pentagon Papers, "the system was inundated with paper—far beyond the capacity of any senior official to absorb." Moreover, Kirkpatrick pointed out, the NIEs did not speak with a single voice but contained contradictory viewpoints and interpretations and frequently reflected military service rivalries.[21] Ellsberg, for his part, blamed the failure to use intelligence on politics alone, accusing successive presidents of preferring "endless, escalating stalemate rather than 'failure.'"[22]

Ellsberg leaked the documents to the *New York Times* to reinforce opposition to the war by showing that American presidents had gone against the advice of "their most senior intelligence officials" and had made policy in contradiction of the evidence. Official Washington made Ellsberg into a pariah, but the CIA itself may not have been all that upset, because the Papers actually made the Agency "look good." Indeed, catching the spirit of the "clandestine mentality," retired Air Force Colonel Fletcher Prouty (author of *The Secret Team: The CIA and its Allies in Control of the United States and the World*) suggested that Ellsberg had acted "on behalf of the CIA" in delivering the papers to the public. Prouty claimed that Ellsberg was a former "employee and disciple" of Colonel Edward Lansdale, the master covert operator, and wrote, "The release of the Pentagon Papers . . . may have been the opening attack by the CIA to cover its disengagement not only from the physical conflict in Indochina, but also from the historical record of that disastrous event."[23] The clandestine nature of the CIA world, as we have seen, invites such speculation. Prouty's allegations actually achieved credence when CIA partisans, such as former IG Kirkpatrick, commented,

> The publication of the Pentagon Papers did much to ease the fears of responsible critics that the CIA and the intelligence agencies were submissive and servile, tailoring their intelligence estimates to policy needs. The evidence that these documents provide is reassurance that the intelligence community attempts to be dispassionate and objective, presenting the prospects as bleakly as the available facts may require despite the obvious hope at the highest level for more encouraging opinions. The fact that the decision-makers overrode, or ignored, or considered the intelligence estimates just another opinion may well provide those who govern the nation in the future with the incentive to give due weight to the intelligence estimates.[24]

Skeptical reactions to such statements suited the mood of the Vietnam era, stemming from the suspicion (later confirmed) that U.S. intelligence agencies kept close watch over the antiwar movement and other dissenting elements within the United States. The opposition to the Vietnam War seemed well-organized; the draft resistance, the teach-ins and sit-ins on college campuses, the spread of student militancy, and the emergence of the New Left were compounded by the so-called counterculture, the "new" morality, the radicalization of the civil rights movement, and women's liberation. Officials in the Johnson administration became certain that there was therefore a conspiracy. They refused to recognize the protests as legitimate and looked for a subversive foreign presence.

On the pretext of investigating possible foreign funding to and influence among activists during the 1960s, U.S. intelligence spied upon American citizens. The worst fears of the nation's founders had been realized: secrecy in government was facilitating the use of intrusive surveillance techniques—including bugging, mail opening, surreptitious entry ("black bag jobs"), and covert infiltration—in violation of the rights of Americans. Moreover, the evidence was plain that these illegal activities were actually aimed to have a "chilling" effect upon the exercise of individual freedoms and sought to stifle dissent. The FBI committed the most serious offenses, but other intelligence agencies were not blameless. FBI field offices in American cities acted in the same way as CIA clandestine stations abroad. They engaged in espionage and covert action for the purpose of influencing political affairs without appearing to do so.

The FBI carried out covert action against domestic groups through its counterintelligence program (COINTELPRO). Organized by J. Edgar Hoover in 1956 to employ "secret tactics/dirty tricks" to "disrupt" and "neutralize" the Communist Party, U.S.A., the FBI extended COINTELPRO to other targets in the mid-1960s.

> The FBI developed new covert programs for disrupting and discrediting domestic political groups, using the techniques originally applied to the Communists. The most intensive domestic intelligence investigations, and frequently COINTELPRO operations, were targeted against persons identified not as criminals or criminal suspects, but as "rabble rousers," "agitators," "key activists," or "key black extremists" because of their militant rhetoric and group leadership. The Security Index [for detention in time of national emergency] was revised to include such persons.[25]

Every new covert program tended to follow in the wake of a major act of lawlessness or violence on the part of some group or organization. Not all were aimed against leftists. After three civil rights workers disappeared in Mississippi in 1964, the FBI initiated a program against the Ku Klux Klan; at the other end of the political scale, the "Black Nationalist" program came in the wake of the 1967 riots in Newark and Detroit, and the "New Left" program was inspired by 1968 student demonstrations at Columbia University.

Under pressure from President Johnson and Attorney General Robert Kennedy, the FBI transferred its activities against the klan from the General Investigative Division to the Domestic Intelligence Division. The latter was instructed to use the same "disruptive" techniques against the klan "as it had against the Communist Party." Between 1964 and 1971, the FBI authorized 287 proposals for COINTELPRO actions against the klan and other "white hate" groups: "Covert techniques used in the COINTELPRO included creating new Klan chapters to be controlled by Bureau informants and sending an anonymous letter designed to break up a marriage."[26] Hoping to distract one klansman from "time spent in the plots and plans of the organization," the FBI sent a "poison-pen letter" to his wife, informing her, "in language usually reserved for bathroom walls, . . . that her husband had 'taken the flesh of another unto himself,' the other person being a woman named Ruby, with her 'lust filled eyes and smart aleck figure.' "[27]

In taking on the "Black Nationalists" in 1967, the FBI sought to discredit various groups and leaders and render them ineffective. A common tactic involved encouraging "gang warfare" among the Black Panthers, US, Inc., and similar organizations.

> An anonymous letter was sent to the leader of the Blackstone Rangers (a group according to the [Chicago] Field Offices' proposal, "to whom violent-type activity, shooting, and the like are second nature") advising him that "the brothers that run the Panthers blame you for blocking their thing and there's supposed to be a hit out for you." The letter was intended to "intensify the degree of animosity between the two groups" and cause "retaliatory action which could disrupt the BPP or lead to reprisals against its leadership."[28]

Another dirty trick to place a target in risk was the so-called snitch jacket technique, in which a phony story labeling a person as an informant was planted: "On several occasions, the Bureau used this technique against members of the Black Panther Party; it was used at least twice after FBI documents expressed concern over the possible consequences because two members of the BPP had been murdered as suspected informants."[29]

Many of the FBI's counterintelligence programs cast an extremely broad net, but the one launched against the "New Left" in May 1968 was the broadest, "most vaguely defined" of all. When the FBI agent in charge of New Left intelligence was asked what the New Left was, he replied, "It has never been strictly defined, as far as I know. . . . It's more or less an attitude, I would think."[30] Viewing the New Left as "a subversive force" seeking to destroy "traditional values" but with "no definable ideology," the FBI adopted the tactic of exposing its "depraved nature and moral looseness." In July 1968, FBI headquarters instructed field offices to:

1. prepare leaflets using "the most obnoxious pictures" of New Left leaders at various universities;

2. instigate "personal conflicts or animosities" between New Left leaders;

3. create the impression that leaders are "informants for the Bureau or other law enforcement agencies" (the "snitch jacket" technique);

4. send articles from student or "underground" newspapers which show "depravity" ("use of narcotics and free sex") of New Left leaders to university officials, donors, legislators, and parents;

5. have members arrested on marijuana charges;

6. send anonymous letters about a student's activities to parents, neighbors, and the parents' employers;

7. send anonymous letters about New Left faculty members (signed "A Concerned Alumni" or "A Concerned Taxpayer") to university officials, legislators, Board of Regents, and the press;

8. use "cooperative press contacts";

9. exploit the "hostility" between New Left and Old Left groups;

10. disrupt New Left coffee houses near military bases which are attempting to "influence members of the Armed Forces";

11. use cartoons, photographs, and anonymous letters to "ridicule" the New Left;

12. use "misinformation" to "confuse and disrupt" New Left activities, such as by notifying members that events have been cancelled.[31]

This abuse of the functions of intelligence posed a danger to the Constitution that was graver than the often loutish behavior of the targeted individuals. Cloaked in secrecy and lacking precise standards, the FBI programs against subversive and violent elements spread even to those engaged in peaceful political expression. A former White House official testifying before the Church Committee observed that intelligence investigations and surveillance during the Vietnam era "risked moving from the kid with the bomb to the kid with a picket sign, and from the kid with the picket sign to the kid with the bumper sticker of the opposing candidate. And you just keep going down the line."[32] This possibility became realized all too often.

But there is no better/worse example of the "overbreadth" of domestic intelligence activity than the FBI's covert campaign against Dr. Martin Luther King, Jr. If the FBI's tactics against the New Left violated the law, those against King "violated the law and fundamental human decency."[33]

The FBI secretly hounded Dr. King from December 1963 until his death in 1968. It gathered intelligence and kept him under surveillance, and it looked for information to discredit him and destroy his effectiveness as a civil rights leader. Nor did the FBI let up even after his assassination: an Atlanta field agent suggested ways to harass his widow, and bureau officials took steps to prevent his birthday from becoming a national holiday.[34] Shortly after King's "I Have a Dream" speech in Washington in August 1963, the FBI targeted him as the "most dangerous and effective Negro leader in the country."[35] Yet five years later, it described him only as a potential threat.

To the FBI he was a potential threat because he might "abandon his supposed 'obedience' to white liberal doctrines (nonviolence)." In short, a non-violent man was to be secretly attacked and destroyed as insurance against his abandoning non-violence.[36]

Based on such lame reasoning, the FBI pulled out all the stops against Dr. King. During 1964 and 1965, it followed him on his speaking engagements in various cities and planted "bugs" in his hotel rooms, from the Willard in Washington to the Shroeder in Milwaukee and the Hilton Hawaiian Village in Honolulu. In November 1964, after it had eavesdropped and collected material of a potentially embarrassing nature, the FBI mailed a "sterilized" tape to Dr. King with an unsigned warning: "King, there is only one thing left for you to do. You know what it is. . . . You are done. There is but one way out for you."[37] King apparently believed that the FBI was trying to get him to commit suicide, but assistant FBI director William C. Sullivan claimed that the only purpose had been "to blackmail King into silence" by threatening to destroy his marriage. Such an act—carried out on the very eve of King's departure for Europe to receive the Nobel Peace prize—was inexplicable; but no explanation was necessary under a veil of secrecy. When King went abroad to claim his prize, the FBI tried to sabotage receptions in his honor, and upon his return, it continued its "war" against him. It attempted to prevent him from receiving an honorary degree from Marquette University (spring 1964), from having an audience with the pope (August 1964), and from obtaining a three-million-dollar grant for the Southern Christian Leadership Conference from the Ford Foundation (October 1966).[38]

Martin Luther King's prominence gave his case notoriety, but the unfortunate truth is that "hundreds of lesser-known Americans" experienced similar violations of their rights.[39] Nor was the FBI the sole transgressor; Army Intelligence, the NSA, and the CIA also engaged in domestic intelligence operations wherein abuses occurred. Faced with domestic racial violence during the 1960s and concerned that antiwar activism could disrupt military bases and installations, the army collected intelligence about a wide variety of civilian political groups and organizations.

Shortly after the Army was called upon to quell civil disorders in
Detroit and to cope with an antiwar demonstration at the Pentagon in 1967, the Army Chief of Staff approved a recommendation for ''continuous counterintelligence investigations'' to obtain
information on ''subversive personalities, groups or organizations'' and their ''influence on urban populations'' in promoting
civil disturbances. The Army's ''collection plan'' for civil disturbances specifically targeted as ''dissident elements'' (without
further definition) the ''civil rights movement'' and the ''Anti-
Vietnam/anti-draft movements.''[40]

Even this overly broad ''requirement'' was later revised to include
''prominent persons'' who were ''friendly'' with the ''leaders of
the disturbance.''[41] It caused Army Intelligence agents to show
up at ''a Halloween party for elementary school children in Washington, D.C., because they suspected a local 'dissident' might be
present; [monitor] protests of welfare mothers' organizations in
Milwaukee; [infiltrate] a coalition of church youth groups in Colorado; and [attend] a priests' conference in Washington, D.C., held
to discuss birth control measures.''[42] From the mid-1960s to 1971,
Army Intelligence used infiltration and other covert surveillance
techniques to gather files on an estimated 100,000 Americans,[43]
including certain U.S. Senators, such as Sam Ervin (North Carolina), George McGovern (South Dakota), Edmund Muskie (Maine),
Edward Kennedy (Massachusetts), Harold Hughes (Iowa), and
Adlai Stevenson III (Illinois). These investigations also extended
to organizations legitimately engaged in political and social dissent: the Southern Christian Leadership Conference, the NAACP,
the ACLU, CORE, NOW, Operation Breadbasket, the Urban
League, YAF, the American Friends Service Committee, and
SANE.

  If the army justified its surveillance of American citizens on
the basis of its mission to insure domestic tranquillity, the National
Security Agency got involved because Presidents Johnson and
Nixon were growing increasingly desperate in their attempts to
discover evidence of foreign influence over domestic dissent and
thereby discredit it. Lyndon Johnson was simply dying to get
something on Jane Fonda or Students for a Democratic Society.
SIGINT, which had contributed so mightily to victory in World
War II, was now forced to serve such narrow political interests in

the Vietnam era. The NSA, created by executive order in 1952, was authorized to collect foreign intelligence and monitor foreign communications, but in practice it interpreted "foreign communications" to mean that only one message point had to be foreign. The NSA therefore intercepted communications that were either sent or received by Americans, some purposefully, most unintentionally. Between 1967 and 1973, yielding to pressure from the CIA, the FBI, and Army Intelligence, the NSA lengthened its "watch list" specifically to include a wide variety of civil rights and peace activists, and it expanded its intercept program to include "information on U.S. organizations or individuals who are engaged in activities which may result in civil disturbances or otherwise subvert the national security of the United States."[44] Designated Project MINARET, the information was handled as SIGINT but was not identified with the National Security Agency. While investigating MINARET, the Church Committee also discovered the SHAMROCK program, by which the NSA (and its predecessors), in an arrangement with at least two cable companies, between 1947 and 1973 obtained copies of "essentially all cables to or from the United States, including millions of private communications of Americans."[45]

Like the NSA's SHAMROCK program, the CIA's mail-opening program used the same "vacuum cleaner" approach against American citizens during the 1960s and early 1970s.

The overbreadth of the longest CIA mail opening program—the 20 year (1953–1973) program in New York City—is shown by the fact that of the more than 28 million letters screened by the CIA, the exteriors of 2.7 million were photographed and 214,820 letters were opened. This is further shown by the fact that American groups and individuals placed on the Watch List for the project included:

- The Federation of American Scientists;

- authors such as John Steinbeck and Edward Albee;

- numerous American peace groups such as the American Friends Service Committee and Women's Strike for Peace; and

- businesses, such as Praeger Publishers.

By one CIA estimate, random selection accounted for 75 percent of the 200,000 letters opened, including letters to or from American political figures, such as Richard Nixon, while a presidential candidate in 1968, and Senators Frank Church and Edward Kennedy.[46]

The National Security Act of 1947 clearly prohibited the CIA from exercising "police, subpoena, or law-enforcement powers, or internal security functions." But the law was not so clear concerning clandestine intelligence activities within the United States in connection with the CIA's foreign intelligence mission. This ambiguity occasionally caused conflict between the CIA and the FBI, but in the 1966 context of domestic strife, the two agencies agreed to coordinate their efforts. This led to CIA involvement in "internal security functions," particularly when a CIA agent recruited abroad came to the United States and was in a position to report on domestic "dissidents." Not only did the FBI permit the CIA to "handle" the agent in the United States for "foreign intelligence" purposes while providing it (the FBI) with "information" concerning "internal security matters"; the FBI requested the CIA to spy on Americans abroad.

After 1969, the FBI began submitting names of citizens engaged in domestic protest and violence to the CIA not only for investigation abroad, but also for placement on the "watch list" of the CIA's mail opening project. Similar lists of names went from the FBI to the National Security Agency, for use on a "watch list" for monitoring other channels of international communication.[47]

Despite the U.S. intelligence agencies' major effort against domestic dissent and despite the gradual "breakdown" of the distinction between "foreign" and "domestic" intelligence, President Johnson was not satisfied that enough was being done. He literally nagged the CIA into developing its own "domestic" counterintelligence program in August 1967—Operation CHAOS. According to DCI Richard Helms (1966–1973),

the only manner in which the CIA could support its conclusion that there was no significant foreign influence on the domestic dissent, in the face of incredulity at the White House, was to continually expand the coverage of CHAOS. Only by being able to demonstrate that it had investigated *all* anti-war persons and *all* contacts between them and any foreign person could CIA 'prove the negative' that none were under foreign domination.''[48]

Despite this excuse, Helms knew that CHAOS violated the CIA's charter, and he ran it as a deep cover counterintelligence operation. He kept it separate even from James Angleton and the rest of the CI staff. For this purpose, he created the Special Operations Group (SOG) and placed Richard Ober in charge (the CIA officer who had investigated the *Ramparts* flap in February 1967). Hidden in a basement bunker at the CIA's Langley headquarters, the SOG employed the full repertoire of covert surveillance techniques. During Operation CHAOS (1967–73), the SOG prepared thirteen thousand "personality" files, including 7,200 on American citizens, and it generated a computerized index of more than 300,000 names of individuals and groups.

> In addition to collecting information on an excessive number of persons, some of the kinds of information were wholly irrelevant to the legitimate interests of the CIA or any other government agency. For example, one CIA agent supplying information on domestic activities to Operation CHAOS submitted detailed accounts of the activities of women who were interested in "women's liberation."[49]

Though Helms tried to blame the excesses of CHAOS on presidential pressure, the CIA violated its own charter in areas that could not be blamed on Johnson. As opposition to the war in Vietnam increased, the tactics of dissent grew bolder, including highly organized "marches" and the leaking of classified information. Acting on its responsibility for "protecting intelligence sources and methods from unauthorized disclosure," the CIA's Office of Security launched two projects aimed at protecting CIA installations and personnel against disruptive acts and at finding out if CIA employees were leaking sensitive information to the press.

Under Project MERRIMACK (1967–73), the CIA spied upon peace groups and black activist groups in Washington, using infiltration and electronic surveillance, to learn their plans for possible demonstrations against the Agency: "However, the collection requirements were broadened to include general information about the leadership, funding, activities, and policies of the targeted groups."[50] In the same way, Project RESISTANCE (1967–73) also involved the CIA in "internal security functions," this time against "radical groups" on college campuses. Concerned over the safety of CIA contractors, personnel responsible for background investigations, and recruiters, the Agency targeted SDS and similar groups. It exploited "open sources" but also obtained information from "cooperating police departments, campus officials, and other local authorities, some of whom in turn were using collection techniques such as informants."[51]

Closer to home, the CIA's Office of Security conducted a number of special investigations of CIA employees and ex-employees to determine the sources of news leaks. The Ellsberg case was an extreme one, but there was disagreement within the CIA about Vietnam, concerning the CIA's role in it or such programs as CHAOS, which some officials regarded as illegal. The problem of leaks in Washington, fueled by a decade of dissent, led even William Colby to wonder "whether any secrets could be kept. . . . After [Victor] Marchetti and [Philip] Agee I felt I could no longer say that it was inconceivable that anyone in CIA would be guilty of an information leak, a position we had proudly held in earlier times."[52]

But the CIA's Office of Security apparently had already lost confidence. In connection with MERRIMACK, the CIA conducted "special coverage" investigations of its employees, its former employees, employees of other intelligence agencies, and newsmen. Such investigations went beyond routine background checks and even polygraph tests to include "physical and electronic surveillance, unauthorized entry, mail covers and intercepts, and reviews of individual federal tax returns." Without judicial warrants, the CIA installed thirty-two wiretaps and thirty-two bugs, in most cases against its own people; it committed twelve burglaries, some involving the homes or offices of journalists.[53]

This surveillance program, added to CHAOS, COINTEL-PRO, and MINARET among others, suggests what the American people were up against. Never in the history of the republic was so much collected about so many for so long, and in 1972 Senator Stevenson justifiably asked, "At what point do efforts to guard American freedom begin to threaten freedom itself?" Not only did illegal and unconstitutional acts performed in secrecy affect the rights of Americans, but secrecy begat secrecy, resulting in cover-up and breached authority.

But there were limits. Even in the days before the "dissent channels" in government, there had been internal or in-house checks that worked—Colby proclaimed that they were honorable men. Interdepartmental rivalries also served to restrain the over-zealous. This safeguard was a slender thread, but intelligence professionals, especially within the CIA, resisted abuse of the apparatus that they had so painstakingly created. Despite the intelligence community's efforts to avoid deeper involvement in the domestic political scene, President Nixon was more persistent than President Johnson. In the end, the IC's lack of cooperation caused it first to be bypassed and then, ironically, to be drawn into the ensuing Watergate scandal. The Vietnam era certainly changed America, but its effect upon U.S. intelligence was devastating.

23

The Watergate Syndrome

President Lyndon Johnson took extraordinary measures against the protest movements of the 1960s, but President Richard Nixon contemplated doing even more. This was not simply a matter of a new and more conservative administration; a general reaction or "backlash" had set in against the politics of confrontation, as demonstrated by candidate Nixon's effective slogan "Silent Majority" in the 1968 presidential campaign and Vice President Spiro Agnew's open criticism of student protesters as "effete snobs." The changing mood erupted violently in July 1968 in Chicago, where police "rioted" against demonstrators during the Democratic National Convention, and in May 1970, at Kent State University, where Ohio National Guardsmen killed four students who had been participating in a campus antiwar rally. Intense student unrest was touched off by the U.S. invasion of Cambodia in the spring of 1970, and President Nixon ordered U.S. intelligence agencies to collect more information about domestic dissenters and their links to foreign powers, if any. "We are now confronted with a new and grave crisis in our country," Nixon told the directors of the FBI, CIA, NSA, and DIA on June 5, 1970, "one which we know too little about."[1]

The Watergate break-in of June 1972 and the subsequent attempts at cover-up were the culmination of something that began two years before, mainly because Nixon's attitude toward secret intelligence and clandestine operations was loose. He had been vice president during the "glory days" of the CIA under Allen Dulles, and he had been instrumental in promoting covert action against Fidel Castro. According to staff assistant Tom Charles Huston, a kind of siege mentality gripped the White House during that Cambodian spring of 1970:

> We were sitting in the White House getting reports day in and day out of what was happening in this country in terms of the violence, the numbers of bombings [forty thousand in one year], the assassination attempts, the sniping incidents [thirty-nine police officers killed], . . . in the month of May [1970] in a 2-week period [we] were averaging six arsons a day against ROTC facilities.[2]

The White House chief of staff, H.R. Haldeman, gave Huston the task of planning increased domestic intelligence operations. For about a year, Huston had been consulting with William C. Sullivan, assistant director of the FBI and head of the Domestic Intelligence Division. Sullivan had complained that he was being inhibited in his attempts to collect information about dissident activity—specifically, that Director Hoover would not permit him to engage in surreptitious entry ("black-bag jobs" or burglaries), nor to recruit students less than twenty-one years of age as campus informants. Acting essentially on Sullivan's complaints, Huston organized the June 1970 meeting between Nixon and the intelligence chiefs so that the president could make "the intelligence community [aware] of the seriousness with which he viewed the escalating level of revolutionary violence."[3] Nixon instructed the directors of the FBI, CIA, NSA, and DIA to set up an Interagency Committee, under Hoover as chair, to prepare a report on domestic intelligence that would assess the internal security threat, evaluate the adequacy of collection procedures, and suggest ways to improve interagency coordination.

The result of this activity was the Huston Plan, dated July 1970. The forty-three-page document, entitled *Special Report, Interagency Committee on Intelligence (Ad Hoc)*, was prepared and signed by the four intelligence directors, but it was eclipsed by Huston's cover memorandum to Haldeman, "Domestic Intelligence Gathering Plan: Analysis and Strategy." This memo summarized the report and made specific recommendations for presidential action. Huston related that he had initially feared that the CIA (under Helms) would refuse to cooperate but that Hoover was actually "the only stumbling block." "[He] refused to go along with a single conclusion drawn or support a single recommendation made."[4] Though Hoover agreed with the first part of the report, on threat assessment, he disagreed with the recommendation to change existing procedures for intelligence collection, particularly to remove "operational restraints," and he opposed the formation of a "permanent interagency group on domestic intelligence" under the direction of the White House. Hoover signed the report, but he entered his objections in the form of footnotes, which Huston characterized as "inconsistent and frivolous."

> Mr. Hoover is set in his ways and can be bull-headed as hell, but he is a loyal trooper. Twenty years ago he would never have raised the type of objections he has here, but he's getting old and worried about his legend. He makes life tough in this area, but not impossible—for he'll respond to direction by the President and that is all we need to set the domestic intelligence house in order.[5]

Proceeding on this assumption, Huston wrote his memorandum and attached specific recommendations dealing with "operational restraints." But Huston was wrong about Hoover. He had not suddenly become a civil libertarian; given the existence of COINTELPRO, he was concerned about his turf. Testifying later, Huston declared that he had not known about COINTELPRO, MINARET, CHAOS, or the CIA mail openings and insisted that he would not have asked for what was already largely being done ("and we still were not getting any results"[6]). Nonetheless, the Huston Plan was startling, because, in listing all the covert surveillance techniques and asking the president to give his approval, its author boldly and frankly acknowledged that what he was recommending was illegal.

Huston recommended, for example, that the NSA be permitted to broaden its "coverage . . . of the communications of U.S. citizens using international facilities." He argued for the "intensification" of electronic surveillances and penetrations targeted against individuals and groups "who pose a major threat to the internal security." He requested that restrictions on "legal" mail coverage be removed and that restrictions on "covert coverage" (mail opening) be relaxed. "Covert coverage," Huston stated, "is illegal and there are serious risks involved. However, the advantages to be derived from its use outweigh the risks."[7] Huston further recommended that restrictions on surreptitious entry be modified, particularly to acquire "vitally needed foreign cryptographic material" and "to permit selective use . . . against other urgent and high priority internal security targets."

> Use of this technique is clearly illegal: it amounts to burglary. It is also highly risky and could result in great embarrassment if exposed. However, it is also the most fruitful tool and can produce the type of intelligence which cannot be obtained in any other fashion. . . .
>   Surreptitious entry of facilities occupied by subversive elements can turn up information about identities, methods of operation, and other invaluable investigative information which is not otherwise obtainable. This technique would be particularly helpful if used against the Weathermen and Black Panthers.[8]

Huston also suggested the "development of campus sources"—meaning informants. He especially wanted to remove Hoover's restrictions against recruiting individuals of less than twenty-one years of age. This restraint "dramatically reduces the pool," Huston complained. "The campus is the battleground of the revolutionary protest movement. It is impossible to gather effective intelligence about the movement unless we have campus sources."[9] Finally, echoing the *Special Report,* Huston called for the establishment of an Interagency Group on Domestic Intelligence, which would consist of the FBI, CIA, NSA, DIA, and the military counterintelligence agencies, "to provide evaluations of domestic intelligence, prepare periodic domestic intelligence estimates, and carry out the other objectives specified in the report."[10] Huston, speculating that "Edgar's nose [might be] out of joint," suggested that Nixon call Hoover in for a "stroking session" before assembling all the intelligence chiefs and announcing his decision. "An official memorandum setting forth the precise decisions of the President should be prepared so that there can be no misunderstanding."[11]

On July 14, 1970, Haldeman notified Huston by memorandum that the president had approved his recommendations, but that Nixon did not wish to follow the suggested implementation procedure: "He would prefer that the thing simply be put into motion on the basis of this approval."

> I realize this is contrary to your feeling as to the best way to get this done. If you feel very strongly that this procedure won't work you had better let me know and we'll take another stab at it. Otherwise let's go ahead.[12]

On July 23, acting on Haldeman's memo, Huston notified the directors of the FBI, CIA, NSA, and DIA that the president had approved the new plan for domestic intelligence operations. The Huston Plan thus actually existed in its specific form—but only for five days. Hoover, as Senator Howard Baker of Tennessee later phrased it, "put the kibosh" on the Huston Plan. Hoover observed that the "decision memorandum" had not come directly from Nixon and had been around long enough to know why. He went to Attorney General John Mitchell and informed him that, although he opposed "the lifting of the various investigative restraints," he would implement "the instructions of the White House at [the AG's] direction."[13] Mitchell, who had not been previously informed of this activity, "prevailed upon" Nixon and Haldeman to "recall" the Huston Plan on July 28. Nixon could have removed Hoover instead, but that was a political risk he was unwilling to take. If Nixon had fired Hoover at that time, author J. Anthony Lukas has suggested, "the White House might not have found it necessary to get so deeply involved in its own domestic intelligence program."[14]

Much has been made of Hoover's opposition to the Huston Plan, but Helms was apparently not enthusiastic either. Helms's biographer, Thomas Powers, writes that the deliberations of the Interagency Committee on Intelligence "seem to have been something of a boondoggle." Huston and the FBI's Sullivan may have been serious, he adds, but the "other members were simply going through the motions."[15] Helms did not take Huston into his confidence about CHAOS. Moreover, the collapse of the Huston Plan was "more apparent than real."[16] At one point during the Church Committee hearings, Pennsylvania Senator Richard

Schweiker wondered "whether or not the Huston plan ever died."[17]

> Despite the revocation of official approval, many major aspects of the plan were implemented, and some techniques which the intelligence community asked for permission to implement had already been underway. . . .
> The NSA program for covering the communications of Americans [and] the CIA mail-opening program . . . continued without the formal authorization which had been hoped for. . . .
> Two of the specific recommendations in the "Huston Plan" were thereafter implemented by the FBI—the lowering of the age limit for campus informants from 21 to 18 and the resumption of "legal mail covers."[18]

Still, the Nixon White House did not achieve the coordination of domestic intelligence activities that it had sought, nor the direct covert surveillance capability that this implied. In August 1970, John Dean, the presidential counsel, assumed Huston's staff responsibilities for domestic intelligence and internal security to try to salvage the Huston Plan. According to Dean, both he and his former boss, Attorney General Mitchell, saw little value in the project. "John, the President loves all this stuff," Mitchell told Dean, "but it just isn't necessary."[19] The following December, hoping to appease the White House, Mitchell created the inter-agency Intelligence Evaluation Committee (IEC), which was little more than a "study group," a "toothless version" of Huston's proposed interagency group.

> While Mitchell presented the IEC to Hoover as meaningless, I [Dean] was to present it to the White House as a promising first step. True, I would say, it was not the Huston Plan, but it would at least get Hoover back in harness. My report was received without joy, but no wrath fell on me. The Huston Plan was laid to rest, and Huston himself soon [June 1971] left the White House in disgust.[20]

In this context, William Colby's claim "that Nixon had to set up the 'plumbers' in the White House, because such activities would not be carried out by CIA"[21] is understandable. In secret intelligence, what cannot be done in one way may be done in another.

Nixon's "love affair" with dirty tricks continued. In 1969, John D. Ehrlichman (then White House counsel and in time Nixon's chief assistant for domestic affairs) had already engaged the services of John Caulfield and Anthony Ulasewicz, two former New York City policemen, as "special investigators" to dig up dirt on people whom Nixon perceived as threats—the so-called enemies list.[22] In July 1971, after the Huston Plan collapsed and the Pentagon Papers were published, the White House expanded this activity by creating the Special Investigations Unit under two young lawyers and White House protégés, David R. Young and Egil Krogh, who had no experience in secret intelligence. The unit was nicknamed the plumbers because its first principal task was to plug leaks of sensitive information. In its subsequent operations the unit simply ignored the "investigative restraints" that had worried Huston, ultimately bringing ruin to the Nixon presidency. When it hired former CIA employee E. Howard Hunt, the plumbers proved the undoing of the Central Intelligence Agency as well.

Hunt had retired from the CIA in April 1970 after twenty-three years of service. He had played a leading role in the 1954 overthrow of Arbenz in Guatemala and in the Bay of Pigs. During that time, he had also written more than forty spy-adventure novels under various pseudonyms. There was a mixture of fantasy and reality in Hunt's character, and he aspired to be a James Bond. He did not have the looks, but he did have "one of the two great 'black minds' in CIA."[23] Hunt's situation illustrates one dimension of the problem of "bringing a spy in from the cold." He was allegedly "nudged" into early retirement as a "burnt-out case,"[24] but the CIA might have done well to keep him on board to keep him out of trouble. " 'You see, our government trains people like myself to do these things and do them successfully,' [Hunt] explained. . . . 'It becomes a way of life for a person like me.' "[25] Even Huston, when he appeared before the Church Committee in 1975, conceded that his plan had been a bad idea if it had unleashed a Howard Hunt.

What I have learned subsequently is what happens when the person [in charge] . . . is not Dick Helms, but he is Howard Hunt, and that seems to me to be the risk. So there has to be some institutional restraint, in my judgment.[26]

Senator Church agreed and cited the affirmation of John Adams "that our society must have a government of laws and not of men."

Hunt was hired by the White House in July 1971 to discredit Daniel Ellsberg. In typical "big shot" fashion, Hunt flaunted his contacts and experience in the CIA. After his bona fides were established by Ehrlichman, Hunt called on CIA deputy director General Robert E. Cushman to request disguise materials and alias documentation. On July 23, at a CIA safe house in the District of Columbia, an officer from the Technical Services Division provided Hunt with "a wig, a pair of glasses, a speech-altering device, a driver's license and miscellaneous identification cards (not including credit cards)."[27] About a month later, the TSD also approved Hunt's request for "alias business cards" and a tape recorder that was effective "in a noisy environment."[28]

Hunt used these materials to carry out a number of assignments. He took a trip to Providence to check out new leads about Senator Edward Kennedy and the Chappaquiddick affair. He flew to Denver to interview Dita Beard, a lobbyist for ITT, which was at the time a principal in a possible scandal involving a $400,000 campaign contribution and the alleged "fixing" of an antitrust suit. With Helms's approval, the CIA also furnished Hunt with file copies of cables from the Saigon station in the early 1960s; Hunt doctored these in a vain effort to frame President Kennedy for the murder of Diem.[29]

But Ellsberg was Hunt's main target. At Hunt's suggestion and David Young's request, the CIA prepared a "psychological profile" of Ellsberg. Hunt was not pleased with the results. He decided to see for himself what could be found in the files of Dr. Lewis J. Fielding, a Los Angeles psychiatrist who had been treating Ellsberg. By this time (August 1971), G. Gordon Liddy, an ex-FBI agent and another "soldier-of-fortune" type, had joined the "plumbers" unit, and he and Hunt got along beautifully. Hunt and Liddy prepared for the burglary of Dr. Fielding's office by flying to Los Angeles and making a photographic study of the site; the TSD furnished them with a "concealed camera" and additional disguises and when they returned, developed their film. Though this CIA assistance appeared to be indirect, the TSD kept

Xeroxed copies of the finished pictures. (One CIA officer remarked that they "looked like 'casing photographs' to him."[30])

Hunt compromised the CIA more seriously by tapping Agency "assets" in putting together a team for the surreptitious entry. Because Hunt had played a role in the Bay of Pigs affair, he was familiar with the Cuban exile colony in Miami and he knew the people there who had worked with the CIA in clandestine operations. He contacted Bernard L. Barker, who had been one of his top agents ten years before; Barker in turn recruited other veterans of the anti-Castro wars, Felipe DeDiego and Eugenio R. Martínez. Hunt committed a serious breach by exploiting his previous connection with the CIA in this way, but the Cubans regarded their participation as nothing less than honorable. Barker explained, "Mr. Hunt's position in the White House would be a decisive factor at a later date for obtaining help in the liberation of Cuba."[31] These men burglarized the office of Dr. Fielding on Labor Day weekend 1971. Along with an enlarged Barker team and another former CIA officer, James W. McCord, Jr., they were also involved in the effort to bug the Democratic National Committee (DNC) headquarters in the Watergate office building during May and June 1972. At 2:00 A.M. on June 17, 1972, five of them—including McCord—were apprehended by District of Columbia police within the DNC's Watergate offices. The Watergate break-in, carried out for narrow partisan purposes, constituted the ultimate presidential abuse of secret intelligence and opened another round in "the great intelligence debate."

The CIA denied having any responsibility for the Watergate break-ins but it was badly damaged nonetheless. As Thomas Powers wrote, Watergate marked "a violent break in Agency history, the first step in a process of exposure . . . [and] it undermined the consensus of trust in Washington which was a truer source of the Agency's strength than its legal charter."[32] The CIA's linkage with Watergate was significant: two former officers were ringleaders, the burglary team consisted of Bay of Pigs veterans—one of whom (Martínez) was still on Agency "retainer"—and it had rendered technical support in the form of spy gadgetry. The question even arose of whether Hunt was really no longer CIA, since the Agency had helped him find a job immediately upon retirement with Robert R. Mullen and Company, a Washington-based public relations firm that operated abroad and provided cover for CIA officers overseas.

If the CIA had infiltrated the White House, the White House hoped to turn that and related circumstances to its advantage to cover up its part in the Watergate break-in. Nixon suggested that Helms call the FBI off the case, implying that it would "open the whole Bay of Pigs thing up again."[33] Helms rebuffed that suggestion and at the same time, for his own purposes, volunteered no information to the FBI or to the U.S. attorney about the CIA's relationship with Watergate defendants Hunt and McCord. The CIA withheld the information that it had Xeroxed copies of the Fielding "casing photos" and that it had received letters from McCord in July and November 1972 that revealed the pressure being exerted on him and the other Watergate burglars to testify that they had been part of a CIA operation.[34] Even so, Helms paid the price for saying no to President Nixon: he was fired as DCI after the November 1972 election and sent packing to Iran as U.S. ambassador.[35]

In the end, McCord himself "broke the case." McCord warned the White House that if the attempts to blame the CIA persisted, "every tree in the forest will fall. It will be a scorched desert."[36] McCord carried out his threat in March 1973, when he wrote to Watergate judge John J. Sirica and revealed the existence of a cover-up and affirmed that "the Watergate operation was not a CIA operation."[37] Sirica, who believed that without the McCord letter, "the case would never have been broken," explained that McCord was unwilling to go to jail for others and that he had acted to defend the honor of the CIA. "McCord had been a CIA employee for nineteen years and was still fiercely loyal to 'The Company,' " Sirica noted.[38] Ironically, though McCord was seeking to protect the CIA, he actually contributed to the popular image of the CIA as a sinister force. When McCord testified before the Senate Watergate committee in May, displaying his "fierce loyalty" and cold professionalism, he made the American people aware of the concept of "The Company" for the first time. His testimony inspired a popular belief that the CIA was a secret organization that operated under its own rules and was accountable to no one, that blackmailed presidents and employed contract killers. This image would be portrayed in films and TV dramas such as "Scorpio" (1973), "Three Days of the Condor" (1975), "The Killer Elite" (1975), and "The Company" (based on the 1976 novel by John Ehrlichman).

In the meantime, James Schlesinger had replaced Helms as DCI (February–July 1973). According to Colby, Schlesinger "came on strong" and was determined to improve the CIA's reputation by switching its emphasis from Operations to Intelligence. He felt there were too many " 'old boys' around the place doing little more than looking after each other, playing spy games and reliving the halcyon past of their OSS and early Cold War derring-do days."[39] During his short tenure (the shortest of any DCI), Schlesinger went after the "dead wood," firing or forcing into early retirement more than a thousand CIA officers, over a hundred of them "old soldiers" from Clandestine Services.[40] To make the CIA appear more open, he changed the name of the Directorate of Plans to the Directorate of Operations and placed Colby in charge, with orders to continue the purges. On the George Washington Parkway, he replaced the Langley exit sign that read "Bureau of Public Roads" with one that stated what most people already knew: "CIA."

As DCI, Schlesinger also had Colby assemble all the information he could uncover about any CIA connection with Watergate, so as to avoid surprises. He was therefore furious in May, when he learned from newspaper accounts of the Ellsberg trial about the Fielding break-in and a possible CIA connection.

Surprised and chagrined by this and by the Ellsberg trial revelations as well, Colby responded to Schlesinger's threat to "tear the place apart and 'fire everyone if necessary' "[41] by proposing that a thoroughgoing in-house search be made for any more hidden sins from the CIA's past. Approving Colby's proposal, Schlesinger issued a directive on May 9 calling upon all CIA employees, past and present, to report any activities "now going on, or that have gone on in the past," which "might be construed" as a violation of the CIA's legislative charter. Based on the search, the inspector general's office prepared a 693-page report of "potential flap activities" (which Colby referred to as "our skeletons in the closet" but

which came to be more colorfully known as "the family jewels").
The report contained twenty-five years of "misdeeds," "questionable activities," and law breaking, including Operation CHAOS,
the mail-opening program, experimentation on unwitting subjects
with behavior-influencing drugs, and (in a "special annex") various assassination programs against foreign leaders. But in the
supercharged atmosphere of Watergate and the Nixon impeachment hearings, the CIA came out wrong even when it tried to do
something right. The existence of the "jewels" created the risk of
its exposure. As Powers noted, "a kind of momentum had built
up, and the inertia of exposure could not be restrained. . . . [Once]
secrets are gathered together they reach a kind of critical mass and
will out." Too many people had been "let in on the secrets."[42]

It took about a year and a half for the inevitable to happen.
Seymour Hersh of the *New York Times* had been piecing together
bits of the story, especially aspects of Operation CHAOS; his investigation led to an interview with Colby, then DCI, on December 20, 1974. Hersh informed Colby "that he had learned from
several sources that the CIA had been engaged in a 'massive' operation against the antiwar movement involving wiretaps, break-ins,
mail intercepts, and surveillances of American citizens."[43] As
Colby attempted to point out to Hersh that he had the story
"mixed up and distorted," he—Colby—actually "confirmed"
most of Hersh's findings.[44] On December 22, the *New York Times*
published Hersh's account. It stated that the CIA, in "direct violation" of its charter, had "conducted a massive illegal domestic
intelligence operation during the Nixon Administration against the
antiwar movement and other dissident groups in the United States,
according to well-informed Government sources." So began "the
Year of Intelligence." In the first half of the year, "the family
jewels" were placed on public display; in the second half, the operations of the entire intelligence community came under the
"closest and harshest public scrutiny."[45]

On January 4, 1975, President Ford created the Commission
on CIA Activities Within the United States and directed it "to
determine whether any domestic CIA activities exceeded the
Agency's statutory authority and to make appropriate recommendations." After a six-month inquiry, the "blue-ribbon" panel of

prominent Americans, chaired by Vice President Nelson A. Rockefeller and including former California Governor Ronald Reagan, issued its report. Although the Rockefeller Commission declared forthrightly that "the preservation of the United States requires an effective intelligence capability," it acknowledged that "the preservation of individual liberties within the United States requires limitations or restrictions on gathering of intelligence."[46] It showed sensitivity to the American search for reasonable lines "where legitimate intelligence needs end and erosion of Constitutional government begins." But it was not above throwing in a scare, reminding the American people that "the United States remains the principal intelligence target of the communist bloc."[47] Employing an apologetic tone and making a strong defense of counterintelligence, the Rockefeller Commission report nonetheless was quite candid and sensational.

The report publicly confirmed for the first time several of the CIA's covert intelligence activities within the United States. It exposed Operation CHAOS, detailing the sorts of covert surveillance techniques that had been employed and the compiling of secret dossiers and files on U.S. citizens. It told about the related investigations by the CIA's Office of Security and reported the mail-opening programs, as well as the CIA's role in "improper activities for the White House." It even described the DDS&T's research and development projects within the United States, including the testing of behavior-influencing drugs on unsuspecting subjects. During the 1950s, stories had circulated about "brainwashing" and the "Manchurian Candidate," as did reports of Soviet experimentation with drugs for intelligence purposes. The CIA had studied the possibile effects on human behavior of radiation, electric shock, and harassment substances, as well as drugs and hypnosis.[48] In one case in 1953 DDS&T researchers had administered LSD to an unsuspecting employee of the Department of the Army. He developed serious "side effects" and was taken to New York City under CIA escort for psychiatric treatment. The employee leaped to his death from a tenth-floor window several days later.[49]

As the Rockefeller Commission aired the CIA's abuses and excesses in domestic intelligence, it stressed that everything that had happened was over and done with. Confession alone was presented as good-faith evidence that the wrongs would not be repeated—but just to make certain, it recommended several ways that oversight could be improved, including extending the activities of the PFIAB to cover the CIA, expanding the role and giving greater independence to the office of the inspector general, and even congressionally establishing a Joint Committee on Intelligence. The Rockefeller Commission frequently did not pull its punches, but if its plan was to head off a genuinely unfriendly probe, it backfired. The conservative stamp of the commission and suspicion that it had trod only so far tended to intensify the public's demand to know more.

Nor did President Ford help. On January 16, 1975, not quite two weeks after the creation of the Rockefeller Commission, Ford entertained the publisher of the *New York Times* and several of his editors at a White House luncheon. When they asked him about the composition of the Rockefeller Commission, Ford reportedly said that "he didn't want anybody on it who might stray off the reservation and begin rummaging about in the recesses of CIA history." Otherwise, he worried, "they might stumble onto things which would blacken the name of the United States and of every President since Truman."[50] "Like what?" the guests wanted to know.

> "Like Assassination!" Ford shot back. And then it sank in on him what he had said, and to whom he had said it. "That's off the record!" he quickly added.[51]

Having let out the one dark secret that even the "family jewels" had set apart, Ford could not call it back. The *New York Times* did not print the story, but it made the rounds, and TV commentator Daniel Schorr reported a garbled version of it on the CBS *Evening News* in February. In its report, the Rockefeller Commission tried to slough off the story, devoting only two short paragraphs to "alleged plans to assassinate certain foreign leaders." It stated that the "allegations" came to its attention "shortly after its inquiry was under way" and that "time did not permit a full investigation before [its] report was due." It noted that materials in its possession bearing on the allegations had been delivered to the president.[52]

Senator Frank Church, the chairman of the Senate Select Committee on Intelligence, declared that Rockefeller's findings were "the tip of the iceberg." The tiny reference to CIA assassination plots attracted most of the attention immediately, but the *Report to the President by the Commission on CIA Activities Within the United States* (June 1975) did signify a great deal more. It demonstrated that Watergate had not been simply an aberration involving a band of bumbling amateurs operating out of the basement of the Executive Office Building or the Committee for the Reelection of the President but constituted a crisis of constitutional proportions, in which legitimate intelligence agencies of the U.S. government and highly trained professional employees had been committing illegal and improper acts over a long period of time. The Rockefeller Commission confirmed what critics had been charging for some time and created the circumstances for further investigations, heightening demands for the reform of the intelligence community.

24

Torn Cloak/Sheathed Dagger

E ven as the Rockefeller Commission was completing its report, two congressional committees—one in the House of Representatives and the other in the Senate—initiated their own inquiries into the alleged illegal and improper activities of U.S. intelligence agencies. The performances of these two committees were ultimately quite different and had distinctly separate influences upon the movement for the reform of U.S. intelligence.

The House Select Committee on Intelligence was organized in February 1975 under the chairmanship of Lucien Nedzi, who was replaced by Otis Pike in July. It was beset by controversy and wrangling for the year that it existed and contributed little to solving the problems of secret intelligence in the U.S. government. Under Pike, the House committee fought constantly with President Ford over the handling of classified and sensitive information, and it was plagued repeatedly by leaks. In the end, the committee chose not to release its report rather than submit it to the White House for review. The document was leaked nonetheless (again, through CBS correspondent Daniel Schorr) and was published in New York's *Village Voice* under the banner headline, "The Report on the CIA that President Ford Doesn't Want You to Read." Although the report contained damaging information about CIA practices, most of the public reaction to it focused upon the issue of leaks instead of intelligence abuses, which strengthened the position of the president against Congress in the matter of oversight.

The Senate Select Committee to Study Governmental Operations with Respect to Intelligence Activities, chaired by Senator Frank Church of Idaho, undertook a probe that lasted about four-

teen months, from the end of January 1975 to April 1976. The
Church Committee conducted the most serious investigation of the
U.S. intelligence community ever undertaken by the U.S. Congress. Its published findings were extensive, consisting of two
special reports, *Alleged Assassination Plots Involving Foreign Leaders, An
Interim Report* (November 20,1975) and *Covert Action in Chile, 1963–
1973* (December 18, 1975); the *Final Report* (April 1976) in six
books; and seven supplemental volumes of testimony taken during
the committee's public hearings.[1]

The hearings and reports opened up the intelligence community
to public scrutiny as never before. They provided organizational
charts, described functions, defined terms, listed acronyms, and
disclosed capabilities and techniques. The books by Philip Agee,
Victor Marchetti and John Marks, and David Wise and Thomas
Ross had already revealed a great deal, but the Church Committee
hearings provided such a steady stream of information over a period
of more than a year that the IC—the CIA included—tended to lose
its mystique and hence its untouchability. Though the Church
Committee reports covered much the same ground as the Rockefeller Commission had on the CIA's domestic intelligence operations, it investigated the specific collection and surveillance capabilities of the FBI, the NSA, and the military intelligence agencies
as well. On foreign intelligence, the Church Committee studied the
use, tactics, and wisdom of covert action; its investigation of alleged
CIA plots to assassinate foreign leaders absorbed its attention for
the first five months and tended to eclipse the more significant
questions about the "new interventionism."

The Rockefeller Commission had made no report on the assassination allegations; they were in effect "dumped into [the] lap"
of the Church Committee—to the dismay of the staff, who suspected that this might be a "diversionary tactic" on the part of the
CIA "to steer us off course."[2] Church himself seemed to start off
badly. After the secret testimony on July 18, 1975 of John Eisenhower, the former president's son, Church told reporters that "the
CIA may have been behaving like a rogue elephant on a rampage."
The discovery in late August that the CIA had continued to store
deadly poisons (cobra venom and shellfish toxin) five years after
President Nixon had ordered their destruction gave the "rogue

elephant'' theory credence, but the comment haunted Church throughout the remainder of the hearings. According to Miles Copeland, a former clandestine operator, it was standard operating procedure within the CIA to count on someone to ''lose the papers.''[3] Someone ''down the line'' would not believe that the boss really wanted him to dump several million dollars' worth of rare cobra venom down the drain: '' 'The subtlest form of insubordination,' goes the saying 'is to take a stupid order and carry it out to the letter.' ''[4]

In mid-September, on the very first day of public hearings convened to investigate the matter of the poisons and why they had not been destroyed as ordered, Church displayed a CIA dart gun before the cameras. The gun, he explained, was part of a ''delivery system'' that

> entailed first applying poison to a tiny dart the size of a sewing needle (''a nondiscernible microbioinoculator,'' as it had been called by an enterprising scientist in the CIA Directorate of Science and Technology), then using an electric dart gun (''noise-free disseminator'') resembling a large .45 pistol, with a telescopic sight, to propel the dart silently toward the victim. The gun was reputed in CIA documents to be accurate up to 250 feet. Here was the ultimate murder weapon, able to kill without sound and with barely a trace.[5]

In time, the hearings avoided such sensationalism. But the matter of the hidden shellfish toxin provided a lesson, as Church himself noted, in ''how illusive the chain of command can be in the intelligence community.''

> It underscores dramatically the necessity for tighter internal controls; for better record-keeping; for greater understanding of code words, compartmentalization, and the whole range of secrecy requirements. Above all, it emphasizes the necessity for improved mechanisms of accountability all the way from the White House to the outer branches of the intelligence establishment.[6]

It was from the Church Committee's *Assassination Report* that the doctrine of ''plausible denial'' was revealed.

The *Assassination Report* investigated alleged CIA plots against Patrice Lumumba, Ngo Dinh Diem, Fidel Castro, and Rafael Trujillo. After it was issued and the Church Committee went on to study other forms of covert action, the committee raised the sorts of questions that had been troubling Americans since they first became aware that clandestine operations were an instrument of U.S. foreign policy. What is the scope of covert action? Is it an "exceptional or commonplace tool" of U.S. foreign policy? How effective is covert action in achieving foreign policy goals? How have CIA covert operations affected the United States' "capacity for ethical and moral leadership" in world affairs? Are the tactics of covert action compatible with the "principles and ideals" of the American nation? Is covert action justified when "national security interests are at stake"? Does having a covert action capability "distort" the decision-making process, contributing to "an erosion of trust" within the U.S. government and "between the government and the people"? Does the "very existence" of a covert action capability promote its use without adequate deliberation of other policy options? Is covert action an essential option in foreign policy and, if so, what controls, standards, and safeguards should be established?[7]

In its inquiry that examined these questions, the Church Committee "took extensive testimony in executive session and received 14 briefings from the CIA." The staff interviewed over 120 persons, "including 13 former Ambassadors and 12 former CIA Station Chiefs."[8] The committee established special security procedures to protect the secret information it gathered, avoiding the leaks that had afflicted the Pike Committee. It did not make public the details of its study of covert action, concluding that "it was not essential to expose past covert relationships of foreign political, labor and cultural leaders with the United States Government nor to violate the confidentiality of these relationships."[9] Instead, it issued the special report, *Covert Action in Chile, 1963–1973,* as a case study of "the scope, techniques, utility, and propriety of covert action."

Except for the dart-gun episode, the Church Committee's behavior demonstrated that Congress could review sensitive operations without divulging secrets or playing politics. This was demonstrated even though, while the hearings were in progress, Senator Church became an active candidate for the Democratic presidential nomination; or perhaps it was demonstrated because of it, since the senator may have wanted to appear "presidential."[10] (The membership of the Church Committee included several other senators with past, present, or future presidential aspirations: Howard Baker, Barry Goldwater, Gary Hart, Walter Mondale, and John Tower—plus Richard Schweiker, whom Ronald Reagan chose as a running mate *before* the 1976 Republican National Convention.)

Before it issued its final report, the Church Committee considered "proposing a total ban on *all* forms of covert action." But it concluded that the United States needed to "maintain the option" of covert action to meet a future "grave, unforeseen threat" to U.S. national security.[11] But having agreed that covert action is a legitimate function of U.S. foreign policy and having further agreed that "the shield of secrecy . . . must necessarily be imposed on any covert activity if it is to remain covert," the committee was back to "square one" in its search for control and accountability: "The challenge [being] to find a substitute for the public scrutiny through congressional debate and press attention that normally attends government decisions."[12] As it searched for alternative processes of "authorization and review," the committee set certain guidelines for all future covert action. A covert action should be "an exceptional act." It must be "compatible with American principles." It must be "based upon a careful and systematic analysis of a given situation," weighing every possible consequence of acting or not acting. Moreover, "every" covert action proposal should be reviewed by the appropriate NSC committee, and the appropriate congressional oversight committee should be given "prior" notification of "significant" covert operations and should review "all" covert action projects "on a semi-annual basis."[13]

The committee supplemented these guidelines with recommendations to restrict domestic intelligence activities, to preserve the constitutional rights of Americans, and to prohibit the use of private U.S. educational and cultural institutions, the press, publishing houses, and religious groups for clandestine purposes. The committee viewed the need for reform from the perspective of the abuse of authority by the executive branch. But the discussion of the control of secret intelligence soon shifted from the issues of foreign intervention and the protection of individual liberties to the issue of separation of powers. In the dynamics of the great intelligence debate of 1975–76, the focus shifted from abuses, to reforms, and finally to "leaks from Capitol Hill."[14]

This shift occurred because President Ford was becoming alarmed that Congress was overstepping its bounds and was intruding into the presidential prerogative in policymaking, particularly in foreign policy. Ford decided to undertake a "preemptive strike" while the Church Committee was still holding hearings. Taking advantage of "a backlash against the congressional investigations"[15] that had partially resulted from the leak of the Pike Committee report and the murder in December of Richard Welch (the CIA station chief in Athens), President Ford issued Executive Order 11905, "United States Foreign Intelligence Activities," on February 18, 1976.

In issuing EO 11905, President Ford relied upon the Rockefeller Commission report and sought to control the movement for intelligence reform. He stressed the need to "insure a proper *balancing of interests,*" stating that though it was "essential to have the best possible intelligence about the capabilities, intentions, and activities of governments and other entities and individuals abroad," it was "equally as important that the methods [that the U.S. foreign intelligence agencies] employ to collect such information for the legitimate needs of the government conform to the standards set out in the Constitution to preserve and respect the privacy and civil liberties of American citizens."[16] The order sought to establish "clear lines of accountability" by reorganizing the executive command and control structure for U.S. intelligence activities (see figure 24–1).

The order created three new entities for intelligence command and control at the executive level: the Intelligence Oversight Board, the Committee on Foreign Intelligence, and the Operations Advisory Group. Each had distinct responsibilities for the review, management, and authorization of intelligence activities. The *Intelligence Oversight Board (IOB)* resulted from the Rockefeller Commission's concern that "external" controls over the intelligence community (especially the CIA) had to be improved, and specifically its recommendation to strengthen the PFIAB by appointing a full-

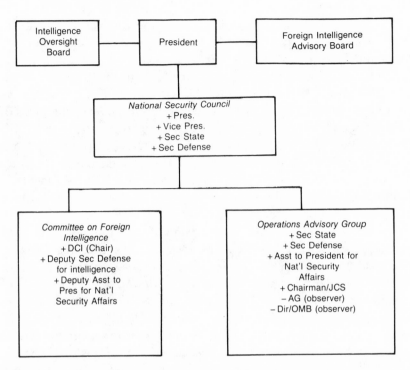

Figure 24–1. *Reorganization of Executive Command and Control/Intelligence Activities, Executive Order 11905, February 18, 1976*

time chairman and staff. Ford decided to keep the part-time PFIAB as it was but added the permanent three-member IOB, which comprised persons from outside government service who could serve concurrently on the PFIAB. It was given the power to receive reports from the CIA's inspector general and general counsel and to notify, in turn, the attorney general about illegal activities and the president about improprieties. Although it was not authorized to conduct investigations on its own, the IOB was at least full time, avoiding the "dog and pony show"/"night-on-the-town" criticism of the PFIAB reported by Patrick McGarvey.

The *Committee on Foreign Intelligence (CFI)* was made up of the DCI as chair, the deputy secretary of defense for intelligence, and the deputy assistant to the president for national security affairs. It was charged with responsibility for "managing" the intelligence community. As a committee of the NSC, the CFI had the authority to "control budget preparation and resource allocation for the National Foreign Intelligence Program" and to "establish policy priorities for the collection and production of national intelligence." The CFI was an effort to enable the DCI to "run" the intelligence community and sought "to specify openly the locus of authority and responsibility for intelligence policy and activity."[17] EO 11905 enhanced the position of the DCI by restoring Donovan's concept of a director of national intelligence and elevating it "to a very high level in the White House."[18] The CFI lacked a representative from the State Department, but neither did it have authority in the matter of covert action.

The responsibility to develop policy recommendations with reference to "special activities" (that is, covert action) resided with the *Operations Advisory Group (OAG),* which consisted of the assistant to the president for national security affairs, the secretaries of defense and state, the chairman of the JCS, and the DCI; the attorney general and the director of the OMB were observer members. The OAG replaced the "40" Committee and its predecessors. It raised the level at which high-risk covert operations were considered up a notch to include cabinet-level officers. In December 1974, Congress amended the Foreign Assistance Act, as proposed by Senator Harold Hughes and Representative Leo Ryan, to provide that the CIA might not expend funds for foreign operations "other than activities intended solely for obtaining necessary intelligence" without a presidential finding that "each such operation" was important to U.S. national security and a report thereof, "in a timely fashion," to the appropriate committees of Congress. Ford intended that the OAG would satisfy the Hughes–Ryan process by examining covert action proposals and making recommendations, "including any dissents," in order to enable him to render a finding. The Church Committee concluded that this was not enough and insisted that the OAG should review "*every* covert action proposal." It felt strongly that "the small nonsensitive covert action proposals which, in the aggregate, establish and maintain the Agency's covert infrastructure around the world should be considered and analyzed by the appropriate NSC committee [that is, the OAG]."[19]

But Ford believed that control over ''nonsensitive'' intelligence operations could be exercised in another way. Indeed, his order set guidelines for the ''conduct'' of senior officials of each organization in the intelligence community. The Rockefeller Commission had concluded that the ''best assurance'' against abuses lay in the ''character'' of the DCI, adding further that the CIA ''must rely on the discipline and integrity of the men and women it employs. Many of the activities that we have found to be improper or unlawful were in fact questioned by lower-level employees.''[20] Ford, in a press release, stated that EO 11905 established ''government-wide direction for the foreign intelligence agencies and [placed] responsibility and accountability on *individuals*, not institutions.''[21] To reinforce this policy of internal monitoring and self-policing, the order ''upgraded'' the investigative and reporting functions of the inspectors general and the legal counsel of the intelligence community, requiring them to report also to the external oversight body, the IOB.

Ford's order, finally, established restrictions on intelligence activities, specifically on collection, experimentation (drug testing), and assistance to U.S. law enforcement agencies. Most of the ''commandments'' pertained to covert surveillance techniques within the United States: physical surveillance, electronic surveillance, unconsented physical search, mail opening, examination of federal tax returns, and ''undisclosed participation in domestic organizations'' (or infiltration). The restrictions also included ''Thou shalt not kill,'' in the single operational restraint upon foreign covert action: ''No employee of the United States Government shall engage in, or conspire to engage in, political assassination.''

Except for this prohibition against assassination, however, the restrictions gave little and kept much.

> They were, undeniably, constraints of a sort, but they amounted merely to executive codification of its own understanding of the existing list of illegalities. They were not substantive concessions on matters debated widely outside the government, and they provided little comfort to those who were already unhappy with the relative generosity of the law concerning intelligence activities.[22]

In fact, the general tone of Ford's executive order was combative. Instead of "backing down" to the critics of foreign intelligence, Ford was fighting back. While making reforms, he intended to preserve and strengthen U.S. foreign intelligence. Moreover, he declared, he was "proposing legislation to impose criminal and civil sanctions on those who are authorized access to intelligence secrets and who willfully and wrongfully reveal this information." He explained that "it is essential that the irresponsible and dangerous exposure of our Nation's intelligence secrets be stopped."[23] "Just as" the Ford Administration believed "that the age of operational abuses had passed, so also it believed that the age of tolerating promiscuous leakage of intelligence secrets had passed."[24]

Ford even took a swipe at Congress in this regard. He conceded that congressional oversight of the foreign intelligence agencies was "essential," but he affirmed that it was equally essential for both the House and the Senate to "establish firm rules to insure that foreign intelligence secrets will not be improperly disclosed." To this end, he recommended that Congress "centralize" the responsibility for oversight by establishing "a joint Foreign Intelligence Oversight Committee." He lectured that "the more committees and subcommittees dealing with highly sensitive secrets, the greater the risk of disclosure."[25] As it turned out, the Congress did not heed his advice. Each chamber chose to establish a separate oversight committee. The Senate, by resolution, created the Select Committee on Intelligence on May 19, 1976, and the House, by Rules of the House, organized the Permanent Select Committee on Intelligence on July 14, 1977.

As far as President Ford was concerned, he had put his house in order. In the November before he issued EO 11905, he had nominated George Bush to be DCI (January 30, 1976–January 20, 1977), replacing William Colby, who had suffered through the "Year of Intelligence" (including three major investigations of the CIA); there was no way that Colby could have emerged unscathed. It took two months to secure Bush's confirmation, largely because he had been chairman of the Republican National Committee (which made him too "political," as Church argued). His appointment conformed to the Rockefeller Commission ideal of a DCI, an individual "of stature, independence, and integrity."

> In making this appointment, consideration should be given to individuals from outside the career service of the CIA, although promotion from within should not be barred. Experience in intelligence service is not necessarily a prerequisite for the position; management and administrative skills are at least as important as the technical expertise which can always be found in an able deputy.[26]

Ford had followed the Rockefeller Commission report as his guide and was satisfied that he had achieved a "balancing of interests." If Ford had been elected president in 1976, it is likely that EO 11905 would have governed the conduct of U.S. foreign intelligence for the next four years. But the election of Jimmy Carter made more extensive reform of the intelligence community inevitable. Carter's reaction to the Church Committee investigation (in which his running mate Walter Mondale had participated) was that the intelligence agencies had to be opened up more and that stronger curbs on their activities were necessary. Intelligence wrongdoing had not been a partisan issue—Kennedy and Johnson were as culpable as Eisenhower and Nixon—but Carter made intelligence *reform* a campaign issue. He stood as a Washington "outsider" and condemned what he described as the three national disgraces: "Watergate, Vietnam, and the CIA."[27]

After his election, Carter quickly signaled that he intended to shake up the CIA. He nominated Theodore Sorensen, the former special counsel to President Kennedy, as DCI. Bush had done a good job and wanted to stay on, but Carter was determined to remove him. This was the first change in DCI to be directly related to a change in the presidency. But the Sorensen appointment became too controversial—he was a "Kennedy liberal" who believed "that moral and legal standards must govern national security decisions."[28] Sorensen decided to withdraw rather than put up with personal attacks during the confirmation hearings (including the fact that he had been a conscientious objector to military service.)

Carter next nominated Admiral Stansfield Turner, his Annapolis classmate, to be DCI (1977–81). Turner was a career naval officer with experience in fleet operations, not intelligence; that is, he had been a consumer of intelligence, never a producer, and he

viewed intelligence performance from the perspective of efficiency
and effectiveness. Turner's appointment appeared less threatening
to the intelligence community than Sorensen's, but aside from the
fact that he wanted to run the place "like a battleship,"[29] he
shared Carter's view that "intelligence agencies, like all arms of
government, must reflect the mores of the nation and abide by its
laws."[30] During 1977, Carter, Turner, and National Security
Adviser Zbigniew Brzezinski made several alterations in the control and direction of U.S. foreign intelligence, while preparing a
major overhaul of American intelligence.

The Carter reforms of U.S. foreign intelligence were contained
in Executive Order 12036, *United States Intelligence Activities,*
January 24, 1978. The order made the president, specific cabinet
officers, and senior officials accountable for "special activities"
("activities conducted abroad in support of national foreign policy
objectives . . . planned and executed so that the role of the United
States Government is not apparent or acknowledged publicly,"
aka covert action) and gave the DCI "full responsibility" for the
collection, production, and dissemination of U.S. foreign intelligence. The organization of the "Direction, Duties and Responsibilities With Respect to the National Intelligence Effort" (see
figure 24-2), as framed by EO 12036, demonstrated Carter's
intention to improve the performance of the intelligence community and to exercise strict control over covert action, guided additionally by the Church Committee's concept that covert action was
"exceptional."

EO 12036 eliminated the PFIAB altogether as so much fluff or
PR, and it retained the Intelligence Oversight Board as the more
substantive means of external oversight. It consisted of three persons "from outside the government" and functioned permanently
within the White House. Carter's IOB still had no independent
investigative authority, but section 3 of EO 12036, which specified
the duties of the IOB for reviewing intelligence activities, instructed
the inspectors general and general counsel, who had responsibility
for agencies within the IC, to "transmit timely reports to the IOB"
and to "formulate practices and procedures for discovering and
reporting to the IOB intelligence activities that raise questions of
legality or propriety."[31]

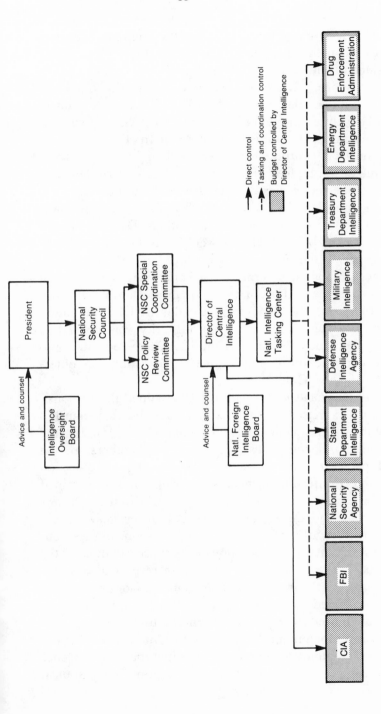

Source: *Time*, February 6, 1978. Copyright 1978 Time Inc. Reprinted by permission.

Figure 24–2. *Direction, Duties, and Responsibilities with Respect to the National Intelligence Effort, Executive Order 12036, January 24, 1978*

EO 12036 designated the NSC "as the highest Executive Branch entity [to provide] review of, guidance for, and direction to the conduct of all national foreign intelligence and counterintelligence activities." It created two new committees to assist it in carrying out its responsibilities: the Policy Review Committee and Special Coordination Committee. The *Policy Review Committee (PRC)* replaced Ford's Committee on Foreign Intelligence except that, while the DCI continued to serve as chair, its membership included some of the highest officers of the U.S. government: the vice president, the secretaries of state, treasury, and defense, the assistant to the president for national security affairs, and the chairman of the JCS. With this lineup, even William Donovan would have been impressed by the DCI's power within the National Foreign Intelligence Program to set priorities and requirements, review budget proposals, determine the appropriate allocation of resources, and review and evaluate the quality of the intelligence product. Yet chairing the PRC did not make the DCI an "intelligence czar," as some suggested; his authority was limited to Intelligence policy and to managing the IC. The responsibility to recommend covert action in support of U.S. foreign policy objectives rested with the SCC.

The *Special Coordination Committee (SCC)* assumed the responsibilities formerly exercised by the OAG. Under the chairmanship of the assistant to the president for national security affairs, the SCC considered independently, with variable membership, the questions of special activities, sensitive foreign intelligence collection operations, and counterintelligence. Aside from a more restrained administration policy toward the use of covert action and sensitive spy missions and the inclusion of the attorney general as a permanent member, the SCC's duties and responsibilities concerning high-risk clandestine operations were similar to those of the OAG. But its charge to "develop policy with respect to counterintelligence activities" *was* new. The Church Committee had actually recommended that an NSC Counterintelligence Committee be established, chaired by the attorney general, to "coordinate and review" the law enforcement duties of the FBI and the intelligence mission of the CIA and to enforce the principle that "intelligence agencies are subject to the rule of law." Assigning this responsibility to the SCC was a compromise (mainly because of new concern over terrorism), but it demonstrated the Carter administration's determination to prevent a recurrence of programs like COINTELPRO, CHAOS, and MINARET. Another section of the order enumerated specific restrictions on intelligence activities, particularly within the United States.

At the next level of the national intelligence effort, EO 12036 created the National Foreign Intelligence Board and the National Intelligence Tasking Center to assist the DCI in carrying out the policies established by the PRC. The *National Foreign Intelligence Board (NFIB)* was chaired by the DCI and consisted of the appropriate officers of the IC agencies. The NFIB was to advise the DCI in achieving the "intelligence cycle" (planning and direction, collection, processing, production and analysis, and dissemination) and in preparing the budget for the National Foreign Intelligence Program. The *National Intelligence Tasking Center (NITC),* under the "direction, control and management" of the DCI, finally provided the mechanism by which the DCI gave the IC its "marching orders" in national foreign intelligence. Further, the Carter order empowered the DCI to act as "the primary advisor to the President and NSC on national foreign intelligence" and as the IC's "principal spokesperson to the Congress, the news media and the public."[32]

Besides firming up the management and control of U.S. foreign intelligence, Carter's order also included specific "restrictions on intelligence activities." In the matter of restricting "certain collection techniques" (bugging and wiretapping, mail and communications interception, surreptitious entry, "tailing," and infiltration), the Carter order resembled Ford's, except that it banned any surveillance activity "for which a warrant would be required if undertaken for law enforcement rather than intelligence purposes," unless the president authorized it and the attorney general "both approved the particular activity and determined that there is probable cause to believe that [any] United States person [affected] is an agent of a foreign power."[33] Beyond this general constraint, EO 12036 instructed operators to gather information "by the least intrusive means possible." This meant that in the choice of methods, the "potential impact" on private citizens took precedence over "operational effectiveness." [34] EO 12036 retained the prohibition on assassination and added the further restriction that special activity/covert action could be conducted only by agencies within the IC.

Carter's restrictions on intelligence activities, like Ford's, may seem to have outlawed only what was already illegal. But they were, in spirit, less the achieving by tacit consent to do what was not explicitly banned and more a genuine effort to end abusive intelligence practices. It was not that Carter abandoned Ford's concept of balancing the interests and values of secret intelligence and American democracy, but he tilted it toward achieving "the *proper* balance between protection of individual rights and acquisition of essential information."

> Information about the capabilities, intentions and activities of foreign powers, organizations, or persons and their agents is essential to informed decision-making in the areas of national defense and foreign relations. The measures employed to acquire such information should be responsive to legitimate government needs and must be conducted in a manner that preserves and respects established concepts of privacy and civil liberties. [35]

Or, as Stansfield Turner expressed this concept,

> Those who criticize our intelligence as a threat to our society's values and those who would condone any kind of intrusion into our personal privacy for the sake of the nation's security are both wrong. Between those outlooks is the mature appreciation that there is a need for good intelligence capabilities, but the need cannot justify abuse of the secrecy that must surround intelligence activities. [36]

Similarly, the Carter administration sought the middle path between banning all forms of covert action (as the Church Committee had contemplated) and retaining the capability: it established the strictest procedures for authorization and review and made clear the president's ultimate accountability.

EO 12036 thus had two purposes: first, to streamline the vast intelligence bureaucracy and to set it to the task of producing quality national intelligence; and second, to eliminate intelligence abuses

at home and restrict covert intervention abroad—particularly the
dirty tricks and paramilitary operations that had undermined
America's moral authority and President Carter's commitment to
human rights. Both aims were intended to restore public confidence in U.S. intelligence.

But intelligence professionals argued that Carter's operational
limitations were "too confining" and that he had permitted "the
policy pendulum [to swing] too far against the interests of the
nation in maintaining potent intelligence capabilities."[37] In addition to EO 12036, the Hughes-Ryan Amendment was passed in
1974, congressional intelligence committees were established in
1976 and 1977, and the Foreign Intelligence Surveillance Act of
1978 ("which in general required a court order for electronic monitoring of signals in the United States, even in national security
cases"[38]) was enacted. All these tended to polarize conservative
and liberal attitudes toward intelligence, which compounded Carter's foreign policy setbacks. Carter's good foreign policy intentions produced mainly the perception that America was weak—
especially in events in Iran and Nicaragua—and critics blamed
much of this on the president's "hobbling" of the CIA. "By
1979," Ray Cline wrote, "nearly everyone was complaining about
shortcomings in foreign intelligence operations rather than about
domestic transgressions."[39]

The complaints reflected an impression that American strength
was declining and Soviet power was growing, based on evidence of
a Soviet weapons buildup, Cuban actions in Angola, Ethiopia, and
Yemen, a formal alliance between the Soviet Union and Vietnam,
the Russian invasion of Afghanistan, and the fall of the shah in
Iran.[40] The rise to power of the Ayatollah Ruhollah Khomeini
and the harrowing Iranian hostage crisis (November 1979–January
1981) came to be associated with the "handcuffing of the CIA."
When Cline saw "the pendulum . . . swinging back," he was
delighted that it cut down in its path Frank Church, "the investigative scourge of the U.S. intelligence community"; Church failed
to win reelection to the Senate in 1980. Nor did Cline mourn Carter's defeat the same year: "Whatever other things voters may
have wanted, they appear to have demanded a new agenda for the
CIA."[41]

John Ranelagh, an Englishman who wrote a history of the CIA, judged Carter's performance even more harshly. He described Carter's policy as "neo-isolationist," since "the inevitable result of the withdrawal behind a human-rights-directed foreign policy and the termination of covert-action capability was a quiet American disengagement that produced some noisy .American 'failures.' " [42] Ranelagh was referring particularly to Iran; he characterized the shah's fall as "a colossal intelligence failure all around" and agreed with Cline that "the alteration in perceptions that flowed from [the Teheran hostage crisis] was to sweep Carter aside and put Ronald Reagan in the White House." [43] He concluded that Carter "was a profoundly ignorant (though by no means unintelligent) American, especially in the areas of economics, international affairs, and history, who assumed that the economic and moral strength of the United States meant that it did not have to behave like other countries or protect itself in hidden ways." [44] Ranelagh conceded that Carter and Turner strove to maintain a strong TECHINT capability, but he still found fault in that "they took no precautions to avoid human surprises."

> When the Soviet Union invaded Afghanistan in December 1979, Carter was horrified to discover that [Leonid] Brezhnev, who had assured him for months that he did not intend to invade, had "lied" to him. With a President who was so limited, the CIA had little chance of being properly used or appreciated. [45]

Without debating these judgments of Carter's leadership and ability, it must be noted that "intelligence had become dramatically a partisan political issue [by] 1979." [46] The truth is that Carter's foreign policy "failures" had little to do with restrictions on domestic intelligence activities or with tighter controls on covert action. In fact, the Foreign Intelligence Surveillance Act probably contributed to the apprehension and conviction of spies in the 1980s (see chapter 25) by establishing procedures for admitting wiretap evidence in court. [47] The troubles abroad, rather, stemmed from policy decisions (in which Intelligence itself gave input) and from new challenges in the aftermath of the United States' withdrawal from Vietnam and the economic and geopolitical crises caused by the OPEC oil embargo. It was clearly counterproductive to insist upon human rights compliance and unload associations with dictators without developing viable alternatives. However, such policy decisions could be firmly pursued through open diplomacy (without returning to the days of Cord Meyer and the covert funding of the non-Communist left, as much to deceive the Congress and the American people as to protect secrets). Carter's failure to force Anastasio Somoza to leave Nicaragua in January 1979 was a policy error and had no relationship to the status of Clandestine Services.

That Clandestine Services had declined, there was little doubt. Even the Carter administration tried "to resurrect covert action" in 1980,[48] after events brought President Carter around to George Kennan's thinking of thirty years earlier. The idea of a contingency force was updated, as stated by Stansfield Turner: "the talent necessary for covert action is available in the CIA and it must be preserved."[49] Carter extended covert support "to opponents of the Sandinistas," including "newsprint and funds to keep the [opposition] newspaper *La Prensa* alive,"[50] and he responded to the Soviet invasion of Afghanistan in December 1979 with covert arms shipments to Afghan rebels. U.S. intelligence was not caught unawares by the Soviet invasion of Afghanistan, as Carter's critics charged, but Carter, shocked by Soviet recklessness, resorted to covert action to "punish the Soviets," since going to war "wasn't feasible."[51] The tragic clandestine rescue mission that was aborted in the Iranian desert in April 1980 was a failure, but it was no more a failure than the Bay of Pigs in the heyday of Allen Dulles.

If Carter's "failures" were also "intelligence failures," the problem was in the function of clandestine intelligence collection (HUMINT). In reforming Clandestine Services, no one had made clear the distinction between foreign intelligence or espionage and covert action. When Ranelagh affirmed that the CIA under Carter and Turner had "lost the quality of being special,"[52] he overlooked the fact that the FI people had lost out a long time before (to say nothing of the DDI analysts). Turner's purge of two hundred covert operators did not ruin the CIA, and Carter's problems in foreign affairs were more complex than his obvious disdain for covert action.

During the 1970s, Americans seriously confronted the contra-dictory issue of secret intelligence and American democracy. The outcome was not perfect, its shortcomings obvious, but presidents would never again be so freewheeling. Retaining the covert action option, however, was no guarantee against further abuses; having a little covert action capability is like being a little bit pregnant.

Despite the machinery and the procedures, the attitude of the president was critical, as a comparison of Ronald Reagan's uses of foreign intelligence with those of Jimmy Carter shows: "Where Carter made one big paramilitary play, his successor Ronald Reagan . . . used covert techniques widely."[53] Because Carter was unpopular and perceived as inept, Reagan's task of undoing EO 12036 was relatively easy. It was assisted greatly by effective lobbying by ex-intelligence officers, such as Ray Cline and David Phillips, and their organizations, the Association of Former Intelligence Officers and the National Intelligence Study Center. More amazing was that it was done so quickly. Allen Dulles was fond of the metaphor about spies folding their tents after each war. Now it was more like a sidewalk salesman folding his suitcase until the cop passes by and being back on the street again.

25

The Rise and Fall of
William Casey

The Rockefeller Commission report to President Ford had
emphasized that the "character" of the DCI is critical in
preventing abuses by U.S. intelligence agencies, particularly the
CIA. The report concluded that "the best assurance against misuse of the agency [CIA] lies in the appointment to that position of
persons with the judgment, courage, and independence to resist
improper pressure and importuning, whether from the White
House, within the agency, or elsewhere."[1] Ronald Reagan (who
had served on the Rockefeller Commission), after becoming president of the United States, nominated his presidential campaign
director, William J. Casey, a New York attorney and "self-made"
millionaire, to be DCI (January 1981–January 1987), giving the
impression that the position of DCI had become another "patron-
age plum."[2]

Casey was a throwback to William Donovan and the OSS.
Although he had been a member of Ford's PFIAB, Casey was
an "ex-spook" whose ideas of intelligence were "fundamentally
forty years old."[3] He described as "superficial" the critics who
ridiculed his experience as Secret Intelligence chief at OSS/London
during World War II, but he resembled Donovan in attitude and
influence more than any previous DCI. In an interview early in his
directorship, Casey revealed that he was not a passive adviser on
the issue of covert action. "Through all the investigations and
examinations of covert activities," he told Philip Taubman of the
New York Times, "very few people came away with the conclusion

that the nation should deprive itself of the ability to move quietly in private channels to react to or influence the policies of other countries.

> To be, or to be perceived as, unable or unwilling to act in support of friendly governments facing destabilization or insurgency from aggressor nations, or to prevent groups acting or standing for American interests or values from being snuffed out, would be damaging to our security and leadership.[4]

Jimmy Carter may have politicized the CIA by firing George Bush, but William Casey was a thoroughly "political animal." He dusted off all the old Donovan psychwar techniques, particularly disinformation, to serve an activist foreign policy reminiscent of the early cold war. Like Donovan, he was an "empire builder." He hired ("Oh, how he hired!"), "overseeing the biggest peace-time buildup in the American intelligence community since the early 1950's." After Casey had been on the job for two years, Taubman reported that

> the C.I.A. is indisputably on the rebound. The staff has increased and morale has improved. A quarter of a million Americans, many of whom saw the C.I.A.'s sophisticated ("We May Have a Career for You") recruiting ads in newspapers and magazines, got in touch with the agency about jobs last year [1982]. Ten thousand . . . submitted formal applications and 1,500 were hired.[5]

This expansion seems to have been a "true measure" of Casey's influence with the president, and a contemporary comment reinforces this: "Reagan thinks Casey is a damn smart guy who elected him. It's the way an actor feels about his agent. This is his agent—he has got to believe the guy is good."[6] At the same time, Casey perfectly suited an administration whose "transition team" for studying the CIA and the intelligence community recommended that "national intelligence capabilities be improved and used more aggressively, . . . [including] an expanded role for covert action."[7] He was a poor choice given the Rockefeller Commission's conclusion that the DCI ought to be a person who would not permit the CIA to be "misused." Casey would have preferred to be appointed secretary of state or defense, but settling for DCI, he received extraordinary power, including cabinet rank (the first DCI to achieve it).

The Reagan administration moved quickly to "restore" the CIA. It prepared three executive orders dealing with intelligence during its first year. Executive Order 12331 (October 20, 1981) reestablished the PFIAB; Executive Order 12333 (December 4, 1981), "United States Intelligence Activities," revised Carter's EO 12036; and Executive Order 12334 (December 4, 1981) reconstituted the IOB. The three measures laid the groundwork for President Reagan's intelligence organization (see figure 25-1), in which authorization and review of intelligence activities occurred at a lower level, "substantially [decreasing] the personal involvement of the president in the control framework."[8]

Reagan revived the PFIAB for external oversight, while retaining the Intelligence Oversight Board. The intelligence "transition team" had recommended that "the President's Foreign Intelligence Advisory Board should be reestablished and its watchdog function should be strengthened."[9] In reality, the PFIAB was a "bigger joke" than before; it had no specific watchdog function beyond suggesting ways to enhance the "performance" of the U.S. intelligence effort and to achieve increased effectiveness "in meeting national intelligence needs." In recommending that the PFIAB be given "a quality control mission," Reagan's "transition team" had actually declared that the board "should be permitted wide-ranging authority to review the intelligence product of the *last four years* to identify erroneous information and to locate the individuals chiefly responsible for those areas."[10]

If restoring the PFIAB gave the impression of increased external oversight, the reality was that the IOB was significantly weakened. Under Carter, the IOB had had the duty to "report in a timely manner to the President any intelligence activities that raise serious questions of legality or propriety." Moreover, the inspectors general and general counsel within the intelligence community had the responsibility "to transmit timely reports to the IOB concerning any intelligence activities . . . that raise questions of legality or propriety." Under Reagan, "propriety" disappeared "as a

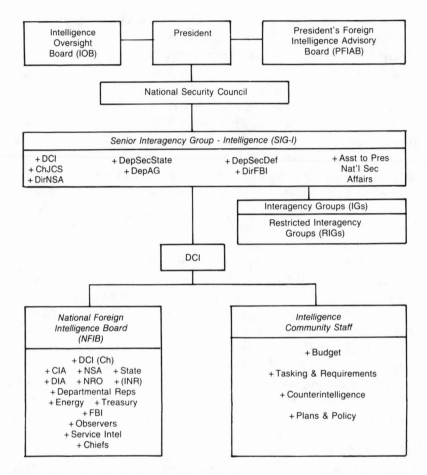

Source: John Patrick Quirk, *The Central Intelligence Agency: A Photographic History,* Foreign Intelligence Press, 1986. Reprinted with permission.

Figure 25-1. *President Reagan's Intelligence Organization. Executive Order 12333, December 4, 1981*

standard for evaluating activities."[11] Reagan's EO 12334 instructed IOB to concern itself with intelligence activities that it believed might be "unlawful." It was to review the "lawfulness of intelligence activities." Neither the PFIAB nor the IOB raised any alarms in the Iran-contra affair.

EO 12333, "United States Intelligence Activities," reaffirmed the primacy of the NSC in directing national foreign intelligence programs and authorized it to establish "such committees as may be necessary to carry out its functions and responsibilities" under the order. By not specifically creating "such committees," EO 12333 effectively eliminated the NSC Policy Review Committee and Special Coordination Committee and paved the way for radical change in the authorization and review of intelligence activities.

In January 1982, Reagan created the *Senior Interagency Group— Intelligence (SIG-I)*. Chaired by the DCI, it was charged with submitting policy recommendations on covert action and reviewing "proposals for other sensitive intelligence operations."[12] Casey, who had the power to act "as the primary advisor to the President and NSC on national foreign intelligence and provide the President and other officials in the Executive Branch with national foreign intelligence," also headed a group that contained no other cabinet officer, since SIG-I consisted of the assistant to the president for national security affairs, the deputy secretary of state, the deputy secretary of defense, the chairman of the JCS, the deputy attorney general, the director of the FBI, and the director of the NSA.

Although "the Reagan order provided evidence that the impetus to move responsibility upward and away from intelligence officials had begun to dissipate,"[13] the bureaucratic structure was more complex. In time, various *interagency groups (IGs)*, made up of representatives of the SIG-I members, were established as subcommittees to assist in considering individual policy issues, such as national foreign intelligence, counterintelligence, or international terrorism. "The IGs, in turn, [established] working groups as needed to provide support to the approved mechanisms of the NSC for [particular] matters."[14]

Certain IGs were transformed into *restricted interagency groups (RIGs)* to deal with covert operations. At the same time, the *National Security Planning Group (NSPG)* evolved, consisting of the president, the vice president, the assistants to the president, the secretaries of state and defense, and the DCI. In accordance with the informal and personal character of the Reagan White House, the NSPG became "the meat-and-potatoes gathering, the foreign-policy inner circle, hashing out overt and covert policy."[15] The president remained accountable for "special activities" under the Hughes-Ryan Amendment, but EO 12333 effectively took the secretaries of state and defense out of the authorization and review process and reduced the role of the assistant to the president for national security affairs. This virtually gave the DCI a free hand in formulating and conducting secret foreign policy. As an activist, Casey concentrated principally upon covert action, but EO 12333 also enhanced his authority as DCI to manage the National Foreign Intelligence Program.

EO 12333 gave the DCI "full responsibility" for producing and disseminating national foreign intelligence. To carry out this responsibility, and to fix tasking priorities and determine the consolidated National Foreign Intelligence Program budget, Reagan's order empowered the DCI to create "appropriate staffs, committees, or other advisory groups," as well as to "establish mechanisms [to translate] national foreign intelligence objectives and priorities approved by the NSC into specific guidance for the Intelligence Community."[16] Accordingly, Casey organized the National Foreign Intelligence Board and the intelligence community staff. The NFIB, chaired by the DCI and made up of senior representatives of the agencies comprising the U.S. intelligence effort, advised the DCI concerning principally the "production, review, and coordination of national foreign intelligence." Casey exercised his powerful management controls through the ICS, supported by the director of the intelligence community staff (D/ICS). The activities of the ICS included "examination of critical cross disciplinary intelligence problems, coordination of Community priorities and requirements, maintenance of Community planning mechanisms, and development of the National Foreign Intelligence Program budget."[17] EO 12333 placed Casey in charge of national foreign intelligence at two levels: the NSC level (policy) through Sig-I and the intelligence community level (performance) through the NFIB and the IC staff.

The order further enhanced "operational performance" by modifying many of the restrictions on intelligence activities that Ford and Carter had imposed.[18] Although many of the "commandments" remained, the balancing of interests was tilted back toward the government's needs for intelligence and away from protecting individual rights. "The word 'restriction,' so prominent in the Carter order, never appears. Provisions are phrased in terms of 'authorizations' (except for a flat prohibition of assassination), and constraints are then stated as exceptions to authorized activity."[19] Section 2 of the order, dealing with operational restraints, even dropped the words "Restrictions on" from its title, substituting "*Conduct of* Intelligence Activities." Moreover, where the Carter order had admonished intelligence agencies to follow procedures that "ensured" that information would be gathered "by the least intrusive means possible" in collecting intelligence within the United States or against U.S. citizens abroad, Reagan instructed them to "use the least intrusive collection techniques feasible." In choice of operational techniques, he thereby altered Carter's emphasis on protecting constitutional rights and privacy to an emphasis "on considerations of effectiveness."[20] EO 12333 "was no timid, self-denying document. It assigned missions and told the agencies to get on with them."[21] If a "Reagan revolution" occurred in domestic affairs, no less a "counter-revolution" occurred in foreign intelligence.

Aside from his popularity, Reagan exploited a number of factors to reverse the "era of reform" in intelligence. He reaped the harvest of the "campaign rhetoric," charging that the congressional investigations of the 1970s had gone too far and that the Carter–Turner restrictions on the CIA had hobbled U.S. intelligence, resulting in such "humiliations" as the seizure of the U.S. embassy in Teheran. Even after the hostages were returned from Iran, the Reagan administration reminded Americans of the need to remain alert against the threat of international terrorism.[22] (Such expressions of concern about terrorism caused John Shattuck of the American Civil Liberties Union to remark that " 'a new talisman, "terrorism," may come to center stage in Washington' to sanctify the reinstatement of dangerous investigative powers in the government."[23]) Reagan also stepped up his rhetoric against the Soviet Union, referring to it as "an evil empire" in a speech in March 1983. Finally, the United States experienced an epidemic of espionage and security cases that reinforced the impression that U.S. intelligence had gone to pot in the 1970s and that made Reagan's "stand-tall" policies look good.

From the 1977 case of Edwin P. Wilson to the November 1985 arrest of Ronald W. Pelton, no other brief period in American history produced so many traitors. Four cases (Wilson, Christopher Boyce and Daulton Lee, William Kampiles, and David H. Barnett) had broken before Reagan's presidency, and the remainder (nine) occurred during his term. They served to vindicate his stand for a stronger, more vigorous intelligence capability. Wilson, a renegade ex-CIA officer, received a fifty-two-year prison term for conspiring to illegally ship guns and forty tons of high explosives to Muammar el-Qaddafi's Libya and for conspiring to murder two U.S. prosecutors and six other people.[24] Boyce, a college dropout working at a clerk's job for the TRW Corporation in California, and his friend Lee managed to pass highly classified secrets about U.S. communications satellites to the Soviet Union. The so-called "Falcon and the Snowman" pair apparently spied for drug money, which provided Reagan with an array of powerful arguments for his policies. Kampiles, a former CIA employee who was allegedly looking for "excitement," sold the Russians a manual for the KH-11 reconnaissance satellite for $3,000, receiving a forty-year jail sentence for his effort. Barnett resigned from the CIA in 1970 after twelve years of service and spied for the Soviets between 1976 and 1980, when he was arrested and sentenced to ten years in prison: "He had identified CIA personnel and divulged how the CIA tracked Soviet shipments of armaments to Indonesia. . . . Money appeared to be his motive. Fortunately, there is no evidence that he was a mole while on active service, when he could have done even more harm."[25]

Almost all the espionage cases that became public during Reagan's term occurred during 1985—the "Year of the Spy." On Sunday, December 1, 1985, "The Week in Review" section of the *New York Times* summarized them in the following grim lineup:

Richard W. Miller, an F.B.I. agent for 20 years, charged in October 1984 with selling counterintelligence secrets to a Soviet émigré woman with whom he was having an affair.

Karl F. Koecher, a former Central Intelligence Agency employee, charged in November 1984 with spying for the Czechoslovak intelligence service.

Thomas P. Cavanagh, a Northrup Corporation engineer, charged in December 1984 with attempting to sell classified documents on "stealth" aircraft technology to Soviet agents.

John A. Walker, Jr., a retired Navy warrant officer, charged in May 1985 with spying for the Soviet Union for nearly 20 years.

Michael Walker, John Walker's son and a Navy yeoman aboard the aircraft carrier Nimitz, charged with providing classified documents to his father.

Arthur J. Walker, John Walker's brother and a retired Navy lieutenant commander, also charged with delivering classified documents to his brother.

Jerry A. Whitworth, a retired Navy enlisted man, charged in June 1985 with passing classified materials to his friend, John Walker. Federal officials conclude that the Walker spy ring was the largest and most damaging in recent American history.

Sharon M. Scranage, a clerk in the C.I.A.'s Ghana station, charged in July 1985 with passing intelligence information to her Ghanaian lover.

Edward L. Howard, a former C.I.A. officer, charged in October 1985 with passing intelligence information to the Soviet Union in 1984. He fled the United States.

Jonathan Jay Pollard, a civilian employee of the Naval Investigative Service, charged in November 1985 with spying for Israel. Mr. Pollard's wife, *Anne Henderson-Pollard,* charged with unauthorized possession of national defense information.

Larry Wu-Tai Chin, a retired C.I.A. analyst, charged with spying for China for 30 years.

Ronald W. Pelton, a former communications specialist for the National Security Agency, charged with spying for the Soviet Union while working for the N.S.A. from 1965 to 1979.[26]

The Walker "family spy ring" constituted a major breach of American secrets, particularly navy cryptographic systems. It is quite possible that the Soviet Union had its own MAGIC or ULTRA operating against the United States for at least a decade. After the arrest of John Walker and Jerry Whitworth, "the U.S. Armed Forces were reported to be replacing their coding machines at a cost of more than $100 million."[27] The Edward Lee Howard case was just as damaging in another way: espionage in the Moscow station was undone and the execution of at least one Russian agent-in-place was caused.

Howard and Ronald W. Pelton were both delivered to U.S. authorities by Soviet KGB officer Vitaly Yurchenko, who defected to the United States in August 1985 and redefected to the Soviet Union the following November. The Yurchenko affair remains unresolved at this writing. He established his bona fides by denouncing Howard and Pelton—"both no longer employed by an intelligence agency, both lacking current access to secrets, and both already thoroughly debriefed by the KGB."[28] Speculation remains whether Yurchenko's return to the Soviet Union was a case of "defector blues"[29] or was part of a "preplanned Soviet intelligence operation."[30] In any event, in March 1986, Yurchenko—alive and well—gave a street interview to West German cameramen in Moscow. Howard, too, managed to flee to the Soviet Union.

The relationship of these spy cases to Reagan's "revitalization" of U.S. intelligence was not cause-and-effect; but they did tend to overcome Reagan's critics in the ongoing debate. Lyndon Johnson and Richard Nixon had only dug their holes deeper when they misused U.S. intelligence in a desperate search for foreign influence in protest movements. But Reagan's evidence was dropped into his lap that the Soviets were a *real* threat—they were spying! The subsequent espionage disclosures involving U.S. Marine guards in the American embassy in Moscow (January 1987) were made in a context when the American people had had enough with being spied upon and when Reagan's own "failures" were coming to the surface.

William Casey had tremendous power as DCI. But as the saying goes, power corrupts, and he proved to be a bungler as well. The only barrier to his absolute power was Congress—specifically, the Hughes-Ryan Amendment and the Accountability for Intelligence Activities Act (the 1980 Intelligence Oversight Act), which restricted CIA operations abroad to intelligence collection unless the president "finds" that an operation "is important to the national security of the United States" and informs the intelligence committees "in a timely fashion."

Casey had an obsession with the Sandinista government of Nicaragua, and he was determined to "make the bastards sweat"[31]—that is, to harass their regime and overthrow it. His powerful ally, Secretary of State Alexander Haig, believed that Cuba was the source of the trouble—in Nicaragua and in the growing insurgency in El Salvador—and he wanted to "go to the source."[32] Casey, having to contend with those in the administration who wanted to do nothing and with Haig, who favored military action against Cuba, decided upon a "middle course." He proposed a covert action program in El Salvador to help the government of José Napoleón Duarte and other moderate elements resist "the export of revolution" from Nicaragua. He engineered a top-secret finding to this effect for the president's signature on March 4, 1981.[33]

To prepare the way for the finding, Casey engaged in a bit of disinformation, working with Haig. On February 23, 1981, the State Department issued an eight-page White Paper, "Communist Interference in El Salvador," which was accompanied by a thick volume of "Documents Demonstrating Communist Support of the Salvadoran Insurgency." The documents were purportedly part of "document caches" that had been recovered from the Communist party of El Salvador (PCS) in November 1980 and from the Peoples' Revolutionary Army in January 1981. The White Paper accused "the Soviet Union, Cuba, and their Communist allies" of rendering "clandestine military support . . . to Marxist-Leninist guerrillas" in El Salvador. It cited the published documents as evidence that PCS secretary-general Shafik Handal had gone on an "arms-shopping expedition" between June 2 and July 22, 1980, to the Soviet Union, Vietnam, East Germany, Czechoslovakia, Bulgaria, Hungary, and Ethiopia and that nearly two hundred tons of arms had been covertly delivered to El Salvador, "mostly through Cuba and Nicaragua."[34] Although Cuba and Nicaragua clearly were aiding the Salvadoran guerrillas, the White Paper was a clumsy effort. According to a report in the *Wall Street Journal* on June 8, 1981, "much of the information in the White Paper [could] not be found in the documents at all." Jon D. Glassman, a State Department official who had helped prepare it, admitted that the White Paper was "possibly misleading" and "overembellished."[35]

The internal evidence of the nineteen published documents suggests that Handal may not have made the trip as described—the authorship of some of the documents was not clear; nor was there any specific data to support the claim that two hundred tons of arms had been delivered. Glassman conceded that the two-hundred-ton figure was "a bit of extrapolation."[36] The *Washington Post* joined in the following day, charging that the documents did not support the conclusions of the White Paper, which was based on "mistranslations, ambiguities, and errors."[37] But by then the White Paper had been forgotten, overtaken by events in El Salvador. This enabled Casey to develop a strategy of covert action within covert action, concealing his and Reagan's purpose even within a presidential finding (or "stretching" the finding[38]).

On December 1, 1981, a few days before he issued his Executive Order on U.S. Intelligence Activities, Reagan signed a finding authorizing the CIA to "support and conduct . . . paramilitary operations against the Cuban presence and Cuban Sandinista support infrastructure in Nicaragua and elsewhere in Central America." The Reagan administration informed the congressional intelligence committees that its purpose was "the interdiction of arms from Nicaragua to the leftist insurgents in El Salvador."[39] It thereby cloaked its real intention: to use $19 million to prepare a counterrevolutionary ("contra") force of Nicaraguans in Honduras to overthrow the Sandinistas. Casey had been working directly with Duane Clarridge, chief of the Latin American division of the Directorate of Operations, bypassing Deputy Director Bobby Ray Inman and DDO John Stein, to organize the contra force, "buying into" an operation that the Argentine military had already begun. In the convoluted politics of Latin America, the Argentines had been training about five hundred Nicaraguan exiles in Honduras in retaliation against the Sandinistas, who were supporting the Montoneros, an antigovernment guerrilla force in Argentina.[40]

Casey paid a high price for his duplicity. Deputy Director Inman became suspicious: "If the real goal was to halt the arms flow from Nicaragua to El Salvador that had already been substantially stopped."[41] But he remained on board until March, when Eden Pastora, "Comandante Cero," became part of the action.

Pastora's base was in Costa Rica; Inman, knowing his geography, concluded that Pastora had little to do directly with intercepting arms shipments to El Salvador. "Inman knew that assistance to Pastora was intended to demolish and oust the Sandinistas.

> . . . He began to question the underlying reasons for making the Nicaragua program covert. He concluded that the Administration did not want it out in the open where they would have to pay the domestic political price. It was covert in order *to avoid a public debate.*[42]

The Rockefeller Commission report had placed great emphasis on individuals as a means of preventing intelligence abuses. Inman, a respected career naval officer and former director of the NSA, had been favored by many for the position of DCI. As deputy director, however, he could not do what he might have done as DCI—keep the CIA out of politics, and he resigned. Shortly thereafter, the Falklands/Malvinas war between Argentina and Great Britain occurred (April–June 1982). Angry that the United States had given sympathy and support to the British in the war, Argentina withdrew from the Nicaragua operation. Despite this loss of the "fig leaf" of Argentine cover, Clarridge took charge of the operation and built up a force of four thousand by the end of the year.[43]

In December 1982, a new era in the history of U.S. foreign intelligence began. The contra force was too large to hide. Congress and the executive branch entered into a sparring match over the relationship between the United States and the Nicaraguan anti-Sandinista elements. Representative Edward P. Boland, chairman of the House Permanent Select Committee on Intelligence, believed that CIA support for the contra operations in Nicaragua entailed more than simply interdicting the flow of arms from Nicaragua to El Salvador. He proposed the first of the so-called Boland amendments, which used Congress's power over the purse to define and limit the CIA's relationship with the contras. Boland I (an amendment to the defense appropriations bill for fiscal year 1983, adopted in December) prohibited CIA use of funds "for the purpose of overthrowing the Government of Nicaragua." "Congress had not cut Contra funding; it merely had legislated an impermissible purpose."[44]

During 1983, the sparring between Congress and the Reagan administration intensified as the CIA continued to build the contra force (up to 5,500 by the spring). House members doubted that the administration was complying with the Boland amendment. The Reagan administration created the State Department Office for Public Diplomacy for Latin America and the Caribbean (S/LPD) to promote popular opposition to Boland I. Casey coordinated this public relations campaign; recognizing the need for a "broader rationale" for supporting the contras—beyond arms interdiction— he prepared a new finding for Reagan's signature in September, explaining that "covert aid was intended to pressure the Sandinistas to negotiate a [peace] treaty with nearby countries."[45] Congress, unconvinced of the sincerity of this new objective, voted in December to place a cap of $24 million on contra funding for 1984, subject to reconsideration if the Sandinistas "thwarted" negotiations for a peace treaty. Knowing that the funding would likely run out by midyear, Reagan, at an NSPG meeting on January 6, agreed with a SIG recommendation that the "covert action program [in Nicaragua] should proceed with stepped-up intensity."[46]

Casey had already been doing just that. He had ordered special speedboat attacks against oil depot facilities on Nicaragua's Pacific coast. In these commando-style raids, the CIA acted directly, deploying UCLAs—"unilateral controlled Latino assets"—not contras. The raiders hit the port of Corinto on October 11, 1983, destroying most of Nicaragua's oil reserves: "About twenty thousand residents of Corinto had to be evacuated because of fires."[47] This operation occurred in the same month as the bombing of the U.S. Marine barracks in Beirut, which killed 241 American servicemen, and the U.S. invasion of Grenada, demonstrating that Central America was not Casey's sole concern. He nonetheless pushed hard to bring matters to a head in Nicaragua.

Casey beseeched the RIG comprising Clarridge, L. Anthony Motley (the assistant secretary of state for inter-American affairs), and Lieutenant Colonel Oliver North of the NSC staff to come up with new ideas, "directing them to think big."[48] During the first quarter of 1984, the group planned increased speedboat attacks, the destruction of transmission towers and power lines along the "entire Pacific coast of Nicaragua," an offensive by Pastora on the southern front, and the mining of Nicaraguan harbors. Although the mines were designed to have "more bark than bite," simply to frighten off shipping, this action, when it was disclosed publicly in April, did more than any other to cause Congress to cut off aid to the contras. Senator Barry Goldwater, chairman of the Senate Select Committee on Intelligence, was furious, proclaiming, "It is indefensible on the part of the Administration to ask us to back its foreign policy when we don't even know what is going on."[49] Casey apologized and pledged to keep the intelligence committees fully informed (the so-called Casey accords), but Congress enacted Boland II in October 1984 as an amendment to an omnibus appropriations bill. It prohibited the CIA and other members of the intelligence community from spending or obligating U.S. funds "for the purpose or which would have the effect of supporting, directly or indirectly, military or paramilitary operations in Nicaragua by any nation, group, organization, movement or individual."[50]

Casey's "apology" had just been crocodile tears. He had been ignoring oversight and avoiding debate for more than two years, pursuing what one CIA official implied was "Casey's war." "Casey cooked this whole thing up," the official told *Washington Post* writer Bob Woodward.[51] And Casey kept right on cooking. According to National Security Adviser Robert McFarlane (October 17, 1983—December 4, 1985), even when the money started to run out before Boland II, President Reagan "directed the NSC staff to keep the Contras together 'body and soul.'"[52]

If Boland II prohibited the CIA and other intelligence agencies from aiding the contras, Casey boldly moved clandestine operations up a notch to the NSC, following the precedent set by Richard Nixon and Henry Kissinger's covert action in Chile. From his position on the NSC (the NSPG, in particular) and as chair of its principal intelligence committee (SIG-I), with its extra bureaucratic layer of IGs and RIGs, Casey both influenced and carried out secret foreign policy. He was, as Secretary of State George Shultz complained, "a shadow Secretary of State."[53] He was also Oliver North's "case officer."[54]

As case officer, Casey guided the activities of Colonel North, "the chief [NSC] staff officer on Central America . . . responsible for carrying out the President's general charter to keep the Contras alive."[55] Casey suggested ways to solve the problem of money and the problem of keeping "USG fingerprints" off the contra operation. He recommended obtaining "third-country" financing, raising contributions from private sources, and generating profits from clandestine operations. He put North in touch with Retired U.S. Air Force Major General Richard V. Secord, who had had experience in special operations with the CIA in Laos and who at the time (June 1984) was head of a private company (Stanford Technology Trading Group) that was capable of arms procurement and military supply operations. With the North–Secord connection established, the proprietary networking was vintage George Doole and the Pacific Corporation. They even chartered planes from the Southern Air Transport, the CIA proprietary that had been sold off in 1973. "North called the organization 'Project Democracy.' Secord and his partner, Albert Hakim, referred to it as *the Enterprise*."[56]

For more than two years, the organization kept the contras fighting—in violation of Boland II (though North did not believe that Boland II applied to NSC staff) and with no notification to the congressional intelligence committees, as was required by Hughes-Ryan and the intelligence oversight law. (After first "stretching" presidential findings, the Reagan administration eventually dispensed with them altogether.) Congress appropriated $27 million in "humanitarian aid" in June 1985 (keeping the contras "in food and clothing"), and assisted by the "things left behind" by U.S. National Guard units that trained in Honduras, North concentrated his efforts on "lethal assistance."

North operated suspiciously like an old pro in covert action techniques. In collaboration with National Security Advisers McFarlane and Admiral John Poindexter (December 4, 1985–November 25, 1986), he did secure contra funding from third countries. Saudi Arabia's contributions—totaling $32 million between July 1984 and the end of March 1985—probably enabled the contras to survive during that time.[57] He also sought private contributions with the help of Retired U.S. Army Major General John K. Singlaub (head of the World Anti-Communist League), and he retained professional fund-raisers Carl R. Channell and

Richard R. Miller. Their National Endowment for the Preservation of Liberty raised $10 million and engaged in "public education" (using some of the same people who had been active in S/LPD). Channell and Miller, however, got into trouble with the Internal Revenue Service for making "lethal aid" tax-deductible.

Finally, North used the profits generated (so-called residuals) from the secret sale of arms to Iran in 1985 and 1986 to finance covert action in Nicaragua. North, the latest of the "swashbucklers of secret wars," came very close to achieving Casey's goal of building "something you could pull off the shelf and use at a moment's notice."

> The DCI spoke with some conviction about having a stand-alone, off-shore, self-financing entity that would operate independent of Congress and its appropriations. It would operate in real secrecy, either alone or jointly with other friendly intelligence services. Apparently he had in mind the Saudis and Israelis. Plausible deniability would be reestablished. In the best tradition of capitalism, this would be a revenue producer, "a full-service covert operation," Casey called it.[58]

This scheme was a far cry from the concept of a last-resort covert action option with presidential accountability fixed through clear procedures of authorization and review.

Under Casey's influence, the Reagan administration developed a secret international antiterrorist network; plotted against Qaddafi of Libya (probably in violation of the ban on assassination); tried to free American hostages in Lebanon (in an incredible blunder, the CIA assigned William Buckley as station chief in Beirut, after he had been identified as a CIA officer; he was kidnapped in March 1984); and dealt with Iran.

Iran was central to many of these other problems. Reagan's declared policy was that the United States would not deal with terrorists and an arms embargo against Iran existed. But the United States, on the initiative of the Israeli government, entered into secret negotiations with Iran for the purpose of exchanging arms for the release of American hostages in Lebanon. In the absence of a presidential finding or notification of Congress, Reagan authorized the covert shipment (through Israel) of certain arms to Iran, beginning in August 1985. For more than a year afterward, Casey, North, and Poindexter watched over the activities of "the Enterprise" in selling and shipping arms to Iran. North "diverted" profits from these sales to support the contras in Nicaragua.[59]

The operation was labyrinthine, as one might expect, with offshore companies, laundered money, and Swiss bank accounts. It attracted a number of unsavory persons, giving it the ambiance of a 1980s version of *Casablanca* or the Boom Boom Room of 1961, where poison capsules were delivered to Mafia hit men. In time, North became convinced that the arms sales would not secure the release of all the hostages (only three were freed during the entire operation) or improve relations with Iran. But he continued to support the arms deal nonetheless, believing "that the prospect of generating funds for the Contras was 'an attractive incentive.' "[60] He later claimed to have learned to his chagrin that most of the profits had remained with "the Enterprise" and did not reach the contras at all.

The covert operations in Iran and Nicaragua demonstrated once again the dilemma of governmental secrecy in American democracy. The report of the congressional committees that investigated the Iran-contra affair noted,

> The common ingredients of the Iran and Contra policies were secrecy, deception, and disdain for the law. A small group of senior officials believed that they alone knew what was right. They viewed knowledge of their actions by others in the Government as a threat to their objectives.[61]

This judgment of DCI Casey and members of the NSC staff left the question of the president's responsibility unanswered. EO 12333 had done much that made it very difficult to find that answer.

Toward the end of 1986, Congress voted $100 million in aid, including military assistance, to the contras. Two events rendered this victory moot: the shootdown on October 5 of a C-123 cargo plane belonging to SAT over Nicaragua, with the capture of crewmember Eugene Hasenfus (an ex-marine and former employee of Air America); and the publication in the Beirut weekly *Al-Shiraa* on

November 3 of an account of McFarlane's secret mission to Teheran the preceding May. The Iran-contra matter abruptly became
public knowledge. Disclosure of these events caused a furor. The
president's denials of any illegalities and of the existence of an
arms-for-hostages deal were generally disbelieved, so Reagan
ordered Attorney General Edwin Meese to conduct an inquiry.

Casey, McFarlane, North, and Poindexter got together to get
their stories straight, and North and Poindexter destroyed material
evidence. Still, Meese's fact-finders "found a 'diversion memorandum' that had escaped the shredder." Meese announced at a press
conference on November 25 that profits from the sale of arms to
Iran had been diverted to the Nicaraguan contras "and that the
President did not know of it."[62] As a scandal clearly threatened,
Reagan established a Special Review Board on December 1, 1986,
that comprised former Senators John Tower (as chair), Edmund
Muskie, and former national security adviser Brent Scowcroft.
Their instructions were "to examine the proper role of the National
Security Council staff in national security operations, including the
arms transfers to Iran." Before the matter was concluded, the U.S.
Senate Select Committee on secret Military Asssistance to Iran and
the Nicaraguan Opposition joined with the U.S. House of Representatives Select Committee to Investigate Covert Arms Trans-
actions with Iran for a comprehensive probe of the Iran-contra
affair, formally beginning on January 6, 1987.

As the Tower Board reported, Reagan affirmed on January 26,
1987, that he had not known that the NSC staff was active in helping the contras. The board also stated that it had no evidence that
suggested the President knew, but it added that he should have
known: "The NSC system will not work unless the President
makes it work. After all, this system was created to serve the President of the United States in ways of his choosing. By his actions,
by his leadership, the President therefore determines the quality of
its performance."[63] The Congressional Committees Investigating
the Iran-Contra Affair reached the same conclusion, declaring that
"the ultimate responsibility for the events in the Iran-Contra
Affair must rest with the President.

> It is his responsibility to communicate unambiguously to his sub-
> ordinates that they must keep him advised of important actions

they take for the Administration. The Constitution requires the President to "take care that the laws be faithfully executed." This charge encompasses a responsibility to leave the members of his Administration in no doubt that the rule of law governs.[64]

Despite the scolding, the questions "what did the President know, and when did he know it" remained unanswered. National Security Adviser John Poindexter affirmed that "the buck stops here with me," and told the Iran-contra committees flat out that he had not told the president about the diversion in order to "insulate [him] from the decision and provide some future deniability for [him] if it ever leaked out." He added, however, that he was certain the president would have endorsed the plan.[65] It is difficult to imagine Poindexter assuming this kind of responsibility, but he clearly was willing to take risks to protect his president. He had destroyed the only copy of a December 5, 1985, finding because it would have "embarrassed" the president by showing that the Iran affair was a straight arms-for-hostages deal.[66] Moreover, according to North's testimony before the Iran-contra committees, Casey had a "fall guy plan" that possibly called for Poindexter to take full responsibility for the clandestine operations in Central America and for the diversion.[67]

If Reagan did not know about the diversion, he knew about a great deal else: the funding of the contras by third countries, the raising of private contributions in their behalf, and the general status of the contras during the period of Boland II (October 1984 to December 1985, prohibiting any CIA contact) and Boland III (December 4, 1985, to October 17, 1986, authorizing the CIA to provide the contras with communications equipment and to exchange intelligence). According to the Tower Board, Reagan "attended almost all of the relevant meetings regarding the Iran initiative."[68] He personally supported the plan developed at the end of 1985 to provide weapons for Iran directly from U.S. stocks, placing the NSC staff in charge and "relegating the Israelis to a secondary role," and he signed a finding to that effect on January 17, 1986 (but he did not forward it to Congress). These matters alone raise serious questions about the president's conduct, and it is difficult to argue that he was not privy to the diversion scheme, since so many diverse people in and out of the U.S. government were in on it, including North, Poindexter, Secord, and DCI Casey.

Casey, North's mentor, had almost unlimited access to the president. Without Casey, the Iran-contra operation as it evolved would have been impossible. As DCI and director of the CIA, sitting atop SIG-I, he was the one person capable of marshaling the covert assets of the U.S. government. North could never have created the infrastructure he did or made use of CIA personnel (Joseph Fernández, aka Tomás Castillo, station chief in San José) and U.S. diplomatic representatives (Louis Tambs, U.S. ambassador to Costa Rica) without Casey's awareness and approval. In Central America, the Enterprise "controlled five aircraft, including C-123 and C-7 transports.

> It had an airfield in one country [Costa Rica], warehouse facilities at an airbase in another [Honduras], a stockpile of guns and military equipment to drop by air to the Contras, and secure communications equipment obtained by North from the National Security Agency (NSA).[69]

Ambassador Tambs (July 1985–January 1987) asserted that he had acted on specific orders from a Washington-based RIG, comprising principally of North, Elliot Abrams (Motley's successor at State), and Alan D. Fiers (who replaced Clarridge as DO Latin American division chief after the harbor-mining flap). Before testifying before the Iran-contra congressional committees, Tambs told the *New York Times,* "Now the people who gave us the orders are trying to paint us as running amok. It's insane."[70]

Three days after Tambs's complaint, on May 6, 1987, Casey died. Casey was never formally questioned about his role in Iran-contra as the story emerged; he had been incapacitated since the previous December after surgery to remove a malignant brain tumor. The Tower Board censured him for permitting North to exercise direct operational control over a covert action program (Casey was willing to surrender the CIA's monopoly over clandestine operations in order to create a real, deep cover capability) and for failing to assess "the assumptions presented by the

Israelis on which the program was based" and "the effect of the transfer of arms and intelligence to Iran on the Iran/Iraq military balance." (Like "Wild Bill" Donovan, Casey was committed to Operations more than to Intelligence.)[71]

The congressional committees investigating the Iran-contra affair were more blunt than the Tower Board on these points. The committees described Casey's plan for an "off-the-shelf" covert capacity as "contradictory" to the Constitution: "The decision to use the Enterprise to fight a war with unappropriated funds was a decision to combine the power of the purse and the power of the sword in one branch of government."[72] They also went further than the Tower Board in the matter of intelligence analysis, reporting that the problem had not been the failure to provide intelligence but the "misuse of intelligence." "The democratic processes," the committees concluded, "also are subverted when intelligence is manipulated to affect decisions by elected officials and the public. . . . There is evidence that Director Casey misrepresented or selectively used available intelligence to support the policy he was promoting, particularly in Central America."[73] By skewing intelligence and withholding information from Congress, the committees concluded, Casey had "showed contempt for the democratic process."[74]

The resolution of the Iran-contra affair was inconclusive, except that the American Constitution survived another shock from those who judged it inadequate in seeking to defend it. Oliver North, a much-decorated marine officer who excited the popular imagination as a combination of Rambo and Jimmy Stewart; John Poindexter, with his "the buck stops here"; and William Casey's death upstaged the perennial dilemma of governmental secrecy and American democracy. The congressional committees concluded that the affair had "resulted from the failure of individuals to observe the law, not from deficiencies in existing law or in our system of governance." The committees determined, therefore, to recommend not new laws but "a renewal of the commitment to constitutional government and sound processes of decisionmaking." In this, they emphasized that "the President must 'take care' that the laws be faithfully executed."[75]

There are two fundamental problems with these recommendations. First, the existing laws governing covert action are not adequate—specifically, as they apply to procedures for the authorization and review of intelligence activities and accountability. Second, they put too much faith in the president and disregard, at the very least, the experiences of Watergate and the Iran-contra affair itself. The Congress is active now in oversight, having created permanent intelligence committees—in the Senate (1976) and House (1977)—and enacted Hughes-Ryan and the Accountability for Intelligence Activities Act. But the restraints on the executive branch remain loose in the absence of a legislative charter (revising the National Security Act of 1947) that requires a permanent executive structure for controlling and managing intelligence activities. Recent attempts to reform intelligence activities by executive order have proven most inadequate. The Ford and Carter orders were not perfect, but it was too easy for Reagan to discard them and to ignore the lessons of history. Such a charter would require two additional forms of oversight, which the Iran-Contra Committees partially recognized: first, a strengthened office of the CIA inspector general as "an independent statutory [office] confirmed by the Senate" but with the authority to initiate investigations; and second, a revitalized and strengthened Intelligence Oversight Board, but removed from the White House and possibly having a case-by-case function like a federal grand jury.

The second problem with the committees' recommendations pertains to the president and the absence of specific consequences if care is not taken to execute the laws faithfully. Presidents have historically resorted to covert action to suit their convenience and have frequently abused their powers. The phenomenal growth of the American intelligence community and the bureaucratization of the covert action capability have exacerbated the situation. Lesser officials run the risk of jail sentences (Colonel North apparently overlooked the historical misgiving of military officers about intelligence), but only when the president faces possible impeachment will covert action be controlled. Once it is made clear that covert action could result in impeachment, it is very likely that there will be rigorous review and vetting (a word much favored by the Tower Board), and legal opinions will be solicited on a systematic basis.

Nonetheless, the Iran-contra committees' report reaffirmed covert action as a legitimate tool of foreign policy, sanguine that its negative side could be managed.

> The United States of America, as a great power with worldwide interests, will continue to have to deal with nations that have different hopes, values and ambitions. These differences will inevitably lead to conflicts. History reflects that the prospects for peaceful settlement are greater if this country has adequate means for its own defense, including effective intelligence and the means to influence developments abroad.
>
> Organized and structured secret intelligence activities are one of the realities of the world we live in, and this is not likely to change. Like the military, intelligence services are fully compatible with democratic government when their actions are conducted in an accountable manner and in accordance with the law.[76]

In view of this firm, bipartisan statement, U.S. foreign intelligence and its covert action capability will remain a major element in guaranteeing American power and security. It will provide many moments of triumph (this chapter does not relate all the episodes of intelligence success during the 1980s), but it will also require the vigilance of the American people to avoid the terrible failings that marked the Iran-contra affair. As Secretary of State Shultz phrased it when he heard about Casey's idea of having a stand-alone, self-financed covert capacity to circumvent congressional review, "This is not sharing power, this is not in line with what was agreed to in Philadelphia. This is a piece of junk and it ought to be treated that way."[77] Americans must continue to search for ways to keep the junk out of U.S. foreign intelligence.

Epilogue

A book that seeks to cover the history of U.S. foreign intelligence from beginning to end runs the risk of losing its edge: it can never be current. But this failing is fleeting in the context of the timelessness of the American experience. Startling new events may occur in the future, but most of the basic issues in the problem of governmental secrecy in a democracy are already apparent. It is difficult to imagine abuses of presidential authority more serious than those that have already been committed. The distressing part is that it is not difficult to imagine them happening again. The solution to the problem of secrecy in democracy remains for the future to find, but the past teaches that it will be found in laws, not in men.

It is evident that George Bush is a responsible leader and honorable man. He is also the first U.S. president to have been the director of central intelligence. During the 1988 presidential campaign, Tom Wicker of the *New York Times* asked himself, "Should any ex-[CIA] director be President?" He expressed the opinion that Bush, as president, would "once again give his old comrades of the C.I.A. the green light for their secret, dangerous, often harebrained schemes."[1] It does not seem reasonable to disqualify someone from being president for having been DCI, but it does seem reasonable to suggest that the issue was worthy of serious debate. Wicker wondered if the American people had "really thought about the implications" of electing a president experienced in clandestine operations. Wicker's language is his own, but if he meant to say that George Bush would likely authorize covert actions, he was probably right. (To be sure, one might have predicted the same of Michael Dukakis.)

The congressional committees investigating the Iran-contra affair had already concluded, "Covert operations are a necessary component of [U.S.] foreign policy."[2] When Hugh Tovar, a retired CIA official and clandestine operator, assessed the possible effects of the Iran-contra scandal on the future use of covert action by American presidents, he observed, "U.S. presidents have repeatedly seen fit to use it when faced with problems that have not responded to other pressures. Once the dust settles over the Iran-Contra controversy, it is a safe bet that the next president will follow suit."[3] Indeed, Professor Richard Shultz of the Fletcher School of Law and Diplomacy, in a paper delivered in December 1987 before the Colloquium on Intelligence Requirements for the 1990s, recommended increased U.S. covert action to meet the anticipated international challenges in the decade ahead. Shultz proceeded from the assumption that "covert action is not considered to be a special activity that is employed only in exceptional circumstances. Rather it is one of a number of instruments of statecraft."[4]

If covert action is a legitimate instrument of U.S. foreign policy, then accountability and control are vital (which is really what Tom Wicker was trying to say). The congressional committees affirmed that "covert operations are compatible with democratic government if they are conducted in an accountable manner and in accordance with law."[5] This is a big "if," and the committees were not very explicit about it; they merely added that "Congress must have the *will* to exercise oversight over covert operations."[6] Congressional oversight of intelligence operations is much improved and procedures exist for timely notification about covert operations, but Congress has delegated almost exclusive authority to the executive branch for accountability and control of covert action.

Up to now, the executive orders and various generations of NSC decision directives governing covert action have been contradictory, self-regulating, and transitory. Following the concept of nonattribution, the decision directives created elite committees to mask—not to fix—presidential accountability. From this emerged the doctrine of plausible deniability, with its built-in circuit breakers and circumlocutious communication. In this environment, even if a president made reforms, the next could undo them. Writing in the *New York Times* in February 1989, William Safire claimed that President Bush wanted to "scuttle" PFIAB and asserted that "George Bush, when he ran the C.I.A. in 1976, did not look kindly on a bunch of prestigious outsiders second-guessing him and reporting directly to the President. . . . Now that he is President, he is folding up the prickly panel of C.I.A. watchdogs, just as Jimmy Carter did before him.

> The [PFIAB] staff in Room 340 of the E.O.B. [Executive Office Building] is awaiting the fall of the Bush ax. (Down the hall, at the moribund Intelligence Oversight Committee, you cannot get through the door for the cobwebs.)[7]

It is difficult to imagine a watchdog more "toothless" than the PFIAB or the IOB, but the point here is to suggest that the president may unilaterally alter the oversight process with ease. What has happened in the trial of Lieutenant Colonel Oliver North may ultimately bring an end to this situation.

The fate of North and the future of plausible deniability are closely linked. Colonel North was caught in "the hateful role of a spy" and ought to have been aware that, as Captain Benjamin Bonneville was told in carrying out his mission, "the government would have no official part in it." But the colonel expected "the spy's fate"—an honorable hanging—not to be charged with a felony. Yet because he acted within the context of plausible deniability, with its contrived phantom authority, and had no opportunity to "take the hit" with honor, he was not going to go to jail, one way or another. If a John C. Frémont type who has confessed to lying to Congress and to shredding material evidence is not sentenced to prison, it is even less likely that a by-the-book admiral—John Poindexter—will, either. North's conviction on three counts unrelated to the issues of the Iran-contra affair, and the jury's refusal to convict him of any serious charge involving acts committed before November 1986, in effect, condemn the doctrine of plausible deniability. The decision of federal district judge Gerhard A. Gesell to impose a three-year suspended sentence upon North, plus a $150,000 fine and 1,200 hours of community service, is consistent with the jury's action. The penalty fits the circumstance, with the clear implication of more serious culpability up the line. Ronald Reagan may feel he succeeded in taking a calculated risk, and George Bush may be off the hook as far as a pardon is concerned, but the doctrine of plausible deniability is dead.

If covert action is "one of a number of instruments of statecraft," the president must exercise control and accept responsibility. A president who knows that he will be held accountable is more apt to assert hands-on control over covert operations; at the same time, officials down the line who have appropriate instructions and authorization will be less likely to act out of control. If they do, at least they will go to jail for their own crimes.

President Bush displayed sensitivity to the special problem of secret intelligence in the American political system by holding DCI William Webster over from the previous administration. But Bush's good sense notwithstanding, presidents have not historically done a good job of policing themselves. The factor of secrecy extends presidential power in the conduct of foreign affairs. The National Security Act of 1947, even as amended, lacking specific requirements of oversight and accountability and control of intelligence operations, is not adequate for checking the president's informal or hidden powers. Past presidents have created their own oversight bodies by executive order, setting up the PFIAB, for example, merely to evaluate the "performance" (that is, the effectiveness) of the intelligence community and the IOB to monitor the adequacy of the oversight procedures of the respective intelligence agencies. No president has been willing to establish true oversight—an independent body with access to the president, empowered to receive complaints and initiate investigations, enjoying an unrestricted "need to know."

Presidents have also shunned formal procedures of accountability and control of covert action, creating instead structures designed to evade, not accept, responsibility. The Congress, in the exercise of its oversight function, now requires the president to make a finding authorizing covert action and to report to the intelligence committees in a timely fashion. Yet in the Iran-contra affair, U.S. covert operators armed and equipped ten thousand rebels in Nicaragua and ran a fleet of planes, among other things, and President Reagan insisted that he "didn't know" about it. The lack of formal procedures and the changing composition and nature of the NSC groups and panels that have recommended— and supervised—covert operations have made it possible for a president to make this claim. The U.S. Constitution makes no provision for the excuse "I didn't know" in the exercise of presidential power. Covert action is the most controversial function of intelligence; bringing it under control is vital for the health of the entire intelligence community. The other functions of intelligence need this healing to solve their own serious problems.

At the beginning of this book, the functions of intelligence were broadly identified as collection, production, protection, and covert action. In December 1987, the Consortium for the Study of Intelligence, a private academic group located in Washington, D.C., sponsored the Colloquium on Intelligence Requirements for the 1990s. It organized the program panels under the headings of collection, analysis, counterintelligence, and covert action. This represents a greater specificity concerning the functions of intelligence in line with more current concerns and problems.

Collection, however, remains a major function. Technical collection, especially, is now the "big ticket" item, absorbing a huge portion of the intelligence dollar and causing an "explosion" in military intelligence activity.[8] R.N. Keeler and Miriam Steiner, participants in the 1987 Washington colloquium, largely reaffirmed Patrick McGarvey's 1972 assessment about "the tail wagging the dog." Although the Pentagon spends substantial sums of money on sensor-bearing satellites orbiting the earth, the analysts and duty officers on the ground are "downgraded" because of the "[low] relative status of intelligence work in the services" and because "the intelligence field must compete with lines that are considered more career enhancing."[9] Panelist Robert Butterworth cited the additional anomaly that "requirements are set in response to capabilities."[10] From the late 1950s to the 1980s,

The United States developed the technical capabilities to see, hear, and sense facts about Soviet capabilities. This drove the requirements in a particular direction, concentrating on objects that could be seen, heard, and sensed.[11]

The technical capability to see, hear, and sense facts, according to Donald Nielson, a former DIA official, "may lead the United States to an environment in which it knows everything about a T-72 tank except where it is going to be used."[12] McGarvey's nightmare of U.S. intelligence drowning in a sea of useless data aside, the Washington colloquium expressed the concern that, by concentrating on facts, technical collection was not only wasting resources but was impairing the development of other forms of collection—such as HUMINT—that are needed to determine intentions. Moreover, the colloquium concluded that the rest of the world (the Soviet Union, particularly) has caught up to and onto U.S. TECHINT, largely by stealing U.S. secrets (in the "Year of the Spy" cases).

> By learning about specific U.S. capabilities and methods, Moscow (most importantly) learned where it was vulnerable to U.S. collection. This enabled the Soviet Union (and other countries) not only to take countermeasures limiting the effectiveness of U.S. collection but also to "steer" U.S. collectors in directions they wish us to pursue—and away from others.[13]

In assessing the high cost of technical collection, along with its limitations and even vulnerability to deception, the Washington colloquium concluded that the "collection mission" must be revised, taking into account "one or more intellectual frameworks."[14] Acknowledging the difficulty in peeling away the layered bureaucracy of collection managers, the colloquium reached consensus on the need for a better way of setting collection priorities, suggesting "a greater measure of top-down control of tasking and increased dialogue among collectors, analysts, and policymakers."[15]

The Washington colloquium suggested that intelligence analysts take an active role in setting collection priorities. It showed interest in strengthening the production function (intelligence), although its focus was upon "analysis" (estimates) and tended to ignore research (basic) and reporting (current). Starting with the OSS and continuing into the early CIA, Intelligence lost out to Operations in the struggle to set the fundamental mission of American intelligence. Archibald Roosevelt's recent memoir, *For Lust of*

Knowing: Memoirs of an Intelligence Officer, provides insight into how this happened.

> When I speak of an intelligence officer, . . . I do not mean the analysts toiling in headquarters to make sense of reports from all over the world, but the man "in the field," as they say in CIA. . . .
>
> I have the greatest respect for those who have spent their years studying other nations and cultures. . . . They make an enormous contribution to our knowledge, indispensable for understanding other parts of the world. But that does not qualify them as intelligence officers in the CIA.[16]

The analysts also lost ground during the 1960s and 1970s to the science and technology people. McGarvey wrote in 1972, "The proportion of high grades [top jobs in the DIA] is three times as high on the technical side as on the production side."[17] Henry Kissinger finally got rid of the remnants of Donovan's "100 professors" altogether in 1973, replacing (through DCI Colby) the Office of National Estimates with the national intelligence officers and preferring concise, up-to-the-minute opinion pieces to the "bland, consensus reporting" of estimates.[18] What then passed for analysis was scornfully described as "cable-gisting."[19]

One longs for the William Langers and Sherman Kents, or for the Norman Holmes Pearson types described so delightfully by Robin Winks in *Cloak & Gown,* but it is obvious that the humanists are out of favor. Activist social scientists may have a better chance of restoring to analysis a place in the intelligence cycle. Whereas Sherman Kent believed that "intelligence informs policy"[20] and tried to keep analysts and policymakers apart for the sake of objectivity, the new approach favors greater interaction between analyst and policymaker. In it, the analyst actually "scouts" the opportunities for advancing policy and lays out the options in so-called opportunity-oriented analysis.[21] There has always been a "this is what should be done" syndrome among analysts—the old academics would object to having their methodology characterized as "objectivist passivity."[22] But the sense was that intelligence would have its say, not the last word. Yet if William Langer or Sherman Kent perceived today that their standards of scholarship had become an excuse for playing it safe, they might very likely support the concept of "activist intelligence." To paraphrase Professor Paul Seabury, a former member of PFIAB (1981–85), activist intelligence means not just scanning the horizons but steering toward them; not just predicting earthquakes but making them.[23]

The Washington colloquium pointed to "new personnel" as critical for the "new analysis" of activist intelligence. This tended to reaffirm a certain anti-intellectualism and at the same time expressed disappointment in the product of American graduate schools and educational system in general. It is not true that the old-time analysts "gained their knowledge of foreign countries [exclusively] from academic studies," as Archibald Roosevelt seems to believe, but the Colloquium's Roy Godson and Seabury indeed perceive today's "school-taught" analysts as lacking understanding of other cultures and languages, thereby undermining a tenet of the new analysis: "awareness of the otherness of foreign societies."

To overcome this apparent ethnocentricity, Seabury proposes that "recruitment officers and other searchers must actively go out in the streets to look for people who from experience and background already have qualities enabling them to understand political cultures and move easily within them." He adds, "I would bet that there are far more Farsi, Amharic, and Arab linguists driving taxicabs in Washington, D.C., than there are in the entire U.S. intelligence community."[24] Godson asks, "Why should U.S. intelligence not actively recruit the needed talent that is available in American society, just as universities recruit athletes?"[25] This is certainly a case of apples and oranges; unless the streetwise cab driver is teamed up with the scholar, there will be no worthy analysis, new or otherwise. It is just as vital to recruit the Kents, Langers, and Pearsons once again (though in compliance with affirmative action this time).

But it will not be as easy to do as before. Says "Archie" Roosevelt,

> The intelligence officer, to be effective, must not only know whose side he is on, but have a deep conviction that it is the right one. . . .

He should not imitate the cynical protagonists of John Le Carré's novels, essentially craftsmen who find their side no less amoral than the other.[26]

The "100 professors" of the World War II era would have had no problem with this. But the CIA's controversial history, with interventions in the Third World and the clandestine funding of private academic, research, student, and youth organizations, among others, has changed the relationship between cloak and gown. Most academics know they are on the "right side," but they are reluctant to be compromised by the excesses of secret intelligence. Formalizing procedures for accountability and control of covert action may help restore confidence in the CIA, but to tap the best minds and achieve a pure, tell-it-like-it-is analysis, it is necessary to make analysis independent of Operations and reaffirm the "clearinghouse" concept.

There is a need for an analytical unit like the old ONE at the DCI/Intelligence Community level, a unit that performs much like the State Department's policy planning staff and that receives all-source intelligence. This might be accomplished in conjunction with the creation of an independent national intelligence agency for research and analysis, which would also resuscitate basic intelligence, reorganize current intelligence, and provide the means for centralized guidance of tasking and collection. There may be good reason to remain with the intelligence community concept, but the United States has paid a price for this "loose confederation."

Nowhere has this lack of centralization exacted a higher price than in counterintelligence, according to CI experts George Kalaris and Leonard McCoy.

> Continuation of the piecemeal and parochial approach to counterintelligence can be expected only to perpetuate the great national security damage that the United States has suffered to date.[27]

The Washington colloquium gave special attention to counterintelligence as a particular function of intelligence. The "Year of the Spy" was obviously the cause for the deep concern. Kenneth deGraffenreid, a senior fellow on intelligence at the National Strategy Information Center, addressed the colloquium on the amount of U.S. effort toward countering terrorism. He remarked, "In terms of actual damage to U.S. national security, even the most provocative and emotionally charged terrorist incidents the United States has experienced cannot compare to the magnitude of damage resulting from a single Pelton, Walker, or Whitworth."[28]

Kalaris and McCoy concluded that while departmental CI had generally performed well, the "component parts" did not add up to an effective overall CI program.[29] They affirmed that the CI function needed to be centralized, to the extent of creating a deputy DCI for CI (DDCI/CI). The multidisciplinary dimensions of the threat involve a wide variety of targets and a vast array of human and technical means, Kalaris and McCoy pointed out; so it is essential to have a "multidisciplinary response."[30] Supporting this viewpoint and noting the multidisciplinary nature of U.S. efforts in collection and analysis, deGraffenreid asked, "Why not admit that any competent positive intelligence service is multidisciplinary and that, hence, any CI service that is not multidisciplinary is unlikely to counter that threat?"[31]

Despite the perception of a "diverse and multifaceted" threat to American secrets, the principal cause of damage so far has been the walk-in. Even deGraffenreid, an advocate of the notion of a CI "czar," concedes that "the United States has an espionage threat right here at home that is as serious as any we face." He observes that the Peltons, the Whitworths, the Walkers, and "the other fifty-odd individuals . . . arrested in this country for espionage" were volunteers or walk-ins.[32] U.S. intelligence has a bigger problem with its old-fashioned personnel security than with the new, improved foreign intelligence operations and techniques. John Walker, in offering his services to the Russians, went right in "the front door" of the Soviet embassy in Washington.[33]

When asked how this could happen, James Geer, assistant director in charge of the FBI's intelligence division, replied that the FBI is not going to "put a RAM car in front of the Soviet Embassy," nor can it monitor the financial standing of every person with clearance or check their drinking habits and marital situation. Instead, he insisted, the United States "must concentrate on those active foreign intelligence officers who are in this country attempting to recruit Americans.''[34] Nonetheless, it seems essential to watch ''the front door'' better and to approach the personnel side of the problem with new ideas.

Chapman Pincher, author of *Traitors,* has suggested certain new ideas using information generated by the recent spy cases to profile volunteers and walk-ins and to identify the traits of traitors. He asks, ''If the motivations of traitors . . . could be more deeply understood, would it be possible to take more active countermeasures to thwart them?''[35] Pincher is aware of the pitfalls of this approach. But he dismisses the glib MICE concept (''traitors are motivated by Money or Ideology or Compromise or Ego'') and makes a clear distinction between ''personality traits'' and ''defects of character.'' Nonetheless, after a study of the case histories of John Walker, Edward Howard, Christopher Daulton Lee, and Richard Miller, Pincher affirmed, ''To perform his task and to survive, the traitor has to be fundamentally dishonest.''[36] He summarized other observations, as well.

> There can be little doubt that any record of criminality, however far back, should be a bar to employment in a secret agency. [Walker was arrested as a teenager for a break-in; Lee was a drug pusher] . . . Counterintelligence officers in search of possible traitors or concerned with preventing the employment of potential traitors would be wise to take note of features like undue arrogance or vanity. More importantly, they should look for evidence of chips on the shoulder, and especially of excessive professional disappointment or smouldering animosity to superiors which can be subsumed under the single factor of resentment. [Howard was fired by the CIA; Miller was the butt of his colleagues' jokes in the FBI because of his bumbling.][37]

The process of singling out and identifying a Benedict Arnold personality syndrome could be disastrous in the hands of amateurs and zealots, but it nonetheless focuses the CI emphasis on the walk-in problem, where it needs to be. It could help avoid a repeat of the CIA's excessive ''great mole hunt'' that ruined the career and effectiveness of James Angleton. Angleton turned the CIA upside down between 1964 and 1974 in search of a Soviet penetration agent within the Agency. He never found one, and apparently during his watch he prevented there being one. Nonetheless, when William Colby became DCI, he fired Angleton, feeling that Angleton's witch-hunt had hurt "the careers of too many people."[38] Colby explained that he did not oppose the "role" of the CI staff; "he opposed its scope. His criticism was CI's lack of specificity. He wanted CI to pinpoint problems, not simply to be suspicious of everyone and everything."[39] Pincher's concept is a step in the direction of specificity; it also offers guidance concerning personnel in general and suggests giving more serious attention to counseling and career development, as well as providing more sophisticated educational programs for employees (and military personnel) in security issues.

Just as the Washington colloquium stressed the need for improved coordination among departmental CI units and even the possible creation of a deputy DCI for CI, so CI ought to be involved in more comprehensive planning and tasking with the other functions of intelligence. The possible increased use of covert action to thwart terrorism and drug trafficking, for example, with its implications for the types of persons that it may be necessary to recruit, is a matter of direct concern to counterintelligence.

The Washington colloquium concurred in the need to perfect and formalize the oversight mechanism of covert action, but in favoring "regularizing covert action in U.S. statecraft," it recognized the broader requirement of public support for the use of the covert instrument.[40] The colloquium made a number of suggestions for achieving public consensus. One is the need to overcome public confusion about the nature and scope of covert action. ("Far too many people believe that covert action is basically paramilitary activity. In fact, there are many other types of covert action involving political support, propaganda, and technology transfer that do not involve guns at all."[41]) For another, covert action must not be a substitute for overt policy. ("If U.S. national security policy is well understood and accepted, chances are good that the major means necessary and proper to its success will not be opposed."[42]) For another, covert activities must not contradict U.S. foreign policy. ("Covert action should be undertaken in support of some widely known and understood public policy, . . . and never run counter to it."[43]) Still another: the United States needs to make its foreign policy goals clear. (In this context, "there is likely to be little opposition to most forms of covert action in support of policy."[44]) And: the decision to use covert action cannot be isolated from broad policy considerations. ("Any consideration of a new proposal for covert action must incorporate a deliberate and methodical review of the risk-gain equation as an integral part of the approval process."[45]) Finally, covert action must be compatible with democratic values. ("Reasonableness of purpose, decency of method, and the likelihood that results will satisfy public opinion at both the giving and receiving ends are still valid criteria against which covert action should be weighed."[46])

Adherence to these principles will not ensure that covert action will be effective, but they go a long way toward cleaning up its act if it is to be "one of a number of instruments of statecraft." At the Washington colloquium, Richard Shultz, one of the most outspoken advocates of covert action, argued that "there is a theoretical basis for the exercise of covert action that is not inimical to democratic norms."[47] He regretted that opponents of covert action "have successfully seized the moral high ground" and insisted "this does not have to be the case."

> It will take effective executive leadership to articulate how the instrument of covert action can be used in support of sound policy objectives and within the context of democratic principles.[48]

This is a far cry from many of the past instances of covert action, but if covert action has to be, Shultz's brand has greater merit. Yet Shultz describes covert action as "the clandestine element of policies aimed at helping friends or potential friends in need of advice and support."[49] This recalls the clandestine funding of democratic and reformist groups and organizations during the 1950s and 1960s, which proved to be counterproductive and badly damaged the democratic option. Unilateral intervention, no matter how well intended, mocks the rule of law, and secret funding is "tainted money," lacking an accounting and tending to corrupt the foreign political process and undermine the integrity of local leaders. Controlling the temptation to meddle is a major reason to support the concept of covert action as "a special activity to be used sparingly and selectively."[50]

It is clear that U.S. foreign intelligence has come a long way since World War II. It comprises a huge professional bureaucracy and a wondrous array of hardware. Even in an era of intercontinental ballistic missiles and space technology, one cannot imagine another successful surprise attack of the Pearl Harbor variety. Many of the technical collection programs are at the same time early warning systems and the means for arms control and arms verification (National Technical Means). U.S. foreign intelligence is adaptive and shows an ability to respond to new challenges, such as terrorism (especially state-sponsored terrorism), the international drug trade, and so-called low-intensity conflict. Nonetheless, despite its vast size and sophistication, the United States has not yet achieved a comprehensive national intelligence system. The intelligence community concept has favored departmental intelligence, and national intelligence has been achieved principally in "big ticket" technical collection and in "such other functions" as space reconnaissance (the NRO), signals intelligence (the NSA), and clandestine operations (the CIA/DO). American intelligence has not yet attained the "clearinghouse" ideal for the production of national or strategic intelligence. In Donovan's concept of Intelligence and Operations, one leg is still excessively short. It is unlikely that the functions of intelligence will ever be brought under one roof—and that may be all to the good; but whereas there are national intelligence agencies for technical collection and clandestine operations, there is no national intelligence agency for research and analysis.

Ray Cline complained about this in his 1976 book *Secrets, Spies and Scholars.* He recommended that "an independent, new, purely analytical and estimative agency" be created, which he proposed be named the Central Institute of Foreign Affairs Research (CIFAR).[51] In the 1981 update of his book, retitled *The CIA Under Reagan, Bush and Casey,* Cline seemed satisfied with the 1978 reorganization of the Directorate of Intelligence as the National Foreign Assessment Center, charged with the communitywide responsibility of supervising the work of the national intelligence officers and aimed at a true national intelligence estimates production. His rejoicing was premature; early in the Reagan administration, NFAC became the Directorate of Intelligence again and the NIOs, though placed under the authority of the DCI and given a corporate identity as the National Intelligence Council, fell far short of Cline's ideal of "[consolidating] the work of the main analytical staffs" of the CIA and the departments of Defense and State.[52]

Scott Breckinridge did not support Cline's idea of an independent national intelligence center for research and analysis, feeling that "the present system soundly meets the requirements of running the intelligence business" and that it should not be changed "just because it suffers the malady common to all administrative systems—imperfection."[53] He believed that needs would be met by "evolutionary change," claiming that experience had already shown this to be the case.

In truth, the failure of Intelligence to keep up with Operations is a more fundamental imperfection. It is an imperfection of essential mission. Cline, an OSS veteran and a former DDI, explained that at the "heart" of his proposals was the need "to change the popular image of intelligence by demonstrating that most of the work is neither illegal nor immoral." He went so far as to suggest dropping the name CIA altogether and wrote in 1981 that "NFAC could nominally replace the CIA as the known administrative element at the Langley Headquarters Building, which could then be more open to scholars and journalists interested in consultation and substantive research findings."[54] A name change alone will not accomplish anything, particularly if it is linked in any way with Operations. What is needed is what Cline proposed before: an independent national intelligence agency for research and analysis. It is the only way to restore scholarly integrity to Intelligence.

In the meantime, don't shoot the piano player.

Further Reading

Historical and General

Bakeless, John. *Spies of the Confederacy*. Philadelphia: J.B. Lippincott, 1970.
———. *Turncoats, Traitors and Heroes*. Philadelphia: J.B. Lippincott, 1959.
Bean, Walton. *California: An Interpretive History*. 3rd ed. New York: McGraw-Hill, 1978.
Brown, Charles H. *Agents of Manifest Destiny: The Lives and Times of the Filibusters*. Chapel Hill: University of North Carolina Press, 1980.
Bryan, George S. *The Spy in America*. Philadelphia: J.B. Lippincott, 1943.
Catton, Bruce. *A Stillness at Appomattox*. New York: Pocket Books, 1958.
Central Intelligence Agency. *Intelligence in the War of Independence*. Washington, D.C.: CIA, 1976.
Copeland, Miles. *Without Cloak or Dagger*. New York: Simon and Schuster, 1974.
Dulles, Allen. *The Craft of Intelligence*. New York: Harper and Row, 1963.
Felix, Christopher. *A Short Course in the Secret War*. New York: Dell, 1988.
Goetzmann, William H. *Exploration and Empire: The Explorer and the Scientist in the Winning of the American West*. New York: Vintage Books, 1966.
Hagan, Kenneth J. *American Gunboat Diplomacy and the Old Navy, 1877–1889*. Westport, Conn.: Greenwood Press, 1973.
Jeffreys-Jones, Rhodri. *American Espionage: From Secret Service to CIA*. New York: The Free Press, 1977.
Kahn, David. *The Codebreakers: The Story of Secret Writing*. New York: Signet, 1973.
Kane, Harnett T. *Spies for the Blue and Gray*. Garden City, N.Y.: Hanover House, 1954.
Knightley, Phillip. *The Second Oldest Profession: Spies and Spying in the Twentieth Century*. New York: Penguin Books, 1988.
LaFeber, Walter. *The Panama Canal: The Crisis in Historical Perspective*. New York: Oxford University Press, 1978.
Merk, Frederick. *Manifest Destiny and Mission in American History: A Reinterpretation*. New York: Vintage Books, 1966.

Mogelever, Jacob. *Death to Traitors: The Story of Lafayette C. Baker, Lincoln's Forgotten Secret Service Chief.* Garden City, N.Y.: Doubleday, 1960.

Pincher, Chapman. *Traitors.* New York: Penguin Books, 1988.

Pletcher, David M. *The Diplomacy of Annexation: Texas, Oregon and the Mexican War.* Columbia: University of Missouri Press, 1973.

Pratt, Julius W. *Expansionists of 1898.* Baltimore: The Johns Hopkins Press, 1936.

Price, Glenn W. *Origins of the War with Mexico: The Polk-Stockton Intrigue.* Austin: University of Texas Press, 1967.

Pringle, Henry F. *Theodore Roosevelt.* New York: Harcourt, Brace and Company, 1931.

Roosevelt, Theodore. *The Rough Riders.* New York: Signet, 1961.

Rowan, Richard Wilmer. *Secret Service: Thirty-three Centuries of Espionage.* New York: Hawthorne Books, 1967.

———. *The Story of Secret Service.* New York: Doubleday, 1937.

Ruiz, Ramón Eduardo, ed. *The Mexican War: Was It Manifest Destiny?* New York: Holt, Rinehart and Winston, 1963

Russ, William Adam. *The Hawaiian Revolution (1893-94).* Selinsgrove, Penn.: Susquehanna University Press, 1959.

Stern, Philip Van Doren. *Secret Missions of the Civil War.* Chicago: Rand McNally, 1959.

Utley, Robert M. *Frontier Regulars: The United States Army and the Indian, 1866-1891.* New York: Macmillan, 1973.

Vagts, Alfred. *The Military Attaché.* Princeton: Princeton University Press, 1967.

Volkman, Ernest, and Blaine Baggett. *Secret Intelligence.* New York: Doubleday, 1989.

World War I to World War II

Alsop, Stewart, and Thomas Braden. *Sub Rosa: The O.S.S. and American Espionage.* New York: Reynal and Hitchcock, 1946.

Ambrose, Stephen E., with Richard H. Immerman. *Ike's Spies: Eisenhower and the Espionage Establishment.* Garden City, N.Y.: Doubleday, 1981.

Brown, Anthony Cave, ed. *The Secret War Report of the OSS.* New York: Berkley, 1976. (Also published as *War Report of the OSS.* 2 vols. New York: Walker and Company, 1976.)

Deutsch, Harold C. "The Historical Impact of Revealing the ULTRA Secret." *Parameters, Journal of the US Army War College* 7 (1977):16-32.

———. "The Influence of ULTRA on World War II." *Parameters, Journal of the US Army War College* 8 (1978): 2-15.

Layton, Edwin T., with Roger Pineau and John Costello. *"And I Was There." Pearl Harbor and Midway—Breaking the Secrets.* New York: William Morrow, 1986.

Lewin, Ronald. *ULTRA Goes to War.* New York: McGraw-Hill, 1978.

———. *The American MAGIC.* New York: Penguin Books, 1983.

Loftus, John. *The Belarus Secret.* Nathan Miller, ed. New York: Alfred A. Knopf, 1982.

March, Peyton C. *The Nation at War.* New York: Doubleday, Doran, 1932.

Masterman, John C. *The Double-Cross System in the War of 1939 to 1945.* New Haven: Yale University Press, 1972.

May, Ernest R., ed. *Knowing One's Enemies: Intelligence Assessment Before the Two World Wars.* Princeton: Princeton University Press, 1984.

Murray, Robert K. *Red Scare: A Study in National Hysteria, 1919–1920.* Minneapolis: University of Minnesota Press, 1955.

Prange, Gordon W., with Donald M. Goldstein and Katherine V. Dillon. *At Dawn We Slept: The Untold Story of Pearl Harbor.* New York: McGraw-Hill, 1981.

———. *Pearl Harbor: The Verdict of History.* New York: McGraw-Hill, 1986.

Rout, Leslie B., Jr., and John F. Bratzel. *The Shadow War: German Espionage and United States Counterespionage in Latin America during World War II.* Frederick, Md.: University Publications of America, 1986.

Smith, Bradley F. *The Shadow Warriors: O.S.S. and the Origins of the C.I.A.* New York: Basic Books, 1983.

Spector, Ronald H. *Eagle Against the Sun.* New York: The Free Press, 1985.

Tuchman, Barbara W. *The Zimmermann Telegram.* New York: Bantam Books, 1971.

Winks, Robin W. *Cloak and Gown: Scholars in the Secret War, 1939–1961.* New York: William Morrow, 1987.

Winterbotham, F.W. *The ULTRA Secret.* New York: Dell, 1982.

Wohlstetter, Roberta. *Pearl Harbor: Warning and Decision.* Stanford: Stanford University Press, 1962.

Yardley, Herbert O. *The American Black Chamber.* New York: Blue Ribbon Books, 1931.

Intelligence Organization

Breckinridge, Scott D. *The CIA and the U.S. Intelligence System.* Boulder, Colo.: Westview Press, 1986.

Cimbala, Stephen J., ed. *Intelligence and Intelligence Policy in a Democratic Society.* Dobbs Ferry, N.Y.: Transnational Publishers, 1987.

Godson, Roy, ed. *Intelligence Requirements for the 1990s.* Lexington, Mass.: Lexington Books, 1989.

Hopple, Gerald W., and Bruce Watson, eds. *The Military Intelligence Community.* Boulder, Colo.: Westview Press, 1986.

Kent, Sherman. *Strategic Intelligence for American World Policy.* Princeton: Princeton University Press, 1949.

Kirkpatrick, Lyman B., Jr. *The U.S. Intelligence Community: Foreign Policy and Domestic Activities.* New York: Hill and Wang, 1973.

Lowenthal, Mark M. *U.S. Intelligence: Evolution and Anatomy.* New York: Praeger, 1984.

Maurer, Alfred C., Marion D. Tunstall, and James M. Keagle, eds. *Intelligence: Policy and Process*. Boulder, Colo.: Westview Press, 1985.

Oseth, John M. *Regulating U.S. Intelligence Operations: A Study in Definition of the National Interest*. Lexington, Ky.: University Press of Kentucky, 1985.

Richelson, Jeffrey T. *The U.S. Intelligence Community*. Cambridge, Mass.: Ballinger, 1985.

The CIA and Foreign Affairs

Agee, Philip. *Inside the Company: CIA Diary*. New York: Bantam Books, 1976.

Blight, James G., and David A. Welch. *On the Brink: Americans and Soviets Reexamine the Cuban Missile Crisis*. New York: Hill and Wang, 1989.

Cline, Ray S. *The CIA Under Reagan, Bush and Casey*. Washington, D.C.: Acropolis Books, 1981.

Davis, Nathaniel. *The Last Two Years of Salvador Allende*. Ithaca: Cornell University Press, 1985.

Demaris, Ovid. *The Last Mafioso: The Treacherous World of Jimmy Fratianno*. New York: Times Books, 1981.

Ellsberg, Daniel. *Papers on the War*. New York: Simon and Schuster, 1972.

Emerson, Steven. *Secret Warriors: Inside the Covert Military Operations of the Reagan Era*. New York: G.P. Putnam's Sons, 1988.

Higgins, Trumbull. *The Perfect Failure: Kennedy, Eisenhower, and the CIA at the Bay of Pigs*. New York: W.W. Norton, 1987.

Immerman, Richard H. *The CIA in Guatemala: The Foreign Policy of Intervention*. Austin: University of Texas Press, 1982.

Jeffreys-Jones, Rhodri. *The CIA and American Democracy*. New Haven: Yale University Press, 1989.

Kalb, Madeline G. *The Congo Cables: The Cold War in Africa—From Eisenhower to Kennedy*. New York: Macmillan, 1982.

Kennedy, Robert F. *Thirteen Days: A Memoir of the Cuban Missile Crisis*. New York: W.W. Norton, 1968.

McGarvey, Patrick J. *C.I.A.: The Myth and the Madness*. Baltimore: Penguin Books, 1973.

McCoy, Alfred W. *The Politics of Heroin in Southeast Asia*. New York: Harper and Row, 1972.

Marchetti, Victor, and John D. Marks. *The CIA and the Cult of Intelligence*. New York: Laurel, 1983.

Morris, George. *CIA and American Labor*. New York: International Publishers, 1967.

Newsom, David D. *The Soviet Brigade in Cuba: A Study in Political Diplomacy*. Bloomington: Indiana University Press, 1987.

Paterson, Thomas G., ed. *Kennedy's Quest for Victory: American Foreign Policy, 1961–1963*. New York: Oxford University Press, 1989.

———. *Meeting the Communist Threat: Truman to Reagan*. New York: Oxford University Press, 1988.

Prados, John. *Presidents' Secret Wars: CIA and Pentagon Covert Operations from World War II Through Iranscam*. New York: Quill/William Morrow, 1988.

Quirk, John Patrick, et al. *The Central Intelligence Agency: A Photographic History*. Guilford, Conn.: Foreign Intelligence Press, 1986.

Rabe, Stephen G. *Eisenhower and Latin America: The Foreign Policy of Anticommunism*. Chapel Hill: University of North Carolina Press, 1988.

Ranelagh, John. *The Agency: The Rise and Decline of the CIA*. New York: Touchstone, 1987.

Romualdi, Serafino. *Presidents and Peons: Recollections of a Labor Ambassador in Latin America*. New York: Funk and Wagnalls, 1967.

Roosevelt, Kermit. *Countercoup: The Struggle for the Control of Iran*. New York: McGraw-Hill, 1979.

Schlesinger, Stephen, and Stephen Kinzer. *Bitter Fruit: The Untold Story of the American Coup in Guatemala*. Garden City, N.Y.: Doubleday, 1982.

Sigmund, Paul E. *The Overthrow of Allende and the Politics of Chile, 1964–1976*. Pittsburgh: University of Pittsburgh Press, 1977.

Snepp, Frank. *Decent Interval*. New York: Random House, 1977.

Stockwell, John. *In Search of Enemies: A CIA Story*. London: Futura Publications, 1979.

Treverton, Gregory F. *Covert Action: The Limits of Intervention in the Postwar World*. New York: Basic Books, 1987.

Weissman, Stephen R. *American Foreign Policy in the Congo. 1960–1964*. Ithaca: Cornell University Press, 1974.

Wise, David, and Thomas B. Ross. *The Invisible Government*. New York: Vintage Books, 1974.

Woodward, Bob. *Veil: The Secret Wars of the CIA, 1981–1987*. New York: Simon and Schuster, 1987.

Wyden, Peter. *Bay of Pigs: The Untold Story*. New York: Simon and Schuster, 1979.

Domestic Intelligence and Internal Security

Barron, John. *Breaking the Ring*. Boston: Houghton Mifflin, 1987.

Bernstein, Carl, and Bob Woodward. *All the President's Men*. New York: Simon and Schuster, 1974.

Dean, John W. *Blind Ambition*. New York: Simon and Schuster, 1976.

Johnson, Loch K. *A Season of Inquiry: Congress and Intelligence*. Chicago: Dorsey Press, 1988.

Lukas, J. Anthony. *Night-mare: The Underside of the Nixon Years*. New York: Viking, 1976.

Sirica, John J. *To Set the Record Straight*. New York: Signet, 1979.

Theoharis, Athan. *Spying on Americans: Political Surveillance from Hoover to the Huston Plan*. Philadelphia: Temple University Press, 1978.

Ungar, Sanford J. *FBI*. Boston: Little, Brown and Company, 1975.

Whitehead, Don. *The FBI Story*. New York: Pocket Books, 1956.

Wise, David. *The Spy Who Got Away: The Inside Story of Edward Lee Howard, the CIA Agent Who Betrayed His Country's Secrets and Escaped to Moscow.* New York: Random House, 1988.

Technical Intelligence and Related Issues

Armbrister, Trevor. *A Matter of Accountability: The True Story of the* Pueblo *Affair.* New York: Coward-McCann, 1970.

Bamford, James. *The Puzzle Palace.* New York: Penguin Books, 1983.

Beschloss, Michael R. *Mayday: Eisenhower, Khrushchev and the U-2 Affair.* New York: Harper and Row, 1986.

Bucher, Lloyd M., with Mark Rascovich. *Bucher: My Story.* Garden City, N.Y.: Doubleday, 1970.

Burrows, William E. *Deep Black: Space Espionage and National Security.* New York: Random House, 1986.

Dallin, Alexander. *Black Box: KAL 007 and the Superpowers.* Berkeley: University of California Press, 1985.

Ennes, James M., Jr. *Assault on the* Liberty: *The True Story of the Israeli Attack on an American Intelligence Ship.* New York: Random House, 1979.

Hersh, Seymour M. *"The Target is Destroyed." What Really Happened to Flight 007 and What America Knew About It.* New York: Random House, 1986.

Johnson, R.W. *Shootdown: Flight 007 and the American Connection.* New York: Viking, 1986.

Kahn, David. *Kahn on Codes.* New York: Macmillan, 1983.

Varner, Roy, and Wayne Collier. *A Matter of Risk: The Incredible Story of the CIA's* Hughes Glomar Explorer *Mission to Raise a Russian Submarine.* New York: Random House, 1978.

Documents and References

Becket, Henry S.A. *The Dictionary of Espionage: Spookspeak into English.* New York: Stein and Day, 1986.

Cline, Majorie W., Carla E. Christensen, and Judith M. Fontaine, eds. *Scholar's Guide to Intelligence Literature: Bibliography of the Russell J. Bowen Collection.* Frederick, Maryland: University Publications of America, 1983.

Commission on CIA Activities Within the United States. *Report to the President.* Washington, D.C.: Government Printing Office, 1975.

Constantinides, George C. *Intelligence and Espionage: An Analytical Bibliography.* Boulder, Colo.: Westview Press, 1983.

House Committee on Foreign Affairs. *The Story of Panama.* Washington, D.C.: Government Printing Office, 1913.

House and Senate. *Report of the Congressional Committees Investigating the Iran-Contra Affair.* 100th Cong., 1st sess., 1987, H. Rept. 100-433, S. Rept. 100-216.

Operation ZAPATA: The "Ultrasensitive" Report and Testimony of the Board of Inquiry on the Bay of Pigs. Frederick, Md.: University Publications of America, 1981.

O'Toole, G.J.A. *The Encyclopedia of American Intelligence and Espionage: From the Revolutionary War to the Present.* New York: Facts on File, 1988.

Senate Select Committee to Study Governmental Operations. *Alleged Assassination Plots Involving Foreign Leaders.* 94th Cong., 1st sess., 1975, Rept. 94-465.

―――. *Covert Action in Chile, 1963–1973.* 94th Cong., 1st sess., 1975, Committee Print.

―――. *Foreign and Military Intelligence.* 94th Cong., 2d sess., 1976, Rept. 94-755, book 1.

―――. *Intelligence Activities and the Rights of Americans.* 94th Cong., 2d sess., 1976, Rept. 94-755, book 2.

―――. *Intelligence Activities—Volume 2: Huston Plan.* 94th Cong., 1st sess., 1975, hearings.

―――. *Supplementary Detailed Staff Reports on Foreign and Military Intelligence.* 94th Cong., 2d sess., 1976, Rept. 94-755, book 4.

―――. *Supplementary Reports on Intelligence Activities.* 94th Cong., 2d sess., 1976, Rept. 94-755, book 6.

The Tower Commission Report: The Full Text of the President's Special Review Board. New York: Bantam Books and Times Books, 1987.

Biographies and Memoirs

Brown, Anthony Cave. *The Last Hero: Wild Bill Donovan.* New York: New York Times Books, 1982.

Colby, William. *Honorable Men: My Life in the CIA.* New York: Simon and Schuster, 1978.

Currey, Cecil B. *Edward Lansdale: The Unquiet American.* Boston: Houghton Mifflin, 1988.

Ford, Corey. *Donovan of OSS.* Boston: Little, Brown, 1971.

Meyer, Cord. *Facing Reality.* New York: Harper and Row, 1980.

Phillips, David Atlee. *The Night Watch.* New York: Atheneum, 1977.

Powers, Thomas. *The Man Who Kept the Secrets: Richard Helms and the CIA.* New York: Alfred A. Knopf, 1979.

Troy, Thomas F. *Donovan and the CIA.* Washington, D.C.: CIA, 1981.

Turner, Stansfield. *Secrecy and Democracy: The CIA in Transition.* Boston: Houghton Mifflin, 1985.

Wright, Peter, with Paul Greengrass. *Spy Catcher: The Candid Autobiography of a Senior Intelligence Officer.* New York: Viking, 1987.

Notes

Chapter 1

1. Spookspeak: "As with most trade talk, intelligence terminology such as clandestine operations, covert action, and black box is highly technical and has developed nuances not easily inferred from the words themselves." Henry S.A. Becket, *The Dictionary of Espionage: Spookspeak into English* (New York: Stein and Day, 1986), p. 10.
2. Senate Select Committee to Study Governmental Operations, *Foreign and Military Intelligence*, 94th Cong., 2nd sess., 1976, Rept. 94-755, book I, p. 624.

Chapter 2

1. Miles Copeland, *Without Cloak or Dagger* (New York: Simon and Schuster, 1974), pp. 126-27, 146-48.
2. Ibid., pp. 140-41.
3. Philip Agee, *Inside the Company: CIA Diary* (New York: Stonehill Publishing Co., 1975), pp. 37-41.
4. Copeland, *Without Cloak*, p. 24.
5. Victor Marchetti and John D. Marks, *The CIA and the Cult of Intelligence* (New York: Alfred A. Knopf, 1974), p. 255.
6. Ibid., pp. 257-58.
7. Copeland, *Without Cloak*, pp. 21, 127-28.
8. Ibid., p. 134.
9. Marchetti and Marks, *Cult of Intelligence*, p. 269.
10. Lyman B. Kirkpatrick, Jr., *The U.S. Intelligence Community: Foreign Policy and Domestic Activities* (New York: Hill and Wang, 1973), p. 114.

Chapter 3

1. George S. Bryan, *The Spy in America* (Philadelphia: J.B. Lippincott, 1943), p. 18.
2. John Bakeless, *Turncoats, Traitors and Heroes* (Philadelphia: J.B. Lippincott, 1959), pp. 74-75.

3. Ibid., pp. 22–23.
4. Ibid., pp. 107–9.
5. Bryan, *Spy in America*, p. 51.
6. Ibid., p. 52.
7. Ibid., p. 82.
8. Bakeless, *Turncoats*, pp. 197–98.
9. Ibid., p. 197.
10. Ibid., p. 189.
11. Richard Wilmer Rowan, *The Story of Secret Service* (New York: Doubleday, 1937), p. 133.
12. Allen Dulles, *The Craft of Intelligence* (New York: Harper & Row, 1963), pp. 34–36.
13. CIA, *Intelligence in the War of Independence* (Washington: 1976), p. 38.
14. Bakeless, *Turncoats*, pp. 364–65.

Chapter 4

1. George S. Bryan, *The Spy in America* (Philadelphia: J.B. Lippincott, 1943), p. 105.
2. John Bakeless, *Turncoats, Traitors and Heroes* (Philadelphia: J.B. Lippincott, 1959), pp. 360–61.
3. Bryan, *Spy in America*, pp. 115–16.
4. Thomas A. Bailey, *A Diplomatic History of the American People*, 7th ed. (New York: Appleton-Century-Crofts, 1964), pp. 201–2.
5. Charles H. Brown, *Agents of Manifest Destiny* (Chapel Hill: University of North Carolina Press, 1980), p. 411.
6. William H. Goetzmann, *Exploration and Empire* (New York: Vintage Books, 1966), pp. 4–5.
7. Ibid., p. 5.
8. Ibid., p. 41.
9. Ibid., p. 47.
10. Ibid., p. 50.
11. Ibid., p. 139.
12. Ibid., p. 149.
13. Ibid., p. 157.
14. Ibid., p. 240.

Chapter 5

1. Richard R. Stenberg, "The Failure of Polk's Mexican War Intrigue of 1845," in Ramón Eduardo Ruiz, ed., *The Mexican War. Was It Manifest Destiny?* (New York: Holt, Rinehart, and Winston, 1963), p. 69.
2. Ibid., pp. 69–70.
3. Glenn W. Price, *Origins of the War with Mexico: The Polk–Stockton Intrigue* (Austin: University of Texas Press, 1967), pp. 150–51.

4. Thomas A. Bailey, *A Diplomatic History of the American People,* 7th ed. (New York: Appleton-Century-Crofts, 1964), pp. 256–57.
5. Ibid., p. 253.
6. Frederick Merk, *Manifest Destiny and Mission in American History* (New York: Vintage Books, 1966), p. 74.
7. Ibid., pp. 65–66.
8. Ibid., p. 75.
9. Ibid., pp. 79–80.
10. Walton Bean, *California: An Interpretive History,* 3rd ed. (New York: McGraw-Hill, 1978), pp. 81–85.
11. George S. Bryan, *The Spy in America* (Philadelphia: J.B. Lippincott, 1943), p. 118.

Chapter 6

1. Richard Wilmer Rowan, *The Story of Secret Service* (New York: Doubleday, 1937), p. 265.
2. Ibid., p. 268.
3. Ibid., p. 286.
4. Jacob Mogelever, *Death to Traitors* (Garden City, N.Y.: Doubleday, 1960), p. 111.
5. Senate Select Committee to Study Governmental Operations, *Supplementary Reports on Intelligence Activities,* 94th Cong., 2d sess., 1976, Rept. 94-755, book 6, p. 45.
6. George S. Bryan, *The Spy in America* (Philadelphia: J.B. Lippincott, 1943), p. 137.
7. Ibid., p. 136.
8. Ibid., p. 140.
9. Senate Select Committee, *Intelligence Activities,* pp. 46–47.
10. Rowan, *Secret Service,* p. 290.
11. Bryan, *Spy in America,* p. 145; see also John Bakeless, *Spies of the Confederacy* (Philadelphia: J.B. Lippincott, 1970), p. 133.
12. Bakeless, *Spies of the Confederacy,* p. 131. Bakeless points out that since many commanders on opposing sides had been classmates at West Point, the identity of the commanding officer was significant information.
13. Ibid., p. 132.
14. Bruce Catton, *A Stillness at Appomattox* (New York: Pocket Books, 1958), pp. 318–19.
15. Ibid., p. 319.
16. Bryan, *Spy in America,* pp. 146–49.
17. David Kahn, *The Codebreakers* (New York: Macmillan, 1967), pp. 154–55.
18. Bryan, *Spy in America,* p. 179.
19. Bakeless, *Spies of the Confederacy,* p. 141.
20. Ibid., p. 148.
21. Rowan, *Secrèt Service,* p. 294.

22. Bryan, *Spy in America,* p. 189.
23. Ibid., pp. 186–87.
24. Rowan, *Secret Service,* p. 297.
25. Bryan, *Spy in America,* p. 193.
26. Ibid., pp. 194–96. Van Lew had concealed Colonel Revere, an escaped POW, in her secret room.

Chapter 7

1. Robert M. Utley, *Frontier Regulars: The United States Army and the Indian, 1866–1891* (New York: Macmillan, 1973), p. 50.
2. Ibid., p. 179.
3. Ibid., p. 54.
4. Ibid., p. 261.
5. Ibid., p. 253.
6. Kenneth J. Hagan, *American Gunboat Diplomacy and the Old Navy, 1877–1889* (Westport, Conn.: Greenwood Press, 1973), p. 80.
7. Ibid., p. 37.
8. Senate Select Committee to Study Governmental Operations, *Supplementary Reports on Intelligence Activities,* 94th Cong., 2d sess., 1976, Rept. 94-755, book 6, pp. 59–60.
9. Hagan, *Gunboat Diplomacy,* p. 131.
10. Ibid., p. 54.
11. Alfred Vagts, *The Military Attaché* (Princeton: Princeton University Press, 1967), p. 3.
12. Ibid.
13. Ibid., p. xi. See also Rhodri Jeffreys-Jones, *American Espionage: From Secret Service to CIA* (New York: The Free Press, 1977), pp. 27–28.
14. Vagts, *Military Attaché,* p. 11.
15. Ibid.
16. Ibid., p. 12.
17. Ibid.
18. Ibid., p. 13.
19. Ibid., pp. 13–14.

Chapter 8

1. Ruhl J. Bartlett, ed., *The Record of American Diplomacy* (New York: Alfred A. Knopf, 1964), pp. 387–88.
2. Ibid., p. 360.
3. Ibid.
4. Ibid., p. 361.
5. William Adam Russ, *The Hawaiian Revolution (1893–94)* (Selinsgrove, Pa.: Susquehanna University Press, 1959), p. 75.

6. Bartlett, *Record,* p. 363.
7. Ibid.
8. Thomas A. Bailey, *A Diplomatic History of the American People,* 7th ed. (New York: Appleton-Century-Crofts, 1964), p. 431.
9. Bartlett, *Record,* p. 364.
10. Ibid., pp. 365–66.
11. Bailey, *Diplomatic History,* p. 435.
12. Rhodri Jeffreys-Jones, *American Espionage: From Secret Service to CIA* (New York: The Free Press, 1977), pp. 16–17, 29–30.
13. George S. Bryan, *The Spy in America* (Philadelphia: J.B. Lippincott, 1943), pp. 201–2.
14. Richard Wilmer Rowan, *The Story of Secret Service* (New York: Doubleday, 1937), p. 418.
15. Bryan, *Spy in America,* p. 203.
16. Senate Select Committee to Study Governmental Operations, *Supplementary Reports on Intelligence Activities,* 94th Cong., 2d sess., 1976, Rept. 94-755, book 6, pp. 67–68.
17. Bryan, *Spy in America,* pp. 206–12.
18. Ibid., pp. 212–16.
19. Philippe Bunau-Varilla, *Panama: The Creation, Destruction, and Resurrection* (New York: McBride, Nast and Company, 1914), p. 319.
20. Charles D. Ameringer, "Philippe Bunau-Varilla: New Light on the Panama Canal Treaty," *Hispanic American Historical Review* 46 (February 1966): 32.
21. House Committee on Foreign Affairs, *The Story of Panama* (Washington: Government Printing Office, 1913), p. 371.
22. Ibid.
23. Ibid., p. 383.
24. Ibid.
25. Ibid., p. 393.
26. Ibid.
27. Quoted in Bailey, *Diplomatic History,* p. 497.
28. *Story of Panama,* pp. 589–90.
29. Ibid., pp. 582–83.
30. Ibid., pp. 703–4.
31. Ibid., p. 704.
32. Ibid., pp. 704–6.
33. Ibid., pp. 369–70.

Chapter 9

1. James Bamford, *The Puzzle Palace* (New York: Penguin Books, 1983), p. 448.
2. David Kahn, *The Codebreakers* (New York: Macmillan, 1967), p. 76.
3. Ibid., p. 77.
4. Ibid., pp. 90–94.
5. Ibid., pp. 97–100.

6. Ibid., pp. 114–16.
7. Ibid., pp. 328–30.

Chapter 10

1. David Kahn, *The Codebreakers* (New York: Signet, 1973), p. 155.
2. Barbara W. Tuchman, *The Zimmermann Telegram* (New York: Bantam Books, 1971), p. 14.
3. Kahn, *Codebreakers,* pp. 158–65.
4. Tuchman, *Zimmermann,* pp. 196–99.
5. See George J. Rausch, Jr., "The Exile and Death of Victoriano Huerta," *Hispanic American Historical Review* 42 (May 1962): 133–51; James A. Sandos, "German Involvement in Northern Mexico, 1915–1916: A New Look at the Columbus Raid," *Hispanic American Historical Review* 50 (February 1970): 70–88; and Charles H. Harris and Louis R. Sadler, "The Plan of San Diego and the Mexican–United States War Crisis of 1916: A Reexamination," *Hispanic American Historical Review* 58 (August 1978): 381–408.
6. Tuchman, *Zimmermann,* p. 13.
7. Kahn, *Codebreakers,* p. 133.
8. Ibid., pp. 142–43.
9. Tuchman, *Zimmermann,* p. 194.
10. Kahn, *Codebreakers,* p. 153.
11. Tuchman, *Zimmermann,* pp. 82–84.
12. Ibid., p. 84.
13. Rhodri Jeffreys-Jones, *American Espionage: From Secret Service to CIA* (New York: The Free Press, 1977), pp. 44–46.
14. Harris and Sadler, "Plan of San Diego," p. 403.
15. Ibid.
16. Robert K. Murray, *Red Scare: A Study in National Hysteria, 1919–1920* (Minneapolis: University of Minnesota Press, 1955), p. 13.
17. Mary Beth Norton et al., *A People and a Nation: A History of the United States,* vol. 2, *Since 1865,* 2d ed. (Boston: Houghton Mifflin, 1986), pp. 665–66.
18. Ibid., p. 666.
19. Murray, *Red Scare,* p. 16.
20. Ibid., p. 17.
21. Ibid., p. 193.
22. Ibid., p. 213.
23. Peyton C. March, *The Nation at War* (New York: Doubleday, 1932), p. 226.
24. Ibid.
25. Kahn, *Codebreakers,* p. 168.
26. Ibid., pp. 169–70.
27. Otto L. Nelson, Jr., *National Security and the General Staff* (Washington, D.C.: Infantry Journal Press, 1946), pp. 264–65.
28. Ibid., p. 265.

29. Richard Wilmer Rowan, *Secret Service: Thirty-three Centuries of Espionage* (New York: Hawthorne Books, 1967), p. 613.
30. Ibid., p. 615.

Chapter 11

1. James Bamford, *The Puzzle Palace* (New York: Penguin Books, 1983), p. 24.
2. Herbert O. Yardley, *The American Black Chamber* (New York: Blue Ribbon Books, 1931), p. 240.
3. Bamford, *Puzzle Palace*, p. 29.
4. Ibid., p. 25.
5. David Kahn, *The Codebreakers* (New York: Signet, 1973), p. 168.
6. Yardley, *The Black Chamber*, p. 332.
7. Ibid., p. 313.
8. Ibid., pp. 313-14.
9. Bamford, *Puzzle Palace*, p. 31.
10. Senate Select Committee to Study Government Operations, *Supplementary Reports on Intelligence Activities*, 94th Cong., 2d sess., 1976, Rept. 94-755, book 6, p. 118.
11. Kahn, *Codebreakers*, p. 178. Rhodri Jeffreys-Jones speculates that Stimson's action was a ''ruse'' to make other nations think that the United States was abandoning cryptanalysis, when it was not. See Rhodri Jeffreys-Jones, *American Espionage: From Secret Service to CIA* (New York: The Free Press, 1977), pp. 134-35.
12. Kahn, *Codebreakers*, p. 179.
13. Ronald Lewin, *The American MAGIC* (New York: Penguin Books, 1983), pp. 34-35.
14. Kahn, *Codebreakers*, pp. 25-26.
15. Lewin, *MAGIC*, p. 41.
16. Bamford, *Puzzle Palace*, pp. 56-57.
17. Don Whitehead, *The FBI Story* (New York: Pocket Books, 1956), p. 191. In time, FDR also had the FBI place certain isolationist groups (America First, for example) under surveillance, in search of Nazi connections. See Richard W. Steele, ''Franklin D. Roosevelt and His Foreign Policy Critics,'' *Political Science Quarterly* 94 (1979): 15-32.
18. Whitehead, *FBI Story*, p. 190.
19. Ibid., pp. 198-99.
20. Ibid., p. 200.
21. Richard Wilmer Rowan, *Secret Service: Thirty-three Centuries of Espionage* (New York: Hawthorne Books, 1967), p. 613.
22. Whitehead, *FBI Story*, p. 205.
23. Ibid.
24. Ibid., p. 217.

Chapter 12

1. Gordon W. Prange et al, *At Dawn We Slept* (New York: McGraw-Hill, 1981).
2. Ronald Lewin, *The American MAGIC* (New York: Penguin Books, 1983), p. 50.
3. David Kahn, *Kahn on Codes* (New York: Macmillan, 1983), p. 252.
4. Roberta Wohlstetter, "Cuba and Pearl Harbor: Hindsight and Foresight," *Foreign Affairs* 43 (July 1965): 691.
5. Quoted in Roberta Wohlstetter, *Pearl Harbor: Warning and Decision* (Stanford: Stanford University Press, 1962), p. 284.
6. Quoted in ibid., p. 231.
7. Ibid., p. 284.
8. John F. Bratzel and Leslie B. Rout, Jr., "Pearl Harbor, Microdots, and J. Edgar Hoover," *The American Historical Review* 87 (December 1982): 1343.
9. Ibid., p. 1347.
10. Lewin, *MAGIC*, pp. 54–55.
11. David Kahn, *The Codebreakers* (New York: Signet, 1973), p. 9.
12. Ibid., pp. 35–37.
13. Ibid.; Lewin, *MAGIC*, p. 66.
14. Kahn, *Codebreakers*, p. 36.
15. Lewin, *MAGIC*, pp. 68–69.
16. Ibid., p. 67.
17. Kahn, *On Codes*, p. 262.
18. James Bamford, *The Puzzle Palace* (New York: Penguin Books, 1983), p. 58.
19. Wohlstetter, *Pearl Harbor*, p. 213.
20. Kahn, *Codebreakers*, p. 34.
21. Ibid., pp. 59–64.
22. Ibid., p. 64.
23. Ibid., p. 57.
24. Ibid., p. 31.
25. Wohlstetter, "Cuba and Pearl Harbor," p. 704.
26. Wohlstetter, *Pearl Harbor*, p. 380.
27. Wohlstetter, "Cuba and Pearl Harbor," p. 705.
28. Kahn, *Codebreakers*, pp. 59–60.
29. Wohlstetter, "Cuba and Pearl Harbor," p. 699.

Chapter 13

1. Ronald Lewin, *The American MAGIC* (New York: Penguin Books, 1983), p. 96.
2. David Kahn, *The Codebreakers* (New York: Signet, 1973), p. 314.
3. Ibid., p. 332.
4. Ibid., p. 330.
5. Ibid., p. 331.
6. Lewin, *MAGIC*, p. 138.

7. James Bamford, *The Puzzle Palace* (New York: Penguin Books, 1983), pp. 62–63.
8. Kahn, *Codebreakers,* p. 316.
9. Ibid., p. 318.
10. Lewin, *MAGIC,* p. 132.
11. Ronald Lewin, *ULTRA Goes to War* (New York: McGraw-Hill, 1978), pp. 97–98.
12. F.W. Winterbotham, *The ULTRA Secret* (New York: Dell, 1974), pp. 92–93.
13. Ibid., p. 76.
14. Lewin, *ULTRA Goes to War,* p. 87.
15. Harold C. Deutsch, "The Historical Impact of Revealing the ULTRA Secret," *Parameters* 7 (1977): 20.
16. Winterbotham, *ULTRA,* p. 126.
17. Lewin, *ULTRA Goes to War,* p. 218.
18. Ibid., pp. 217–18.
19. Lewin, *MAGIC,* p. 132n.
20. Bamford, *Puzzle Palace,* p. 397.
21. Lewin, *ULTRA Goes to War,* p. 245. See also Stephen E. Ambrose, with Richard H. Immerman, *Ike's Spies: Eisenhower and the Intelligence Establishment* (New York: Doubleday, 1981), p. 37.
22. Winterbotham, *ULTRA,* p. 145.
23. Ibid., p. 146.
24. Lewin, *ULTRA Goes to War,* pp. 279–80.
25. Winterbotham, *ULTRA,* p. 163.
26. Lewin, *ULTRA Goes to War,* p. 282.
27. Harold C. Deutsch, "The Influence of ULTRA on World War II," *Parameters* 8 (1978): 3–4.
28. Ibid., pp. 4–5.
29. Ibid., p. 14.
30. Ibid.
31. Kahn, *Codebreakers,* p. 340.

Chapter 14

1. Thomas F. Troy, *Donovan and the CIA* (Washington: CIA, 1981), p. 42.
2. Anthony Cave Brown, ed., *The Secret War Report of the OSS* (New York: Berkley, 1976), p. 62.
3. Ibid., p. 77.
4. Ibid., p. 74.
5. Richard Wilmer Rowan, *Secret Service: Thirty-three Centuries of Espionage* (New York: Hawthorne Books, 1967), p. 617.
6. Stewart Alsop and Thomas Braden, *Sub Rosa: The O.S.S. and American Espionage* (New York: Reynal and Hitchcock, 1946), p. 41.
7. Brown, *Secret War Report,* p. 328.
8. Ibid., p. 162.

9. Ibid., p. 96.
10. Ibid., p. 310.
11. Alsop and Braden, *Sub Rosa,* p. 18.
12. Ray S. Cline, *The CIA Under Reagan, Bush and Casey* (Washington: Acropolis Books, 1981), p. 80.
13. Brown, *Secret War Report,* p. 100.
14. Ibid., pp. 100–101.
15. Ibid., p. 102.
16. Ibid., p. 391.
17. Alsop and Braden, *Sub Rosa,* p. 229.
18. Brown, *Secret War Report,* pp. 226–27. Brown wrote that Holohan's body was placed in the Lake of Orta in *The Last Hero: Wild Bill Donovan* (New York: New York Times Books, 1982), p. 809.
19. Brown, *Secret War Report,* pp. 190–91.
20. Ibid., p. 208.
21. Troy, *Donovan,* p. 168.
22. Brown, *Secret War Report,* p. 190.
23. Ibid., p. 114.
24. Ibid., p. 106.
25. Ibid., pp. 108–9.
26. Ibid., p. 108.
27. Ibid., p. 109.
28. Ibid., p. 118.
29. Ibid., p. 138.
30. Ibid., p. 142.
31. Ibid., p. 145.
32. Stephen E. Ambrose, with Richard H. Immerman, *Ike's Spies: Eisenhower and the Intelligence Establishment* (New York: Doubleday, 1981), pp. 54–56.
33. Troy, *Donovan,* p. 445.
34. Ibid., p. 225.

Chapter 15

1. Senate Select Committee to Study Governmental Operations, *Supplementary Reports on Intelligence Activities,* 94th Cong., 2d sess., 1976, Rept. 94-755, book 6, p. 8.
2. Ibid.
3. Ibid., pp. 14–15.

Chapter 16

1. Jeffrey Richelson, *The U.S. Intelligence Community* (Cambridge, Mass.: Ballinger, 1985), pp. 263–65.
2. Ibid., p. 289.
3. Victor Marchetti and John D. Marks, *The CIA and the Cult of Intelligence* (New York: Laurel, 1983), pp. 287–88.

4. Patrick J. McGarvey, *C.I.A.: The Myth and the Madness* (Baltimore: Penguin Books, 1973), p. 212.
5. Marchetti and Marks, *Cult of Intelligence,* p. 286.
6. Lyman B. Kirkpatrick, Jr., *The U.S. Intelligence Community: Foreign Policy and Domestic Activities* (New York: Hill and Wang, 1973), p. 51.
7. Marchetti and Marks, *Cult of Intelligence,* p. 91.
8. Ibid.
9. Richelson, *U.S. Intelligence,* p. 275; John Prados, *Presidents' Secret Wars* (New York: Quill/William Morrow, 1986), pp. 111–12.
10. Marchetti and Marks, *Cult of Intelligence,* p. 69.
11. McGarvey, *Myth and Madness,* p. 69.
12. Ibid., p. 72.
13. Senate Select Committee to Study Governmental Operations, *Foreign and Military Intelligence,* 94th Cong., 2d sess., 1976, Rept. 94-755, Book 1, p. 326.
14. McGarvey, *Myth and Madness,* pp. 214–15.
15. Ibid., p. 227.
16. *Foreign and Military Intelligence,* p. 349.
17. Kirkpatrick, *Intelligence Community,* p. 36.
18. Marchetti and Marks, *Cult of Intelligence,* p. 79.
19. Richelson, *U.S. Intelligence,* pp. 187–89.
20. James Bamford, *Puzzle Palace,* p. 509.
21. Marchetti and Marks, *Cult of Intelligence,* p. 79, and Richelson, *U.S. Intelligence,* pp. 12–15.
22. Marchetti and Marks, *Cult of Intelligence,* p. 79.
23. Ibid.
24. Ibid., pp. 167–68.
25. Ray S. Cline, *The CIA Under Reagan, Bush and Casey* (Washington: Acropolis Books, 1981), p. 241.
26. Kirkpatrick, *Intelligence Community,* p. 84.
27. Senate Select Committee to Study Governmental Operations, *Supplementary Reports on Intelligence Activities,* 94th Cong., 2d sess., 1976, Rept. 94-755, book 6, p. 287.
28. Ibid., p. 244.
29. Ibid., p. 284.
30. Ibid., pp. 290–91.
31. Quoted in Marchetti and Marks, *Cult of Intelligence,* p. 294.
32. Marchetti and Marks, *Cult of Intelligence,* p. 296.
33. Cline, *The CIA,* pp. 284–85.

Chapter 17

1. Senate Select Committee to Study Governmental Operations, *Supplementary Detailed Staff Reports on Foreign and Military Intelligence,* 94th Cong., 2d sess., 1976, Rept. 94-755, book 4, pp. 14–15.
2. Ibid., p. 23.

426   U.S. Foreign Intelligence

4. Ibid., p. 30.
5. Ibid., p. 31.
6. Ibid., pp. 31–32.
7. Ibid., p. 38.
8. Ibid.
9. Ibid., pp. 40–41.
10. Quoted in David Wise and Thomas B. Ross, *The Invisible Government* (New York: Vintage Books, 1974), p. 96.
11. Ibid.
12. Victor Marchetti and John D. Marks, *The CIA and the Cult of Intelligence* (New York: Laurel, 1983), p. 268.
13. Senate Select Committee to Study Governmental Operations, *Foreign and Military Intelligence,* 94th Cong., 2d sess., 1976, Rept. 94-755, book 1, pp. 289–90.
14. Ibid., p. 297, fn. 73.
15. Ibid., p. 297.
16. Ibid., p. 282.
17. Ibid.
18. Marchetti and Marks, *Cult of Intelligence,* pp. 292–93.
19. Ibid., p. 58.
20. Ibid., p. 246.
21. Ibid., p. 245.
22. *Foreign and Military Intelligence,* p. 257.
23. Marchetti and Marks, *Cult of Intelligence,* p. 65.
24. Wise and Ross, *Invisible Government,* p. 240.
25. Marchetti and Marks, *Cult of Intelligence,* p. 65.
26. Patrick J. McGarvey, *C.I.A.: The Myth and the Madness* (Baltimore: Penguin Books, 1973), p. 189.
27. Marchetti and Marks, *Cult of Intelligence,* p. 236.
28. John Ranelagh, *The Agency: The Rise and Decline of the CIA* (New York: Touchstone, 1987), p. 578.
29. *Foreign and Military Intelligence,* p. 262.
30. McGarvey, *Myth and Madness,* pp. 139–40. McGarvey wrote that the "CIA simply did not trust their uniformed brethren to deal honestly with [military intelligence]," referring to the "bomber gap" and "missile gap" controversies of the mid-1950s and early 1960s.
31. *Detailed Staff Reports,* p. 77.
32. Marchetti and Marks, *Cult of Intelligence,* p. 67.
33. Ibid., pp. 166–67.
34. Ibid., p. 68. The annual budget was placed at about $1 billion in 1985. See Ranelagh, *The Agency,* p. 677.
35. Glenn P. Hastedt, "Organizational Foundations of Intelligence Failures," in *Intelligence: Policy and Process,* ed. Alfred C. Maurer, Marion D. Tunstall, and James M. Keagle (Boulder, Colo.: Westview Press, 1985), p. 152.

Chapter 18

1. Lyman B. Kirkpatrick, Jr., *The U.S. Intelligence Community: Foreign Policy and Domestic Activities* (New York: Hill and Wang, 1973), p. 114.
2. David Wise and Thomas B. Ross, *The Invisible Government* (New York: Vintage Books, 1974), pp. 97–98.
3. Senate Select Committee to Study Governmental Operations, *Supplementary Detailed Staff Reports on Foreign and Military Intelligence*, 94th Cong., 2d sess., 1976, Rept. 94-755, Book 4, p. 42.
4. Wise and Ross, *Invisible Government*, p. 99.
5. Allen Dulles, *The Craft of Intelligence* (New York: Harper and Row, 1963), pp. 53, 95.
6. *Detailed Staff Reports*, pp. 52–53, fn.
7. John Prados, *Presidents' Secret Wars: CIA and Pentagon Covert Operations From World War II Through Iranscam* (New York: Quill/William Morrow, 1988), p. 108.
8. Stephen E. Ambrose, with Richard H. Immerman, *Ike's Spies: Eisenhower and the Intelligence Establishment* (New York: Doubleday, 1981), p. 188.
9. Prados, *Secret Wars*, p. 108.
10. Philip Agee published two organization charts of the DDP, one dated 1959, and the other 1964–68. See Philip Agee, *Inside the Company: CIA Diary* (New York: Bantam Books, 1976), pp. 656–58.
11. In the CIA's latest (1989) recruiting brochure, the work of the DO described covers the traditional activities—espionage, counterespionage, and covert action—but with some fudging: "Although the primary focus of operations officers is the *collection* of foreign intelligence, they are also involved in *counterintelligence* abroad. . . . A very small percentage of operations overseas involves *covert action*, where diplomacy will not work and military force is inappropriate." (Emphasis added)
12. Victor Marchetti and John D. Marks, *The CIA and the Cult of Intelligence* (New York: Laurel, 1983), p. 178.
13. Ibid., pp. 181–82.
14. Senate Select Committee to Study Governmental Operations, *Foreign and Military Intelligence*, 94th Cong., 2d sess., 1976, Rept. 94-755, book 1, pp. 171–72. See also Peter Wright, *Spy Catcher* (New York: Viking, 1987), pp. 303–9, 376–77.
15. Marchetti and Marks, *Cult of Intelligence*, pp. 22–23.
16. Kirkpatrick, *Intelligence Community*, p. 127.
17. Marchetti and Marks, *Cult of Intelligence*, p. 38.
18. *Detailed Staff Reports*, p. 47.
19. Patrick J. McGarvey, *C.I.A.: The Myth and the Madness* (Baltimore: Penguin Books, 1973), p. 53.
20. Marchetti and Marks, *Cult of Intelligence*, p. 197.
21. *Foreign and Military Intelligence*, p. 193.

22. Marchetti and Marks, *Cult of Intelligence,* pp. 95–96.
23. Ibid., p. 53.
24. Ibid., p. 24.
25. *Foreign and Military Intelligence,* p. 207.
26. Marchetti and Marks, *Cult of Intelligence,* pp. 118–19.
27. Ibid., p. 119. See also Prados, *Secret Wars,* p. 34.
28. *Foreign and Military Intelligence,* p. 239.
29. Ibid., p. 237.
30. Marchetti and Marks, *Cult of Intelligence,* p. 133.
31. *Foreign and Military Intelligence,* p. 227.
32. Marchetti and Marks, *Cult of Intelligence,* p. 63.
33. Ibid., pp. 64–65.
34. McGarvey, *Myth and Madness,* p. 164.
35. Marchetti and Marks, *Cult of Intelligence,* p. 64.
36. Ibid.
37. *Foreign and Military Intelligence,* p. 207.
38. See Marchetti and Marks, *Cult of Intelligence,* pp. 242–45.
39. John J. Sirica, *To Set The Record Straight* (New York: Signet, 1979), p. 74.
40. Marchetti and Marks, *Cult of Intelligence,* p. 23.

Chapter 19

1. John Prados, *Presidents' Secret Wars: CIA and Pentagon Covert Operations From World War II Through Iranscam* (New York: Quill/William Morrow, 1988), pp. 37–44, 52–60, 45–52.
2. John Ranelagh, *The Agency: The Rise and Decline of the CIA* (New York: Touchstone, 1987), p. 137.
3. Ibid., p. 156.
4. Prados, *Secret Wars,* p. 37. See John Loftus, *The Belarus Secret* (New York: Alfred A. Knopf, 1982).
5. Victor Marchetti and John D. Marks, *The CIA and the Cult of Intelligence* (New York: Laurel, 1983), p. 25. A biography of Lansdale is now available: Cecil B. Currey, *Edward Lansdale: The Unquiet American* (Boston: Houghton Mifflin, 1988).
6. Marchetti and Marks, *Cult of Intelligence,* p. 122.
7. David Wise and Thomas B. Ross, *The Invisible Government* (New York: Vintage, 1974), p. 107.
8. Prados, *Secret Wars,* p. 73. Downey and Fecteau might have gotten off earlier had Secretary of State Dulles been willing to cooperate. Ibid., p. 131.
9. Senate Select Committee to Study Governmental Operations, *Supplementary Detailed Staff Reports on Foreign and Military Intelligence,* 94th Cong., 2d sess., 1976, Rept. 94-755, book 4, p. 36.
10. Marchetti and Marks, *Cult of Intelligence,* p. 139.
11. Wise and Ross, *Invisible Government,* p. 131; Prados, *Secret Wars,* p. 77.
12. Marchetti and Marks, *Cult of Intelligence,* p. 100.

13. Ibid., pp. 101-2.
14. Ibid., p. 129.
15. Ibid., p. 102; see also Prados, *Secret Wars,* p. 170.
16. Senate Select Committee to Study Governmental Operations, *Foreign and Military Intelligence,* 94th Cong., 2d sess., 1976, Rept. 94-755, book 1, p. 147.
17. Marchetti and Marks, *Cult of Intelligence,* p. 205.
18. Prados, *Secret Wars,* pp. 271-76.
19. Marchetti and Marks, *Cult of Intelligence,* p. 29.
20. Prados, *Secret Wars,* pp. 276-78.
21. Marchetti and Marks, *Cult of Intelligence,* p. 101; and Wise and Ross, *Invisible Government,* pp. 140-41.
22. Ray S. Cline, *The CIA Under Reagan, Bush and Casey* (Washington: Acropolis Books, 1981), p. 206.
23. Wise and Ross, *Invisible Government,* pp. 110-13; Prados, *Secret Wars,* pp. 95-97.
24. Thomas Powers, *The Man Who Kept the Secrets* (New York: Alfred A. Knopf, 1979), p. 85.
25. Stephen Schlesinger and Stephen Kinzer, *Bitter Fruit: The Untold Story of the American Coup in Guatemala* (Garden City, N.Y.: Doubleday, 1982), p. 132.
26. Wise and Ross, *Invisible Government,* p. 177.
27. Richard H. Immerman, *The CIA in Guatamala: The Foreign Policy of Intervention* (Austin: University of Texas Press, 1982), pp. 174-77.
28. Charles D. Ameringer, *Don Pepe: A Political Biography of José Figueres of Costa Rica* (Albuquerque: The University of New Mexico Press, 1979), pp. 121-25.
29. Ibid., pp. 146-47.
30. Senate Select Committee to Study Governmental Operations, *Alleged Assassination Plots Involving Foreign Leaders,* 94th Cong., 1st sess., 1975, Rept. 94-465, p. 211.
31. Ibid., p. 209.
32. Ibid., pp. 191, 213.
33. Ibid., p. 215.
34. Cord Meyer, *Facing Reality* (New York: Harper and Row, 1980), p. 85.
35. Drew Pearson, "Washington Merry-go-round," syndicated, February 24, 1967; George Morris, *CIA and American Labor* (New York: International Publishers, 1967), p. 157.
36. Philip Agee, *Inside the Company: CIA Diary* (New York: Bantam Books, 1976), pp. 244-46.
37. Serafino Romualdi, *Presidents and Peons* (New York: Funk and Wagnalls, 1967), p. 352.
38. Morris, *CIA and Labor,* p. 89.
39. Senate Select Committee to Study Governmental Operations, *Covert Action in Chile, 1963-1973,* 94th Cong., 1st sess., 1975, Committee Print, pp. 7-10.
40. Ibid., p. 21.
41. Ibid., p. 23.
42. *Assassination Plots,* pp. 225-26.

43. *Covert Action in Chile,* pp. 28, 33.
44. Ibid., p. 13.
45. Ibid., pp. 38–39.
46. Ibid., pp. 47–48.
47. Ibid., p. 53.
48. Ibid., p. 55.
49. Agee, *CIA Diary,* pp. 516–17.
50. Wise and Ross, *Invisible Government,* pp. 124–28.
51. Meyer, *Facing Reality,* pp. 103–4.
52. *Foreign and Military Intelligence,* p. 184.
53. Ibid., p. 184 fn.
54. Ibid., p. 184.
55. Ibid., p. 185.
56. Ibid., p. 187.
57. Ibid., pp. 187–88.
58. Wise and Ross, *Invisible Government,* p. 183.

Chapter 20

1. David Wise and Thomas B. Ross, *The Invisible Government* (New York: Vintage Books, 1974), pp. 75–76.
2. Victor Marchetti and John D. Marks, *The CIA and the Cult of Intelligence* (New York: Laurel, 1983), pp. 259–60.
3. Wise and Ross, *Invisible Government,* p. 345.
4. Ibid., p. 336.
5. Peter Wyden, *Bay of Pigs: The Untold Story* (New York: Simon and Schuster, 1979), p. 170.
6. *Operation ZAPATA: The "Ultrasensitive" Report and Testimony of the Board of Inquiry on the Bay of Pigs* (Frederick, Md.: University Publications of America, 1981), p. 326.
7. Ibid., p. 111.
8. Ibid., p. 253.
9. Ibid., p. 220.
10. Ibid., pp. 112–13.
11. Terry Southern, "How I Signed Up at $250 a Month for The Big Parade through Havana Bla-Bla-Bla and Wound Up in Guatemala with the CIA," *Esquire* 59 (June 1963): 68.
12. Wyden, *Bay of Pigs,* p. 309.
13. *Operation ZAPATA,* p. 22.
14. Wyden, *Bay of Pigs,* p. 270.
15. *Operation ZAPATA,* p. 40.
16. Ibid., p. 42.
17. Ibid., p. 249.
18. Ibid., pp. 19–20. Bradley F. Smith, in writing on the OSS, warned of limitations of covert action that seem germane to the Bay of Pigs failure and to sim-

ilar operations that followed: "It behooves Americans to put aside romance and mind the two most important facts of the O.S.S. story: despite the best efforts of Donovan and his successors, no shadow warrior ever found a magic wand and the great power game was always too demanding to allow 'secret shenanigans' to do 'what armies are supposed to do.' " Bradley F. Smith, *The Shadow Warriors: O.S.S. and the Origins of the C.I.A.* (New York: Basic Books, 1983), p. 419.

19. Lawrence C. Soley and John S. Nichols, *Clandestine Radio Broadcasting* (New York: Praeger, 1987), p. 181.
20. Lyman B. Kirkpatrick, Jr., *The U.S. Intelligence Community: Foreign Policy and Domestic Activities* (New York: Hill and Wang, 1973), p. 88.
21. Marchetti and Marks, *Cult of Intelligence*, p. 263.
22. Wise and Ross, *Invisible Government*, p. 293.
23. Robert F. Kennedy, *Thirteen Days* (New York: W.W. Norton, 1968), pp. 1–2.
24. Ibid., p. 1.
25. Kirkpatrick, *Intelligence Community*, p. 97. See Thomas G. Paterson, "Fixation with Cuba: The Bay of Pigs, Missile Crisis, and Covert War Against Fidel Castro," in *Kennedy's Quest for Victory: American Foreign Policy, 1961–1963*, ed. Thomas G. Paterson (New York: Oxford University Press, 1989), pp. 140–52, for a discussion of the foreign policy of the Cuban missile crisis.
26. Senate Select Committee to Study Governmental Operations, *Alleged Assassination Plots Involving Foreign Leaders*, 94th Cong., 1st sess., 1975, Rept. 94-465, p. 72.
27. Ibid., p. 75.
28. Ibid., p. 77.
29. Ibid., pp. 77–79; Wyden, *Bay of Pigs*, p. 44.
30. *Assassination Plots*, p. 80.
31. Ibid., pp. 80–82.
32. Ibid., p. 82.
33. Ibid., pp. 83–85.
34. Ovid Demaris, *The Last Mafioso: The Treacherous World of Jimmy Fratianno* (New York: Times Books, 1981), p. 193.
35. *Assassination Plots*, pp. 85–86.
36. Ibid., pp. 88–89.
37. Ibid., p. 91.
38. Ibid., p. 92.
39. Ibid., p. 108.
40. Thomas Powers, *The Man Who Kept the Secrets* (New York: Alfred A. Knopf, 1979), pp. 153–54.
41. *Assassination Plots*, pp. 11–12.
42. Ibid., p. 55.
43. Ibid., p. 52.
44. Ibid., p. 61.
45. Ibid., p. 66.

46. Ibid., pp. 51–52.
47. Ibid., p. 264.
48. Ibid., p. 186.
49. Ibid., p. 141.
50. Powers, *Secrets,* p. 155.
51. Ibid.
52. *Assassination Plots,* p. 130.
53. Ibid., p. 180, n. 1.
54. Powers, *Secrets,* pp. 151–52.
55. *Assassination Plots,* p. 179.

Chapter 21

1. David Atlee Phillips, *The Night Watch* (New York: Atheneum, 1977), p. 277.
2. William Colby, *Honorable Men: My Life in the CIA* (New York: Simon and Schuster, 1978), p. 294.
3. William E. Burrows, *Deep Black: Space Espionage and National Security* (New York: Random House, 1986), pp. vii–viii.
4. Ibid., p. 76, and photographs following p. 166.
5. James Bamford, *The Puzzle Palace* (New York: Penguin Books, 1983), pp. 210–11.
6. Ibid., p. 253.
7. Ibid., p. 254.
8. Burrows, *Deep Black,* pp. 177–79.
9. Ibid., p. 183.
10. Victor Marchetti and John D. Marks, *The CIA and the Cult of Intelligence* (New York: Laurel, 1983), p. 164.
11. Burrows, *Deep Black,* pp. 80–81.
12. Ibid., p. 76.
13. Ibid.
14. Ibid., pp. 165–66.
15. Ibid., p. 241.
16. Ibid., p. 352.
17. Ibid., p. 251.
18. Patrick J. McGarvey, *C.I.A.: The Myth and the Madness* (Baltimore: Penguin Books, 1973), pp. 94–95.
19. Ibid., pp. 69–70.
20. Ibid., p. 94.
21. Ibid., p. 115.
22. Eliot Cohen, "The 'No Fault' View of Intelligence," in *Intelligence Requirements for the 1990s,* ed. Roy Godson (Lexington, Mass.: Lexington Books, 1989), p. 90.
23. Roy Godson, "Intelligence for the 1990s," in *Intelligence Requirements for the 1990s,* ed. Roy Godson (Lexington, Mass.: Lexington Books, 1989), p. 15.

24. Roy Godson, ed., *Intelligence Requirements for the 1990s* (Lexington, Mass.: Lexington Books, 1989), p. 68.
25. Michael R. Beschloss, *Mayday: Eisenhower, Khrushchev and the U-2 Affair* (New York: Harper and Row, 1986), p. 16.
26. Bamford, *Puzzle Palace,* p. 281.
27. McGarvey, *Myth and Madness,* p. 17.
28. Bamford, *Puzzle Palace,* p. 283.
29. McGarvey, *Myth and Madness,* p. 99.
30. Ibid., p. 102.
31. Ibid., pp. 104-5.
32. Ibid., pp. 106-7.
33. Senate Select Committee to Study Governmental Operations, *Foreign and Military Intelligence,* 94th Cong., 2d sess., 1976, Rept. 94-755, pp. 341-42.
34. Ibid., p. 343.
35. Bamford, *Puzzle Palace,* p. 301.
36. Godson, "Intelligence for the 1990s," p. 15.
37. Marchetti and Marks, *Cult of Intelligence,* p. 169.
38. Burrows, *Deep Black,* p. 173.
39. Ibid., pp. 172-73.
40. Jeffrey T. Richelson, *The U.S. Intelligence Community* (Cambridge, Mass.: Ballinger, 1985), p. 338.

Chapter 22

1. Lyman B. Kirkpatrick, Jr., *The U.S. Intelligence Community: Foreign Policy and Domestic Activities* (New York: Hill and Wang, 1973), p. 123.
2. William Colby, *Honorable Men: My Life in the CIA* (New York: Simon and Schuster, 1978), p. 148.
3. Frank Snepp, *Decent Interval* (New York: Random House, 1977), pp. 11-14.
4. Senate Select Committee to Study Governmental Operations, *Foreign and Military Intelligence,* 94th Cong., 2d sess., 1976, Rept. 94-755, p. 228.
5. Catherine Lamour and Michel R. Lamberti, *The International Connection: Opium from Growers to Pushers* (New York: Pantheon Books, 1974), pp. 142-43.
6. Alfred W. McCoy, *The Politics of Heroin in Southeast Asia* (New York: Harper and Row, 1972), p. 217.
7. *Foreign and Military Intelligence,* pp. 230-31.
8. Ibid., p. 227. See also John Prados, *Presidents' Secret Wars* (New York: Quill/William Morrow, 1988), pp. 286-87.
9. Victor Marchetti and John D. Marks, *The CIA and the Cult of Intelligence* (New York: Laurel, 1983), pp. 206-7.
10. Colby, *Honorable Men,* p. 276.
11. Marchetti and Marks, *Cult of Intelligence,* p. 209.
12. Colby, *Honorable Men,* pp. 246-47.

13. Ibid., p. 291.
14. Kirkpatrick, *Intelligence Community*, p. 108.
15. Ibid., p. 97.
16. Ibid., p. 101.
17. Ibid., p. 104.
18. Ibid., p. 105.
19. Ibid., p. 104.
20. Ibid., p. 98.
21. Ibid., p. 111.
22. Daniel Ellsberg, *Papers on the War* (New York: Simon and Schuster, 1972), p. 35.
23. L. Fletcher Prouty, *The Secret Team: The CIA and its Allies in Control of the United States and the World* (New York: Prentice-Hall, 1973), p. 195.
24. Kirkpatrick, *Intelligence Community*, p. 185.
25. Senate Select Committee to Study Governmental Operations, *Intelligence Activities and the Rights of Americans*, 94th Cong., 2d sess., 1976, Rept. 94-755, p. 69.
26. Ibid., p. 87.
27. Ibid., pp. 216–17.
28. Ibid., p. 218.
29. Ibid.
30. Ibid., p. 72.
31. Ibid., p. 89.
32. Ibid., p. 177.
33. Ibid., p. 219.
34. Ibid., p. 223.
35. Ibid., p. 11.
36. Ibid., pp. 11–12.
37. Ibid., p. 221.
38. Ibid., pp. 221–22.
39. Ibid., p. 219.
40. Ibid., p. 77.
41. Ibid.
42. Ibid., p. 8.
43. Ibid., p. 6.
44. Ibid., pp. 104–5.
45. Ibid., p. 104.
46. Ibid., p. 168.
47. Ibid., p. 99.
48. Ibid., pp. 101–2.
49. Ibid., p. 102.
50. Ibid.
51. Ibid., p. 103.
52. Colby, *Honorable Men*, p. 356.
53. Commission on CIA Activities Within the United States, *Report to the President* (Washington, D.C.: Government Printing Office, 1975), pp. 161–68.

Chapter 23

1. Senate Select Committee to Study Governmental Operations, *Intelligence Activities and the Rights of Americans,* 94th Cong., 2d sess., 1976, Rept. 94-755, p. 113.
2. Senate Select Committee to Study Governmental Operations, *Intelligence Activities—Volume 2: Huston Plan,* 94th Cong., 1st sess., 1975, hearings, p. 32.
3. Ibid., p. 4.
4. Ibid., p. 189.
5. Ibid., p. 192.
6. Ibid., p. 17.
7. Ibid., p. 194.
8. Ibid., pp. 194-95.
9. Ibid., p. 196.
10. Ibid., p. 197.
11. Ibid., pp. 191-92.
12. Ibid., p. 198.
13. *Rights of Americans,* pp. 114-15.
14. J. Anthony Lukas, *Night-mare: The Underside of the Nixon Years* (New York: Viking, 1976), p. 34.
15. Thomas Powers, *The Man Who Kept the Secrets: Richard Helms and the CIA* (New York: Alfred A. Knopf, 1979), pp. 248-49.
16. Ibid., p. 249.
17. *Huston Plan,* p. 42.
18. *Rights of Americans,* pp. 111-16.
19. John W. Dean, *Blind Ambition* (New York: Simon and Schuster, 1976), p. 37.
20. Ibid., p. 38.
21. William Colby, *Honorable Men: My Life in the CIA* (New York: Simon and Schuster, 1978), p. 341.
22. Lukas, *Night-mare,* pp. 12-15.
23. Powers, *Helms,* p. 253.
24. Lukas, *Night-mare,* p. 78.
25. Ibid.
26. *Huston Plan,* p. 40.
27. Commission on CIA Activities Within the United States, *Report to the President* (Washington, D.C.: Government Printing Office, 1975), p. 178. Hereafter cited as *Rockefeller Commission.*
28. Ibid., p. 179.
29. Powers, *Helms,* p. 253.
30. Ibid., p. 256.
31. Lukas, *Night-mare,* p. 97.
32. Powers, *Helms,* p. 258.
33. Ibid., pp. 260-61.
34. *Rockefeller Commission,* p. 201.
35. Colby, *Honorable Men,* p. 328.

36. John J. Sirica, *To Set The Record Straight* (New York: Signet, 1979), p. 74.
37. Ibid.
38. Ibid.
39. Colby, *Honorable Men,* p. 332.
40. Powers, *Helms,* p. 279.
41. Colby, *Honorable Men,* p. 338.
42. Powers, *Helms,* p. 288.
43. Colby, *Honorable Men,* p. 389.
44. Powers, *Helms,* p. 288.
45. Colby, *Honorable Men,* p. 391.
46. *Rockefeller Commission,* p. 5.
47. Ibid., p. 7.
48. Ibid., p. 226.
49. Ibid., p. 227.
50. Powers, *Helms,* p. 290.
51. Ibid., p. 291.
52. *Rockefeller Commission,* p. xi.

Chapter 24

1. The following six books constitute the *Final Report.* Book 1, *Foreign and Military Intelligence,* surveys the intelligence community and intelligence functions and includes a discussion of the CIA's proprietaries. Book 2, *Intelligence Activities and the Rights of Americans,* is a detailed report on covert surveillance techniques in domestic intelligence, including the FBI's COINTELPRO and its operations against Martin Luther King, Jr.; the CIA's Operation CHAOS and mail-opening programs; and the NSA's monitoring (MINARET and SHAMROCK). It contains a discussion of the Huston Plan. Book 3 is *Supplementary Detailed Staff Reports on Intelligence Activities and the Rights of Americans.* Book 4, *Supplementary Detailed Staff Reports on Foreign and Military Intelligence,* is a history of the CIA written by staff member Anne Karalekas, including a discussion of how clandestine operations had taken over the CIA by 1953. Book 5 is *The Investigation of the Assassination of President John F. Kennedy: Performance of the Intelligence Agencies.* Book 6, *Supplementary Reports on Intelligence Activities,* consists of two reports: "The Evolution and Organization of the Federal Intelligence Function: A Brief Overview (1776–1975)" and "Executive Agreements: A Survey of Recent Congressional Interest and Action," prepared by Harold C. Relyea and Marjorie Ann Brown, respectively, of the Congressional Research Service, the Library of Congress. The seven additional volumes of public testimony are: *Unauthorized Storage of Toxic Agents* (vol. 1); *Huston Plan* (vol. 2); *Internal Revenue Service* (vol. 3); *Mail Opening* (vol. 4); *The National Security Agency and Fourth Amendment Rights* (vol. 5); *Federal Bureau of Investigation* (vol. 6); and *Covert Action* (vol. 7). Many of these volumes are cited throughout this study as its principal source. See also Loch

K. Johnson, *A Season of Inquiry: Congress and Intelligence* (Chicago: Dorsey Press, 1988), pp. 306–7.

2. Johnson, *Inquiry,* p. 54.
3. Miles Copeland, *Without Cloak or Dagger* (New York: Simon and Schuster, 1974), p. 303.
4. Ibid.
5. Johnson, *Inquiry,* p. 73.
6. Ibid., p. 76.
7. Senate Select Committee to Study Governmental Operations, *Foreign and Military Intelligence,* 94th Cong., 2d sess., 1976, Rept. 94-755, book 1, pp. 141–42.
8. Ibid., p. 143.
9. Ibid.
10. Johnson, *Inquiry,* p. 269.
11. *Foreign and Military Intelligence,* p. 159.
12. Ibid.
13. Ibid., pp. 160–61.
14. Johnson, *Inquiry,* p. 184.
15. Ibid., p. 182.
16. Office of the White House Press Secretary, *The White House,* February 18, 1976 (mimeographed).
17. John M. Oseth, *Regulating U.S. Intelligence Operations: A Study in Definition of the National Interest* (Lexington, Ky.: The University Press of Kentucky, 1985), p. 93.
18. Ray S. Cline, *The CIA Under Reagan, Bush and Casey* (Washington: Acropolis Books, 1981), p. 263.
19. *Foreign and Military Intelligence,* pp. 160–61.
20. Commission on CIA Activities Within the United States, *Report to the President* (Washington, D.C.: Government Printing Office, 1975), p. 93.
21. White House Press Release, Feb. 18, 1976.
22. Oseth, *Regulating U.S Intelligence,* p. 95.
23. White House Press Release, Feb. 18, 1976.
24. Oseth, *Regulating U.S. Intelligence,* p. 92.
25. White House Press Release, Feb. 18, 1976.
26. *Report to the President,* p. 93.
27. Cline, *The CIA,* p. 268.
28. Oseth, *Regulating U.S. Intelligence,* p. 106.
29. Cline, *The CIA,* p. 270.
30. Stansfield Turner, *Secrecy and Democracy: The CIA in Transition* (Boston: Houghton Mifflin, 1985), p. 26.
31. Executive Order No. 12036, *United States Intelligence Activities* (January 24, 1978, 43 F.R. 3674, 50 U.S.C. 401 note).
32. Ibid.
33. Ibid. *United States person* means a citizen of the United States, an alien lawfully admitted for permanent residence, an unincorporated association organized in the United States or substantially composed of United States citizens

or aliens admitted for permanent residence, or a corporation incorporated in the United States.

34. Oseth, *Regulating U.S. Intelligence,* p. 117.
35. EO 12036.
36. Turner, *Secrecy and Democracy,* pp. 1–2.
37. Oseth, *Regulating U.S. Intelligence,* p. 121.
38. Cline, *The CIA,* p. 273.
39. Ibid., p. 274.
40. Ibid., p. 273.
41. Ibid., p. 275.
42. John Ranelagh, *The Agency: The Rise and Decline of the CIA* (New York: Simon and Schuster, 1987), p. 642.
43. Ibid., p. 633.
44. Ibid., pp. 632–33.
45. Ibid., p. 644.
46. Harry Howe Ransom, "Intelligence and Partisan Politics," in *Intelligence: Policy and Process,* ed. Alfred C. Maurer, Marion D. Tunstall, and James M. Keagle (Boulder, Colo.: Westview Press, 1985), p. 34.
47. See Alfred C. Maurer, "National Security and the Right to Know," in ibid., pp. 93–94.
48. John Prados, *Presidents' Secret Wars* (New York: Quill/William Morrow, 1988), p. 356.
49. Ibid., p. 355.
50. Bob Woodward, *Veil: The Secret Wars of the CIA, 1981–1987* (New York: Simon and Schuster, 1987), p. 113.
51. Prados, *Secret Wars,* pp. 357–58.
52. Ranelagh, *The Agency,* p. 643.
53. Prados, *Secret Wars,* p. 357.

Chapter 25

1. Commission on CIA Activities Within the United States, *Report to the President* (Washington, D.C.: Government Printing Office, 1975), p. 93.
2. Philip Taubman, "Casey and His C.I.A. On the Rebound," *The New York Times Magazine* (January 16, 1983), p. 34.
3. John Ranelagh, *The Agency: The Rise and Decline of the CIA* (New York: Simon and Schuster, 1987), p. 675.
4. Taubman, "Casey," pp. 46–47.
5. Ibid., p. 21.
6. Joseph Lelyveld, "The Director: Running the C.I.A.," *The New York Times Magazine* (January 20, 1985), p. 19.
7. John M. Oseth, *Regulating U.S. Intelligence Operations: A Study in Definition of the National Interest* (Lexington, Ky.: The University Press of Kentucky, 1985), p. 148.
8. Ibid., p. 156.

9. Ranelagh, *The Agency,* p. 662.
10. Ibid. (Emphasis added.)
11. Oseth, *Regulating U.S. Intelligence,* p. 155.
12. Executive Order No. 12333, *United States Intelligence Activities* (December 4, 1981, 46 F.R. 59941).
13. Oseth, *Regulating U.S. Intelligence,* p. 157.
14. Central Intelligence Agency, *Intelligence: The Acme of Skill* (Washington, D.C.: CIA, 1981).
15. Bob Woodward, *Veil: The Secret Wars of the CIA, 1981–1987* (New York: Simon and Schuster, 1987), p. 253. Woodward observes, "For practical purposes the NSPG replaced the NSC as the chief decision-making body in the Reagan Administration" (pp. 21–22).
16. EO 12333.
17. Central Intelligence Agency, *Fact Book on Intelligence* (Washington, D.C.: CIA, 1987), p. 15.
18. Oseth, *Regulating U.S. Intelligence,* p. 159.
19. Ibid., p. 153.
20. Ibid., p. 159.
21. Ibid., p. 155.
22. Woodward, *Veil,* p. 92.
23. Oseth, *Regulating U.S. Intelligence,* p. 151.
24. Stansfield Turner, *Secrecy and Democracy: The CIA in Transition* (Boston: Houghton Mifflin, 1985), p. 58.
25. Ibid., p. 63.
26. Joel Brinkley, "Seeking Cures for an Epidemic of Espionage," *New York Times,* December 1, 1985, sec. 4, p. 1E. "Copyright 1981/85 by The New York Times Company. Reprinted by permission."
27. The Maldon Institute, *America's Espionage Epidemic* (Washington, D.C.: The Maldon Institute, 1986), p. 43.
28. Ibid., p. 56.
29. Woodward, *Veil,* p. 423.
30. Maldon Institute, *Espionage,* p. 56.
31. Woodward, *Veil,* p. 281.
32. Ibid., p. 117.
33. Ibid.
34. U.S. Department of State, "Communist Interference in El Salvador," Special Report no. 80 (Washington, D.C.: Government Printing Office, February 23, 1981).
35. *Wall Street Journal,* June 8, 1981.
36. Ibid.
37. *Washington Post,* June 9, 1981.
38. House and Senate, *Report of the Congressional Committees Investigating the Iran-Contra Affair,* 100th Cong., 1st sess., 1987, H. Rept. 100-433, S. Rept. 100-216, p. 379.
39. Ibid.
40. Woodward, *Veil,* pp. 172–73.

41. Ibid., p. 175.
42. Ibid., pp. 205–6 (Emphasis added).
43. Ibid., p. 212.
44. *Iran-Contra Affair,* p. 33.
45. Ibid., p. 35.
46. Ibid., p. 36.
47. Woodward, *Veil,* p. 281.
48. Ibid., p. 282.
49. *Iran-Contra Affair,* p. 37.
50. Ibid., p. 41.
51. Woodward, *Veil,* p. 329.
52. *Iran-Contra Affair,* p. 37.
53. Woodward, *Veil,* p. 490.
54. See ibid., p. 46.
55. *Iran-Contra Affair,* p. 77.
56. Ibid., p. 59 (Emphasis added).
57. Ibid., pp. 45, 133.
58. Woodward, *Veil,* p. 467. See also *Iran-Contra Affair,* p. 332.
59. *Iran-Contra Affair,* pp. 6–7.
60. Ibid., p. 7.
61. Ibid., p. 11.
62. Ibid., pp. 10–11.
63. *The Tower Commission Report* (New York: Bantam Books, 1987), p. 79.
64. *Iran-Contra Affair,* p. 21.
65. Ibid., p. 271.
66. Ibid., pp. 195–97.
67. Ibid., pp. 11 and 291.
68. *Tower Report,* p. 81.
69. *Iran-Contra Affair,* p. 327.
70. *New York Times,* May 3, 1987.
71. *Tower Report,* p. 82.
72. *Iran-Contra Affair,* p. 413.
73. Ibid., p. 382.
74. Ibid., p. 375.
75. Ibid., p. 423.
76. Ibid., p. 384.
77. Ibid., p. 413.

Epilogue

1. *New York Times,* November 4, 1988.
2. House and Senate, *Report of the Congressional Committees Investigating the Iran-Contra Affair,* 100th Cong., 1st sess., 1987, H. Rept. 100-433, S. Rept. 100-216, p. 383.

3. B. Hugh Tovar, "Covert Action II," in *Intelligence Requirements for the 1990s,* ed. Roy Godson (Lexington, Mass.: Lexington Books, 1989), p. 208.
4. Richard H. Shultz, Jr., "Covert Action I," in *Intelligence Requirements,* ed. Roy Godson, p. 194.
5. *Iran-Contra Affair,* p. 383.
6. Ibid., pp. 383–84 (Emphasis added).
7. *New York Times,* February 16, 1989.
8. See Jeffrey T. Richelson, *The U.S. Intelligence Community* (Cambridge, Mass.: Ballinger, 1985), chapters 12, 14, and especially 16.
9. R. Keeler and E. Miriam Steiner, "Collection II," in *Intelligence Requirements,* ed. Roy Godson, pp. 50–51.
10. Robert Butterworth, "Collection I," in *Intelligence Requirements,* ed. Roy Godson, p. 35.
11. Roy Godson, "Intelligence for the 1990s," in *Intelligence Requirements,* ed. Roy Godson, p. 12.
12. Donald Nielson, "Collection/Discussion," in *Intelligence Requirements,* ed. Roy Godson, p. 64.
13. Godson, "Intelligence," p. 13.
14. Ibid., p. 14.
15. Roy Godson, "Collection/General Discussion," in *Intelligence Requirements,* ed. Roy Godson, p. 68.
16. Archibald Roosevelt, Jr., *For Lust of Knowing: Memoirs of an Intelligence Officer* (Boston: Little, Brown, 1988), pp. 431, 476.
17. Patrick J. McGarvey, *C.I.A.: The Myth and the Madness* (Baltimore: Penguin Books, 1973), p. 115.
18. John Prados, "Central Intelligence and the Arms Race," in *Intelligence: Policy and Process,* eds. Alfred C. Maurer, Marion D. Tunstall, and James M. Keagle (Boulder, Colo.: Westview Press, 1985), p. 325.
19. Stafford T. Thomas, "Intelligence Production and Consumption: A Framework of Analysis," in *Intelligence,* eds. A.C. Maurer, M.D. Tunstall, and J.M. Keagle, p. 119.
20. Prados, "Central Intelligence," p. 324.
21. Godson, "Intelligence," p. 6.
22. Paul Seabury, "Analysis II," in *Intelligence Requirements,* ed. Roy Godson, p. 101.
23. Ibid., p. 103.
24. Ibid., p. 105.
25. Godson, "Intelligence," p. 11.
26. Roosevelt, *For Lust,* p. 430.
27. George Kalaris and Leonard McCoy, "Counterintelligence I," in *Intelligence Requirements,* ed. Roy Godson, pp. 134–35.
28. Kenneth deGraffenreid, "Counterintelligence/Discussion," in *Intelligence Requirements,* ed. Roy Godson, pp. 147–48.
29. Kalaris and McCoy, "Counterintelligence I," pp. 127–28.
30. Ibid., p. 130.

31. DeGraffenreid, "Discussion," p. 148.
32. Ibid., p. 149.
33. Chapman Pincher, *Traitors* (New York: Penguin Books, 1988), p. ix.
34. James Geer, "Counterintelligence/Discussion," in *Intelligence Requirements,* ed. Roy Godson, pp. 156-57.
35. Pincher, *Traitors,* p. xiv.
36. Ibid., p. 166.
37. Ibid., p. 174.
38. John Ranelagh, *The Agency: The Rise and Decline of the CIA* (New York: Simon and Schuster, 1987), p. 567.
39. Ibid., p. 572, fn.
40. Godson, "Intelligence," p. 24.
41. Roy Godson, "Covert Action/General Discussion," in *Intelligence Requirements,* ed. Roy Godson, p. 234.
42. Godson, "Intelligence," pp. 24-25.
43. Tovar, "Covert Action II," p. 215.
44. Godson, "Intelligence," p. 27.
45. Tovar, "Covert Action II," p. 215.
46. Ibid., p. 208.
47. Shultz, "Covert Action I," p. 170.
48. Ibid., pp. 172-73.
49. Ibid., p. 171.
50. Tovar, "Covert Action II," p. 214.
51. Ray S. Cline, *Secrets, Spies and Scholars* (Washington: Acropolis Books, 1976), p. 265.
52. Ray S. Cline, *The CIA Under Reagan, Bush and Casey* (Washington, D.C.: Acropolis Books, 1981), p. 319.
53. Scott D. Breckinridge, *The CIA and the U.S. Intelligence System* (Boulder, Colo.: Westview Press, 1986), p. 320.
54. Cline, *The CIA,* p. 322.

Index